Economic Theory and International Trade

Economic Theory and International Trade

Essays in Honour of Murray C. Kemp

Edited by

Alan D. Woodland

Professor of Econometrics, School of Economics and Political Science, University of Sydney, Australia

Edward Elgar

Cheltenham, UK • Northampton, MA, USA

Published by
Edward Elgar Publishing Limited
Glensanda House
Montpellier Parade
Cheltenham
Glos GL50 1UA
UK

Edward Elgar Publishing, Inc.
136 West Street
Suite 202
Northampton
Massachusetts 01060
USA

A catalogue record for this book
is available from the British Library

Library of Congress Cataloguing in Publication Data

Economic theory and international trade : essays in honour of Murray C. Kemp / edited by Alan D. Woodland.
p. cm.
Includes bibliographical references and index.
1. International trade–Econometric models. 2. Commercial policy–Econometric models. 3. Economics–Econometric models. I. Woodland, A. D. II. Kemp, Murray
C.

HF1379 .E276 2002
382'.104–dc21

2002024724

ISBN 1 84064 294 7

Printed and bound in Great Britain by MPG Books Ltd, Bodmin, Cornwall

Contents

PART THREE
MARKET STRUCTURE

PART FOUR
ECONOMIC DYNAMICS

List of Contributors

Carl Chiarella	*University of Technology, Sydney*
Partha Gangopadhyay	*Europa Universität Viadrina*
Joshua S. Gans	*University of Melbourne*
Horst Herberg	*University of Kiel*
Seiichi Katayama	*Kobe University*
Murray C. Kemp	*University of New South Wales*
Alexander Khomin	*University of Technology, Sydney*
Yoshio Kimura	*Gifu Shotokugakuen University*
Kenji Kondoh	*Chukyo University*
Wing-fai Leung	*City University of Hong Kong*
Ngo Van Long	*McGill University*
Siang Ng	*Monash University*
Yew-Kwang Ng	*Monash University*
Hiroshi Ohta	*Kobe University*
Michihiro Ohyama	*Keio University*
Koji Okuguchi	*Gifu Shotokugakuen University*
Makoto Okamura	*Kobe City University of Foreign Studies*
Masayuki Okawa	*Ritsumeikan University*
Takao Ohkawa	*Ritsumeikan University*
Albert G. Schweinberger	*University of Konstanz*
Koji Shimomura	*Kobe University*
Robin Stonecash	*University of New South Wales*
Makoto Tawada	*Nagoya University*
Binh Tran-Nam	*University of New South Wales*
Cong Nghe Truong	*University of Western Sydney, Nepean*
Arja H. Turunen-Red	*University of New Orleans*
Yasuo Uekawa	*Now Deceased*
Henry Wan Jr	*Cornell University*
Kar-yiu Wong	*University of Washington*
Alan D. Woodland	*University of Sydney*

Introduction

Alan D. Woodland

This volume of research is published as a tribute to Murray C. Kemp.

Murray is one of the world's best-known and leading international trade theorists, with a distinguished career spanning over half a century. His published work is both familiar to and highly valued by international trade theorists and generations of graduate students. He has published 17 books, beginning with *The Demand for Canadian Imports, 1926-1955* and including his well-known international trade textbooks *The Pure Theory of International Trade* and *The Pure Theory of International Trade and Investment*, the first comprehensive modern, graduate-level textbooks in the area of international trade. His research papers have been published in all of the major economics journals and cover virtually every aspect of international trade. While international trade is the subject matter of most of his research, many of Murray's publications extend into other areas of economics. Indeed, as an illustration, his first paper published in the Australian *Economic Record* in 1949 was entitled 'Interest and the Money Supply in Keynes' Economics'.

Murray Kemp's devotion to the discipline of economics and his research output show no signs of wavering. Elsewhere in this volume I have provided a list of recent publications (since 1991), which attest to Murray's energetic research activities since his 'retirement'.

Others have previously provided formal recognition of Murray Kemp's contributions to economics, of course. He was elected a Fellow of the Econometric Society in 1971 and a Distinguished Fellow of the Economic Society of Australia in 1989. In its own small way, the present volume adds to these formal and prestigious awards. In particular, the volume provides recognition of Murray's numerous and important professional contributions by many of his former graduate students, colleagues and friends who constitute the authors of its various chapters.

Many of us have benefited immensely from professional and personal contacts with Murray. Australians, in particular, are especially grateful that Murray decided to return to his country of birth for most of his career and to share his insights and knowledge with us. This volume is therefore a tribute to Murray Kemp as a colleague and friend.

The idea for this volume was initially struck in 1996. Professor Duc-Tho (Tom) Nguyen organised a special section (Economic Theory) of the 1996 Economic Society of Australia (Queensland) conference in honour of Murray Kemp on the occasion of his seventieth birthday year. This conference attracted the attendance and participation of many of Murray's former students and colleagues both from within Australia and from countries (most notably, Japan) around the globe. Some time later, Henry Wan Jr and I put the idea of a volume to honour Murray into motion and this book is the end result of our efforts.

Although conceived in 1996, the volume has had a long gestation period and is now published at the time of Murray's seventy-fifth birthday year. The volume may therefore be regarded as a timely sequel to the previous volume entitled *Trade, Welfare, and Economic Policies* and edited by Horst Herberg and Ngo Van Long in honour of Murray on the occasion of his sixty-fifth birthday in 1991.

In the early stages of the planning for this volume, Henry Wan Jr had the misfortune to suffer medical problems that prevented his full participation in the project. With characteristic generosity Henry insisted that, not being able to contribute as much as he would wish, I should continue as the sole editor of the volume. In doing so, I wish to acknowledge the support, encouragement and wisdom that Henry gave to the project. Henry gave a tribute to Murray Kemp at the 1996 conference mentioned above and I feel that it is fitting to reproduce that short tribute here.

A Tribute to Murray

Now that the twentieth century is approaching its end, we have witnessed the drawing-together of the world economy in this century, with international trade playing an essential role in this drama.

The study of international trade is both challenging and important: challenging, because its complexity demands a general equilibrium approach; important, because the welfare of so many persons are directly and indirectly at stake. It takes a scholar with supreme analytic skill and a particular sensitivity to do research in this field.

Professor Murray Kemp, a foremost leader of research in international trade, is such a scholar. He demonstrates both the skill to extract relevant implications out of the complexities of the general equilibrium framework and the concern over what impact trade can impose on individuals and how to adjust and compensate for it so that, as far as possible, no one will be harmed by trade.

Murray came from Australia and received training in both America and Britain. After a period of teaching at McGill and MIT, he decided, 35 years ago, to return to the shore of the Pacific and set up his base at the University of New South Wales. I was there when he made his decision. It was a decision not easily made and not without difficulties and costs for himself and his family. Since his return to Australia, he has exercised profound impact throughout all shores of the Pacific. The profession acknowledges his achievements as economists gather across the world to come here today to pay him honour.

It is my honour to pay tribute to Murray, and to thank all those organisers and

participants of this event.
Henry Wan
July 1996

The volume brings together the results of research by some of Murray Kemp's many colleagues and former students. The topics chosen for the various chapters are primarily in the area of international trade and the techniques of analysis are firmly grounded in economic theory. The contents of the volume therefore reflect, in a fundamental way, the approach that Murray brought to his own analysis of economic problems and issues.

This volume provides a collection of papers that address important issues in economic theory and international trade, written by internationally renowned researchers in the field. The volume is divided into four parts. These parts are entitled: Classical Trade Theory, International Trade Policy, Market Structure and Economic Dynamics. While the volume does not claim to be a comprehensive account of international trade theory, the topics covered encompass a wide range of enquiry into international trade issues that form the backbone of modern international trade.

The first part of this volume, entitled Classical Trade Theory, deals with various issues in the pure theory of international trade and related areas. It is perhaps fitting, given Murray Kemp's propensity to engage in joint research, that the first chapter in the volume is authored jointly by Murray and Koji Shimomura. The first two chapters of Part One are concerned with the role played by increasing returns-to-scale in the analysis of international trade issues. Kemp and Shimomura deal with a new approach to international trade theory under increasing returns-to-scale, based upon the assumption that the economy is comprised of homogeneous agents each of whom is aware that they are part of what the authors call an 'egalitarian' society. The subsequent chapter by Horst Herberg deals with a more traditional issue, namely the question of how the shape of the production possibilities curve is affected by the existence of variable returns-to-scale in the production of goods. Attention then turns to other issues. Kemp, Kimura and Shimomura introduce the concept of a second correspondence principle to replace Samuelson's famous concept when a market-clearing, resource-using dynamic process replaces a tâtonnement process for the re-establishment of equilibrium. In the final chapter of Part One, Yew-Kwang Ng provides a novel examination of welfare economics when the population is endogenous and shows that the resulting population size may be sub-optimal in the sense of Pareto.

Part Two of the volume is concerned with international trade policy issues. This is a very important area of research that has induced a vast literature. The topics covered in the present volume are concentrated primarily upon the welfare implications of various multilateral trading arrangements and national trade policies. The first chapter, by Michihiro Ohyama, deals with international trade policy from a multilateral point of view and examines the economic significance, particularly the welfare gains, of the trading and policy rules that form part of the GATT/WTO (General Agreement on Tariffs and Trade/World Trade Organisation) framework. By contrast, Okawa uses a small-scale model of world trade with monopolistic behaviour to analyse the welfare implications of voluntary export restraints. The remaining chapters in Part Two are focused on various aspects of trade policy in small open economies. Schweinberger's chapter shifts the emphasis away from multilateral trading arrangements towards special economic zones within a small open economy and the evaluation of the welfare effects thereof. Long and Shimomura are concerned with the dynamics of redistributive taxation policies in small open economies. The welfare implications of various unilateral trade and environmental policy reforms provide the subject matter for Turunen-Red and Woodland's analysis.

The purpose of Part Three is the modelling and analysis of the relationship between market structure and international trade. The first two chapters of this Part are primarily concerned with innovation and technology. Wong and Leung are concerned with the role played by international joint ventures and technology spillovers, while Gans and Stonecash concentrate on the interaction between market structure and technology innovation. The subsequent chapters are concerned with duopoly and oligopoly market structures and international trade. Okuguchi analyses the structure of comparative statics in such models. The interactions between market structure and trade policies are the major concerns of the chapters by Uekawa, Katayama and Ohta and by Ohkawa, Okamura and Tawada. Gangopadhyay explores the interaction with the political economy of trading economies.

Economic dynamics forms the subject matter of the final Part, Part Four. The chapters span a wide range of topics and issues. This Part begins with an investigation by Chiarella and Khomin into the dynamic paths generated by a macroeconomic model of exchange rates when agents learn about the economy over time. The next two chapters deal with growth and immigration (Kondoh) and growth and environmental externalities (Tran-Nam and Truong). Henry Wan returns to the issue of learning, but this time within the context of learning as a mechanism for the transmission of technical knowledge from one nation to another. Finally, Siang Ng introduces an empirical aspect to the volume by assessing the spillover effects of growth of its trading partners upon Malaysia.

This brief overview of the volume cannot do justice to the contributions contained in each of the chapters. It does, however, indicate the breadth and nature of the research that is the subject matter of this book. Readers from all strands of international trade will find much of value and interest in the chapters of this volume.

The production of this volume involved a large number of people, whose efforts are gratefully acknowledged.

The chapters in this volume were subjected to a rigorous refereeing and revision process. The authors and I are greatly indebted to the referees for their generous contributions of their valuable time and expertise to this important task. The resulting chapters owe much to the comments and suggestions offered by the referees. Those people who undertook refereeing for the volume include:

Satya Das, Indian Statistical Institute, New Delhi
Rod Falvey, University of Birmingham, Birmingham
Richard Harris, Simon Fraser University, Vancouver
Christian Keuschnigg, University of Saarland, Saarbruecken
Carsten Kowalczyk, Tufts University, Medford
Kala Krishna, Pennsylvania State University, Pittsburg
Sajal Lahiri, University of Essex, Colchester
Peter Lloyd, University of Melbourne, Melbourne
Yoshivasu Ono, Osaka University, Osaka
Pascalis Raimondos-Møller, Copenhagen Business School, Copenhagen
Martin Richardson, University of Otago, Otago
Nicolas Schmitt, Simon Fraser University, Vancouver
Albert Schweinberger, University of Konstanz, Konstanz
Jeffrey Sheen, University of Sydney, Sydney
Koji Shimomura, Kobe University, Kobe
Arja Turunen-Red, University of New Orleans, New Orleans
Neil Vousden, Australian National University, Canberra (now deceased)
Don Wright, University of Sydney, Sydney.

The production of this volume was greatly assisted at various stages by administrative assistants Sheilah Whyte, Ruth Williams and Kristi Chambers and research assistants Jane Healy and Veronica Livera. Their cheerful and dedicated contributions are gratefully acknowledged. The assistance of editorial staff of Edward Elgar Publishing Limited is likewise much appreciated and acknowledged. Kerrie and Ray Legge expertly performed the task of proof-reading the penultimate versions of the chapters at the University of Sydney. Thanks also go to Narelle Woodland for her valuable editorial advice and encouragement throughout the duration of this project.

Finally, the volume owes its essential content to the authors, who enthusiastically offered their research as a tribute to Murray. For their co-operation and patience, I am grateful.

Publications of Murray C. Kemp from 1992

1992

'Some properties of egalitarian economies', *Journal of Public Economics*, **49** (3), 383-87. With N.V. Long.

'The static welfare economics of foreign aid: a consolidation', *Equity and Efficiency in Economic Development: Essays in Honour of Benjamin Higgins*, D.J. Savoie, R. Brecher, eds, Montreal; London and Buffalo: McGill-Queen's University Press, 289-314. Reprinted in M.C. Kemp, *The Gains from Trade and the Gains from Aid*, 333-355. London: Routledge, 1995.

'Errata: variable returns to scale, non-uniqueness of equilibrium and the gains from international trade', *Review of Economic Studies*, **59** (1), 227. With A.G. Schweinberger.

'Gains from trade in monetary economies', in P. Newman, M. Milgate and J. Eatwell, eds, *The New Palgrave Dictionary of Money and Finance*, 215-16. London: Macmillan. With K.-Y. Wong.

'A dynamic model of the distribution of wealth among households and nations', *Annals of Operations Research*, **37**, 245-72. With K. Shimomura.

1993

The Welfare Economics of International Trade, Chur, London, Paris and New York: Harwood. With Henry Y. Wan, Jr.

'The welfare gains from international migration', *Keio Economic Studies*, **30** (1), 1-5. Reprinted in M.C. Kemp, *The Gains from Trade and the Gains from Aid*, 147-51. London: Routledge, 1995.

'Paradoxes associated with the administration of foreign aid', *Journal of Development Economics*, **42** (1), 197-204. With K.-Y. Wong.

'The international diffusion of the fruits of technical progress', *International Economic Review*, **34** (2), 381-85. With Y.-K. Ng and K. Shimomura. Reprinted in M.C. Kemp, *The Gains from Trade and the Gains from Aid*, 160-64. London: Routledge, 1995.

'Cyclical and noncyclical redistributive taxation', *International Economic Review*, **34** (2), 415-29. With N.V. Long and K. Shimomura.

'Labour unions and the theory of international trade', in K. Shimomura, *Essays on the Economic Analysis of Labour Unions*, 55-92. Kobe: Research Institute for Economics and Business Administration, Kobe University. With K. Shimomura.

'Tariffs and employment in union-ridden economies I', in K. Shimomura, *Essays on the Economic Analysis of Labour Unions*, 121-33. Kobe: Research Institute for Economics and Business Administration, Kobe University. With K. Shimomura.

'Tariffs and employment in union-ridden economies II', in K. Shimomura, *Essays on the Economic Analysis of Labour Unions*, 135-43. Kobe: Research Institute for Economics and Business Administration, Kobe University. With K. Shimomura.

1994

'The transfer problem in the context of public goods', *Economics Letters*, **45** (2), 223-26. With K. Abe. Reprinted in revised form, and with Makoto Tawada as co-author, in M.C. Kemp, *The Gains from Trade and the Gains from Aid*, 360-64. London: Routledge, 1995.

1995

The Gains from Trade and the Gains from Aid: Essays in International Trade Theory, London and New York: Routledge.

'Conditions for the local impotence of lumpsum transfers to effect a redistribution of welfare between nations', *The Gains from Trade and the Gains from Aid: Essays in International Trade Theory*, M.C. Kemp, London and New York: Routledge, 356-59.

'Lumpsum compensation in a context of overlapping generations', *The Gains from Trade and the Gains from Aid: Essays in International Trade Theory,* M.C. Kemp, London and New York: Routledge, 323-29. With N. Wolik.

'Lumpsum compensation in a context of incomplete markets', *The Gains from Trade and the Gains from Aid: Essays in International Trade Theory*, M.C. Kemp, London and New York: Routledge, 317-22. With H.Y. Wan, Jr.

'On lumpsum compensation', *The Gains from Trade and the Gains from Aid: Essays in International Trade Theory*, M.C. Kemp, London and New York: Routledge, 296-316. With H.Y. Wan, Jr.

'Does the set of imperfectly competitive general equilibria depend on the choice of price normalization?', *The Gains from Trade and the Gains from Aid: Essays in International Trade Theory*, M.C. Kemp, London and New York: Routledge, 271-73.

'The international diffusion of the fruits of technical progress under imperfect competition', *The Gains from Trade and the Gains from Aid: Essays in International Trade Theory*, M.C. Kemp, London and New York: Routledge, 253-70. With M. Okawa.

'The gains from international trade under imperfect competition: a conjectural variations approach', *The Gains from Trade and the Gains from Aid: Essays in International Trade Theory*, M.C. Kemp, London and New York: Routledge, 242-52. With M. Okawa.

'The gains from international trade in a context of overlapping generations', *The Gains from Trade and the Gains from Aid: Essays in International Trade Theory*, M.C. Kemp, London and New York: Routledge, 129-46. With N. Wolik.

'The gains from trade for a monetary economy when markets are possibly incomplete', *The Gains from Trade and the Gains from Aid: Essays in International Trade Theory*, M.C. Kemp, London and New York: Routledge, 78-100. With K.-Y. Wong.

'The gains from trade when markets are possibly incomplete', *The Gains from Trade and the Gains from Aid: Essays in International Trade Theory*, M.C. Kemp, London and New York: Routledge, 47-72. With K.-Y. Wong.

'The gains from trade and the gains from aid: essays in international trade theory: introduction', *The Gains from Trade and the Gains from Aid: Essays in International Trade Theory*, M.C. Kemp, London and New York: Routledge, ix-xvii.

The Gains from Trade and the Gains from Aid: Essays in International Trade Theory, London and New York: Routledge, xvii, 398.
'Gains from trade with overlapping generations', *Economic Theory*, **6** (2), 283-303. With K.-Y. Wong. Reprinted in '*The Gains from Trade and the Gains from Aid: Essays in International Trade Theory*, M.C. Kemp, London and New York: Routledge, 105-28.
'The apparently innocuous representative agent', *Japanese Economic Review*, **46** (3), 247-56. With K. Shimomura.
'On representative agents: reply to Kaneko and Suzumura', *Japanese Economic Review*, **46** (3), 300. With K. Shimomura.
'Why must we always follow Nash?: a further reply', *Japanese Economic Review*, **46** (3), 302. With K. Shimomura.
'The gains from free trade under imperfect competition', in S. Katayama and W. Chang, eds, *Imperfect Competition in International Trade*, 53-62. Norwell, Mass.: Kluwer Academic Publishers. With M. Okawa.
'The international diffusion of the fruits of technical progress', in S. Katayama and W. Chang, eds, *Imperfect Competition in International Trade*, 79-98. Norwell, Mass.: Kluwer Academic Publishers. With M. Okawa.

1997
'High youth wages can generate general and persistent unemployment', *Essays in Honour of Geoff Harcourt. Volume 2. Markets, Unemployment and Economic Policy*, Philip Arestis; Gabriel Palma; Malcolm Sawyer, eds, *Frontiers of Political Economy*, Vol. 7, London and New York: Routledge, 315-27. With N.V. Long and K. Shimomura.
'Symposium on the welfare economics of international trade and investment: introduction', *Japanese Economic Review*, **48** (2), 119-20. With K. Shimomura.
'Trade gains: a unified exposition based on duality', *Japanese Economic Review*, **48** (2), 121-31. With K. Shimomura.
'Voluntary export restraints and economic welfare: a general equilibrium analysis', *Japanese Economic Review*, **48** (2), 187-98. With K. Shimomura and M. Okawa.
'Factor price equalization under imperfect competition', *Review of International Economics*, **5** (2), 153-78. With M. Okawa.

1998
'On the evaluation of social income in a dynamic economy: generalizations', *Trade, Growth, and Economic Policy in Open Economies: Essays in Honour of Hans-Jurgen Vosgerau*, Karl-Josef Koch; Klaus Jaeger, eds, Heidelberg and New York: Springer, 101-10. With N.V. Long.
'Market structure and factor price equalization', *Japanese Economic Review*, **49** (3), 335-39. With M. Okawa.
'Variable returns to scale and factor price equalization', in *Increasing Returns and Economic Analysis*, K.J. Arrow; Y.-K. Ng; X. Yang, eds, New York: St. Martin's Press; London: Macmillan Press, 409-12. With M. Okawa and M. Tawada.
'Foreword' to S. Paul, ed., *Trade and Growth: New Theory and the Australian Experience*, Sydney: Allen and Unwin.

1999
'Pareto's compensation principle', *Social Choice & Welfare*, **16** (3), 441-44. With P. Pezanis-Christou.
'The internationalization of the world economy and its implication for national

welfare', *Review of International Economics*, **7** (1), 1-7. With K. Shimomura.
'Trade gains in chaotic equilibria', *Review of International Economics*, **7** (3), 403-9. With K. Shimomura.
'On lumpsum compensation', *Trade, Theory and Econometrics: Essays in Honor of John S. Chipman*, James R. Melvin; James C. Moore; Raymond Riezman, eds, *Studies in the Modern World Economy*, vol. 15. London and New York: Routledge, 185-205. With H.Y. Wan Jr.

2000
'The gains from free trade when workers are not indifferent to their occupations', *Journal of Post Keynesian Economics*, **23** (2), 299-300. With K. Shimomura.
'Increasing returns and international trade', *Review of International Economics*, **8** (4), 614-18. With K. Shimomura.
'An antiquarian note on optimal tariffs', *History of Political Economy*, **32** (3), 415-20. With K. Shimomura.
'A simple model of privately profitable but socially useless speculation', *Japanese Economic Review*, **51** (1), 84-94. With H.-W. Sinn.
'Welfare comparisons of customs unions and other free trade associations', *Pacific Economic Review*, **5** (1), 1-3.
'A note on Tomkinson's losses-from-trade proposition', *Kobe Economic and Business Review*, **1**, 77-87. With K. Shimomura. In Japanese.

2001
'A second elementary proposition concerning the formation of customs unions', *Japanese Economic Review*, **52** (1), 64-69. With K. Shimomura.
'Trade gains when the opportunity to trade changes the state of information', *Review of International Economics*, **9** (1), 24-28. With K. Shimomura and H.Y. Wan Jr.
'Factor market distortions, dynamic stability, and paradoxical comparative statics', *Review of International Economics*, **9** (3), 383-400. With M. Yamada.
'Factor price equalization when the world equilibrium is not unique', *Review of Development Economics*, **5** (2), 205-10.
'Gains from trade in a Cournot-Nash general equilibrium', *Japanese Economic Review*, **52** (3), 284-302. With Koji Shimomura.
International Trade and National Welfare, London: Routledge, 2001.
'Economic development and the gains from international trade and investment', in M. Chatterji and P. Gangopadhay, eds, *Globalization and Economic Reform*, London: Edward Elgar, 2001.

Forthcoming
'The Sonnenschein-Debreu-Mantel proposition and the theory of international trade', *Review of International Economics*. With Koji Shimomura.
'A dynamic Heckscher-Ohlin model: the case of costly factor movement', *Japanese Economic Review*. With Koji Shimomura.
'A theory of voluntary unrequited international transfers', *Japanese Economic Review*. With Koji Shimomura.

PART ONE

Classical Trade Theory

1. A New Approach to the Theory of International Trade under Increasing Returns: The Two-Commodities Case

Murray C. Kemp and Koji Shimomura

1. INTRODUCTION

It is our purpose to develop a new model of international trade in a context of increasing returns to scale. In constructing the model we are thoroughly conventional in confining attention to 'egalitarian' or 'representative agent' economies, that is, economies in which all agents have the same preferences, the same access to technologies and the same factor endowments; moreover, it is assumed that each agent is aware that he is part of an egalitarian economy.[1] However we avail ourselves of some little-known properties of such economies. Thus in representative-agent economies it is in each agent's interest to cooperate in forming a single utility-maximising firm to produce those commodities subject to increasing returns. Moreover, under autarkic conditions, the monopoly firm will engage in marginal-cost pricing; see Kemp and Long (1992) and Kemp and Shimomura (1995). Under free trade, on the other hand, the several utility-maximising monopolists (one for each trading country) are supposed to engage in a Cournot-Nash game in quantities.

In this chapter we restrict attention to the canonical case in which there are just two trading countries and two traded commodities, with constant returns to scale in one industry and increasing returns to scale in the other industry. It is shown that if preferences are everywhere identically homothetic and if production functions are everywhere homothetic (but not necessarily identically homothetic), then each country gains from trade; and it is shown that if, in addition, the two countries differ only in their factor endowments and if the endowments differ only by a positive scalar multiplier, then the larger country exports the increasing-returns commodity.

The model is presented in Section 2. In Section 3 we provide a sufficient condition for the existence of a Cournot-Nash trading equilibrium. In Section

4 we take up the question of trade gains and in Section 5 we address the question of trade patterns.

2. A MODEL OF AN AUTARKIC ECONOMY

Two consumption goods, x and y, are produced with the aid of two primary factors, labour and capital. The production of good x is subject to increasing returns to scale described by the homothetic production function

$$x = G\left(f^x\left(\ell_x, k_x\right)\right), \tag{1.1}$$

where the function f^x is increasing, homogeneous of degree one and strictly quasi-concave in the inputs of labour and capital and where G is an increasing and strictly convex function of f^x, with $G(0) = 0$. (Notice that, in the economy under study and in industry x, returns to scale are related to that economy's output of x but not to the other economy's output of x. In other words, economies of scale respect national boundaries.) The production function for good y, $y = f^y\left(\ell_y, k_y\right)$, has the same properties as f^x. As already noted in Section 1, all agents have the same preferences, the same access to technologies and the same factor endowments.

Under the foregoing assumptions we may write the aggregate budget and market-clearing equations as

$$HE(p,u) = px + F(x) \text{ and } HE_p(p,u) = x, \tag{1.2}$$

where H is the population of the autarkic economy, $E(p,u)$ is the expenditure function of each agent, u is the utility of each agent, p is the price of good x in terms of good y, $y = F(x)$ is the equation of the production possibility curve and $E_p \equiv \partial E/\partial p$. For simplicity, we normalise H to unity.

Taking income effects into account, the consumer-owned monopoly firm seeks to maximise the utility u of each agent subject to (1.2). Totally differentiating (1.2), we find that

$$\begin{aligned} E_u du &= (p + F')dx \\ E_{pp}dp + E_{pu}du &= dx, \end{aligned} \tag{1.3}$$

where

$$E_u \equiv \partial E/\partial u \ , \ E_{pu} \equiv \partial^2 E/\partial p \partial u \text{ and } E_{pp} \equiv \partial^2 E/\partial p^2 .$$

Thus, setting $du = 0$, we obtain the first-order condition for an interior maximum as

$$p + F'(x) = 0. \tag{1.4}$$

Since the slope of the production possibility curve is equal to minus the ratio of the marginal cost of good x to that of good y, and since good y is the numeraire, (1.4) means that the price of the oligopolistic good is equal to its marginal cost. This confirms a proposition established by Kemp and Long (1992). The second-order condition is

$$\frac{\partial p}{\partial x} + F''(x) = \frac{1}{E_{pp}(p,u)} + F''(x) < 0, \tag{1.5}$$

where use has been made of the second member of (1.3), with $du = 0$. This inequality is satisfied if the production possibility set is convex. However, it is well known (Herberg and Kemp 1969, Wong 1995a) that, under increasing returns to scale, it is possible that the set has a non-convex part. In what follows, therefore, we simply assume that the second-order condition is always satisfied, whatever the sign of F''.

3. A TWO-COUNTRY MODEL: THE EXISTENCE OF EQUILIBRIUM

Let us now allow the two countries, the 'home' and the 'foreign', to trade freely with each other. It is assumed that the countries share the same homothetic preferences but that agents can cooperate only within their own national borders. It follows that, when trade is opened, two giant firms (one for each country) compete with each other in the world market. The world market-clearing condition is

$$\frac{e'(p)}{e(p)}\left[px + F(x)\right] + \frac{e'(p)}{e(p)}\left[px^* + F^*(x^*)\right] = x + x^*, \tag{1.6}$$

where $e(p)$ is the common unit expenditure function and asterisks (*) indicate that the variables belong to the foreign country. Equation (1.6) can be rewritten as

$$\frac{e(p)}{e'(p)} - p = \frac{F(x)+F^*(x^*)}{x+x^*}. \tag{1.7}$$

The left hand side of (1.7) is monotonically increasing in p. Hence we can write the inverse demand function as

$$p = g\left(\frac{F(x)+F^*(x^*)}{x+x^*}\right) \equiv P(x,x^*). \tag{1.8}$$

Since $g' = -(e')^2/(ee'') > 0$ and $F(x)$ and $F^*(x^*)$ are decreasing in x and x^*, respectively, $P(x,x^*)$ is a decreasing function of x and x^*.

As explained in Section 2, the objective of each giant firm is to maximise the utility of each agent in the relevant country. Substitution from (1.8) into the indirect utility functions

$$\begin{aligned} u &= \frac{1}{e(p)}\left[px + F(x)\right] \\ u^* &= \frac{1}{e(p)}\left[px^* + F^*(x^*)\right] \end{aligned} \tag{1.9}$$

yields the objective functions

$$\begin{aligned} u &= \frac{1}{e(P(x,x^*))}\left[P(x,x^*)x + F(x)\right] \equiv u(x,x^*) \equiv U(P(x,x^*),x) \\ u^* &= \frac{1}{e(P(x,x^*))}\left[P(x,x^*)x^* + F^*(x^*)\right] \\ &\equiv u^*(x,x^*) \equiv U(P(x,x^*),x^*). \end{aligned} \tag{1.10}$$

Partially differentiating $u(x,x^*)$ and $u^*(x,x^*)$ with respect to x and x^*, respectively, we finally obtain the Cournot-Nash equilibrium conditions

$$\begin{aligned} \frac{\partial u}{\partial x} = \frac{1}{e}\Bigg[& P(x,x^*) + F'(x) + \frac{\partial P(x,x^*)}{\partial x}\Bigg\{ x \\ & - \frac{e'(P(x,x^*))}{e(P(x,x^*))}\left(P(x,x^*)x + F(x)\right) \Bigg\}\Bigg] = 0, \end{aligned}$$

$$\frac{\partial u^*}{\partial x^*}=\frac{1}{e}\left[P(x,x^*)+F^{*\prime}(x^*)+\frac{\partial P(x,x^*)}{\partial x^*}\left\{x^* -\frac{e'(P(x,x^*))}{e(P(x,x^*))}\left((P(x,x^*)x^*+F^*(x)\right)\right\}\right]=0. \tag{1.11}$$

It must be shown that (1.11) has a solution. The question of existence in general equilibrium with increasing returns and oligopolistic markets has not been adequately treated by trade theorists. Accordingly, in this chapter we take the question seriously. For a detailed commentary on earlier attempts to resolve the issue, the reader is referred to Kemp and Shimomura (2001).

In view of (1.1), the production possibility curve can be written as

$$F(x)\equiv T(z(x)),\quad z(x)\equiv G^{-1}(x) \tag{1.12}$$

where $y=T(\cdot)$ is the equation of the production possibility curve under the condition that $G(\cdot)$ is the identity mapping. (Wong (1995b) called $T(\cdot)$ the 'virtual' production possibility curve.) Thus $T(\cdot)$ has all the properties of the standard production possibility curve. Since we assume that $G(0)=0$, there are positive values, $\bar{x}$ and $\bar{x}^*$, such that $0=F(\bar{x})=F^*(\bar{x}^*)$.

Consider Figure 1.1. The strategy space is the rectangular area $0\bar{x}A\bar{x}^*$. Let us fix x^* at some value in the interval $[0,\bar{x}^*]$. Then, from the first member of (1.11),

$$\frac{\partial u(0,x^*)}{\partial x}=\frac{1}{e}\left[P(0,x^*)+F'(0)+\frac{\partial P(0,x^*)}{\partial x}\left\{-\frac{e'(P(0,x^*))}{e(P(0,x^*))}F(0)\right\}\right]$$

$$\frac{\partial u(\bar{x},x^*)}{\partial x}=\frac{1}{e}\left[P(\bar{x},x^*)+F'(\bar{x})+\frac{\partial P(\bar{x},x^*)}{\partial x}\left\{1-\frac{P(\bar{x},x^*)e'(P(\bar{x},x^*))}{e(P(\bar{x},x^*))}\right\}\bar{x}\right]. \tag{1.13}$$

Since

$$\frac{\partial P(x,x^*)}{\partial x}<0 \text{ and } \frac{\partial P(x,x^*)}{\partial x^*}<0 \tag{1.14}$$

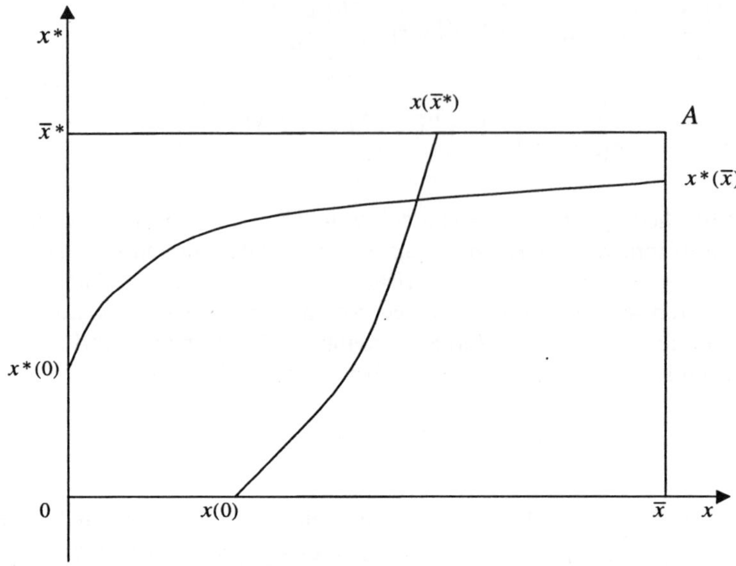

Figure 1.1 Reaction Curves

for any (x,x^*) in the rectangle $0\overline{x}A\overline{x}^*$, (1.13) implies that if

$$P(0,x^*)+F'(0)>0 \text{ and } P(\overline{x},x^*)+F'(\overline{x})<0$$

then

$$\frac{\partial u(0,x^*)}{\partial x}>0 \text{ and } \frac{\partial u(\overline{x},x^*)}{\partial x}<0.$$

It follows that there is an internal maximum point $x(x^*)\in(0,\overline{x})$ such that

$$\frac{\partial u(x(x^*),x^*)}{\partial x}=0, \quad \frac{\partial^2 u(x(x^*),x^*)}{\partial x^2}\leq 0 \tag{1.15}$$

and

$$u(x(x^*),x^*)\geq u(x,x^*) \text{ for all } x\in[0,\overline{x}]. \tag{1.16}$$

In view of (1.14),

$$P(0,\bar{x}^*)+F'(0)>0 \text{ and } P(\bar{x},x^*)+F'(\bar{x})<0. \tag{1.17}$$

We can devise a parallel argument concerning $u^*(x,x^*)$. Therefore, if (1.17) and

$$P(\bar{x},0)+F^{*\prime}(0)>0 \text{ and } P(0,\bar{x}^*)+F^{*\prime}(\bar{x}^*)<0 \tag{1.18}$$

are satisfied, we can depict the reaction curves $x(x^*)$ and $x^*(x)$ as in Figure 1.1, with

$$0<x(0),\quad x(\bar{x}^*)<\bar{x} \text{ and } 0<x^*(0),\quad x^*(\bar{x})<\bar{x}^*. \tag{1.19}$$

It follows that the two reaction curves must intersect somewhere inside the rectangle $0\bar{x}A\bar{x}^*$. Thus we arrive at the required existence proposition.

Proposition 1: *If preferences are everywhere identically homothetic, if production functions are everywhere homothetic (but not necessarily identically homothetic), and if* (1.17) *and* (1.18) *are satisfied, there exists a Cournot-Nash equilibrium point* (x_e, x_e^*) *of the duopoly game played by the two monopolistic firms.*

Remark 1: Proposition 1 guarantees existence but says nothing about uniqueness. As we shall see, uniqueness is not needed for Proposition 2; and Proposition 3 is based on assumptions, which imply uniqueness.

4. GAINS FROM TRADE

In this section, we show that, under the assumptions of Proposition 1, each country gains from trade. Partially differentiating (1.10) with respect to $P(x,x^*)$, we obtain

$$\frac{\partial U(P(x,x^*),x)}{\partial P(x,x^*)}=\frac{1}{e(P)^2}\left[xe(P)-e'(P)\{P(x,x^*)x+F(x)\}\right]$$

$$\frac{\partial U^*\left(P(x,x^*),x^*\right)}{\partial P(x,x^*)}=\frac{1}{e(P)^2}\left[x^*e(P)-e'(P)\left\{P(x,x^*)x^*+F^*(x^*)\right\}\right]. \tag{1.20}$$

Let (p_a, x_a) be an autarkic equilibrium pair for the home country. Then

$$\left.\frac{\partial U(P,x)}{\partial P}\right|_{(p_a,x_a)}=\frac{1}{e(p_a)^2}\left[x_a e(p_a)-e'(p_a)\left\{p_a x_a+F(x_a)\right\}\right]=0. \tag{1.21}$$

Moreover,

$$\left.\frac{\partial^2 U(P,x)}{\partial P^2}\right|_{\frac{\partial U}{\partial P}=0}=-\frac{e''(P)}{\left(e(P)\right)^2}\left[Px+F(x)\right]>0. \tag{1.22}$$

Thus, for given x_a, $P=p_a$ minimises $U(P,x_a)$. Hence

$$U(p_a,x_a)\le U\left(P\left(x_a,x_e^*\right),x_a\right). \tag{1.23}$$

On the other hand, from the definition of a Cournot-Nash equilibrium,

$$U\left(P\left(x_a,x_e^*\right),x_a\right)\le U\left(P\left(x_e,x_e^*\right),x_e\right). \tag{1.24}$$

It follows from (1.23) and (1.24) that

$$U(p_a,x_a)\le U\left(P\left(x_e,x_e^*\right),x_e\right). \tag{1.25}$$

A parallel argument can be applied to the foreign country, completing the proof of the gains-from-trade proposition.

Proposition 2: *Under the assumptions of Proposition 1, both countries gain from trade.*

Remark 2: As already noted in Remark 1, Proposition 2 is valid whether or not the world equilibrium is unique.

Remark 3: Given existence, the proposition is robust enough to cover the case in which the numbers of increasing-returns-to-scale goods, constant-returns-to-scale goods and countries are arbitrary; for a proof, see Kemp and Shimomura (2000).

5. TRADE PATTERNS

In this section we examine the equilibrium pattern of trade when the two countries differ in just one respect: each of the two aggregate endowment vectors is a positive scalar multiple of the other or, equivalently, the pair of foreign production functions is a positive scalar multiple of the pair of home production functions, so that one country is uniformly more productive than the other. For concreteness only, we confine our attention to the case in which the foreign endowment is b $(b>0)$ times the home endowment. Preferences and production functions are everywhere identically homothetic.

From the definitions of $T(\cdot)$ and $z(\cdot)$, we easily obtain

Lemma 1: *If the home production possibility function is* $y=T(z(x))$ *then the foreign production possibility function is* $y^*=bT(z(x^*)/b)$.

In view of Lemma 1, (1.11) reduces in the present case to

$$\frac{\partial u}{\partial x}=\frac{1}{e}\left[P(x,x^*;b)+T'(z(x))z'(x)+\frac{\partial P}{\partial x}\left\{x-\frac{e'(P(x,x^*;b))}{e(P(x,x^*;b))}(P(x,x^*;b)x+T(z(x))\right\}\right]=0$$

$$\frac{\partial u^*}{\partial x^*}=\frac{1}{e}\left[P(x,x^*;b)+T'\left(\frac{z(x^*)}{b}\right)z'(x^*)+\frac{\partial P}{\partial x^*}\left\{x^*-\frac{e'(P(x,x^*;b))}{e(P(x,x^*;b))}\left(P(x,x^*;b)x^*+bT\left(\frac{z(x^*)}{b}\right)\right)\right\}\right]=0, \quad (1.26)$$

where

$$P(x,x^*;b) \equiv g\left(\left(T(z(x))+bT\left(\frac{z(x^*)}{b}\right)\right)\Big/(x+x^*)\right).$$

The following result, concerning the *local* trade pattern, also will be useful.

Lemma 2: *There is a small positive number, say* ε, *such that if* $b \in (1, 1+\varepsilon)$ [*respectively,* $b \in (1-\varepsilon, 1)$] *then the home country imports* [*respectively, exports*] *the increasing-returns good x.*

Our proof of Lemma 2 is tedious and contains no useful intermediate results; hence it is confined to the Appendix.

With the aid of Lemma 2, we can prove the following proposition concerning the *global* trade pattern.

Proposition 3: *If the two countries differ only in the size of their factor endowments and if preferences and production functions are everywhere identically homothetic then the bigger country exports the increasing-returns good.*

Proof. Lemma 2 implies that if b is greater (respectively, smaller) than but sufficiently close to one then the larger country exports (respectively, imports) the increasing-returns good. We now show that the trade pattern is the same for all b greater than (respectively, smaller than) one.

Suppose that there exists $\tilde{b} \neq 1$ such that

$$x(\tilde{b})-\frac{e'\left(P\left(x(\tilde{b}),x^*(\tilde{b});\tilde{b}\right)\right)}{e\left(P\left(x(\tilde{b}),x^*(\tilde{b});\tilde{b}\right)\right)}\left(P\left(x(\tilde{b}),x^*(\tilde{b});\tilde{b}\right)x(\tilde{b})+T\left(z\left(x(\tilde{b})\right)\right)\right)=0, \tag{1.27}$$

that is, such that the home production of commodity x is equal to its home consumption. Evidently (1.27) implies that the foreign production and consumption of x also are equal, that is, that

$$x^*(\tilde{b})-\frac{e'\left(P\left(x(\tilde{b}),x^*(\tilde{b});\tilde{b}\right)\right)}{e\left(P\left(x(\tilde{b}),x^*(\tilde{b});\tilde{b}\right)\right)}\left(P\left(x(\tilde{b}),x^*(\tilde{b});\tilde{b}\right)x^*(\tilde{b})+\tilde{b}T\left(\frac{z\left(x^*(\tilde{b})\right)}{\tilde{b}}\right)\right)$$
$$=0. \tag{1.28}$$

In view of (1.26), (1.27) and (1.28) imply that

$$P\left(x(\tilde{b}),x^*(\tilde{b});\tilde{b}\right)+T'\left(z\left(x(\tilde{b})\right)\right)z'\left(x(\tilde{b})\right)=0$$

$$P\left(x(\tilde{b}),x^*(\tilde{b});\tilde{b}\right)+T'\left(\frac{1}{\tilde{b}}z\left(x^*(\tilde{b})\right)\right)z'\left(x^*(\tilde{b})\right)=0$$

$$x^*(\tilde{b})-\frac{e'\left(P\left(x(\tilde{b}),x^*(\tilde{b});\tilde{b}\right)\right)}{e\left(P\left(x(\tilde{b}),x^*(\tilde{b});\tilde{b}\right)\right)}\left[P\left(x(\tilde{b}),x^*(\tilde{b});\tilde{b}\right)x^*(\tilde{b})+\tilde{b}T\left(\frac{z\left(x(\tilde{b})\right)}{\tilde{b}}\right)\right]$$
$$=0. \tag{1.29}$$

And, in view of the definition of $P(x,x^*;b)$ attached to (1.26), equations (1.27)-(1.29) together imply that

$$g\left(\frac{T\left(z\left(x(\tilde{b})\right)\right)}{x(\tilde{b})}\right)+T'\left(z\left(x(\tilde{b})\right)\right)z'\left(x(b)\right)=0,$$

$$g\left(\frac{\tilde{b}T\left(\frac{1}{\tilde{b}}z\left(x^*(\tilde{b})\right)\right)}{x^*(\tilde{b})}\right)+T'\left(\frac{1}{\tilde{b}}z\left(x^*(\tilde{b})\right)\right)z'\left(x^*(\tilde{b})\right)=0, \tag{1.30}$$

$$\frac{T\left(z\left(x(\tilde{b})\right)\right)}{x(\tilde{b})}=\frac{\tilde{b}T\left(\frac{1}{\tilde{b}}z\left(x^*(\tilde{b})\right)\right)}{x^*(\tilde{b})}.$$

We now show that (1.30) cannot hold unless $\tilde{b}=1$. First, $x(\tilde{b})$ must be the solution to the first equation of (1.30); hence the value of $x(\tilde{b})$ does *not* depend on the value of $\tilde{b}$. Second, it follows from the remaining members of (1.30) that each of the values

$$T'\left(\frac{1}{\tilde{b}}z\left(x^*(\tilde{b})\right)\right)z'\left(x^*(\tilde{b})\right) \text{ and } \tilde{b}T\left(\frac{1}{\tilde{b}}z(x^*)\right)\Big/x^*$$

is independent of the value of $\tilde{b}$.

Let us draw the graphs of

$$\text{constant} = T'\left(\frac{1}{\tilde{b}}z(x^*)\right)z'(x^*) \tag{1.31}$$

and

$$\text{constant} = bT\left(\frac{1}{b}z(x^*)\right)\Big/x^* \tag{1.32}$$

on the (x^*, b)-plane in such a way that the two graphs intersect at $b = 1$; see Figure 1.2. Totally differentiating (1.31) and (1.32) with respect to x^* and b, we find that, at any intersection of the graphs,

$$\begin{aligned}\left.\frac{b}{x^*}\frac{dx^*}{db}\right|_{(31)} - \left.\frac{b}{x^*}\frac{dx^*}{db}\right|_{(32)} &= \frac{T''zz'}{x^*\left(T''(z')^2 + bT'z''\right)} - \frac{bT - T'z}{bT - T'x^*z'} \\ &= \frac{T''bTz'(z - xz') - (bT - zT')x^*bT'z''}{x^*\left(T''(z')^2 + bT'z''\right)(bT - T'x^*z')} \\ &= -\operatorname{sign}\left(T''(z')^2 + bT'z''\right).\end{aligned} \tag{1.33}$$

If there is no inflection point on the production possibility curve

$$y^* = bT(z(x^*)/b)$$

then the sign of

$$\left(T''(z')^2 + bT'z''\right)$$

does not change. In that case, the graphs of (1.31) and (1.32) intersect at most once. Since the graphs intersect at $b = 1$, there is no other b at which the graphs intersect, which is incompatible with the assumption that there exists $\tilde{b} \neq 1$ which satisfies (1.30). If, on the other hand, there is an inflection point on the production possibility curve then we can draw the locus of (1.31) as either *AEB* or *A′EB′* in Figure 1.2. Thus there is no point of intersection other than *E*. If there are multiple inflection points, the locus can be drawn like the dashed curve of Figure 1.2. However, noting that $T'' < 0$, $T' > 0$ and $z' > 0$, we see from (1.30) that if

$$\left.\frac{b}{x^*}\frac{dx^*}{db}\right|_{(31)} > 0 \ (< 0)$$

then

$$\left.\frac{b}{x^*}\frac{dx^*}{db}\right|_{(31)} > \quad (<) \quad \left.\frac{b}{x^*}\frac{dx^*}{db}\right|_{(32)}.$$

Hence multiple intersections of *CD* and the dashed curve are impossible; *E* is again the only possible point of intersection. □

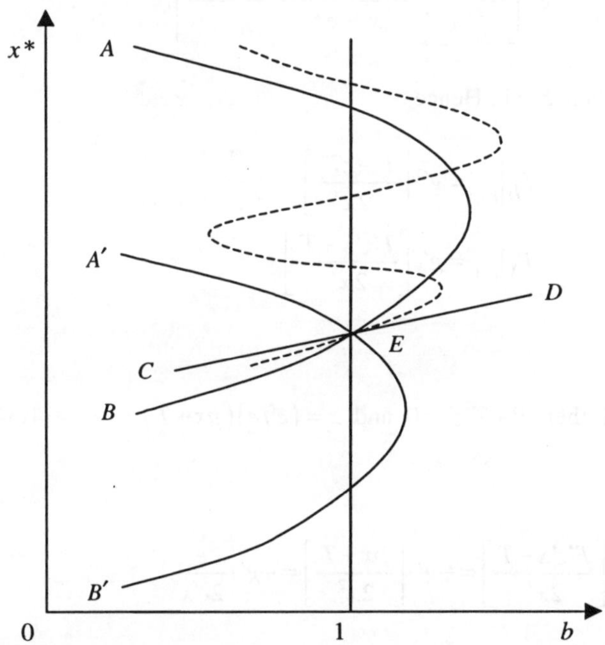

Figure 1.2 Locus of Equation (1.31) *(AEB , A′EB′) and Locus of Equation* (1.32) *(CD)*

Propositions bearing a superficial resemblance to Proposition 3 have been available for some time; see for example, Markusen and Melvin (1981). However those results were derived in a context of external economies and perfect competition whereas Proposition 3 relates to a world economy in which two giant duopolists compete strategically in quantities.

APPENDIX

Proof of Lemma 2. By definition,

$$P(x,x^*;b) \equiv g\left(\frac{T(z(x))+bT(z(x^*)/b)}{x+x^*}\right).$$

We begin by evaluating $P_b \equiv \partial P/\partial b$ and $P_x \equiv \partial P/\partial x$ at $b=1$. We have

$$P_b\big|_{b=1} = g' \cdot \left[\frac{T(z(x^*)) - z(x^*)T'(z(x^*))}{x+x^*}\right].$$

However, $x = x^*$ when $b=1$. Hence

$$P_b\big|_{b=1} = g' \cdot \left[\frac{T - zT'}{2x}\right]$$

$$P_x\big|_{b=1} = g' \cdot \left[\frac{T'z'x - T}{2x^2}\right].$$

However,

$$\text{if } b=1 \text{ then } P + T'z' = 0 \text{ and } x = (e'/e)(px+T). \tag{1.34}$$

Hence

$$g' \cdot \left[\frac{T'z'x-T}{2x^2}\right] = -g' \cdot \left[\frac{px+T}{2x^2}\right] = -g' \cdot \frac{e}{2e'x}.$$

Finally, we note that, since $g' = -(e')^2/(ee'')$,

$$P_x \cdot \left(\frac{e''}{e}\right)(px+T)\bigg|_{b=1} = \frac{1}{2}\left[\frac{1}{x} \cdot \frac{e'}{e} \cdot (px+T)\right] = 1/2. \tag{1.35}$$

Let us return to the Cournot-Nash equilibrium conditions (1.26), which we now rewrite as

$$\Gamma(x,x^*;b) \equiv P(x,x^*;b) + T'(z(x))z'(x)$$
$$+P_x(x,x^*;b)\left\{x - \frac{e'(P(x,x^*;b))}{e(P(x,x^*;b))}\left(P(x,x^*;b)x + T(z(x))\right)\right\} = 0 \tag{1.36}$$

$$\Gamma^*(x,x^*;b) \equiv P(x,x^*;b) + T'\left(\frac{z(x^*)}{b}\right)z'(x^*)$$
$$+P_{x^*}(x,x^*;b)\left\{x^* - \frac{e'(P(x,x^*;b))}{e(P(x,x^*;b))}\left(P(x,x^*;b)x^* + bT\left(\frac{z(x^*)}{b}\right)\right)\right\} \tag{1.37}$$
$$= 0.$$

The key terms are those in braces. When $b = 1$, both terms vanish. To establish Lemma 2, therefore, it suffices to show that, for sufficiently small ε, both terms are negative if $b \in (1, 1+\varepsilon)$ and positive if $b \in (1-\varepsilon, 1)$. Thus, differentiating the term in braces in (1.36) with respect to *b*, we obtain

$$\frac{d}{db}\left[x - \frac{e'(P(x,x^*;b))}{e(P(x,x^*;b))}\left(P(x,x^*;b)x + T(z(x))\right)\right]$$
$$= \left[1 - P_x(e''/e)(px+T)\right]\frac{dx}{db} - P_x(e''/e)(px+T)\frac{dx^*}{db} - P_b(e''/e)(px+T)$$
$$= \frac{1}{2}\frac{dx}{db} - \frac{1}{2}\frac{dx^*}{db} - \frac{1}{2}\frac{P_b}{P_x}. \tag{1.38}$$

To evaluate dx/db and dx^*/db we totally differentiate (1.36) and (1.37) with respect to *x*, *x** and *b*, evaluate at $b = 1$ and recall (1.34), obtaining

$$\left[P_x + \left(T''(z')^2 + T'z''\right) + P_x\{1 - P_x(e''/e)(px+T)\}\right]dx$$
$$+\left[P_x - (P_x)^2(e''/e)(px+T)\right]dx^* + P_b\left[1 - P_x(e''/e)(px+T)\right]db = 0, \tag{1.39}$$

$$P_x\left[1 - P_x(e''/e)(px+T)\right]dx$$
$$+\left[P_x + \left(T''(z')^2 + T'z''\right) + P_x\{1 - P_x(e''/e)(px+T)\}\right]dx^* \tag{1.40}$$
$$\left[P_b\{1 - P_x(e''/e)(px+T)\} - \{T''zz' + (e''/e)P_x(T - zT')\}\right]db = 0,$$

or, in view of (1.34),

$$\begin{bmatrix} \frac{3}{2}P_x + T''(z')^2 + T'z'' & \frac{1}{2}P_x \\ \frac{1}{2}P_x & \frac{3}{2}P_x + \left(T''(z')^2 + T'z''\right) \end{bmatrix} \begin{bmatrix} dx \\ dx^* \end{bmatrix} = \begin{bmatrix} -\frac{1}{2}P_b \\ -\frac{1}{2}P_b + \{T''zz' + (e''/e)P_x(T - zT')\} \end{bmatrix} \tag{1.41}$$

where the determinant of the coefficient matrix is

$$\begin{aligned} \Delta &\equiv \begin{vmatrix} \frac{3}{2}P_x + T''(z')^2 + T'z'' & \frac{1}{2}P_x \\ \frac{1}{2}P_x & \frac{3}{2}P_x + \left(T''(z')^2 + T'z''\right) \end{vmatrix} \\ &= \left[\frac{3}{2}P_x + \left(T''(z')^2 + T'z''\right) + \frac{1}{2}P_x\right]\left[\frac{3}{2}P_x + \left(T''(z')^2 + T'z''\right) - \frac{1}{2}P_x\right] \\ &= \left[P_x + \left(T''(z')^2 + T'z''\right) + P_x\right]\left[P_x + \left(T''(z')^2 + T'z''\right)\right] \\ &> 0. \end{aligned}$$

(The final inequality follows from the negativity of each of the square-bracketed terms, which in turn follows from the second-order conditions for the two giant firms.) Hence

$$\Delta\frac{dx}{db} = -\begin{vmatrix} \frac{1}{2}P_b & \frac{1}{2}P_x \\ \frac{1}{2}P_b - \{T''zz' + (e'/e)P_x(T - zT')\} & \frac{3}{2}P_x + T''(z')^2 + T'z'' \end{vmatrix} \tag{1.42}$$

and

$$\Delta\frac{dx^*}{db} = -\begin{vmatrix} \frac{3}{2}P_x + T''(z')^2 + T'z'' & \frac{1}{2}P_b \\ \frac{1}{2}P_x & \frac{1}{2}P_b - \{T''zz' + (e'/e)P_x(T - zT')\} \end{vmatrix}. \tag{1.43}$$

Substituting from (1.42) and (1.43) into (1.38), omitting the inessential multiplier ½, we obtain

$$
\begin{aligned}
&-\frac{1}{\Delta}\begin{vmatrix} \frac{1}{2}P_b & \frac{1}{2}P_x \\ \frac{1}{2}P_b-\{T''zz'+(e'/e)P_x(T-zT')\} & \frac{3}{2}P_x+T''(z')^2+T'z'' \end{vmatrix} \\
&+\frac{1}{\Delta}\begin{vmatrix} \frac{3}{2}P_x+T''(z')^2+T'z'' & \frac{1}{2}P_b \\ \frac{1}{2}P_x & \frac{1}{2}P_b-\{T''zz'+(e'/e)P_x(T-zT')\} \end{vmatrix}-P_b/P_x \\
&=\frac{1}{\Delta}\begin{vmatrix} \frac{1}{2}P_x & \frac{1}{2}P_b \\ \frac{3}{2}P_x+T''(z')^2+T'z'' & \frac{1}{2}P_b-\{T''zz'+(e'/e)P_x(T-zT')\} \end{vmatrix} \\
&+\frac{1}{\Delta}\begin{vmatrix} \frac{3}{2}P_x+T''(z')^2+T'z'' & \frac{1}{2}P_b \\ \frac{1}{2}P_x & \frac{1}{2}P_b-\{T''zz'+(e'/e)P_x(T-zT')\} \end{vmatrix}-P_b/P_x \\
&=\frac{1}{\Delta}\begin{vmatrix} \frac{3}{2}P_x+\left(T''(z')^2+T'z''\right)+\frac{1}{2}P_x & \frac{1}{2}P_b \\ \frac{3}{2}P_x+\left(T''(z')^2+T'z''\right)+\frac{1}{2}P_x & \frac{1}{2}P_b-\{T''zz'+(e'/e)P_x(T-zT')\} \end{vmatrix}-P_b/P_x \\
&=-\frac{1}{\Delta}\left\{2P_x+\left(T''(z')^2+T'z''\right)\right\}\{T''zz'+(e'/e)P_x(T-zT')\}-P_b/P_x \\
&=-\frac{1}{\Delta P_x}\left\{\left(2P_x+\left(T''(z')^2+T'z''\right)\right)\left(T''zz'+(e'/e)P_x(T-zT')\right)P_x+\Delta P_b\right\} \\
&=-\frac{1}{\Delta P_x}\left\{\left(2P_x+\left(T''(z')^2+T'z''\right)\right)\left(T''zz'+(e'/e)P_x(T-zT')\right)P_x\right. \\
&\quad\left.+P_b\left(2P_x+\left(T''(z')^2+T'z''\right)\right)\left(P_x+\left(T''(z')^2+T'z''\right)\right)\right\} \\
&=-\frac{1}{\Delta P_x}\left[2P_x+\left(T''(z')^2+T'z''\right)\right]\left[P_x\left(T''zz'+(e'/e)(T-zT')\right)\right. \\
&\quad\left.+P_b\left(P_x+\left(T''(z')^2+T'z''\right)\right)\right].
\end{aligned}
\tag{1.44}
$$

Now the term enclosed by the braces in (1.44) can be re-written as

$$\left\{P_b+(e'/e)P_x(T-zT')\right\}P_x+T''z'\left(P_xz+P_bz'\right)+P_bT'z''. \qquad (1.45)$$

The final term of (1.45) is positive, since P_b is positive and each of T' and z'' is negative. On the other hand,

$$\begin{aligned} P_b+(e'/e)P_x(T-xT') &= \frac{g'(T-zT')}{2x}-(e'/e)g'\frac{px+T}{2x^2}(T-zT') \\ &= \frac{g'(T-zT')}{2x}-g'\frac{(T-zT')}{2x}<0 \end{aligned} \qquad (1.46)$$

and

$$\begin{aligned} P_xz+P_bz' &= -\frac{g'(px+T)}{2x^2}z+\frac{g'(T-zT')}{2x}z'=\frac{g'}{2x}\left\{z'(T-zT')-\left(\frac{px+T}{x}\right)z\right\} \\ &= \frac{g'T}{2x^2}(z'x-z)<0. \end{aligned}$$

It follows from this last inequality and from the negativity of $T''z'$ that

$$T''z'\left(P_xz+P_bz'\right)>0. \qquad (1.47)$$

Hence (1.45), and therefore the term enclosed by braces in (1.44), is positive. Hence(1.38), with $b=1$, also is positive and we may conclude that, for a sufficiently small $\varepsilon>0$, $x-(e'/e)(px+T)<0$ for $b\in(1,1+\varepsilon)$ and $x-(e'/e)(px+T)>0$ for $b\in(1-\varepsilon,1)$. □

NOTE

1. This assumption plays no role in a Walrasian economy. In such an economy agents know nothing about each other; their actions are coordinated by market prices alone. In an egalitarian economy, on the other hand, the assumption is a natural one; it is also quite mild, falling far short of the game theoretical assumption that the egalitarian status of the agents is common knowledge.

REFERENCES

Herberg, H. and Kemp, M.C. (1969), 'Some implications of variable returns to scale', *Canadian Journal of Economics*, **2**, 403-15.

Kemp, M.C. and Long, N.V. (1992), 'Some properties of egalitarian economies', *Journal of Public Economics*, **49**, 383-7.

Kemp, M.C. and Shimomura, K. (1995), 'The apparently innocuous representative agent', *Japanese Economic Review*, **46**, 247-56.

Kemp, M.C. and Shimomura, K. (2000), 'Increasing returns and international trade: a new approach', *Review of International Economics*, **8**, 614-18.

Kemp, M.C. and Shimomura, K. (2001), 'Gains from trade in a Cournot-Nash general equilibrium', *Japanese Economic Review*, **52**, 284-302.

Markusen, J.R. and Melvin, J.R. (1981), 'Trade, factor prices, and gains from trade with increasing returns to scale', *Canadian Journal of Economics*, **14**, 450-69.

Wong, K.-y. (1995a), 'Curvature in the production possibility frontier under external economies of scale: was Tinbergen wrong?', University of Washington.

Wong, K.-y. (1995b), *International Trade in Goods and Factor Mobility*, Cambridge, Mass.: MIT Press.

2. On the Shape of Production Possibility Loci under Variable Returns to Scale: The *n* Commodity *m* Factor Case

Horst Herberg

1. INTRODUCTION

Until the late 1960s it was a common tenet among economists that, in the two-commodity, two-factor case with different factor intensities and totally inelastic factor supplies, sufficiently weak increasing returns to scale in one or both sectors leave the production possibility locus (PPL) conventionally bowed-out, i.e. strictly convex from above, and thus do not endanger the convexity of the production possibility set; see e.g., Caves (1960), Kemp (1964) and Savosnick (1958).

This tenet was proved to be incorrect by Murray Kemp and me in two papers, the first one, Herberg (1969), dealing with homogeneous production functions, the other one, Herberg and Kemp (1969), dealing with the more general case of homothetic production functions. More specifically, it was shown in the second paper that the following proposition holds: *Whenever for small enough or all levels of its output one of the commodities is produced under increasing (decreasing) returns to scale, however weak, then close to the axis of the other good the PPL is strictly concave (strictly convex) from above, and this is true whatever the returns to scale in the other industry;* see Herberg and Kemp (1969, p. 409, theorem 2(a)).[1]

A graphical representation of this proposition is given in Figure 2.1 for the two-by-two case with homogeneous Cobb-Douglas production functions and increasing returns in the first and decreasing returns in the second industry.[2]

The purpose of the present chapter is to demonstrate that this proposition holds for any number of commodities and any number of fixed or mobile factors provided that the production functions are homothetic with respect to the mobile factors and the returns to scale refer to these factors only.

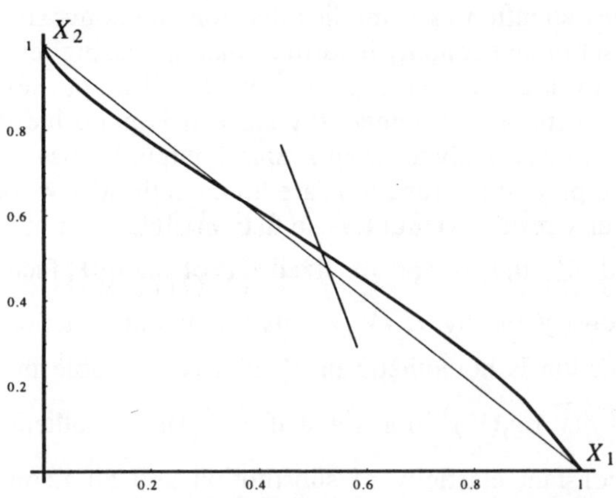

Figure 2.1 Transformation Curve for Cobb-Douglas Functions $X_1 = (C_1^{1/4} L_1^{3/4})^{3/2}$, $X_2 = (C_2^{3/4} L_2^{1/4})^{3/4}$ *and Factor Endowments* $C = L = 1$.

Figure 2.2 gives a first impression of what the PPL for three commodities looks like if the production functions are homogeneous and if there are increasing returns in the first sector and constant or decreasing returns in the second and third sectors. This diagram exemplifies a general result: *The production possibility set of an economy is non-convex if its production functions are all homothetic with respect to the mobile factors and if one or more of these functions are non-concave at least for small output levels. Consequently, for given positive commodity prices the total output value need not be highest at an interior point of tangency of the PPL and the price plane.*

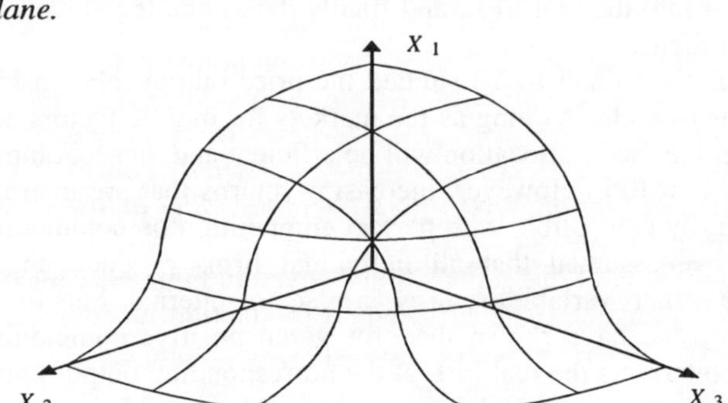

Figure 2.2 The Production Possibility Locus with Increasing Returns to Scale in the First Sector and Constant or Decreasing Returns in the Second and Third Sector

This conclusion deserves attention as it implies that for non-convexity of the production possibility set of an economy it suffices that increasing returns prevail in a single sector, even a tiny one and even for small output levels only. The last observation seems to be noteworthy since it is plausible that increasing returns, if any, are most likely to occur at *small* output levels.

The requirement that the production functions are homothetic with respect to the mobile factors is clearly restrictive but less so than might appear at first sight. Denote by $\overline{V_i}$ and V_i the vector of fixed or of mobile factors, respectively, of the *i*-th industry and by $H_i^*(\overline{V_i}, V_i)$ its production function. It is easy to see that this function is homothetic in V_i if it is separable in the sense that $H_i^*(\overline{V}_i, V_i) = \Gamma_i\left(f_i(\overline{V_i}), g_i(V_i)\right)$ holds and if $g_i(V_i)$ is homothetic in V_i. Obviously, e.g., all constant elasticity of substitution and all Leontief functions or combinations thereof have this property and thus belong to the category of production functions for which the findings reported here apply.

As in Herberg (1969) and Herberg and Kemp (1969), the proof of the main theorem is based on the following idea. A homothetic production function[3] $H_i(V_i)$ is a monotonously increasing transformation $G_i(Y_i)$ of a linear homogeneous function $Y_i = F_i(V_i)$; see e.g., Takayama (1994, p. 147). Call $H_i(\cdot)$ the *real* and $F_i(\cdot)$ the *virtual* production functions.[4] Since any pair of $H_i(\cdot)$ and $F_i(\cdot)$ defines the same isoproduct loci, an efficient factor allocation for the virtual production functions is also an efficient factor allocation for the real production functions, and vice versa. Hence the real PPL is simply a transformation of the virtual PPL, based on the functions G_i. Therefore, one can start by analysing the slope and curvature of the virtual PPL, then transform it into the real PPL, and finally determine the slope and curvature of the latter locus.

In our 1969 paper, Kemp and I also studied the price-output relationship under variable returns to scale. As long as the markets for mobile factors are perfectly competitive, the factor allocation will be efficient and, hence, output points will lie on the real PPL. However, increasing returns that are internal to single firms are hardly compatible with perfect competition on commodity markets. Therefore, we assumed that all individual firms produce under constant returns, i.e., that variable returns are sector-internal but firm-external. For this case we have shown that, for given positive commodity prices, the price line intersects the real PPL at the corresponding output point unless the two local returns to scale happen to coincide; see Herberg and Kemp (1969, theorem 6). A consequence is that the price-output reaction can normally not be inferred from the curvature of the real PPL. Mutatis mutandis, this result also continues to hold.

The chapter is organised as follows. In the next section the assumptions on which the analysis is based are listed and some basic implications are mentioned. In section 3 I state a lemma and a theorem about the properties of the virtual and the real PPL, respectively. Section 4 deals with the relationship between pairs of commodity prices and the corresponding slopes of the real PPL. Some extensions will be presented in the final section. All proofs are relegated to appendices as they are partly rather tedious. They can be skipped by readers interested only in my findings and trusting my mathematical competence.

2. ASSUMPTIONS AND SOME BASIC RESULTS

The following notation will be used:

R^n_+; R^n_{++}: non-negative and positive orthants of the n-dimensional Euclidean space

$V=(V_1,...,V_m)$: vector of the country's overall factor endowment

$V_i=(V_{i1},...,V_{im})$: input vector of sector i

$X=(X_1,...,X_n)$: vector of real outputs

$X_i=H_i(V_i)$: real production function of sector i

$Y=(Y_1,...,Y_n)$: vector of virtual outputs

$Y_i=F_i(V_i)$: virtual production function of sector i

$z_i=(z_{i2},...,z_{im})$, $z_{ij}=V_{ij}/V_{i1}$: vector of factor intensities of sector i

$F_{ij}=\partial F_i/\partial V_{ij}$, $F_{ijk}=\partial F_{ij}/\partial V_{ik}$, $\beta_i=(\beta_{i2},...,\beta_{im})$, $\beta_{ij}=F_{ij}/F_{i1}$.

Some additional notation will be introduced later.

The assumptions are:

(A1) There are n domestic sectors or industries, each producing a single final commodity $i=1,...,n$ and using m factors of production $j=1,...,m$.

(A2) These factors are mobile between sectors and their supply is completely inelastic.

(A3) The real production function $X_i=H_i(V_i)\equiv G_i(F_i(V_i))$ of sector i is homothetic with respect to V_i, where the function G_i is defined over R^1_+ with $G_i(0)=0$ and twice continuously differentiable over R^1_{++} with $G_i'>0$. The virtual production function $F_i(V_i)$ is defined, linear homogeneous and strictly quasi-concave over R^m_+ and twice continuously differentiable over R^m_{++} with $F_{ij}>0$ for $j=1,...,m$.

(A4) All factors are essential for producing any good, i.e. $F_i=0$ if $V_{ij}=0$ for at least one j.[5]

(A5) β_i is a vector-valued function of V_i with domain R^m_{++} and range R^{m-1}_{++}.

Some comments on these assumptions and their immediate implications seem to be called for:

(a) As already mentioned, a sector's real and virtual production functions define the same isoproduct loci. These loci are strictly convex from below as the functions F_i are assumed to be strictly quasi-concave.

(b) Due to the linear homogeneity of F_i, the partial derivatives F_{ij} depend only on the factor intensity vector z_i, and they are positive and finite for any $z_i \in R^{m-1}_{++}$. Hence, the slopes of the isoproduct loci, i.e., the marginal rates of factor substitution, $\partial V_{i1} / \partial V_{ij} = -F_{ij} / F_{i1} = -\beta_{ij}$, are well-defined functions of z_i : $\beta_{ij} = B_{ij}(z_i)$.

(c) Since F_i is assumed to be twice continuously differentiable its isoproduct loci are smooth surfaces. This implies that the functions $B_{ij}(z_i)$ are continuously differentiable over R^{m-1}_{++}.

(d) Because of assumption (A5), $B_i(z_i) = \left(B_{i2}(z_i), \ldots, B_{im}(z_i)\right)$ defines a univalent, i.e., one-to-one, mapping of R^{m-1}_{++} onto itself. Efficient factor allocation requires $\beta_1 = \ldots = \beta_n$ and thereby establishes an univalent relationship between any pair z_i and z_k of factor intensity vectors. These relationships hold irrespective of the output levels, and they map any positive, finite z_i into an equally positive, finite z_k.

(e) Finally, due to assumption (A4), $Y_i > 0$ implies $z_i > 0$. Hence, whenever a factor allocation is efficient and thus the output vector Y is a point on the virtual PPL, it follows from the last conclusion that *all* factor intensity vectors $z_1, \ldots, z_n$ are positive and finite.

3. PROPERTIES OF THE VIRTUAL AND THE REAL PRODUCTION POSSIBILITY LOCUS

To formulate the findings some additional notation is needed. Denote by S_v and S_r the virtual and the real PPL, respectively, and by S^o_{ik} the curve on S_r passing through some point X^o on that surface with only X_i and X_k varying. Hence, S^o_{ik} is a transformation curve between the i-th and the k-th commodity with all other output levels remaining constant.

The following two elasticities of the transformation functions are of some importance:

$$\eta_i = Y_i G_i' / G_i, \quad \delta_i = Y_i G_i'' / G_i'. \qquad (2.1)$$

η_i is, of course, the local scale elasticity of the i-th sector's production function. δ_i is closely related to it by the relationship

$$\delta_i = \eta_i - 1 + (Y_i \eta_i' / \eta_i) . \tag{2.2}$$

For reasons which will become clear later I shall call returns to scale locally increasing (decreasing) in *the strict sense* whenever both $\eta_i - 1$ and δ_i are positive (negative).[6]

To analyse the curvature of the real PPL one needs to know the slopes and curvature of the virtual PPL and to show that they are subject to certain finite bounds. As shown in the Appendix the following lemma holds.

Lemma: *Let assumptions* (A1)-(A5) *be satisfied. Then the virtual production possibility locus, S_v, can be described by a concave, twice continuously differentiable function $Y_1 = \Psi(Y_2,...,Y_n)$. Over the domain of Ψ, i.e., for points of S_v,*

(i) its first-order partial derivatives $\Psi_i = \partial\Psi / \partial Y_i$ have negative upper and finite lower bounds, and

(ii) its second-order differential $d^2\Psi = \sum_{i,k=2}^{n} \Psi_{ik} dY_i dY_k$ is non-positive due to the concavity of Ψ and bounded from below for given values of dY_i and dY_k, $i,k = 1,...,n$.[7]

This lemma is the basis for proving, as is done in the Appendix, the following theorem describing the main properties of the real PPL. It generalises Theorem 2 in Herberg and Kemp (1969) and its predecessor, the lemma in Herberg (1969), to any number of commodities and mobile factors.

Theorem: *Assumptions* (A1)-(A5) *imply for the real production possibility locus S_r and for the transformation curves S_{ik}^o, passing through any point X^o on S_r with positive X_i^o and X_k^o:*

(i) The real PPL is uniformly convex from above if in each sector and for all feasible output levels the returns to scale are locally non-increasing in the strict sense. The real PPL is even strictly convex if the same is true for the virtual PPL. Moreover, if the k-th sector produces under locally decreasing returns to scale for all feasible output levels, all curves S_{ik}^o are uniformly strictly convex from above.

(ii) Suppose that low output levels of the k-th commodity are produced under locally decreasing returns to scale in the strict sense, i.e. that

$\lim_{Y_k \to 0} \delta_k < 0$ holds. Then for sufficiently small output levels of the k-th commodity the transformation curves S^o_{ik} are strictly convex from above, and this is so irrespective of the returns to scale in the other sectors.[8]

(iii) *Suppose that low output levels of the k-th commodity are produced under locally increasing returns to scale in the strict sense, i.e., that $\lim_{Y_k \to 0} \delta_k > 0$ holds. Then for sufficiently small output levels of the k-th commodity the transformation curves S^o_{ik} are strictly concave from above, and this is so irrespective of the returns to scale in the other sectors. Consequently, the real PPL is non-convex from above close to the coordinate plane $X_k = 0$.*[9]

(iv) *Suppose that none of the commodities is produced under decreasing returns to scale in the strict sense. Then all curves S^o_{ik} are uniformly strictly concave from above if the k-th commodity is produced under sufficiently strongly increasing returns to scale, i.e., δ_k exceeds zero by a sufficient margin. (This does not mean, however, that the real PPL itself is uniformly concave or even strictly concave from above.)*

(v) *These results also hold for all lower-dimensional PPL, including transformation curves, associated with zero output levels of one or more of the commodities.*

Two short comments seem to be called for.

(a) It seems worthwhile to compare the present conditions for strict concavity or strict convexity of the transformation curves S^o_{ik} close to their endpoints with those stated in Herberg and Kemp (1969). There the production functions were written as $X_i = g_i(X_i)Y_i$ with the elasticity $\omega_i = X_i\, g_i'/g_i$ assumed to be less than unity. As shown in the Appendix

$$\eta_i = (1-\omega_i)^{-1}, \quad \delta_i / Y_i = (1-\omega_i)^{-2}\left[(1-\omega_i)(g_i\omega_i / X_i) + g_i\omega_i'\right]. \quad (2.3)$$

Hence, not surprisingly, the terms determining the curvature of the transformation curve in the former paper and of the curves S^o_{ik} in the present one are the same.

(b) Parts (ii) and (iii) of the theorem remain silent about the shape of the transformation curves S^o_{ik} for low output levels of the *i*-th sector if δ_i is negative (positive) but $\lim_{Y_i \to 0} \delta_i = 0$. Under such circumstances it cannot be ruled out that the surface is strictly concave (convex) from above for small output levels of the *i*-th good since then the signs of the other δ_j also matter. In the simplest possible case of just two final goods and a single mobile factor the virtual PPL is a straight line with $\Psi_2 = -1$. Then equation (2.15) in the Appendix implies

$$\operatorname{sgn} \partial^2 X_1 / \partial X_2^2 = \operatorname{sgn}\left[(\delta_1/Y_1)+(\delta_2/Y_2)\right]. \tag{2.4}$$

Of course, $\delta_1 < 0$ and $\delta_2 > 0$ with $\lim_{Y_i \to 0} \delta_i = 0$ are compatible with the right hand side of (2.4) being positive for small Y_1 and negative for small Y_2. Only in this rather exceptional case is Tinbergen correct in asserting that the transformation curve is bowed-in close to the axis of the commodity produced under increasing and bowed-out close to the axis of the other commodity produced under decreasing returns: see Tinbergen (1945, p. 192). An example with rather odd 'production functions' is given by Wong (1995, pp. 210-11).

4. COMMODITY PRICES AND SLOPES OF THE REAL PRODUCTION POSSIBILITY LOCUS

As already mentioned, another result derived in Herberg and Kemp (1969) also carries over to the general case. Assuming that all firms within a sector have individual production functions that are linear homogeneous in the mobile factors but that the sector's total output may be subject to variable returns to scale, we have shown for the two-commodity, two-factor case that price lines intersect the real PPL at the corresponding output points unless there the local returns to scale of the two sectors happen to coincide. Here the equivalent relationship

$$\left|\partial X_i / \partial X_k\right| = (\eta_i / \eta_k)(p_k / p_i) \geq (\leq)\, p_k / p_i \quad \text{if} \quad \eta_i \geq (\leq)\, \eta_k \tag{2.5}$$

holds provided that X_i and X_k are both positive. The proof is quite simple and left to the reader. Thus, under these circumstances, theorems 5 and 6 of Herberg and Kemp (1969) also continue to hold. Especially, for given positive commodity prices, the real PPL is usually cut by the price plane.

5. SOME EXTENSIONS

Although the theorem stated above deals with the general case of n commodities and m mobile factors it should not be overlooked that it is based on assumptions, which partly are rather restrictive. In particular, this is true for assumption (A4). Closer inspection of the steps taken to prove the lemma reveals, however, that (A4) can be weakened to:

(A4a) There is at least one factor that is indispensable in producing each commodity, and there is also at least one commodity for which all factors are indispensable.

Let these be, without loss, the first factor and the first commodity. Assumption (A4a) guarantees that the factor intensities z_{ij} are well defined and that all elements of the vector z_i are positive if $Y_1 > 0$. Assumption (A5) again implies the existence of a univalent relationship mapping positive, finite z_1 into equally positive, finite z_i, $i = 2,...,n$. Thus, all conclusions drawn in the Appendix continue to hold at least for $Y_1 > 0$ and the lemma remains valid. Any further weakening of (A4) seems, however, to be difficult.

Assumption (A3) postulates, inter alia, unrestricted factor substitutability but the lemma can also be proved if (A3) and (A5) are replaced by:

(A3a) (last sentence) The virtual production function F_i is linear homogeneous, strictly quasi-concave and twice continuously differentiable with $F_{ij} > 0, j = 1,...,m$, over some open convex cone $C_i \in R_+^m$ which also contains the endowment vector V.

(A5a) β_i is a vector-valued function of V_i with domain C_i and with some open convex cone in R_{++}^{m-1}, the same for $i = 1,...,n$, as its range.

Corollary: *The theorem remains valid if assumptions* (A3), (A4) *or* (A5) *are replaced by* (A3a), (A4a) *or* (A5a), *respectively.*

Taking also into account my earlier observation that quite a number of different types of production functions are homothetic with respect to proper subsets of their inputs, it appears safe to assert that the theorem is rather generally applicable. The same can be said for the findings mentioned in section 4.

APPENDIX

Proof of the Lemma. The lemma evidently holds if there is only one mobile factor, say the first one, as then the virtual production functions can be chosen to be $Y_i = V_{i1}$ and S_v is that part of the hyperplane $\sum_i Y_i = V_1$ lying in R_+^n.

The proof proceeds in several steps for the case where $m > 1$. Consider first the virtual production possibility set D_v. It is well known that it is non-empty, compact and convex; see, e.g., Woodland (1982, p. 52). S_v is the outer boundary of D_v and hence convex from above.

More precisely, S_v can be defined as follows. Denote by D_v^* the projection of D_v onto the plane $Y_1 = 0$. Thus D_v^* is a subset of R_+^{n-1}. Denote its points by $Y^* = (Y_2, \ldots, Y_n)$. Then,[10]

$$S_v = \left\{ Y : Y^* \in D_v^*, Y_1 = \max F_1(V_1) \; s.t. \; Y_i \leq F_i(V_i), i = 2, \ldots, n; \sum_{i=1}^{n} V_i \leq V \right\}. \quad (2.6)$$

As the highest possible value of Y_1 corresponding to any one $Y^* \in D_v^*$ is uniquely determined, it can be inferred that S_v is the graph of a function $Y_1 = \Psi(Y^*)$ with domain D_v^*. Moreover, this function is concave as S_v is convex from above.

The next step is to show that the input vectors V_i and factor intensity vectors z_i, $i = 1, \ldots, n$, corresponding to some given output vector Y on S_v are also uniquely determined, i.e., are functions of Y^* with domain D_v^*. Assume the contrary. Let Y be a point on S_v and suppose that there exist two different input vectors V' and V'' for producing this output vector. Define $V^\alpha = \alpha V' + (1-\alpha)V'', 0 < \alpha < 1$. Obviously, these vectors satisfy the factor restriction $\sum_{i=1}^{n} V_i^\alpha \leq V$. Since $Y_i = F_i(V_i') = F_i(V_i'')$, strict quasi-concavity of F_i implies $F_i(V_i^\alpha) > Y_i$ for $i = 1, \ldots n$ and $0 < \alpha < 1$. Thus factors could be reallocated to raise, say, Y_1 without lowering any other Y_j. This contradicts the definition of S_v. Thus, the V_{ij} are indeed uniquely determined by, and functions of, Y^*: $V_{ij} = \varphi_{ij}(Y^*), Y^* \in D_v^*$.

Obviously, for $Y \in S_v$ at least one Y_k is positive. Since, by assumption (A4), all corresponding inputs V_{kj} are positive, the same holds true for the factor intensities z_{kj}. Hence the factor intensity vector z_k is positive and uniquely determined by Y^*. Points on S_v require efficient factor allocation. Therefore, the univalent relationships between all pairs z_k and z_j imply that all factor intensities z_{ij} are positive functions of Y^*: $z_{ij} = \xi_{ij}(Y^*)$, $Y^* \in D_v^*$. It should also be noted that, due to the smoothness of the isoproduct loci, the functions φ_{ij} and ξ_{ij} are continuously differentiable.

The next step is to look at the first-order conditions characterising S_v. As equation (2.6) indicates they can be derived from the Lagrangean function[11]

$$L = Y_1 + \sum_{i=1}^{n} \lambda_i \left[F_i(V_i) - Y_i \right] + \sum_{j=1}^{m} \mu_j \left[V_j - \sum_{i=1}^{n} V_{ij} \right]. \tag{2.7}$$

These conditions and the envelope theorem imply

$$F_{11} = \lambda_i F_{i1}, \quad \partial Y_1 / \partial Y_i = -\lambda_i = -F_{11} / F_{i1} \text{ if } Y_1 > 0, Y_i > 0. \tag{2.8}$$

Thus for $Y_1 > 0$, $Y_i > 0$ and also for $Y_1 \to 0$ or $Y_i \to 0$

$$\Psi_i = \partial Y_1 / \partial Y_i = -F_{11} / F_{i1}. \tag{2.9}$$

Since all z_{ij} are continuous, positive functions of Y^* over D_v^*, the same holds true for the partial derivatives F_{11} and F_{i1}. Therefore, all Ψ_i are continuous, negative functions over the compact domain D_v^*, and it follows from the Weierstrass theorem (see, e.g., Takayama 1994, p. 36) that each Ψ_i has a negative upper and a finite lower bound. This completes the proof of part (i) of the lemma.

The final step is straightforward. The concavity of Ψ implies $d^2\Psi \leq 0$. Remembering that F_{i1} depends on z_i only, one finds

$$\begin{aligned} \Psi_{ik} = \partial \Psi_i / \partial Y_k = (F_{i1})^{-1} \sum_{j=2}^{m} (\partial F_{11} / \partial z_{1j})(\partial \xi_{1j} / \partial Y_k) \\ - F_{11}(F_{i1})^{-2} \sum_{j=2}^{m} (\partial F_{i1} / \partial z_{ij})(\partial \xi_{ij} / \partial Y_k). \end{aligned} \tag{2.10}$$

All derivatives on the right hand side of (2.10) are continuous over D_v^* with F_{i1} being positive. Hence Ψ_{ik} is continuous over D_v^* as well. Invoking the Weierstrass theorem once again it follows that all Ψ_{ik}, $i,k = 2,\ldots,n$, are bounded. This establishes part (ii) of the lemma and completes its proof.

Proof of the Theorem. The virtual PPL, S_v, can be converted into the real one, S_r, by applying the mapping $X_i = G_i(Y_i)$:

$$X_1 = \Theta(X_2,...,X_n) = G_1\left(\Psi\left(G_2^{-1}(X_2),...,G_n^{-1}(X_n)\right)\right). \qquad (2.11)$$

The function Θ is defined for $X^* = (X_2,...,X_n) \in D_r^*$ where D_r^* is the image of D_v^* under the mappings $X_i = G_i(Y_i)$, $i = 2,...,n$. Since $G_i' > 0$ and $dY_i = (1/G_i')dX_i$ it follows that

$$dX_1 = \sum_{i=2}^{n} \Theta_i dX_i = \sum_{i=2}^{n} (G_1'/G_i')\Psi_i dX_i . \qquad (2.12)$$

Hence, as was to be expected, S_r is also negatively sloped in every direction. Moreover,

$$d^2X_1 = \sum_{i,k=2}^{n} \Theta_{ik} dX_i dX_k$$
$$= \sum_{i,k=2}^{n} [G_1'\Psi_{ik} + G_1''\Psi_i\Psi_k](G_i'G_k')^{-1} dX_i dX_k - \sum_{i=2}^{n} G_1'G_i''(G_i')^{-3}\Psi_i dX_i^2 . \qquad (2.13)$$

Using the elasticities δ_i, defined in equation (2.1), yields a more useful version of the last relationship:

$$d^2X_1 = G_1'\left\{\sum_{i,k=2}^{n}\left[\Psi_{ik} + (\delta_1/Y_1)\Psi_i\Psi_k\right]dY_i\,dY_k - \sum_{i=2}^{n}(\delta_i/Y_i)\Psi_i dY_i^2\right\}. \qquad (2.14)$$

Taking the lemma into account it follows immediately that $\delta_i \le 0$ for $Y_i \ge 0$ and $i = 1,...,n$ is a sufficient, but not necessary, condition for $d^2X_1 \le 0$ for any $X^* \in D_r^*$. This implies that then Θ is a concave function over D_r^*, i.e., that the real PPL S_r is convex from above and the real production possibility set D_r is convex.

A different situation arises if, say, the elasticity δ_1 takes positive values and has a positive lower bound for small Y_1. Then δ_1/Y_1 tends to plus infinity as Y_1 approaches zero.[12] Take an output point $X^o \in S_r$ with positive X_1^o and X_k^o, and consider the transformation curve S_{1k}^o passing through X^o.

Equation (2.14), $dY_k = (1/G_k')dX_k$ and $dY_i = 0$, $i \neq 1,k$, imply for the curvature of S_{1k}^o:

$$\partial^2 X_1 / \partial X_k^2 = G_1'(G_k')^{-2}\left[\Psi_{kk} + (\delta_1 / Y_1)(\Psi_k)^2 - (\delta_k / Y_k)\Psi_k\right]. \quad (2.15)$$

Remember that, according to the lemma, $a \leq \Psi_k \leq b$, $c \leq \Psi_{kk} \leq 0$ where *a, b, c* are finite, negative bounds. Starting from X^o let the output point move along S_{1k}^o with X_1 declining and X_k rising. The corresponding values of X_k form a positive compact interval. Over this interval δ_k / Y_k is bounded since it is a continuous function of Y_k and hence of X_k. At the same time δ_1 / Y_1 increases without limit if $X_1 \to 0$ and $\lim_{Y_1 \to 0} \delta_1 > 0$. Therefore, equation (2.15) then implies that $\partial^2 X_1 / \partial X_k^2$ is positive at least for sufficiently small outputs of the first commodity, and this is true whatever the signs and values of δ_k or the other δ_i. This means that under these circumstances any such curve S_{1k}^o is strictly concave from above close to the coordinate plane $X_1 = 0$ and that the real PPL is there not convex from above. (It does not mean, however, that the real PPL is concave or even strictly concave for sufficiently small output levels of the first commodity; see Figure 2.2 for a counter-example). Similar arguments imply that $\partial^2 X_1 / \partial X_k^2$ is negative for small enough X_1 if $\lim_{Y_1 \to 0} \delta_1 < 0$.

Looking at the other end of the curve S_{1k}^o one can similarly infer that $\partial^2 X_1 / \partial X_k^2$ is positive (negative) for small enough X_k if $\lim_{Y_k \to 0} \delta_k$ is positive (negative). Again, these signs do not depend on the signs and values of δ_1 and of the other δ_i.

It will be noted that all these conclusions hold (a) for all similarly defined transformation curves S_{ik}^o,[13] (b) for any lower-dimensional real PPL, i.e., for any part of S_r with a zero output of one or more commodities, and (c) for any number of mobile factors, *m*, including *m* = 1.[14] □

Proof of Equation (2.3). To simplify the notation the subscript is omitted. Now

$$X = g(X)Y \Rightarrow dX = Yg'dX + gdY \Rightarrow dX / dY = g/(1 - Yg') \Rightarrow$$
$$\eta = (Y/X)(dX/dY) = (gY/X)/(1 - Yg') = 1/(1 - Yg') = 1/(1 - \omega).$$

Moreover,

$$\eta' = d\eta / dY = \omega'(1-\omega)^{-2}(dX/dY) = g\omega'(1-\omega)^{-1}$$
$$\eta'/\eta = g\omega'(1-\omega)^{-2}$$
$$(\eta-1)/Y = (g\omega/X)(1-\omega)^{-1}.$$

Hence, equation (2.3) does indeed follow. □

ACKNOWLEDGEMENTS

I dedicate this chapter to Murray C. Kemp since it deals again with a problem, now for the $n \times m$ case, which for the 2×2 case had been the reason for the first contact between Murray and me back in 1968 and which we then solved in our first joint paper. It was the beginning of a productive and most enjoyable cooperation – and of a close friendship, which includes our families. For helpful comments I am grateful to Bettina Peters, Ngo Van Long, Hans-Werner Sinn, Frank Stähler, Makoto Tawada, Hans-Jürgen Vosgerau, Hans-Werner Wohltmann and Kar-yiu Wong. The usual caveat applies.

NOTES

1. Some years later, Kemp and I proved that this conclusion remains valid in the presence of sector-specific factors if there are at least two mobile ones; see Herberg and Kemp (1991). The case of a single mobile factor has been studied by Panagariya (1981) and Wong (1996).
2. The straight line is a price line intersecting the curve at the corresponding output point.
3. Fixed or sector-specific factors need not be explicitly referred to and, to simplify the notation, they will not be symbolised.
4. The terms 'real' and 'virtual' are borrowed from Wong (1995, p. 203).
5. It will be argued later that this assumption can be considerably weakened.
6. For production functions which are homogeneous of degree η_i, obviously $\delta_i = \eta_i - 1$ holds and hence the notions of returns to scale in the normal and in the strict sense coincide. For other homothetic functions this coincidence remains true, e.g., if the local returns to scale do not change too strongly with the output level, i.e., if η_i' is close enough to zero.
7. Dealing with the two-commodity case Wong (1995, p. 209) has formulated a condition *A*, which he uses to determine the curvature of the real PPL close to the axes. According to the lemma, assumptions (A1)–(A5) guarantee that this condition and its higher-dimensional counterpart are satisfied.
8. The length of such an convex part of the transformation curves S_{ik}^o, however, does depend on the other returns to scale. The same is true for the concave part referred to under (iii).
9. As already mentioned, this result is noteworthy since, if a homothetic production function is characterised by increasing returns over some output interval, the interval can be expected to comprise at least all output levels close to zero.

10. The reader may wonder why in defining S_v by equation (2.1) the first commodity is singled out. The reason simply is that thereby all functions to be studied are defined over D_v^*, which is, like D_v, a non-empty, convex and compact set.
11. See, e.g., Takayama (1994, p. 92, theorem 2.2). Note that these conditions are both necessary and sufficient as all constraint functions are concave.
12. Remember that $Y_k \to 0$ implies $X_k \to 0$ and vice versa.
13. To see this one only needs to interchange the numbering of the *i*-th and the first commodity.
14. This immediately follows since in the present section this number did not matter.

REFERENCES

Caves, R.E. (1960), *Trade and Economic Structure*, Cambridge, Mass: Harvard University Press.

Herberg, H. (1969), 'On the shape of the transformation curve of homogeneous production functions', *Zeitschrift für die gesamte Staatswissenschaft,* **125**, 202-10.

Herberg, H. and M.C. Kemp (1969), 'Some implications of variable returns to scale', *Canadian Journal of Economics,* **2,** 403-15, reprinted in M.C. Kemp (ed.), *Production Sets*, New York: Academic Press, 1982, pp. 69-87.

Herberg, H. and M.C. Kemp (1991), 'Some implications of variable returns to scale: the case of industry-specific factors', *Canadian Journal of Economics,* **24**, 681-82.

Kemp, M.C. (1964), *The Pure Theory of International Trade*, Englewood Cliffs: Prentice Hall.

Panagariya, A. (1981), 'Variable returns to scale in production and patterns of specialisation', *American Economic Review,* **71,** 221-30.

Savosnick, K.M. (1958), 'The box diagram and the production possibility curve', *Ekonomisk Tidskrift,* **60,** 183-97.

Takayama, A. (1994), *Analytical Methods in Economics*, New York: Harvester-Wheatsheaf.

Tinbergen, J. (1945), *International Economic Cooperation*, Amsterdam: Elsevier.

Wong, K. (1995), *International Trade in Goods and Factor Mobility*, Cambridge, Mass.: MIT Press.

Wong, K. (1996), 'Some implications of variable returns to scale: the case of industry-specific factors: A comment', *Canadian Journal of Economics,* **29**, 240-44.

Woodland, A. (1982), *International Trade and Resource Allocation,* Amsterdam-New York-Oxford: North-Holland Publishing Company.

3. A Second Correspondence Principle

Murray C. Kemp, Yoshio Kimura and Koji Shimomura

Paul Samuelson's *Correspondence Principle* (CP henceforth) first appeared in a pair of wartime articles (see Samuelson 1941, pp. 97-120 and 1942, pp. 1-25). The CP asserts that economic dynamics and comparative statics stand in a two-way relationship of mutual support and dependence. In particular, the precision of comparative statics may be enhanced by imposing the assumption of dynamic stability.

Since its appearance sixty years ago, the CP has been widely accepted, especially by economists who work primarily with Heckscher-Ohlin or other two-by-two models. However, the CP has been subjected to criticism, principally on two grounds.

1. For systems only slightly larger than two-by-two, the assumption of dynamic stability typically adds little to the precision of comparative statics.
2. The dynamic models in terms of which Samuelson illustrated the potential usefulness of the CP were of the *tâtonnement* variety. Similarly, nearly all later applications of the CP have been in the context of a *tâtonnement* process. Now, in such models, costless adjustment takes place at a finite pace. However, if adjustment is costless then, given any finite speed of adjustment, there is a profit or utility incentive to increase the speed. In short, *tâtonnement* models are internally inconsistent. That this was not recognised long ago is a bit of a puzzle, best explained perhaps in terms of our failure to ask whose maximising behaviour is being modeled.

The first of these two criticisms has long been recognised; but we have learned to live with it. The second criticism is more fundamental. What can be done about it? Recently, Kemp and Shimomura (1999) have examined a possible escape route. Specifically, they have proposed that *tâtonnement* models be abandoned in favour of models in which markets always clear and in which the dynamics are both resource using and rooted in the choices of resource owners.

In Appendix 1, we present and examine a modified version of Kemp and Shimomura (1999), in which the effect of learning associated with the movement of factors is explicitly recognised. Naturally, the modified version relaxes but cannot extinguish the destructiveness to Samuelson's CP, which the modelling changes introduced by Kemp and Shimomura (1999) brought about. Let us explain.

Consider an arbitrary initial allocation of resources to industries. The rewards earned by any particular factor may differ from industry to industry. Indeed they may differ by more than the marginal cost of moving the factor. Hence there may be incentives for the owners of the factor to move it from one industry to another. Each owner of a factor must consider the control problem of choosing the optimal employment path for each factor owned, given the paths of expected factor rewards in each industry and given the (positive) marginal costs of moving factors. Over time, the inter-industrial earnings disparities may increase or decrease; but, whatever happens, the disparities will remain. In fact, the phase diagram (Figure 3.3) shows that any optimal trajectory ceases its motion at a certain point on the corridor $H'J'M'R'$ surrounding the point E where the disparities vanish or at one of the points A, B, C, and D.

On the other hand, all of the well-known general equilibrium comparative-static propositions (for example, the Stolper-Samuelson, Rybczynski, Heckscher-Ohlin Factor Price Equalisation and Hicks-Ikema propositions) rely on each factor earning the same reward in all industries, both before and after the relevant disturbance. Hence none of those propositions survives the replacement of *tâtonnement* by market-clearing, resource-using dynamic processes. This is the second CP, announced in our title. Perhaps it would be as appropriately called the non-CP.

Whereas Samuelson's CP was put forward in a spirit of constructive optimism about the possibility of deriving broad comparative-static results from purely theoretical considerations, the second CP is compatible only with a profound pessimism. The second CP does not signal the end of general-equilibrium comparative statics. Indeed it never denies the idea, immanent in Samuelson's CP, that the thorough analysis of dynamic or transitional process can help establish meaningful comparative statics. However, it does signal the end of traditional general equilibrium comparative statics, which rest on theoretical specifications of the Heckscher-Ohlin type.

Having admitted the second CP, we must be satisfied with fairly attenuated versions of the traditional comparative-static propositions. For example, with the aid of the observation that the corridor (or diamond) $H'J'M'R'$ is narrower than the Kemp-Shimomura corridor (or diamond) HJMR obtained by putting $\gamma = 0$ (see Figure 3.3), the revised Stolper-Samuelson Proposition of Kemp and Shimomura (1999) is slightly relaxed to read as follows.

Re-revised Stolper-Samuelson Proposition: *Given any constant-returns production functions and any initial and final values of the commodity price ratio p, say* p' and p'', *and a positive rate* γ *of technical progress in the* *technology associated with the movement of factors, there exists a sufficiently small but positive rate of time preference, say* $\rho(p', p'', \gamma)$ *such that, for all* $\rho \le \rho(p', p'', \gamma)$ *and comparing the initial and final steady states, the Stolper-Samuelson conclusions remain intact. Moreover, the larger the value of* γ*, the larger the value of* $\rho(p', p'', \gamma)$.

The remaining comparative static propositions listed above may be similarly attenuated.

We bring this short chapter to an end by arguing the robustness of the second CP. A close scrutiny of the analysis of the appendices reveals that, if and only if (a) the cost of moving each factor can be extinguished by learning and (b) the process of learning lasts long enough to achieve that end, the destructive conclusions of the second CP would need to be abandoned. However, assumption (a) is completely implausible; and in many plausible situations assumption (b) would not be satisfied. Thus the second CP is intrinsically robust.

APPENDIX 1

In this appendix we present a modified version of Kemp and Shimomura (1999), which is henceforth abbreviated as the K-S paper, and construct the phase diagram, making use of the lemmas stated and proved in Appendix 2.

The modified K-S model

Consider a small and fully-employed open economy, which potentially produces two final goods (labelled 1 and 2) with the aid of two factors of production (labour and land, available in amounts L and T). The short-run gross national product (GNP) function for the economy is defined as

$$Y(p, L_1, T_1) = Y^1(L_1, T_1) + pY^2(L - L_1, T - T_1), \qquad (3.1)$$

where p is the given and constant relative price of the second commodity and Y^i is the output of industry i, i=1,2. It is assumed that each production function is increasing, strictly quasi-concave, homogeneous of degree one in the two factor inputs and satisfies the Inada conditions.

To move a factor of production from one industry to the other requires inputs of commodities 1 and 2. The production functions are defined by

$$|\dot{X}_1| = G(y_{1X}, y_{2X}, \tilde{I}(t)), \; X = L, T,$$

where $\dot{X}_1$ is the (positive or negative) rate of re-allocation of factor X from industry 2 to industry 1, y_{iX} is the amount of commodity i (i=1,2) employed in reallocating factor X and production function $G(.)$ is supposed to satisfy the same conditions as the production function $Y^i(\cdot)$ with respect to y_{1X} and y_{2X} and to be increasing in the indicator $\tilde{I}(t)$ of learning by watching.

A rational owner of a factor of production would naturally take into account the observations cumulated from the outset of moving the factor. $\tilde{I}(t)$ is, so to speak, a measure of the cumulated observations. In what follows, we assume that

$$\tilde{I}(t) \equiv \exp[\gamma \int_0^t \left[|\dot{L}_1(s)| + |\dot{T}_1(s)| \right] ds],$$

where γ is a given positive constant. We further assume that the cumulated observations work like Hicksian neutral technical progress. Thus, the production functions related to the movement of factors take the form

$$|\dot{X}_1| = \tilde{I}(t) G(y_{1X}, y_{2X}), \; X = L, T. \tag{3.2}$$

Given (3.2), the minimum cost, in terms of the first commodity, of a pair of inter-industrial factor movements $(\dot{L}_1, \dot{T}_1)$ is

$$\alpha(p) I(t) [|\dot{L}_1| + |\dot{T}_1|], \tag{3.3}$$

where $I(t)$ denotes the reciprocal of $\tilde{I}(t)$.

All households are identical, that is, at all times they have the same homothetic preferences, own the same amounts of the two factors of production, and allocate those amounts in the same way. Bearing in mind these assumptions, the competitive market may be viewed as solving the control problem

$$\max_{\dot{L}_1, \dot{T}_1} \int_0^\infty \frac{\exp[-\rho t]}{e(p)} u[Y(p, L_1, T_1) - \alpha(p) I(t)(|\ell| + |h|)] dt \tag{3.4}$$

subject to the constraints

$$\dot{L}_1 = \ell, \; \dot{T}_1 = h,$$
$$0 \le T_1 \le T, \; 0 \le L_1 \le L,$$
$$L_1(0), T_1(0) \text{ given},$$

where $e(p)$ is the unit expenditure function, $u(.)/e(p)$ is the indirect utility function and ρ is the given, constant and positive rate of time preference.[1] It is assumed that $u(\cdot)$ is increasing and strictly concave and that it satisfies the Inada conditions.

Normalising $e(p)$ to be unity for simplicity, associated with (3.4) is the Hamiltonian

$$H \equiv u[Y(p, L_1, T_1) - I\alpha(p)(|\ell| + |h|)] + \mu_L \ell + \mu_T h \,. \tag{3.5}$$

The optimal trajectories

Take a look at Figure 3.1, which is the same as Figure 2 in the K-S paper. As Figure 3.1 shows, we can divide the Edgeworth box diagram into four sub-regions. Let us concentrate on the case in which the initial condition $(L_1(0), T_1(0))$ is in Region I. The other three cases can be treated in a similar manner.

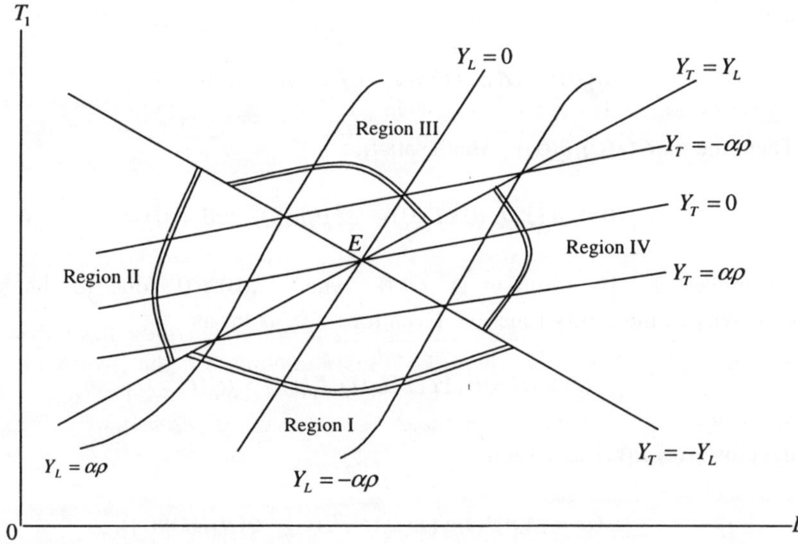

Figure 3.1 Edgeworth Box

Before actually deriving the optimal trajectory, let us explain the principle involved in the derivation. First, considering the assumed properties of the functions $Y(\cdot)$ and $u(\cdot)$, and the definition of $|\;|$, it is clear that the

Hamiltonian (3.5) is *strictly* concave in state variables (L_1, T_1) and instrument variables (ℓ, h). Therefore, by virtue of Mangasarian's sufficiency theorem for the *unique* existence of an optimal trajectory, we can be sure that any trajectory $(L_1(t), T_1(t))$ that (i) starts from the initial condition, (ii) satisfies the first-order conditions for maximising the Hamiltonian, (iii) involves the co-state variables each of which satisfies the solution of the differential equation

$$\dot{\mu}_{X_1} = \rho\mu_{X_1} - \frac{\partial \mathrm{H}}{\partial X_1},\ X = L, T,$$

and (iv) satisfies the transversality condition, is optimal. If the state variables converge to constant values and the growth rate of each co-state variable is less than ρ, then the transversality condition must be satisfied. Hence, our aim is to obtain such a trajectory.

Now let us consider the case in which the initial condition is not only in Region I but also below the locus $Y_T = \alpha p$. Choose $\mu_X(0), X = L, T,$ such that

$$\mu_T(0) > \alpha(p)u'(Y(L_1(0), T_1(0))) > \mu_L(0) > 0.$$

Then, the pair $(\ell(0), h(0))$, which satisfies

$$\mu_T(0) = u'(Y(L_1(0), T_1(0)) - \alpha(p)h(0)) \text{ and } \ell(0) = 0,$$

maximises the Hamiltonian at $t = 0$, where $h(0) > 0$, due to the strict concavity of the utility function. Even for $t > 0$, as far as

$$\mu_T(t) > \alpha(p)I(t)u'(Y(L_1(t), T_1(t))) > \mu_L(t) > 0,$$

the pair $(\ell(t), h(t))$ satisfying

$$\begin{aligned} &\mu_T(t) = \alpha(p)I(t)u'(Y(L_1(t), T_1(t)) - \alpha(p)I(t)h(t)) \\ &\ell(t) = 0 \end{aligned} \tag{3.6}$$

maximises the Hamiltonian at $t > 0$. It follows that $L_1(t) = L_1(0)$. Note also that the co-state variables are the solutions of the differential equations

$$\begin{aligned}\dot{\mu}_T(t) &= \rho\mu_T(t) - u'[Y(L_1(0), T_1(t)) - \alpha(p)I(t)h(t)]Y_T(L_1(0), T_1(t)) \\ &= \mu_T(t)[\rho - \frac{Y_T(L_1(0), T_1(t))}{\alpha(p)I(t)}]\end{aligned} \tag{3.7}$$

$$\begin{aligned}\dot{\mu}_L(t) &= \rho\mu_L(t) - u'[Y(L_1(0), T_1(t)) - \alpha(p)I(t)h(t)]Y_L(L_1(0), T_1(t)) \\ &= \mu_L(t)[\rho - \frac{\mu_T(t)Y_L(L_1(0), T_1(t))}{\mu_L(t)\alpha(p)I(t)}].\end{aligned} \tag{3.8}$$

Note finally that $Y_T > \alpha I(t)\rho$ below the locus $Y_T = \alpha I(t)\rho$. Hence, it follows from (3.7) that below the locus we see that $\dot{\mu}_T(t)/\mu_T(t) < 0$. The trajectory can be depicted like the vertical arrow ll' in Figure 3.2.

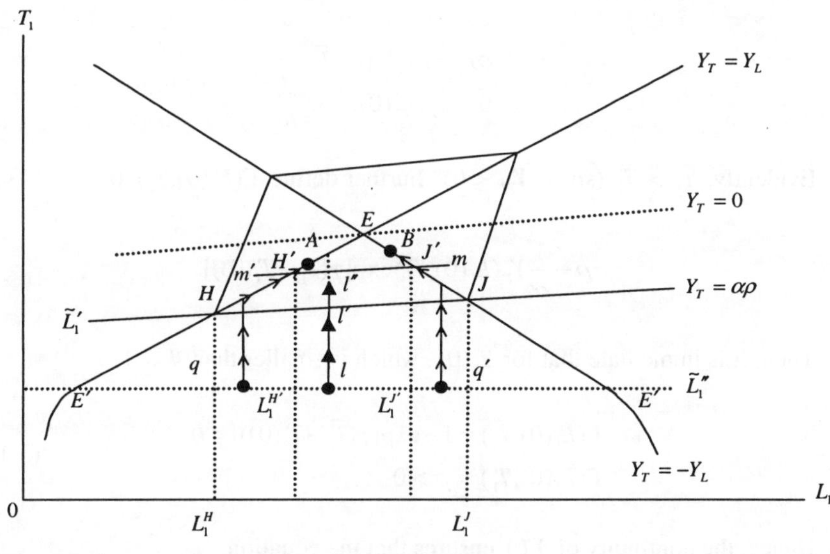

Figure 3.2 Optimal Trajectory

The present analysis differs from the Kemp-Shimomura paper in that the locus $Y_T = \alpha I(t)\rho$ itself gradually shifts toward the locus $Y_T = 0$, since, from the definition of $I(t)$,

$$I(t) = \exp[-\gamma \int_0^t \dot{T}(s)ds] = \exp[-\gamma\{T_1(t) - T_1(0)\}] \tag{3.9}$$

Substituting (3.9) into (3.6), (3.7) and (3.8) we have

$$\dot{T}_1 = \frac{\exp[\gamma(T_1 - T_1(0))]}{\alpha}[Y(T_1, L_1(0)) - \beta(\frac{\mu_T \exp[\gamma(T_1 - T_1(0))]}{\alpha})] \quad (3.10)$$

$$\dot{\mu}_T = \mu_T[\rho - \frac{Y_T(T_1, L_1(0))\exp[\gamma(T_1 - T_1(0))]}{\alpha}] \quad (3.11)$$

$$\dot{\mu}_L = \rho\mu_L - \frac{\mu_T Y_L(T_1, L_1(0))\exp[\gamma(T_1 - T_1(0))]}{\alpha}, \quad (3.12)$$

where $\beta(\cdot) \equiv (u')^{-1}$. The differential equations (3.10)-(3.12) is the system on which our argument is based.

Notice that for any given $L_1(0)$ between $L_1^{H'}$ and $L_1^{J'}$, there exist $\overline{T}_1$ and $\tilde{T}_1$ which satisfy

$$\alpha\rho = Y_T(L_1(0), \overline{T}_1)$$
$$0 = Y_T(L_1(0), \tilde{T}_1).$$

Evidently, $\tilde{T}_1 > \overline{T}_1$ (since $Y_{TT} < 0$). Further define $\Gamma(L_1(0), T_1)$ by

$$\rho - \frac{1}{\alpha} Y_T(L_1(0), T_1)\exp[\gamma(T_1 - T_1(0))].$$

Then, it is immediate that for $T_1(0)$, which is smaller than $\overline{T}_1$,

$$\begin{aligned} \Gamma(L_1(0), \overline{T}_1) &= 1 - \exp[\gamma(\overline{T}_1 - T_1(0))] < 0 \\ \Gamma(L_1(0), \tilde{T}_1) &= \rho > 0. \end{aligned} \quad (3.13)$$

Hence, the continuity of $\Gamma(\cdot)$ ensures that the equation

$$\Gamma(L_1(0), T_1) = 0 \quad (3.14)$$

has a solution T_1^S. Since $\Gamma(\cdot)$ is not necessarily increasing in T_1, T_1^S may be multiple. In such a case, it suffices to define T_1^S as the minimum of the solutions of (3.14). Since $Y_{TT} < 0$ and $Y_{TL} > 0$, both $\overline{T}_1$ and $\tilde{T}_1$ are increasing in $L_1(0)$. Moreover, a direct computation, coupled with the facts that $Y_{TL} > 0$ and that $\dot{T}_1 > 0$ (or $T_1 > T_1(0)$), yields

$$\Gamma(L_1(0),T_1) - \Gamma(L_1'(0),T_1) = \frac{\exp[\gamma(T_1 - T_1(0))]}{\alpha}[Y_T(L_1'(0),T_1) - Y_T(L_1(0),T_1)] > 0,$$

provided that $L_1'(0) > L_1(0)$. Therefore, the locus $(L_1(0), T_1^S)$, or the line $m'H'J'm$ of Figure 3.2 is positively sloped, or algebraically, $Y_{TT} + Y_T < 0$, along the locus.

Once we derive the locus to which the optimal trajectory converges, the rest of our argument basically follows the Kemp-Shimomura paper.

(i) First, suppose that the initial condition ($L_1(0)$, $T_1(0)$) is on the segment $L_1^{H'} L_1^{J'}$. Lemmas 3 and 4 (see Appendix 2) imply that, if we choose positive $\mu_T(0)$ and $\mu_L(0)$ such that $\mu_T(0) > \mu_L(0)$, the optimal trajectory must follow the system (3.10)–(3.12). The steady state of the system (3.10)–(3.12), which corresponds to point l'' in Figure 3.2, is the solution to the system of equations

$$\dot{T}_1 = \frac{\exp[\gamma(T_1 - T_1(0))]}{\alpha}[Y(T_1, L_1(0)) - \beta(\frac{\mu_T \exp[\gamma(T_1 - T_1(0))]}{\alpha})] = 0 \quad (3.10)'$$

$$\dot{\mu}_T = \mu_T[\rho - \frac{Y_T(T_1, L_1(0))\exp[\gamma(T_1 - T_1(0))]}{\alpha}] = 0 \quad (3.11)'$$

$$\mu_L = \rho\mu_L - \frac{\mu_T Y_L(T_1, L_1(0))\exp[\gamma(T_1 - T_1(0))]}{\alpha} = 0. \quad (3.12)'$$

As we discussed above, T_1^S satisfies (3.11)'. Substituting T_1^S into (3.10)', μ_T is uniquely determined. Then, from (3.12)' so is μ_L. Note that $Y_T > Y_L$ on the segment $H'J'$ except for point H', where $Y_T = Y_L$. It follows from (3.11)' and (3.12)' that $\mu_T > \mu_L$ on the segment $H'J'$ except for point H' where $\mu_T = \mu_L$.

Let $f(x)$ be the characteristic equation of the Jacobian matrix evaluated at the steady state of the system (3.10)–(3.12). Then,

$$f(x) \equiv (x-\rho)[x^2 - (Y_T - \frac{\gamma\beta' e^{\Delta}}{\alpha})\frac{e^{\Delta}}{\alpha}x - \frac{e^{2\Delta}\beta'\mu_T(Y_{TT} + \gamma Y_T)}{\alpha^2}] = 0 \quad (3.15)$$

where $\Delta \equiv \gamma(T_1 - T_1(0))$. From (3.14),

$$-\frac{e^{2\Delta}\beta'\mu_T(Y_{TT}+\gamma Y_T)}{\alpha^2}<0.$$

Hence, the characteristic equation (3.15) has two positive and one negative real roots, which means that there exists a one-dimensional stable arm crossing the steady state. Since the number of state variables is one, the foregoing result means that the steady state is saddlepoint stable.

Next, let us consider the case in which the initial condition ($L_1(0)$, $T_1(0)$) is either (ii) on $\tilde{L}_1'L_1^{H'}$ or (iii) on $\tilde{L}_1''L_1^{J'}$ in Figure 3.2.

(ii) If the initial condition is on the segment $\tilde{L}_1'L_1^{H'}$, then the optimal trajectory follows the system (3.10)–(3.12) until it reaches the locus $Y_T=Y_L$ at some finite time $\bar{t}$ at which $\mu_T(\bar{t})=\mu_L(\bar{t})$, and then the trajectory converges to a point along the locus $Y_T=Y_L$ by following the system of differential equations (using Lemma 3 of Appendix 2)

$$Y_T(T_1,L_1)=Y_L(T_1,L_1) \tag{3.16}$$

$$\dot{L}_1+\dot{T}_1=\frac{1}{\alpha l}[Y(T_1,L_1)-\beta(\frac{\mu}{\alpha l})] \tag{3.17}$$

$$\dot{\mu}=\mu[\rho-\frac{Y_T(T_1,L_1)}{\alpha l}]. \tag{3.18}$$

Differentiating (3.16) with respect to time, we have

$$(Y_{TL}-Y_{LL})\dot{L}_1=(Y_{LT}-Y_{TT})\dot{T}_1 \tag{3.19}$$

or

$$\dot{L}_1=\frac{(Y_{LT}-Y_{TT})}{(Y_{TL}-Y_{LL})}\dot{T}_1. \tag{3.20}$$

Let us denote by $L_1=\eta(T_1)$ the relation between L_1 and T_1 which is defined by (3.16). Equation (3.20) means that

$$\eta'=\frac{Y_{LT}-Y_{TT}}{Y_{TL}-Y_{LL}}>0.$$

Therefore, along the locus $Y_T = Y_L$, both L_1 and T_1 are increasing, which implies that

$$\begin{aligned} I(t) &= \exp[-\gamma\{(T_1(t)-T_1(0))+(L_1(t)-L_1(\bar{t}))\}] \\ &= \exp[-\gamma\{(T_1(t)-T_1(0))+(\eta(T_1(t))-L_1(\bar{t}))\}]. \end{aligned} \tag{3.21}$$

Note that $L_1(\bar{t}) = L_1(0)$. Substituting (3.21) into (3.17) and (3.18), we see that

$$\dot{T}_1 = \frac{Y(T_1,\eta(T_1)) - \beta(\frac{\mu}{\alpha})\exp[\gamma\{(T_1-T_1(0))+(\eta(T_1)-L_1(\bar{t}))\}]}{\alpha(1+\eta')\exp[-\gamma\{(T_1-T_1(0))+(\eta(T_1)-L_1(\bar{t}))\}]} \tag{3.22}$$

$$\dot{\mu} = \mu[\rho - \frac{Y_T(T_1,\eta(T_1))\exp[\gamma\{(T_1-T_1(0))+(\eta(T_1)-L_1(\bar{t}))\}]}{\alpha}]. \tag{3.23}$$

To consider whether the system (3.22) and (3.23) has a steady state or not, we verify that at point H'

$$\begin{aligned} &\rho - \frac{Y_T(T_1,\eta(T_1))\exp[\gamma\{(T_1-T_1(0))+(\eta(T_1)-L_1(\bar{t}))\}]}{\alpha} \\ &< \rho - \frac{Y_T(T_1,\eta(T_1))\exp[\gamma(T_1-T_1(0))]}{\alpha} = 0. \end{aligned} \tag{3.24}$$

On the other hand, since $Y_T = Y_L = 0$ at point E, we see that

$$\rho - \frac{Y_T(T_1,\eta(T_1))\exp[\gamma\{(T_1-T_1(0))+(\eta(T_1)-L_1(\bar{t}))\}]}{\alpha} = \rho > 0. \tag{3.25}$$

Equations (3.24) and (3.25) imply that there exists a point on $E'E$ such that

$$\rho - \frac{Y_T(T_1,\eta(T_1))\exp[\gamma\{(T_1-T_1(0))+(\eta(T_1)-L_1(\bar{t}))\}]}{\alpha} = 0. \tag{3.26}$$

Denote by T_1^{SS} the minimum value of T_1 that satisfies (3.26). Substituting it into

$$0 = Y(T_1,\eta(T_1)) - \beta(\frac{\mu}{\alpha})\exp[-\gamma\{(T_1(t)-T_1(0))+(\eta(T_1(t))-L_1(\bar{t}))\}], \tag{3.27}$$

we can determine the steady-state value of μ uniquely. The differentiation of the left side of (3.26) with respect to T_1 yields

$$-\frac{(1+\eta')}{\alpha}[Y_{TT}+\gamma Y_T]\exp[\gamma\{(T_1(t)-T_1(0))+(\eta(T_1(t))-L_1(\bar{t}))\}], \quad (3.28)$$

which is positive.

Once we verify the existence of the steady state of the system (3.22) and (3.23), we can proceed to check the saddlepoint stability of it. We see that at the steady state

$$\partial\dot{T}_1/\partial\mu = \frac{-\frac{1}{\alpha}\beta'\exp[\gamma\{(T_1-T_1(0))+(\eta(T_1)-L_1(\bar{t}))\}]}{\alpha(1+\eta')\exp[-\gamma\{(T_1-T_1(0))+(\eta(T_1)-L_1(\bar{t}))\}]}>0 \quad (3.29)$$

$$\partial\dot{\mu}/\partial T_1=\mu\times(3.25)>0\,. \quad (3.30)$$

Thus, the determinant of the Jacobian matrix of the system (3.22) and (3.23) evaluated at the steady state, which is –(3.29)× (3.30), is negative. It follows that the characteristic equation has one positive and one negative real root. Therefore, the steady state is saddlepoint stable.

(iii) Third, suppose that the initial condition is on the segment $L_1^{J'}\tilde{L}_1''$. Then the optimal trajectory follows the system (3.10)–(3.12) until it reaches the locus $-Y_T=Y_L$ at some finite time $\tilde{t}$ at which $\mu_T(\tilde{t})=\mu_L(\tilde{t})$, and then the trajectory converges to a point along the locus $-Y_T=Y_L$ by following the system of differential equations (using Lemma 3 of Appendix 2)

$$-Y_T(T_1,L_1)=Y_L(T_1,L_1) \quad (3.31)$$

$$|\dot{L}_1|+|\dot{T}_1|=\frac{1}{\alpha I}[Y(T_1,L_1)-\beta(\frac{\mu}{\alpha I})] \quad (3.32)$$

$$\dot{\mu}=\mu[\rho-\frac{Y_T(T_1,L_1)}{\alpha I}]. \quad (3.33)$$

Here we focus on the case in which the locus $-Y_T(T_1,L_1)=Y_L(T_1,L_1)$ is negatively sloped as in the Figure 3.2. Then, if the trajectory proceeds toward point *E* along the locus, L_1 decreases and T_1 increases. Thus (3.32) can be rewritten as

$$-\dot{L}_1 + \dot{T}_1 = \frac{1}{\alpha I}[Y(T_1, L_1) - \beta(\frac{\mu}{\alpha I})]. \tag{3.34}$$

Moreover, in this case we see that

$$I = \exp[-\gamma\{(L_1(\tilde{t}) - L_1(t)) + (T_1(t) - T_1(0))\}]. \tag{3.35}$$

Note that $L_1(\tilde{t}) = L_1(0)$. Totally differentiating (3.31) with respect to time, we have

$$\Delta_L \dot{L}_1 + \Delta_T \dot{T}_1 = 0, \tag{3.36}$$

where $\Delta_L \equiv Y_{LL} + Y_{TL}$ and $\Delta \equiv Y_{LT} + Y_{TT}$. A direct calculation yields

$$\Delta \equiv \Delta_L + \Delta_T < 0,$$

and (3.36), together with the fact that $\dot{L}_1 < 0$ and $\dot{T}_1 > 0$, assert that $\Delta_L \Delta_T > 0$. Hence, it is sure that

$$\Delta_L < 0 \text{ and } \Delta_T < 0. \tag{3.37}$$

Solving (3.34) and (3.36), we derive

$$\dot{L}_1 = \frac{-\Delta_T}{\Delta \alpha I}[Y(T_1, L_1) - \beta(\frac{\mu}{\alpha})\exp[\gamma\{(L_1(\tilde{t}) - L_1(t)) + (T_1(t) - T_1(0))\}]] \tag{3.38}$$

$$\dot{T}_1 = \frac{\Delta_L}{\Delta \alpha I}[Y(T_1, L_1) - \beta(\frac{\mu}{\alpha})\exp[\gamma\{(L_1(\tilde{t}) - L_1(t)) + (T_1(t) - T_1(0))\}]] \tag{3.39}$$

$$\dot{\mu} = \mu[\rho - \frac{Y_T(T_1, L_1)}{\alpha}\exp[\gamma\{(L_1(\tilde{t}) - L_1(t)) + (T_1(t) - T_1(0))\}]]. \tag{3.40}$$

The steady state is determined by

$$-Y_T(T_1, L_1) + Y_L(T_1, L_1) = 0 \tag{3.41}$$

$$Y(T_1, L_1) - \beta(\frac{\mu}{\alpha})\exp[\gamma\{(L_1(\tilde{t}) - L_1(t)) + (T_1(t) - T_1(0))\}] = 0 \tag{3.42}$$

$$\rho - \frac{Y_T(T_1, L_1)}{\alpha} \exp[\gamma\{(L_1(\tilde{t}) - L_1(t)) + (T_1(t) - T_1(0))\}] = 0\,, \qquad (3.43)$$

First, at point J' in Figure 3.2,

$$0 = \rho - \frac{Y_T(T_1, L_1)}{\alpha} \exp\{\gamma(T_1(t) - T_1(0))\}\,.$$

Thus,

$$0 > \rho - \frac{Y_T(T_1, L_1)}{\alpha} \exp[\gamma\{(L_1(\tilde{t}) - L_1(t)) + (T_1(t) - T_1(0))\}]\,. \qquad (3.44)$$

Second, at *E*,

$$\rho - \frac{Y_T(T_1, L_1)}{\alpha} \exp[\gamma\{(L_1(\tilde{t}) - L_1(t)) + (T_1(t) - T_1(0))\}] = \rho > 0\,. \quad (3.45)$$

Therefore, there exists a point on the locus $Y_T(T_1, L_1) + Y_L(T_1, L_1) = 0$ such that (3.43) holds. Let (T_1^s, L_1^s) be such that T_1^s is smallest among such points. Totally differentiating the right hand of (3.43) with respect to time, we have

$$0 < -[(\gamma Y_T + Y_{TT})\dot{T}_1 + (-\gamma Y_T + Y_{TL})\dot{L}_1]\,. \qquad (3.46)$$

The sign of (3.46) results from (3.44) and (3.45). Since $\dot{T}_1 > 0$, it follows from (3.36) and (3.37) that at the steady state

$$0 > (\gamma Y_T + Y_{TT})\Delta_L + (\gamma Y_T - Y_{TL})\Delta_T\,. \qquad (3.47)$$

Using (3.47), we can prove that the steady state is saddlepoint stable. The characteristic equation corresponding to the Jacobian matrix evaluated at the steady state of the system (3.38)–(3.40) is

$$g(x) \equiv x[x^2 - \frac{2\Delta_T \beta'}{\alpha\beta I\Delta}(Y_L + \frac{\gamma\mu\beta'}{\alpha I})x + \frac{\beta'}{\alpha I\Delta}\{\Delta_T(Y_{YL} - \gamma Y_T) + \Delta_L(Y_{TT} + \gamma Y_T)\}] = 0.$$

Because of $\beta' < 0$, $\Delta < 0$, $\mu > 0$ and (3.47),

$$\frac{\beta'}{\alpha I \Delta}\{\Delta_T(Y_{YL} - \gamma Y_T) + \Delta_L(Y_{TT} + \gamma Y_T)\} < 0\,.$$

Therefore, the characteristic equation has a zero root, a positive real root and a negative real root. This guarantees that the steady state is saddlepoint stable.

We have just considered the case in which the initial condition is in Region I. The case in which the initial condition is in one of the other three regions can be treated in a similar way. Thus, the desired phase diagram is shown in Figure 3.3.

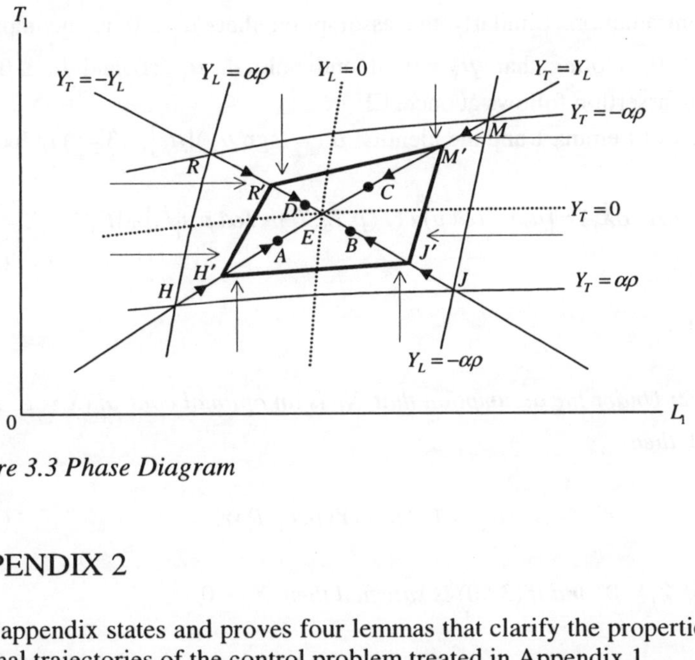

Figure 3.3 Phase Diagram

APPENDIX 2

This appendix states and proves four lemmas that clarify the properties of the optimal trajectories of the control problem treated in Appendix 1.

As preliminary observations, we draw attention to: (i) the convention that X denotes any one member of the set $\{L, T\}$, the remaining member of the set being denoted by Z and vice versa, and (ii) the fact that, if the Hamiltonian is differentiable,`

$$\left(\partial H / \partial \dot{X}_1\right) = -\left(\operatorname{sgn} \dot{X}_1\right)\alpha(p) I u'\left(Y(p, L_1, T_1) - I\alpha(p)\left\{\left|\dot{L}_1\right| + \left|\dot{T}_1\right|\right\}\right) + \mu_X,\ X = L, T, \tag{3.48}$$

where sgn x means the sign of variable x.

Lemma 1: *For any optimal plan, if* $\mu_X \geq 0$ $(\mu_X \leq 0)$ *then* $\dot{X}_1 \geq 0$ $(\dot{X}_1 \leq 0)$, $X = L, T$. *Consequently,* $\mu_X = 0$ *implies that* $\dot{X}_1 = 0$.

Proof. Consider the case $\mu_X \geq 0$ and suppose that $\dot{X}_1 < 0$. Then the assumed optimality and (3.48) imply that

$$0 = (\partial H / \partial \dot{X}_1) = \alpha(p) I u'(Y(p, L_1, T_1) - I\alpha(p)\{|\dot{L}_1| + |\dot{T}_1|\}) + \mu_X > 0,$$

a self-contradiction. Similarly the assumption that $\mu_X \leq 0$ is incompatible with $\dot{X}_1 > 0$. Noting that $\mu_X = 0$ if and only if $\mu_X \geq 0$ and $\mu_X \leq 0$, the remaining assertion follows at once. □

In view of Lemma 1 and the identity $\mu_X = (\operatorname{sgn} \mu_X)|\mu_X|$, (3.48) reduces to

$$(\operatorname{sgn} \mu_X)(\partial H / \partial \dot{X}_1) = |\mu_X| - I\alpha(p) u'(Y(p, L_1, T_1) - I\alpha(p)\{|\dot{L}_1| + |\dot{T}_1|\}), \quad X = L, T \tag{3.49}$$

if $\dot{X}_1 \neq 0$.

Lemma 2: *Under the assumption that* $\dot{X}_1$ *is an optimal control (X = L, T), (i) if* $\dot{X}_1 \neq 0$ *then*

$$|\mu_X| > I\alpha(p) u'(Y(p, L_1, T_1)), \tag{3.50}$$

and (ii) if $\dot{Z}_1 = 0$ *and if* (3.50) *is satisfied then* $\dot{X}_1 \neq 0$.

Proof. (i) Arguing by contradiction, assume that $\dot{X}_1 \neq 0$ and that

$$|\mu_X| \leq I\alpha(p) u'(Y(p, L_1, T_1)) \tag{3.51}$$

Then, the assumed optimality, (3.51) and the strict concavity of $u(\cdot)$ imply that

$$\begin{aligned} 0 = (\operatorname{sgn} \mu_X)(\partial H / \partial \dot{X}_1) &= |\mu_X| - I\alpha(p) u'(Y(p, L_1, T_1) - I\alpha(p)\{|\dot{X}_1| + |\dot{Z}_1|\}) \\ &< |\mu_X| - I\alpha(p) u'(Y(p, L_1, T_1)) \leq 0, \end{aligned}$$

a self-contradiction.

We verify that the assumed conditions are incompatible with $\dot{X}_1 = 0$. Suppose that $\mu_X \geq 0$. Then the assumed optimality requires that there exists a positive number d such that the Hamiltonian viewed as a function of $\dot{X}_1$ is monotonically non-increasing in the open interval $(0,d)$. Letting $\dot{X}_1 \in (0,d)$ tend to zero, the differentiability of the Hamiltonian in this interval, the assumed optimality and the assumption that $\dot{Z}_1 = 0$ imply that

$$\mu_X - I\alpha(p)u'(Y(p,L_1,T_1)) \leq 0.$$

This violates (3.50).

When μ_X is nonpositive, it suffices to note that there can be found an open interval $(-d,0)$ in which the Hamiltonian is differentiable as well as non-decreasing and to proceed as above, *mutatis mutandis.* □

Lemma 3: *Along the optimal path, the following assertions hold true:*
(i) if $|\mu_X| > |\mu_Z|$ *then* $\dot{Z}_1 = 0$,
(ii) if $|\mu_X| > \max\{|\mu_X|, I\alpha(p)u'(Y(p,L_1,T_1))\}$ *then* $\dot{X}_1 \neq 0$ *and* $\dot{Z}_1 = 0$,
(iii) if $\dot{X}_1 \neq 0$ *then* $|\dot{X}_1| + |\dot{Z}_1| = (Y(p,L_1,T_1) - \beta(|\mu_X| / I\alpha(p))) / I\alpha(p)$, *and if, in addition,* $|\mu_X| = |\mu_Z|$ *then*

$$|\dot{X}_1| + |\dot{Z}_1| = (Y(p,L_1,T_1) - \beta(|\mu_Z| / I\alpha(p))) / I\alpha(p),$$

and, finally,
(iv) if $\dot{X}_1 \neq 0$ *and* $\dot{Z}_1 = 0$ *then*

$$\dot{X}_1 = (\operatorname{sgn} \mu_X)\{Y(p,L_1,T_1) - \beta(|\mu_X| / I\alpha(p))\} / I\alpha(p).$$

Proof. (i) Suppose the contrary. Then $\dot{Z}_1 \neq 0$. If $\dot{X}_1 \neq 0$, we obtain

$$\begin{aligned} 0 &= (\operatorname{sgn} \mu_X)(\partial H / \partial \dot{X}_1) \\ &= |\mu_X| - I\alpha(p)u'(Y(p,L_1,T_1) - I\alpha(p)\{|\dot{X}_1| + |\dot{Z}_1|\}) \\ &> |\mu_Z| - I\alpha(p)u'(Y(p,L_1,T_1) - I\alpha(p)\{|\dot{X}_1| + |\dot{Z}_1|\}) \\ &= (\operatorname{sgn} \mu_Z)(\partial H / \partial \dot{Z}_1), \end{aligned}$$

because $\dot{Z}_1 \neq 0$ and from (3.49). Hence $(\partial H / \partial \dot{Z}_1) \neq 0$, which contradicts the assumed optimality.

Now consider the case $\dot{X}_1 = 0$. Since $\dot{Z}_1 \neq 0$, the assumed optimality, with the aid of (3.49), yields

$$\begin{aligned} 0 &= (\partial H / \partial \dot{Z}_1)(\operatorname{sgn} \mu_Z) \\ &= |\mu_Z| - I\alpha(p)u'(Y(p, L_1, T_1) - I\alpha(p)|\dot{Z}_1|) \\ &< |\mu_X| - I\alpha(p)u'(Y(p, L_1, T_1) - I\alpha(p)|\dot{Z}_1|). \end{aligned}$$

Furthermore, μ_X is either positive or negative for $|\mu_X| > |\mu_Z| \geq 0$. Since the Hamiltonian viewed as a function of $\dot{X}_1$ attains a local maximum at $\dot{X}_1 = 0$, there exists a positive number d_1 such that the Hamiltonian is non-increasing in an open interval $(0, d_1)$ and non-decreasing in $(-d_1, 0)$. Therefore, if $\mu_X > 0$, by letting $X_1 \in (0, d_1)$ tend to zero, we reach a self-contradiction

$$0 < \mu_X - I\alpha(p)u'(Y(p, L_1, T_1) - I\alpha(p)|\dot{Z}_1|) \leq 0.$$

On the other hand, if $\mu_X < 0$, the same reasoning as above applied to $(-d_1, 0)$ leads to a self-contradiction

$$0 > \mu_X + I\alpha(p)u'(Y(p, L_1, T_1) - I\alpha(p)|\dot{Z}_1|) \geq 0.$$

(ii) The implication follows directly from Lemma 1 (ii) and Lemma 3 (i).

(iii) Noticing that $u'(\cdot)$ is monotonously decreasing, the assertion follows from (3.49) and the Inada conditions. The remaining assertion is rather trivial.

(iv) The conclusion is derived directly from (iii) above and the fact that $|\dot{X}_1| = (\operatorname{sgn} \dot{X}_1)\dot{X}_1$. □

Lemma 4: *Along the optimal path, we can assert*
(i) if $\dot{X}_1 \neq 0$ then $\dot{\mu}_X = \mu_X(\rho - ((\operatorname{sgn} \mu_X)Y_X) / I\alpha(p))$, *and*
(ii) if $\dot{X}_1 \neq 0$ *and* $\dot{Z}_1 = 0$, *then*

$$\dot{\mu}_Z = \rho \cdot \mu_Z - ((\operatorname{sgn} \mu_X)\mu_X Y_Z) / I\alpha(p),$$

where $Y_X = (\partial Y / \partial X_1)$, $X = L, T$.

Proof. (i) The optimality and (3.49) imply that

$$|\mu_X| - I\alpha(p)u'(Y(p,L_1T_1) - I\alpha(p)\{|\dot{X}_1| + |\dot{Z}_1|\}) = 0.$$

Hence,

$$u'(Y(p,L_1,T_1) - I\alpha(p)\{|\dot{X}_1| + |\dot{Z}_1|\}) = (\text{sgn}\,\mu_X)\mu_X / I\alpha(p). \quad (3.52)$$

On the other hand, the optimal principle requires that

$$\dot{\mu}_X = \rho \cdot \mu_X - (\partial H / \partial X_1) = \rho \cdot \mu_X - u'(Y(p,L_1,T_1) - I\alpha(p)\{|\dot{X}_1| + |\dot{Z}_1|\})Y_X.$$

Substituting (3.52) into the above equation, the assertion is immediate.

(ii) Using (3.52) with $\dot{Z}_1 = 0$, eliminate $u'(Y(p,L_1,T_1) - I\alpha(p)|\dot{X}_1|)$ from

$$\dot{\mu}_Z = \rho \cdot \mu_Z - u'(Y(p,L_1,T_1) - I\alpha(p)|\dot{X}_1|)Y_Z$$

Then, the assertion is seen to hold trivially. □

NOTE

1. It may be useful to recall three pioneering studies of the costly reallocation of a single primary factor of production. Mussa (1978) analyses the dynamic process of costly movement of a factor service. It is assumed that capital moves between two industries with the aid of labour input and that the mobile factor moves towards the industry in which it is relatively well paid. Thus, workers are employed in three industries. Therefore, if we consider that not only capital but labour is mobile keeping the above two assumptions intact, then there may arise a situation where labour is best paid in two industries so that the industry into which it flows becomes equivocal. On the other hand, our approach, expressed in (3.4), of which a direct predecessor is Kemp and Wan (1974), is free of such a technical difficulty. Furthermore, Mussa (1978) is concerned with the dynamic analysis of a costly adjustment process and mentions little about what his dynamic analysis implies on the comparative static propositions in Heckscher-Ohlin models. Long (1978) also studies the costly regional reallocation of labour, based on the maximisation of the sum of the discounted future utilities. However, Long (1978) was not interested in the robustness of Heckscher-Ohlin comparative statics.

REFERENCES

Kemp, M.C., and H.Y. Wan (1974), 'Hysteresis of long-run equilibrium from realistic adjustment costs', in G. Horwich and P.A. Samue--lson (eds), *Trade, Stability and Macroeconomics,* New York: Academic Press, pp. 221-42.

Kemp, M.C. and K. Shimomura (1999), 'A dynamic Heckscher-Ohlin model: the case of costly factor movement', unpublished paper, University of New South Wales.

Long, N.V. (1978), 'Optimal inter-regional movements of labour: a theoretical analysis', *Australian Economic Papers*, **17**, 290-302.
Mussa, M. (1978), 'Dynamic adjustment in the Heckscher-Ohlin-Samuelson model', *Journal of Political Economy*, **86**, 775-91.
Samuelson, P.A. (1941), 'The stability of equilibrium: comparative statics and dynamics', *Econometrica*, **9**, 97-120.
Samuelson, P.A. (1942), 'The stability of equilibrium: linear and nonlinear systems', *Econometrica*, **10**, 1-25.

4. The Welfare Economics of Encouraging More Births

Yew-Kwang Ng

1. INTRODUCTION

It is well known that, under certain conventional assumptions (including the absence of ignorance and external effects), a perfectly competitive equilibrium is Pareto optimal. However, this first theorem in welfare economics may not be valid if the size of the population is taken as a variable. Nevertheless, rather than showing that a higher population leads to an inferior situation by decreasing the per capita income, increasing congestion or some such other factors, I wish to show that the size of the population by the free and enlightened choices of the relevant rational people (e.g. in having more children) may be less than Pareto optimal. This sounds astonishing but can be demonstrated and explained. It is related to the gain from trade on which Professor Murray Kemp has made important contributions. However, here, the gain from trade is not from trade with existing people but with the newly born. The point does not arise in traditional welfare economics as the set of people is implicitly taken as given. Thus, in the proof of the first welfare theorem, the issue of affecting population size is never considered.

Elsewhere (Ng 1986), I critically reviewed grounds for population control (e.g., resource limitation, reduction in per capita income, congestion, unemployment, etc.) and found them to be wanting (at least if we ignore ignorance and irrational preference). Rather, I found reasons (e.g., external benefits of a larger population through a higher growth rate in knowledge, a public good) in favour of subsidising population growth. In the present chapter, it is argued that a subsidy on population growth may be Pareto optimal even if we ignore factors (external benefits) identified in Ng (1986). In Yang and Ng (1993), we analyse the division of labour to benefit from the economies of specialisation. Again, a higher population may benefit all by allowing more specialisation. However, in this chapter, we ignore such possible benefits of a larger population.

Clarke and Ng (1993) show that, even in the presence of external costs such as congestion, an increase in population (through immigration or natural increase) does not make existing people as a group worse off economically provided an efficient tax is imposed on the congestion; the increase in congestion tax paid outweighs the decrease in consumer surplus of existing people due to a higher congestion and a higher tax. Also, in the presence of uncorrected distortions, it is well known from the theory of second best that peculiar and opposite results may be obtained. Thus, for simplicity, we should ignore such factors and assume a perfectly functioning competitive economy with no external effects or other distortions. We also assume a closed economy to avoid the complication of international redistribution. Finally, individuals are taken to be rational utility maximisers without ignorance. The next two sections argue for subsidy from the viewpoint of pre-existing people. Section 4 brings the additional people into the objective function, with the case for subsidy still sustained, if not strengthened. The concluding section explains why the rather astonishing result is true and discusses some qualifications.

2. THE CASE FOR SUBSIDY: GRAPHICAL ANALYSIS

The basic reason Ng (1986) is able to dismiss arguments for population control such as lowering per capita income may be briefly summarised. Even with constant resources, a larger population need not reduce per capita income. Even for cases where a larger population does reduce the per capita income, it remains a fallacy to believe that population growth through either natural increase or immigration is thus necessarily undesirable. This fallacy is held even by population theorists, including economists and philosophers, as evidenced by the dominant view that the optimal size of the population is one that maximises income per head or average utility.[1] This is a fallacy even if we abstract from such relevant factors as possible preference for family size.

The fallacy is due to the failure to see that, despite a decrease in income per head and/or average utility, an increase in population may yet make everyone better off. Suppose a family of three decides under perfect rationality and full information to have another child. Its per capita income immediately falls by 25%. As a neighbour, do you go to express your condolence or to congratulate them? (See Simon 1977, 1981.)

Despite the benefits through infrastructure cost-sharing and other factors, more people may yet reduce the income per head of a country if they earn somewhat lower levels of income than the existing average. Yet no one in the country (or even in the world) may be made worse off as a result. Even if the income (utility) level of everyone else increases a little, income (utility) per head may yet decrease due to the lower income (utility) levels of the new people. But if no one is made worse off, how could this be regarded as an inferior situation?

If a family decides to have another family member, presumably the family considers itself better off with the new baby. Even if some family member is made worse off, this must be regarded as an intra-family problem. Typically, the society does not interfere with intra-family choices unless violation of basic human rights is involved. Being made somewhat worse off by the birth of a sibling is not regarded as a matter of human rights violation. While some elder children may resent having more siblings, others positively welcome them. The new baby will grow up to earn and get paid their marginal product. Thus, the rest of the society is not made worse off. If there is no serious parental negligence resulting in a negative welfare level for the new born child, no group is made worse off (there could be a minor distributional effect within the group called 'the rest of society' since wages could go down and rents increase), but some people are better off. It is thus at least a quasi-Pareto improvement where each relevant group is better off (Ng 1984).

In fact, if the increase in population is substantial, the rest of the society will benefit by a curvilinear triangular area. Because of diminishing marginal product of labour, all the new people N_0N_1 will receive a lower wage-rate $W_1 = BN_1$, as illustrated in Figure 4.1. Their total contribution to production is measured by AN_0N_1B. Thus, the curvilinear triangle ABC measures the gain to pre-existing people. While the latter also suffers a loss in wage income equal to W_0W_1CA, the increase in non-wage income is measured by W_0W_1BA.

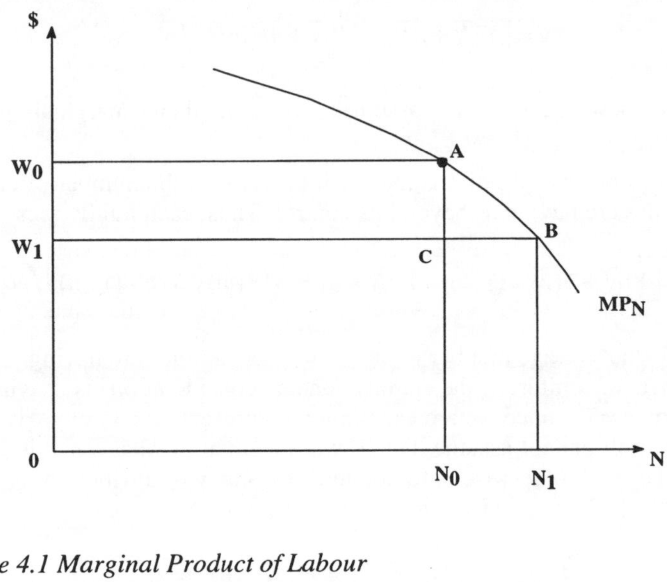

Figure 4.1 Marginal Product of Labour

The argument illustrated in Figure 4.1 is well known in the migration literature (e.g., Berry and Soligo 1969). However, to my knowledge, no one has gone on from here to infer that it may be Pareto optimal to subsidise more births. Yet, it is not difficult to see that this may well be the case, as shown in the next section.

3. INDIVIDUAL VS GROUP OPTIMA: A SIMPLE MODEL

For simplicity, assume that all existing people are identical with, in particular, identical ownership of assets. (The relaxation of this assumption complicates the analysis without reversing our conclusion for most cases; see the second last paragraph in the concluding section.) The utility of a representative family depends on both family income y (of existing members) and the number of children n as given by

$$U = U(y,n), \tag{4.1}$$

where the usual assumptions such as convexity apply.

Since asset ownership is the same across families, the family income y depends on gross national product Y less the income earned by new people divided by the number of existing families $\overline{N}$ as given by

$$y = \left[Y\{\overline{N} + n\overline{N}\} - Y'\{\overline{N} + n\overline{N}\}n\overline{N}\right]/\overline{N}, \tag{4.2}$$

where the new people are assumed to earn their marginal product $Y' \equiv \partial Y/\partial N$, where $N = \overline{N} + n\overline{N}$.

However, the crucial point is that each family sees the number of children other families are having as beyond its control. Thus, each family sees its y as

$$y = \left[Y\{\overline{N} + \overline{n}(\overline{N}-1) + n\} - Y'\{\overline{N} + \overline{n}(\overline{N}-1) + n\}\{\overline{n}(\overline{N}-1) + n\}\right]/\overline{N}, \tag{4.3}$$

where $\overline{n}$ is the average number of children other families are having, and n is the number of children the family under consideration is having. At equilibrium $n = \overline{n}$, since we are examining a representative family. However, the family itself cannot assume that $\overline{n}$ will be equal to whatever n it decides to have. (To think otherwise is to commit the fallacy of attribution discussed in Ng (1982).) The maximisation of (4.1) subject to (4.3) gives

$$U_n/U_y = Y''\{\overline{n}(\overline{N}-1) + n\}/\overline{N} = nY'' \cong 0, \tag{4.4}$$

where $U_n \equiv \partial U/\partial n$ is the net marginal utility of having children, $U_y \equiv \partial U/\partial y$ is the marginal utility of a dollar. Hence U_n/U_y is the net marginal value of children (i.e., marginal benefit minus marginal cost). Also, $Y'' \equiv \partial Y'/\partial N$ is slope of the marginal-product-of-labour curve.

The right-hand side of (4.4) is approximately equal to zero because an increase in one person does not decrease the marginal product of labour appreciably ($Y'' \cong 0$) and *n* is typically a small number (usually around two). Why has Y'' to be multiplied by *n*? This is explained with reference to Figure 4.2.

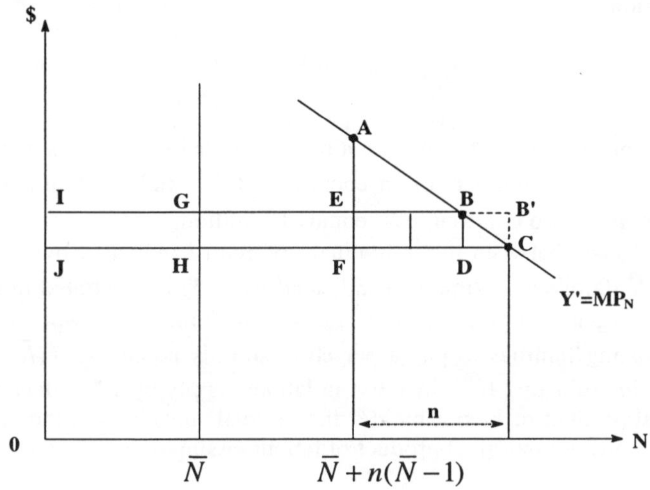

Figure 4.2 Marginal Product of Labour and Family Structure

The family in question takes the number of existing families ($\bar{N}$) and the number of children other families are having ($\bar{n}\bar{N}-\bar{n}$) as given. Hence, it starts from the point *A* and decides to have *n* (equal to 3 in the illustration) children. Consider its decision whether to have the last of these children. Having this last child will decrease the marginal product of labour Y' slightly (almost negligible; exaggerated in Figure 4.2 for visibility) by *BD*. This reduced value of Y' applies not only to this last child but to all other people, including existing families and the newly born. This reduction is measured by the area *IJDB*. For the existing people, while their wage income is reduced by *IJHG*, their non-wage income is increased by *IJCB*. They thus gain the area *GHCB*, which is approximately equal to $GHCB'$. (The slight difference of $BB'C$ is due to a discrete change in *n*; for a marginal change, the divergence vanishes.) However, this gain of $GHCB'$ is equally shared by all $\bar{N}$ families. Thus, each family (including the one making the marginal decision to have the extra child) gains the area $EFCB'$ which equals n times $BD(=Y'')$. This is why Y'' has to be multiplied by n (or $\bar{n}$).

The illustration in Figure 4.2 also shows that, while $EFCB'$ $(= nY'')$ may be negligibly small, the total gain to all the $\bar{N}$ families as a group $GHCB'$ $(= n\bar{N}Y'')$ need not be negligible. The fact that, from the viewpoint of existing people, an extra person generates an indirect gain of $GHCB'$ $(= n\bar{N}Y'')$ is confirmed by maximising (4.1) subject to (4.2), giving the first-order condition

$$U_n / U_y = n\bar{N}Y'' < 0. \tag{4.5}$$

The right-hand side of (4.5) need not be negligible even if Y' is negligible since $n\bar{N}$ is a large number. In an economy of five million families, each with an average of two children, $n\bar{N}$ equals 10 million.

The divergence between the individual optimum I indicated by (4.4) and the group ($\bar{N}$ families) optimum G indicated by (4.5) is illustrated in Figure 4.3. This divergence suggests that it is desirable from the viewpoint of the group of existing families to pay a per child subsidy equal to $-n(\bar{N}-1)Y''$. How big is this subsidy? If an increase in labour supply by 1% reduces long-run marginal product of labour by x%, the optimal subsidy is in the order of $2/3x$% the (life-time) marginal product of labour, assuming $n = 2$, since

$$-n(\bar{N}-1)Y'' = -\frac{n(\bar{N}-1)}{N}\frac{\partial Y'}{\partial N}\frac{N}{Y'}Y' = \frac{n(\bar{N}-1)}{(1+n)\bar{N}}xY' \cong \frac{n}{1+n}xY'. \tag{4.6}$$

Even if x is a relatively small number (say 0.01), and even if we take into account the extra costs of raising revenue and hence, say, half the optimal subsidy, it is still a significant sum and orders of magnitude larger than the 'milk money' (child endowment) paid in Australia.

Some readers may feel uncomfortable that the number of children is a discrete variable (an integer) while we treat it as a continuous variable. While this is true for each family, for the society as a whole the number of children is almost a continuous variable. Moreover, heterogeneity between families and uncertainty effectively mean that the *expected* total number of children born (say with respect to the amount of subsidy) *is* a continuous variable.

We have shown that having more people makes existing people as a group better off and hence it is desirable to subsidise more births from the viewpoint of existing people. What if the welfare of the new people is also allowed into the objective function? The next section shows that a different reason for subsidising more births then arises.

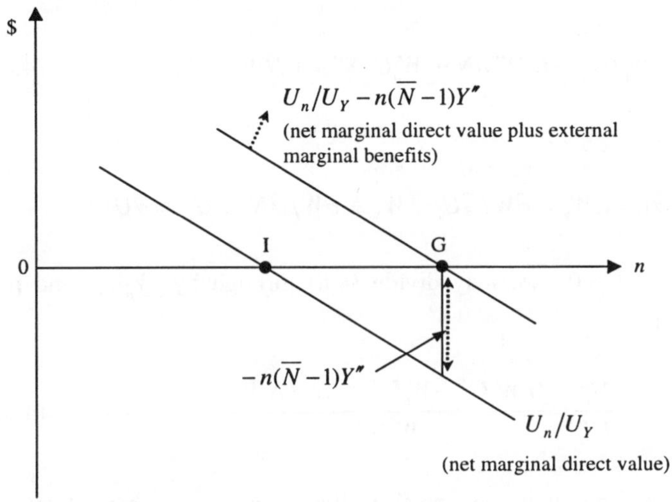

Figure 4.3 Divergence between Social and Group Optima

4. ACCOUNTING FOR THE WELFARE OF THE NEW PEOPLE

Let social welfare be dependent on the utility of pre-existing people U^p, the utility of the new or additional people U^a (each referring to the representative number of the respective group) and the number of new people $N^a = n\overline{N}$. Since the number of existing people is given, we may ignore it in the objective function

$$W = W(U^p, U^a, N^a). \tag{4.7}$$

Over the relevant range, it is assumed, as is consistent with happiness surveys (e.g., Veenhoven 1984) and the feasibility of suicide, that $U^p > 0$, $U^a > 0$ and hence $\partial W/\partial N^a > 0$. In other words, if it is regarded as desirable to have additional happy people (otherwise we are back to the objective function of Section 3 above), it must be more desirable if we can have more additional people of the same level of happiness if the happiness of existing people is not reduced.[2]

U^p is as given in (4.1) above, i.e., $U^p = U^p(y^p, n)$. U^a simply depends on $y^a = Y''$, which still depends on $N = \overline{N} + n\overline{N}$. The family income of an existing family y^p is still as given in (4.2). Then, maximising (4.7) with respect to n and subject to these specifications, we have the first-order condition

$$W_p(U_n^p - U_y^p Y'' n\bar{N}) + W_a U_y^p Y'' \bar{N} + \bar{N} W_N = 0\,, \tag{4.8}$$

where, for example,

$$W_p \equiv \partial W/\partial U^p\,,\ W_a \equiv \partial W/\partial U^a\,,\ W_N \equiv \partial W/\partial N^a\,,\ U_n^p \equiv \partial U^p/\partial n\,.$$

Since $W_p > 0, U_y^p > 0$, we may divide (4.8) through by $W_p U_y^p$ and re-arrange to obtain

$$\frac{U_n^p}{U_y^p} = \frac{(nW_pU_y^p - W_aU_y^a)Y''\bar{N} - \bar{N}W_N}{W_pU_y^p}\,. \tag{4.9}$$

Even if we assume that the social welfare function concerned treats additional people 'at a par' with pre-existing people such that $nW_pU_y^p = W_aU_y^a$ (the n accounting for the fact that there are n times new people as the number of pre-existing family and the fact that U_y^p and U_y^a applies to *all* pre-existing and new people respectively; so if a marginal dollar is valued the same irrespective of whether consumed by a pre-existing family or by new people, the equality before this parenthesis holds), we still have

$$U_n^p/U_y^p = -\bar{N}W_N/W_pU_y^p < 0\,, \tag{4.10}$$

which diverges from (4.4) above. Thus, even if we are maximising an objective function that takes full account of the welfare of the additional people, a subsidy on having more children is still optimal.

If we give additional people less than 'at par' concern in our social welfare function, then $nW_pU_y^p > W_aU_y^a$ and the first term in the numerator of the right-hand side of (4.9) is also negative (as $Y'' < 0$). Intuitively, if additional people are given less than 'at par' valuation, the decrease in their labour income (the area *GHCB*) does not fully offset the corresponding gain to the pre-existing people, making part of this area still a ground for subsidising births.

If we don't take the welfare of additional people into account, a subsidy is desirable due to the externality illustrated in Figure 4.2 (lower income to the new people generating more income to existing people). If we take the welfare of additional people fully into account (i.e., at par), a subsidy is desirable since more happy people increases social welfare. If their welfare is taken into account at less than at par, both considerations for subsidy apply partially.

5. CONCLUDING REMARKS

The source of the sup-optimality may be explained thus. While there is no real externality of any kind in our model, there is a pecuniary externality as more people reduce the marginal product of labour and hence the real wage rate. However, pecuniary externalities do not create distortions in the traditional analysis. At the margin, the loss of a marginal decrease in wage rate is exactly offset by the gain to other factors of production. Nevertheless, this is true only with the set of individuals held unchanged. With the set changing as new people are born (or allowed to enter the border), a part of the external pecuniary cost of a reduced wage rate is sustained by the prospective people. This makes the gain to factor-owners in the existing people more than the external pecuniary costs, explaining the source of the 'problem'. In other words, it is a combination of the pecuniary externality plus the change in the set of population that does the trick of creating the sub-optimality. However, this is a trick that no one has noticed and in a direction opposite to the intuition of most people.

Despite the above explanation, it may still seemed rather paradoxical (as it did to me at first and probably will be to many other economists) that the voluntary choices of knowledgeable and rational families should result in sub-optimality in the absence of any distortion. After some reflections, I was then convinced that the source of the 'problem' is related to the fact that new people enjoy positive welfare. That this is necessary for $W_N > 0$ in Section 4 is obvious. Even for the analysis of Section 3, the fact that new people enjoy positive welfare means that as N is increased and the earning of the new people decreased, they would still prefer to be born and to live (rather than commit suicide). Thus, this allows existing people to increase N to increase their own income, without producing the external costs of bringing about unhappy people into existence. However, if the welfare of new people does not enter the objective function of existing people (i.e., in the framework of Section 3), unhappy people (who may not commit suicide for various reasons) may not be regarded as an external cost. Thus, one may also view the 'problem' as being due to the fact that having additional people provides existing people with more opportunity to trade. Thus, our basic conclusion, which already follows from the analysis of Section 3, is not contingent on the framework of Section 4, which uses a social welfare function with interpersonally comparable utilities. (Even the framework of Section 4 should be acceptable for the problem on hand as reasonable social choice is not possible without interpersonal cardinal utilities; see Kemp and Ng 1976 and Ng 1997.) Some readers may also be troubled by the concept of zero vs. positive/negative utilities. However, this is an essential concept and almost universally used in the issue of optimum population. Moreover, we may 'define the zero on the [utility] scale as the well-being of a person who leads a life without experiences of any sort: a life lived in a coma throughout' (Broome 1996, p. 177).

There are a few considerations that may qualify my conclusions. First, ignorance and irrational choice have been ignored. However, perhaps the decisions to have more children in poor and heavily populated countries of the world may not be utility-maximising. Perhaps we are genetically programmed to want to procreate even if it decreases our welfare. This is debatable. In countries of high income and high education levels, the chosen family sizes are typically very small, being well below replacement levels for many countries. (While a fertility rate, i.e., the number of children an average woman has, of more than two is necessary for replacement, the current figures, which are declining, are: Australia: 1.74, Europe: 1.6, Spain: 1.15.)

Secondly, if external costs are very big and very difficult to internalise through appropriate pricing/taxing, some form of control may be justified. This may become important if intertwined with the issue of ignorance and vicious cycles as may be more applicable for certain very poor countries. (See Dasgupta, 1995.) However, this consideration is hardly applicable to most rich countries.

Thirdly, if we recognise unequal asset ownership among pre-existing people, a distributional effect may qualify our conclusion, though my argument (Ng 1984) for treating a dollar as a dollar in specific issues (leaving the equality objective to be achieved through the general tax/transfer system)[3] make this qualification not important except where the redistributive effect is huge.

To most people, the first issue in optimal population is that of overcrowding. Apart from the issue of the proper taxation of congestion and pollution mentioned in the third paragraph of Section 1 and the mistake of using per capita income discussed at the beginning of Section 2, the following may be added. When one drives in a heavily congested road, it is natural to think 'how nice it would be if there were only 20% of people travelling!' However, with only 20% of people travelling (ignoring the shift to public transport which may be a good solution for many cities), the per capita cost of building the existing road system would be 5-fold or the width of the road might be reduced to one fifth, with probably more serious congestion!

NOTES

1. A contrasting view is that of maximizing total utility (average utility times the number of

people). The long-standing debate between total and average utility maximisation does not seem to have been settled either in the philosophy or the economics cycles. However, I argue elsewhere (Ng 1989) in favour of total utility on ethical grounds (applicable for choices on population sizes not affecting ourselves) but allow for our partiality towards our own utility for actual choices that affect us, thus effectively resolving the dilemma. Most economists (with the notable exception of Meade (1955) and Dasgupta (1969) who favour total utility) discussing optimum population chooses to maximise average utility; see Pitchford (1974), Parfit (1984), Cowen (1996) on issues of optimum population.

2. Broome (1996) believes that creating happy people is morally neutral. But this creates an asymmetry, since creating miserable people is ethically bad. It also leads to unavoidable difficulties as Broome himself realises.
3. While the progressive tax/transfer system has disincentive effects, it is not usually recognised that equality-oriented measures in specific issues also have the same disincentive effects plus additional distortive costs.

REFERENCES

Berry, R. A. and R. Soligo (1969), 'Some welfare aspects of international migration', *Journal of Political Economy*, **77,** 195-221.

Broome, John (1996), 'The welfare economics of population', *Oxford Economic Papers*, **48**, 177-93.

Clarke, H. R. and Y.-K. Ng (1993), 'Immigration and economic welfare: resource and environmental aspects', *Economic Record*, **6**, 59-73.

Cowen, Tyler (1996), 'What do we learn from the repugnant conclusion?' *Ethics*, **106**, 754-75.

Dasgupta, P. (1969), 'On the concept of optimum population', *Review of Economic Studies,* **36**, 295-318.

Dasgupta, P. (1995), 'The population problem: theory and evidence', *Journal of Economic Literature*, **33,** 1879-902.

Kemp, M.C. and Y.-K. Ng (1976), 'On the existence of social welfare functions, social orderings and social decision functions', *Economica,* **43,** 59-66.

Meade, J.E. (1955), *Trade and Welfare*, Oxford: Oxford University Press.

Ng, Y.-K. (1982), 'A micro-macroeconomic analysis based on a representative firm', *Economica*, **49,** 121-39.

Ng, Y.-K. (1984), 'Quasi-Pareto social improvements', *American Economic Review*, **74**, 1033-50.

Ng, Y.-K. (1986), 'On the welfare economics of population control', *Population and Development Review*, **12**, 247-66.

Ng, Y.-K. (1989), 'What should we do about future generations? Impossibility of Parfit's Theory X', *Economics and Philosophy*, **5,** 235-53.

Ng, Y.-K. (1997), 'A case for happiness, cardinalism, and interpersonal comparability', *Economic Journal*, **107,** 1848-58.

Parfit, D. (1984), *Reasons and Persons*, Cambridge: Cambridge University Press.

Pitchford, J.D. (1974), *Population in Economic Growth*, Amsterdam: North-Holland.

Simon, J. L. (1977), *The Economics of Population Growth,* Princeton: Princeton University Press.

Simon, J. L. (1981), *The Ultimate Resource*, Princeton: Princeton University Press.

Veenhoven, R. (1984), *Conditions of Happiness*, Holland: Reidel Dordrecht.

Yang, X. and Y.-K. Ng (1993), *Specialization and Economic Organization*, Amsterdam: North-Holland.

PART TWO

International Trade Policy

5. The Economic Significance of the GATT/WTO Rules

Michihiro Ohyama

1. INTRODUCTION

The General Agreement on Tariffs and Trade (GATT), created in 1947, states in the preamble that the participating governments were desirous of contributing to their declared objectives ... 'by entering into reciprocal and mutually advantageous arrangements directed at the substantial reduction of tariffs and other trade barriers and to the elimination of discriminatory treatment in international commerce'. The GATT successfully contributed to the liberalisation of world trade through eight rounds of multilateral trade negotiations and developed into the World Trade Organisation (WTO) in 1995. While the GATT was formally a mere international agreement, the WTO is an international organisation comparable to the International Monetary Fund (IMF) and the World Bank. The GATT continues to exist as the agreement on a set of rules the member countries are to abide by in exercising their trade policies.

There are, however, views critical or sceptical of the basic stance of GATT, especially among economists. Some argue that GATT was originally based on the spirit of mercantilism rather than on the principle of free trade. There is indeed no explicit statement in GATT that it seeks to realise free trade. On the contrary, the stipulation of countervailing and anti-dumping duties (Article 6), the approval of trade restriction for the reason of balance of payments (Article 12) and the provision of safeguards (Article 19) may be interpreted to reflect the anti-economic mercantilist dogma that exports are beneficial, imports are harmful and the balance of payment deficits are nothing but national disasters. The principle of reciprocity (mentioned in the preamble and article 28) is often construed as the mercantilist rule of negotiation.[1] There is no doubt, however, that GATT has contributed to the realisation of freer trade by prohibiting quantitative trade restriction in principle and arranging a number of rounds to reduce tariff and non-tariff trade barriers. There may be traces of mercantilist ideas in GATT, but as a whole it has served as an extremely useful vehicle of trade liberalisation. This fact seems to suggest that the GATT/WTO rules are basically conducive to the realisation of free trade. Recently, using standard one-good or two-good models of international trade, Bagwell and Staiger (1997, 1999) demonstrated that GATT's principle of reciprocity indeed serves to deliver efficient policy outcomes in combination with that of non-discrimination. In this chapter, I shall similarly argue that the basic rules of the GATT/WTO are economically meaningful and useful for creating freer trade. To discuss broad aspects of the GATT/WTO rules, I shall use an alternative multi-good general equilibrium model of international trade and the method of welfare analysis developed in my previous paper (Ohyama, 1972). I shall also reconsider recent claims for harmonisation of national policies and institutions, posed as a future challenge to the WTO, in the same context.

The chapter is organised as follows. Section 2 provides a basic criterion for comparing the welfare of two distinct situations within the framework of a multi-country, multi-good general equilibrium model of international trade, which I shall employ extensively in subsequent sections. Section 3 clarifies the economic significance of the principle of non-discrimination including the case for free trade. Section 4 considers regional integration agreements (RIA for short) such as free trade areas and customs union, an important exception to the principle of non-discrimination. I shall argue that the existence of industrial adjustment costs also explains GATT's conditional approval of RIA. Furthermore, I shall show that free trade areas, as well as customs unions, can be made potentially beneficial to the world as whole if they adjust tariffs so as to leave their trade with the rest of the world at the level prior to their formation. This extends the incidence of the celebrated Kemp-Wan Theorem concerning the customs unions (see Kemp and Wan, 1976). Section 5 turns to the principle of reciprocity. I shall provide a basis for the conjecture that multilateral tariff negotiations on the basis of reciprocity are likely to produce mutually beneficial concessions if combined with the Most-Favoured-Nation rule. Section 6 reconsiders recent arguments for harmonisation and shows that they can be rationalised on the basis of efficiency rather than equity. Finally, Section 7 concludes the chapter.

2. CRITERION OF WELFARE COMPARISON

To investigate the economic significance of the GATT/WTO rules, it is necessary to employ criteria of welfare comparison in some form or another. One of the criteria most widely accepted among economists is the standard of Pareto comparison, which ranks different economic situations in the order of allocative efficiency. In this section I introduce a method of Pareto comparison useful for the purpose of the present chapter.

Let us consider the economy of a single country (or a union of countries) engaging in external trade. The economy is assumed to be static in the sense that its technology, factor endowment and the preferences of its consumers are all given and fixed. There is a finite number of commodities produced and consumed in competitive markets.[2] The model is general enough to accommodate all kinds of commodities: final consumption goods and services, intermediate goods, factor services, any of which may be traded or non-traded. Consider two distinct economic situations, S' and S'' and their general equilibria.[3] For simplicity, I assume that there are no domestic taxes or subsidies and abstract from domestic distortions arising from external economies and diseconomies. Let p' and p'' denote the domestic consumers' (and producers') equilibrium price vectors and let x' and x'' denote the aggregate equilibrium consumption vectors in situation S' and S'' respectively. Then, one can show that if

$$p''x'' \geq p''x' \tag{5.1}$$

for any relevant set of income distributions, situation S'' is potentially preferable to S' from the viewpoint of the country (or the union of the countries) in the sense that some consumers can be made better off with other consumers being kept not worse-off in S'' than in S'.[4] Note that if a commodity is a pure intermediate good, its consumption is identically zero in all situations. Suppose that the government imposes a tariff at ad valorem rate, t_i'', on the import of commodity i from all sources in situation S''. Let q' and q'' be the international price vectors in S' and S'' respectively and let T'' signify the diagonal matrix with the i-th diagonal element t_i''. In the absence of transportation costs, perfect arbitrage entails

$$p'' = q''(I + T''). \tag{5.2}$$

Let y' and y'' denote the equilibrium output vector, a' and a'' the endowment vector, e' and e'' the excess demand (or net import) vector in situation S' and S'' respectively. By definition, we have

$$e' = x' - y' - a', \tag{5.3}$$

$$e'' = x'' - y'' - a''. \tag{5.4}$$

If a commodity is non-traded, its excess demand becomes identically zero in all situations. The balance of payments is assumed to be in equilibrium in both situations implying

$$q''e'' = 0. \tag{5.5}$$

Noting that $a' = a''$ by assumption, we obtain from equations (5. 2)–(5. 5),

$$p''x'' - p''x' = q''(e'' - e') + q''T''(e'' - e') + p''(y'' - y') \tag{5.6}$$

The assumption of profit maximisation implies $p''y'' \geq p''y'$. In view of (5.6), we have

Theorem 1 (Welfare Comparison): *Consider two distinct situations, S' and S'', with common initial endowment and production set. If*

$$q''(e'' - e') + q''T''(e'' - e') \geq 0 \tag{5.7}$$

holds for all relevant income distributions, situation S'' is potentially preferable to situation S'.

The first term on the left hand side of (5. 7) represents the terms of trade effects and the second term the tariff revenue effects on potential economic welfare of shift from S' to S''. Caveats are in order. First, this theorem is applicable only to the comparison of equilibria in two situations. In evaluating the welfare effects of actual economic reforms such as trade liberalisation and domestic deregulation, it is necessary to take into consideration the costs and benefits arising in the process of transition from S' to S''. To be more specific, the costs of industrial adjustment associated with the transition may be very important in actual policy decision-making. Second, it compares two situations only in terms of potential economic welfare upon allocative efficiency. In fact, S'' may be said to be *actually* preferable to S' not only if the former is potentially preferable to the latter but also if the former is more distributionally equitable than the latter.

3. THE PRINCIPLE OF NON-DISCRIMINATION

The trade policy instruments of a country consist of custom duties, trade subsidies, quantitative trade restrictions and various other non-tariff barriers designed to suppress its imports and promote its exports of goods and services. In contrast, the domestic policy instruments include production and consumption taxes and subsidies and various other quantitative restrictions employed to affect domestic production and consumption. Article 1 of the GATT stipulates that 'any advantage, favour, privileges or immunity by any contracting party to any product originating in or destined for any other country shall be accorded immediately and unconditionally to the like product originating in or destined for the territories of any other parties'. This is the so-called most-favoured nation clause prohibiting discriminatory application of tariffs and other trade policy measures. In addition to this, Article 3 of the GATT rules that 'internal taxes and other internal charges, and laws, regulations and requirements affecting internal sale, offering for sale, purchase, transportation, distribution or use of products, and internal quantitative regulations requiring mixture, processing, or use of products in specific amounts or proportions, should not be applied to imported or domestic products so as to afford protection to domestic production'. This is the so-called national treatment clause ensuring that market access commitments made by any country are not nullified through the introduction of offsetting domestic policies. These two clauses are combined to constitute the principle of non-discrimination of the GATT. It should also be noted that the GATT approves the continued existence of tariffs while generally inhibiting the quantitative restriction of trade by measures other than duties, taxes and other charges (Article 11).

3.1 Free trade proposition

The instruments of discriminatory regulations like tariffs and import quotas hinder the fulfilment of the 'law of one price' that the internationally tradable goods are traded at the same price everywhere in the world (except for the differences due to the costs of transportation and distribution). For simplicity suppose that perfect competition prevails in all markets and there are no external economies. If the price of good i relative to good j is higher in the home country than in the foreign country, one may infer that the buyers' evaluation of good i relative to good j is higher in the home country than in the foreign country, or conversely the buyers' evaluation of good j relative to good i is higher in the foreign country than in the home country. It would then be possible to increase the welfare of both countries by decreasing the usage of good j and increasing that of good i slightly in the home country and increasing the usage of good j and increasing that of good i by the same amount in the foreign country without changing the world production of the two goods. This conclusion is applicable to any pair of goods irrespective of whether they are consumption goods or intermediate goods. Therefore, the breakdown of the law of one price for internationally tradable goods across national borders implies that the situation is not Pareto-optimal from the viewpoint of the world as a whole. In other words, it is *necessary* for the law of one price to hold for all tradable goods throughout the world if the resource allocation of the world is to be efficient in the sense of Pareto.

At the same time, one can easily prove that the fulfilment of the law of one price for all tradable goods is also *sufficient* for the attainment of a Pareto-efficient allocation of world resources.

Proposition 1: *If the prices of all tradable goods are equalised all over the world, the resulting equilibrium is Pareto-optimal for the world as a whole.*

Proof. Recall the theorem of welfare comparison established in the preceding section and apply it to the 'union of all countries in the world', as it were. Suppose that situation S' is an arbitrary non-free trade state saddled with artificial trade impediments in some form or another and situation S'' is the state of free trade. In situation S'' the prices of all tradable goods are equalised internationally so that the proposition of welfare comparison is certainly applicable. Moreover, the 'external' trade of the world union is identically zero, or $e' = e'' = 0$. Therefore, condition (5. 7) is clearly satisfied meaning that the potential welfare of the world as a whole is not lower in the free-trade situation than in any other situation under trade restrictions. □

This conclusion may be interpreted as the theoretical foundation of the free-trade principle underlying the GATT/WTO rules of international trade. An important caveat is, however, in order, to which I now turn.

3.2 The most-favoured-nation rule

As pointed out above, the GATT/WTO approves the imposition of tariffs subject to certain restrictions. The most-favoured-nation rule (MFN rule for short) merely requires that the imports of the same good originating from all member countries be treated equally subject to common border measures such as tariffs and other trade charges. It does *not* require the immediate abolition of border measures, or the immediate realisation of free trade. At the same time, however, the GATT/WTO organises the 'rounds' of trade negotiation in the hope that they lead *gradually* to the ultimate ideal state of non-discrimination, i.e., world free trade. Thus it stipulates the non-discriminatory application of border measures on the other hand and calls for the gradual reduction of such measures. These two dimensions of the GATT/WTO rules are respectively of some economic significance.

Under the most-favoured-nation rule, a member country has the incentive to import goods from the trading partners where it can buy at lowest prices and export goods to the partners where it can sell at the highest prices. We can formalise this point by applying the theorem of welfare comparison to a single country.

Proposition 2: *A country can achieve a given quantity of external trade most efficiently by abiding by the MFN rule.*

Proof. Let S' stand for the situation where a country discriminates between its trading partners by imposing differential tariffs and S'' for the situation where it imposes non-discriminatory tariffs on trades with all countries. Further suppose that the tariffs in situation S'' are adjusted to achieve the external trade of all goods at the same level as in situation S' or $e' = e''$. Clearly, condition (5. 7) is satisfied by equality.

It may not be possible, however, for a country to achieve the same quantity of external trade given in situation S' by means of non-discriminatory tariffs. In fact, a large country with market power may be able to increase gains from trade by discriminating between its trading partners through differential tariffs at the expense of their welfare. The MFN rule serves to eliminate such a case of exploitation by a large country of its trading partners where Proposition 2 becomes vacuous.[5]

4. REGIONAL ECONOMIC COOPERATION

In reality, the existence of industrial adjustment costs may limit the spatial extent of trade liberalisation in a given length of time. Trade liberalisation among a certain set of countries may involve much less adjustment costs than global liberalisation covering all countries. For instance, horizontal integration between countries similar in the structure of factor endowment and usable technology may be realised without major adjustment of their industrial structures and yet lead to consumption diversification because of expansion in intra-industry trade and gains in productivity due to increased competition. Conversely, vertical integration between countries specialising in distinct sets of industries also increases gains from trade at the least costs of industrial adjustment. Furthermore, it may be possible to transfer labour and entrepreneurial resources from contracting industries of one country to expanding industries in another much more smoothly in the case of integration between countries geographically close and similar in cultural backgrounds than in the case of integration of distant countries. Thus the concept of 'deeper integration' involving the liberalisation of factors of production becomes relevant. It should be clear that regional economic integration may be justified when the costs of industrial adjustment are important and differ substantially depending on the extent and incidence of trade liberalisation.

4.1 Customs union

Beside the consideration of adjustment costs, there are also good reasons why the GATT/WTO permits regional economic integration such as customs unions and free-trade areas on certain conditions although they violate the MFN rule. An important condition is that the duties and other regulations of an integration applied to international trade with non-member countries shall not be higher or more restrictive than the corresponding duties and restrictions existing prior to the formation of the integration (Article 24.5). The exact meaning of this condition is not clear, but in the case of a customs union one of the possible interpretations is that the member countries as a whole shall keep the volume of trade with non-member countries at least at the same level prevailing before the union. Kemp (1964) and Vanek (1965) suggested, and later Ohyama (1972) and Kemp and Wan (1976) proved independently using a general competitive equilibrium model comprising many goods and countries, that the customs union satisfying this version of the condition necessarily improves the potential welfare of the world. As regionalism revived and spread all over the world recently, this result received renewed attention and came to be known as the Kemp-Wan Theorem.

Let me first re-establish the Kemp-Wan Theorem by appealing to our theorem of welfare proposition.[6]

Proposition 3 (Kemp-Wan Theorem): *A customs union that adjusts its common external trade so as to keep the total quantity of trade with non-member countries at the level prior to its formation is beneficial to the world as a whole.*

Proof. Let S'' be the situation of the customs union after its formation and S' be its pre-union situation. One may apply the theorem of welfare comparison to the customs union as a whole, since consumers in the union face common consumption prices. By assumption $e' = e''$ so that condition (5.7) is satisfied by equality, which implies that all member countries are potentially better off after the formation of the union. The rest of the world is not affected by the formation of the union. □

The literal interpretation of the GATT's Article 24 does not necessarily mean that a customs union must satisfy the condition of the Kemp-Wan theorem. Thus McMillan (1993) proposed to revise Article 24 on the basis of this theorem to stipulate explicitly that a customs union must not reduce the volume of trade with the rest of the world.

4.2 Free trade area

A free-trade area requires the removal of tariffs and other trade regulations among member countries, but each member retains its own tariffs against outsiders. It differs from a customs union that set up common external tariffs as well. Article 24 of the GATT considers both free trade areas and customs unions as the typical cases of regional preferential arrangement. In reality, free-trade areas are indeed important regional integration agreements as exemplified by the European Free Trade Area (EFTA) and the North American Free Trade Agreement (NAFTA). The Kemp-Wan Theorem is designed to apply only to a customs union. By using the theorem of welfare comparison, however, one can establish a similar proposition with respect to a free-trade area.

Proposition 4: *A free-trade area in which each member country adjusts its tariffs so as to keep the quantity of its trade with non-member countries at the previous level is beneficial to the world as a whole.*

Proof. Let S' stand for the situation of member country i before the formation of the free-trade area and S'' for the situation after that. Let e_{im} be the vector of its total trade with member countries and e_{io} the vector of its total trade with non-member countries. By assumption we have $e_i' = e_{im}' + e_{io}'$ and $e_i'' = e_{im}'' + e_{io}''$. In the free-trade area tariffs between members are abolished so that condition (5.7) as applied to country i may be written as

$$q''(e_i'' - e_i') + q''T_i''(e_{io}'' - e_{io}') \geq 0 \, ,$$

where T_i'' is the diagonal matrix of country i's tariff rates applied to non-member countries. By hypothesis, $e_{io}' = e_{io}''$. Hence, this reduces to

$$q''(e_{im}'' - e_{im}') \geq 0.$$

This condition can be satisfied if appropriate income transfers are made between the member countries. To see this, note that exports of a member country to other member countries must be matched by imports of the latter from the former, or $\sum e_{im}' = \sum e_{im}'' = 0$, where the summation is taken over all member countries of the free-trade area. Therefore, we have

$$q''\sum(e_{im}'' - e_{im}') \geq 0.$$

Thus it should be possible to achieve $q''(e_{im}'' - e_{im}') \geq 0$ through income transfer between member countries. □

Needless to say, the formation of the free-trade area does not affect non-member countries since each member's trade with them is thereby unchanged. I record this result since, to my knowledge, it is not common knowledge in the literature on regional economic integration.

5. THE PRINCIPLE OF RECIPROCITY

Reciprocity is counted as a fundamental principle of the GATT/WTO along with non-discrimination. Loosely defined, it is the practice of making a concession by one party conditional upon a concession by another in the GATT negotiations. Its basis is found in the preambles to the GATT and the

Marakesh Agreement Establishing the WTO, as well as in Article 28 of the GATT, which emphasises the importance of negotiations on a reciprocal and mutually advantageous basis. There are some sceptical views, however, about the role reciprocity plays in trading negotiations. Historically, it has been used by mercantilists and protectionists as a pretext for maintaining one's own trade barriers and later for preventing or punishing free-riding by countries that continued to maintain high trade barriers, or engage in 'unfair trade'. For example, the US 1890 Trade Act enabled the President to impose punitive tariffs upon the imports from the countries who practiced 'unequal and unreasonable' restrictions on US products. After the 1934 Trade Act, however, reciprocity, combined with the MFN rule, came to be recognised as a powerful device to realise multilateral trade liberalisation. This change of views about reciprocity in the United States certainly influenced the process of creating the GATT rules, which respect reciprocity together with non-discrimination.[7]

From a single large country's viewpoint, a unilateral reduction of tariffs and other trade restrictions is not incentive-compatible since it will worsen the country's terms of trade and may lower its potential welfare. If all countries act non-cooperatively without any agreement, the most likely result is an inefficient Nash tariff equilibrium in which some of them are bound to become worse-off than under free trade. If reciprocity is used as a guiding principle in trade negotiations and the resultant concessions are to be applied on the MFN basis, participating countries will be induced to reduce trade barriers and may succeed in getting out of this 'prisoner's dilemma'.

This idea may be formalised to some extent as follows. Suppose that many countries engage in bilateral negotiations simultaneously as in the early rounds of the GATT, and suppose that tariff concessions are made on a reciprocal basis and applied to all contracting parties following the MNF rule. Let S' be the situation of a participating country before the trade negotiations and S'' its situation after that. If tariff concessions are made to an 'equal' degree between any pair of countries and applied to all participants, they, as a whole, will not affect the external terms of trade of each country very much. For definiteness, suppose that the tariff concessions are made so as to leave each country's terms of trade completely unaffected, or $q''(e''-e')=0$. Condition (5.7) is then simplified to

$$q''T''(e''-e')\geq 0.$$

This condition is likely to be satisfied since the reduction of tariffs may be presumed generally to increase the trade volume of products restricted by tariffs, i.e., $e''\geq e'$. It follows that the round of tariff negotiation designed as above is likely to increase the potential welfare of all participating countries.[8] This conjecture also applies to the tariff negotiation by the across-the-board formula approach practised since the Kennedy Round.[9]

6. HARMONISATION

In the face of deepening international economic interdependence and globalisation, there has been increasingly loud clamour for harmonisation of national policies, laws and practices such as labour and environmental standards, domestic distribution systems etc. The concept of harmonisation here seems to be closely related to that of 'fair trade'.[10] A country's labour and environmental standards can be said to be 'unfair' if they are considerably lower than the corresponding standards in its trading partners giving competitive edge to its labour intensive and polluting industries. Similarly, a country's domestic distribution system can be labelled 'unfair'' when it is regulated more severely than its foreign counterparts. In short, these standards and regulations are required to be harmonised to prepare a 'level-playing ground' for products from different countries in the world. These claims for harmonisation can easily be converted into claims for old-fashioned protectionism against social and environmental dumping on the pretext that there is little prospect for their satisfactory fulfilment.

It is, however, questionable that the calls for harmonisation are justified on the ground of 'fairness'. What is 'fair' for producers in a particular industry differs from what is 'fair' for producers in general. More importantly, at least from the viewpoint of Economics, it is consumers rather than producers who should ultimately count in policy decision-making. In fact, it is on the basis of efficiency rather than fairness that harmonisation may be rationalised in some cases. International differences in economic policies and institutions tend to imply differences in, among other things, prices. For instance, the price of gasoline would be, *ceteris paribus*, higher in a country with high environmental standards than in other countries with low standards. It is considered to be desirable to restrict the world total usage of gasoline to alleviate global warming. If so, the most efficient measure to achieve this objective is to tax the usage of gasoline at the same rate in all countries thereby eliminating international differences in the user's price of gasoline.

To establish this point formally, I need to extend Theorem 1 slightly. Let p_c'' be the vector of consumers' prices and p_r'' the vector of producers' prices in the equilibrium of situation S''. For simplicity, I only consider here taxes on the usage of goods either as consumption or as inputs in production. Producers' and consumers' prices coincide and they are now distinguished from and related to the vector of domestic market prices by

$$p_c'' = p_r'' = p''(I + U''), \qquad (5.8)$$

where U'' is the diagonal matrix of the ad valorem rates of usage (either consumption or input in production) tax in situation S''. Note that the i-th diagonal element u_i'' of U'' is the rate of tax on the use in production of good i only when y_i'' is negative. In view of equations (5. 2)–(5. 5), (5. 8) and profit maximisation condition, $p_r''y'' \geq p_r''y'$, we have

$$p_c''(x''-x') \geq q''(e''-e') + q''T''(e''-e') + p''U''[(x''-y'')-(x'-y')] , \quad (5.9)$$

on the assumption that $a''=a'$. By the same logic leading to Theorem 1, I can now state

Theorem 2 (Welfare Comparison): *Consider two distinct situations, S' and S'', with common initial endowments and production sets. If*

$$q''(e''-e') + q''T''(e''-e') + p''U''[(x''-y'')-(x'-y')] \geq 0 \quad (5.10)$$

holds for all relevant income distributions, situation S'' is potentially preferable to situation S'.

This extends Theorem 1 to the case where a country, or a union of countries, imposes a uniform tax on the usage of goods in situation S''. I can now put forward

Proposition 5: *If the world total usage of good i is to be controlled at a given level, free trade with a uniform tax on the usage of good i is most efficient from the viewpoint of the world as a whole in the sense that it is potentially preferable to any situation achieving the same policy goal by other instruments.*

Proof. Applying Theorem 2 to the union of all countries in the world, let the rate of usage tax u_i'' in situation S'' be set such that the total usage of good i is made equal to the given target level. Let S' be any other situation where the total usage of good i is controlled at the same target level by means of other policy instruments and let $u_j''=0$ for all $j \neq i$. We then have $x_i''-y_i''=x_i'-y_i'$. Furthermore, suppose that free trade prevails in situation S'' with users' prices of all tradable goods being equalised throughout the world. Under these circumstances, condition (5.10) is clearly satisfied by equality. □

Thus harmonisation of usage tax is desirable for the sake of efficient allocation of world resources if the world total usage of a *tradable* good is to be controlled at a given level. Note that this conclusion has nothing to do with 'fairness' in any plausible sense of the word. Some qualifications are in order. First, if good i is non-tradable, Proposition 5 is formally valid, but it does not imply that the same rate of tax be imposed on the usage of goods physically similar to good i in all countries. In this case, good i is produced and consumed in a single country and a physically similar good used in any other country must be regarded as a different good. Thus the rate of tax on the usage of these similar goods need not be equalised internationally even though the world total usage of them is to be controlled at a certain level. Second, harmonisation of usage tax may be objectionable because of its 'unfair' effects on the welfare of poor countries. For instance, developing countries usually object with good reasons to a uniform imposition of carbon tax. In such a case, one should introduce some kind of scheme to compensate the loss of welfare falling on developing countries as a result of harmonisation or modify harmonisation in order to secure fair share of carbon usage for them. Third, hasty harmonisation of usage tax should be avoided when it incurs heavy adjustment costs in some countries, just as hasty trade liberalisation is avoided under the GATT/WTO rules. In this respect, the WTO is in the position to promote gradual harmonisation in selected fields in collaboration with other specialised international organisations. At the same time, it is the task of the WTO to suppress disguised protectionism in the name of environmentalism or minimum labour standards.

7. CONCLUDING REMARKS

The GATT has operated successfully for a long time since its initiation in 1947 and continues to be effective under the WTO established in 1995. This fact itself testifies to the general acceptability of its basic rules. From the viewpoint of Economics, the important function of the GATT/WTO may be said to lower artificial trade barriers toward the ultimate goal of global free trade. Except for differences due to transportation and distribution costs, global tree trade realises the law of one price all over the world to achieve efficient allocation of world resources. In this chapter, I discussed various implications of the GATT/WTO rules, to be applied to trade negotiations between member countries, with a view to demonstrating that they, as a whole, constitute powerful instruments to deliver mutually advantageous reduction of tariffs and other trade restrictions. Some of the exceptions to the basic rules permitted under the GATT/WTO are also economically meaningful. In view of short-run structural adjustment costs associated with trade liberalisation, I argued that it is indeed appropriate for the GATT/WTO to support regional integration agreements such as free trade areas and customs unions on the condition that they do not hamper trade with the rest of the world.

Let me discuss briefly some qualifications of the chapter. First, the assumption of perfect competition adopted in the basic model may appear anachronistic, to say the least. As mentioned above, however, our theorem of welfare comparison is applicable to a model of imperfect competition and variable returns provided that in each industry the degree of monopoly is controlled at a given magnitude and firms' profits decline to zero under free entry.[11] This extension may still be unsatisfactory to some. Second, some may question the lack of political economy considerations in the chapter. To be sure, international trade negotiations are greatly influenced by political factors and it would be almost silly to ignore them to understand actual developments in GATT/WTO activities. Even so, one should explore the significance of the basic GATT/WTO rules purely from the viewpoint of economic theory if only to weigh its importance against political issues. Third, I have left out some important exceptions to the basic GATT/WTO rules in the form of safeguards such as anti-dumping and countervailing duties, trade restrictions for balance-of-payments purposes and waivers. Apparently, they belong to the realm of political economy, which is beyond the scope of the present study. The economic significance of these exceptions is at least dubious and the abuse of them would seriously undermine the *raison d'etre* for an organisation like the WTO.

ACKNOWLEDGEMENTS

I thank Murray Kemp, Alan Woodland, Kotaro Suzumura and an anonymous referee for many helpful comments and discussions.

NOTES

1. See Krugman (1991) for instance.
2. The analysis below is also applicable to the models of imperfectly competitive markets with increasing returns to scale under certain conditions. See Ohyama (1999).
3. See Ohyama (1972) for the concept of economic situation and its general equilibria.
4. See Ohyama (1972).
5. See Hoeckman and Kostecki (1995, 26-27).
6. The present proof of this result was originally given by Ohyama (1972) and reproduced here.
7. See Goldstein (1993) for a detailed account of the history of views on reciprocity and MFN rule in the United States.
8. Note that a reciprocal tariff reduction between a pair of countries may not be mutually advantageous *in isolation* since it is likely to deteriorate their terms of trade against the rest of the world.
9. See Bagwell and Staiger (1997) for a demonstration that reciprocity, coupled with the MFN rule, is bound to lead to Pareto-improving trade negotiations. Its basic logic is similar to the reasoning here although it is based on a structured partial equilibrium model of multi-country trade negotiation incorporating elements of political economy.
10. See Bhagwati and Hudec (1996) for a collection of excellent essays on the issue.
11. See Ohyama (1999).

REFERENCES

Bagwell, K. and R.W. Staiger (1997), 'Reciprocity, non-discrimination and preferential agreements in the multilateral trading system', NBER Working Paper 5932.

Bagwell, K. and R.W. Staiger (1999), 'An economic theory of GATT', *American Economic Review*, **89**, 215-48.

Bhagwati, J. and R.E. Hudec (1996) (eds), *Fair Trade and Harmonization,* Vol. 1, Cambridge, MA; MIT Press.

Goldstein, J. (1993), 'Creating the GATT rules: politics, institutions and American policy', in H. Milner and J. Ruggie (eds), *Multilateralism Matters: The Theory and Praxis of an International Form,* New York: Columbia University Press, Chap. 6, pp. 201-32.

Hoekman, B. and M. Kostecki (1995), *The Political Economy of the World Trading System: From GATT to WTO,* New York: Columbia University Press.

Kemp, M.C. (1964), *The Pure Theory of International Trade,* Englewood Cliffs, N.J.: Prentice-Hall.

Kemp, M.C. and H. Wan (1976), 'An elementary proposition concerning the formation of customs unions', *Journal of International Economics*, **6**, 95-97.

Krugman, P. R. (1991), 'The move toward free trade zone', in Federal Reserve Bank of Kansas City (ed.), *Policy Implications of Trade and Currency Zones, Symposium Series*, pp. 7-42.

McMillan, J. (1993), 'Does regional integration foster open trade? Economic theory and GATT's Article XXIV', in Kym Anderson and R. Blackhurst (eds), *Regional Integration and the Global Trading System*, New York: Harvester Wheatsheaf, pp. 292-310.

Ohyama, M. (1972), 'Trade and welfare in general equilibrium', *Keio Economic Studies*, **9**, 37-73.

Ohyama, M. (1999), 'Market, trade and welfare in general equilibrium', *Japanese Economic Review*, **51**, 1-32.

Vanek, J. (1965), *General Equilibrium of International Discrimination: The Case of Customs Unions*, Cambridge, MA: Harvard University Press.

6. Are Special Economic Zones Desirable?

Albert G. Schweinberger

1. INTRODUCTION

Special economic zones exist in many developing and advanced countries. They may be referred to as duty free zones, high tech, export processing zones or free trade areas. For a description of the free trade areas set up in more than eighty countries, see, for example, Grubel (1982). A detailed exposition of the classification of special economic zones can be found in Hamilton and Svensson (1982).

In the theoretical literature it is generally assumed that all trade barriers are retained in the domestic zone after the creation of the special economic zone. Consumers and producers in the domestic zone therefore face tariff-distorted prices. For convenience I assume that trade barriers always take the form of tariffs.[1] Furthermore I concentrate on the analysis of the welfare effects of production special economic zones. This implies that all consumption takes place in the domestic zone. However, all firms in the special economic zone face world market prices.[2] I believe that the assumption of a production special economic zone is not only analytically convenient but also a reasonably good approximation to reality in many cases (see e.g. the special economic zone of Shenzhen in Guangdong Province of the People's Republic of China).

Special economic zones may become less important in some countries in the future. However, it seems probable that at least some transition economies in Eastern Europe will make increasing use of them if they cannot join (in the near future) the European Union.

Special economic zones may be established for many reasons. Possibly the most important one is to attract more foreign investment. This purpose (if it is realised) is at odds with a considerable part of the received literature. Starting with the seminal article by Hamada published in 1974, it would appear that foreign investment in the special economic zone is likely to have an immiserisation effect. It is therefore argued that the setting up of the special economic zone implies a welfare loss. Many extensions (and qualifications) of the basic Hamada result can be found in the literature, see e.g. Rodriguez (1976), Hamilton and Svensson (1982), Wong (1986), Copeland (1994) and most recently, Dévereux and Chen (1995).

There exists another important purpose of the setting up of special economic zones: employment generation. Responding to a previous article by Young (1987) which, inter alia, focuses on imports of intermediate goods, Young and Miyagiwa (1987) show that, in the presence of unemployment of the Harris-Todaro type, a lowering of the tariffs on imports of intermediate goods into the special economic zone generally raises welfare.[3]

The literature on special economic zones contains undoubtedly many interesting insights and results. These insights and results notwithstanding, Dévereux and Chen (1995) have argued that the literature also has some significant weaknesses. In their view a major weakness is that the literature had very little, if any, effect on actual policy making. This is because the literature fails to produce any clear-cut and more general messages. There exist many disparate models with very special assumptions. It is not clear how they are related to each other. What is lacking is a unified framework. For a theory to be influential it must identify the general forces at work in the process of the establishment of a special economic zone. Moreover, the results should be communicable to policy makers.

An important purpose of this chapter is (a) to put forward such a unified general framework and (b) to make use of it to derive results that can be communicated to policy makers. Presumably, governments need economists' advice as to the setting up of welfare improving special economic zones, *ex ante*. But equally important, since welfare is not directly observable, the economist may determine, *ex post*, whether the establishment of a special economic zone was desirable.

The central tenet of this chapter is that, to achieve the purpose defined in the previous paragraph, a global approach is indispensable. The establishment of a special economic zone is a discrete phenomenon because it is a discrete geographic entity. It cannot be analysed using local (calculus) techniques. If we nevertheless insist on calculus techniques we overlook some very important effects (as is the case with all of the received literature).

The main result derivable from my novel global approach is this: subject to Hatta normality, the establishment of a production special economic zone is desirable if and only if the sum of a (to be defined) partition gain (loss), production gain, mobile factor reallocation and gains from factor trade effect is positive. Every one of these effects is shown to have a precise economic meaning. Equally important, several of these effects can be signed making use only of well-known properties of general equilibrium models.

The received literature employing a local (calculus) analysis focuses exclusively on the mobile factor reallocation effect associated with foreign investment, overlooking the partition gain (loss) and the production gain. The key message of the present chapter can be put very simply: foreign investment may have an immiserisation effect as, for example, in Hamada (1974) but this does not imply that the establishment of a special economic zone is not desirable. The partition gain (loss) and the production gain could more than offset the immiserisation effect of foreign investment.

The chapter is structured as follows. It consists of five sections. In section 2 I introduce the reader to the global approach put forward in this chapter. I also derive the basic results. I take a closer look at the partition gain/loss in section 3. The welfare effects of foreign investment are analysed in section 4. The analysis in section 4 focuses on the mobile factor reallocation effect, an effect well known from the literature. Nevertheless, applying a global approach I can offer some novel insights and results in section 4. Finally in section 5 I suggest some other applications of my approach and point out directions for further research in this area.

2. THE WELFARE EFFECTS OF SPECIAL ECONOMIC ZONES: A GLOBAL ANALYSIS

The following assumptions are made throughout section 2:[4]

1. All the special economic zones considered are production special economic zones. The domestic consumption of all goods takes place in the domestic zone.
2. Perfect competition in all goods and factor markets and constant returns to scale production functions.
3. There is only one household type.
4. The economy is a small open economy. All goods are traded internationally.[5]
5. Mobile and immobile factors are used in the special economic zone.

We now turn to the basic model. There are no special assumptions regarding the number of goods and factors (except that it is finite).

A meaningful analysis of the welfare effects of special economic zones must specify the definition of the special economic zone and the corresponding two equilibria: one initial equilibrium (without the special economic zone) and another equilibrium with the special economic zone.[6] The special economic zone is defined in terms of a partition of the factor endowments of the country. This definition takes into account that some factors may be mobile between the domestic and the special economic zone. The country's factor endowment vector v is partitioned into v^D and v^S. The symbol v^D denotes the factors that are used in the domestic and v^S in the special economic zones respectively. I shall return to this later (see also Copeland 1994).

In order to obtain insights I decompose the move of the economy from the original equilibrium (without a special economic zone) to the new equilibrium with a special economic zone and foreign investment into two moves. In the first move immobile and mobile factors are reallocated to the special economic zone. In the second move foreign investment is introduced. This decomposition, of course, does not imply a loss in generality but, as will be shown, yields a rich harvest of novel insights and results.

We proceed to specify the original equilibrium and the equilibrium with a special economic zone but no foreign investment by means of the trade expenditure function (see Schweinberger and Lloyd 1988 or Anderson and Neary 1992). Let

$$B(p,q,v,u) = E(p,u) - R^0(p,v) - (p-q)[E_p(p,u) - x^0] \quad (6.1)$$

$$B(p,q,v^D,v^S,u) = E(p,u) - R^D(p,v^D) - R^S(q,v^S) - (p-q)[E_p(p,u) - x^D] \quad (6.2)$$

where $B(\cdot)$ denotes the trade expenditure function, $E(\cdot)$ the household expenditure function, $R^0(\cdot)$ the revenue function in the original equilibrium, $R^D(\cdot)$ the revenue function of the domestic zone in the new equilibrium, $R^S(\cdot)$ the revenue function of the special economic zone in the new equilibrium, x^0 the output vector in the original equilibrium,[7] x^D the output vector of the domestic zone in the new equilibrium, p and q denote the vectors of domestic (tariff distorted) and world market prices respectively.

If there are no transfers the utility level adjusts so that $B(p,q,v,u^0) = B(p,q,v^D,v^S,u^1) = 0$. The question is, under which conditions will $u^1 \geq u^0$. To answer this question I make use of the following standard *Hatta normality* assumption (see Hatta 1977). Define

$$F = E(p,u) - (p-q)E_p(p,u). \quad (6.3)$$

F is increasing in u. The term $(p-q)E_p(p,u)$ in equation (6.3) may be regarded as the consumption tax revenue associated with a tariff. It is well known that a tariff may be interpreted as a production subsidy and a consumption tax. Setting $B(p,q,v,u) = 0$ in equation (6.1) and rearranging we obtain

$$F^0 = E(p,u) - (p-q)E_p(p,u) = R^0(p,v) - (p-q)x^0. \quad (6.4)$$

Proceeding similarly with equation (6.2) we have

$$F^1 = E(p,u) - (p-q)E_p(p,u) = R^D(p,v^D) + R^S(q,v^S) - (p-q)x^D. \quad (6.5)$$

From equations (6.4) and (6.5) it follows that $u^1 \geq u^0$ if Hatta normality holds and

$$F^1 - F^0 = R^D(p,v^D) + R^S(q,v^S) - (p-q)x^D - R^0(p,v) + (p-q)x^0 \geq 0. \quad (6.6)$$

In fact, subject to Hatta normality, equation (6.6) represents a necessary and sufficient condition for an efficiency improvement.

Since by definition

$$R^0(p,v) = px^0, \quad (6.7)$$

we can rewrite equation (6.6) as

$$R^D(p,v^D) + R^S(q,v^S) - (p-q)x^D - qx^0 \geq 0. \quad (6.8)$$

Also, since $R^D(p,v^D) = px^D$, (6.6) becomes

$$F^1 - F^0 = R^S(q,v^S) + qx^D - qx^0(p,v) \geq 0. \quad (6.9)$$

We now transform equation (6.9) by adding and subtracting:

$$q[x(p,v^D) + x(p,v^S)]. \quad (6.10)$$

This yields

$$R^S(q,v^S) + qx^D - q[x(p,v^D) + x(p,v^S)] + q[x(p,v^D)] - qx^0(p,v) \geq 0. \quad (6.11)$$

Two concepts and definitions are useful in the economic interpretation of equation (6.11): the production gain and the partition gain (loss). The production gain is defined as

$$q[x(q,v^S) - x(p,v^S)], \quad (6.12)$$

and the partition gain as

$$q[x(p,v^D) + x(p,v^S)] - qx^0(p,v). \quad (6.13)$$

The following proposition follows from equation (6.11) and the definitions of the production and partition gains (6.12) and (6.13).

Proposition 1: *(a) The establishment of a production special economic zone without foreign investment is welfare-raising subject to Hatta normality, if and only if the sum of the* ***production gain*** *and the* ***partition gain (loss)*** *is positive. (b) The production gain is positive or at least non-negative. The partition gain may be positive, zero or negative. If the partition satisfies the factor price equalisation theorem (factor prices do not change) then the partition gain is zero.*

Proof. Returning to equation (6.11), we can readily show that

$$R^S(q,v^S)+qx^D-q[x(p,v^D)+x(p,v^S)]$$

is equal to the production gain from the establishment of the special economic zone as stated in Proposition 1.[8] If the partition satisfies the assumptions of the factor price equalisation theorem we have that $x(p,v^D)+(p,v^S)=x(p,v)$. Therefore, the partition gain is zero. □

The partition gain/loss will be analysed in detail in the following section 3. At this point I only want to emphasise that the government normally faces a number of constraints in partitioning the factor endowment vector of the economy. There may be income distributional constraints or constraints which are due to the existence of factors that are mobile between the domestic and the special economic zones. The allocation of the mobile factors to the two zones will be decided by the market mechanism. The allocations must be such that the relevant factor prices or rentals are equalised.[9]

We now turn to the introduction of foreign investment. In this chapter I follow the standard practice of the literature and treat foreign investment as exogenous.

An important assumption in the following analysis is that foreign investment takes place only with regard to factors that are immobile between the domestic and special economic zones. The vector v^F, which stands for the given supplies of the foreign-owned factors, is of the same dimension as v^S but has zero elements for all mobile factors. Furthermore note that foreign investment is assumed to take place only in the special economic zone.

Our first aim now is to isolate and identify the welfare effects of foreign investment. I therefore assume that the original equilibrium is the equilibrium with a special economic zone but no foreign investment. The income/expenditure equality in the original equilibrium is described by equation (6.5). The income/expenditure equality in the new equilibrium is represented by

$$\begin{aligned} F^2 &= E(p,u)-(p-q)E_p(p,u) \\ &= R^D(p,v^D-\Delta v^S)+R^S(q,v^S+\Delta v^S+v^F)-r^*v^F \qquad (6.14) \\ &\quad -(p-q)x^D(p,v^D-\Delta v^S), \end{aligned}$$

where Δv^S is a vector of the same dimension as v^S (however all the elements representing immobile factors are zero in Δv^S). The vector Δv^S may have zero, positive or negative elements. The vector r^* stands for the world market prices of the factors v^F.[10]

Generally, foreign investment changes outputs and factor prices. This induces reallocations of the mobile factors between the domestic and special economic zones. These reallocations are represented by the vector Δv^S. Note, from the assumption that domestic demands for foreign factors are rationed, we know that

$$R_v^S > r^* . \tag{6.15}$$

The case, when foreign-owned factors are rewarded according to domestic factor prices or rentals, is dealt with further below.

We now subtract equation (6.5) from equation (6.14). This yields

$$\begin{aligned} F^2 - F^1 = {} & R^D(p,v^D - \Delta v^S) - R^D(p,v^D) + R^S(q,v^S + \Delta v^S + v^F) \\ & - r^* v^F - R^S(q,v^S) - (p-q)[x^D(p,v^D - \Delta v^S) - x^D(p,v^D)]. \end{aligned} \tag{6.16}$$

Equation (6.16) may be rewritten as

$$\begin{aligned} F^2 - F^1 = {} & R^S(q,v^S + \Delta v^S + v^F) - r^* v^F \\ & - R^S(q,v^S) + q[x^D(p,v^D - \Delta v^S) - x^D(p,v^D)]. \end{aligned} \tag{6.17}$$

Since the revenue function is concave in the factor supplies we can write

$$R^S(q,v^S + \Delta v^S) < R^S(q,v^S + \Delta v^S + v^F) - r^S v^F ,$$

where r^S is the vector of factor prices in the special economic zone with foreign investment. Rearranging the latter expression and deducting $r^* v^F$ we have

$$R^S(q,v^S + \Delta v^S) + (r^S - r^*)v^F < R^S(q,v^S + \Delta v^S + v^F) - r^* v^F . \tag{6.18}$$

Recall that I have assumed that the demand for foreign-owned factors is rationed in the equilibrium without foreign investment and in the final equilibrium. Therefore, each element of r^S is greater than r^*. We also know from the mean value theorem that[11]

$$R^S(q, v^S + \Delta v^S) + (\tilde{r}^S - r^*) = R^S(q, v^S + \Delta v^S + v^F) - r^* v^F, \qquad (6.19)$$

where $\tilde{r}^S$ represents a gradient vector of $R^S(\cdot)$ with respect to v between $v^S + \Delta v^S$ and $v^S + \Delta v^S + v^F$. Equation (6.19) may now be substituted into equation (6.17). This yields

$$\begin{aligned} F^2 - F^1 &= R^S(q, v^S + \Delta v^S) + (\tilde{r}^S - r^*)v^F - R^S(q, v^S) \\ &+ q[x^D(p, v^D - \Delta v^S) - x^D(p, v^D)]. \end{aligned} \qquad (6.20)$$

It follows from equations (6.18) and (6.19) and the assumption that each element of the vector r^S exceeds each element of the vector r^* that

$$(\tilde{r}^S - r^*)v^F > (r^S - r^*)v^F > 0. \qquad (6.21)$$

Equation (6.20) can now be rewritten as

$$\begin{aligned} F^2 - F^1 &= q[x^S(q, v^S + \Delta v^S) - x^S(q, v^S)] \\ &+ q[x^D(p, v^D - \Delta v^S) - x^D(p, v^D)] + (\tilde{r}^S - r^*)v^F. \end{aligned} \qquad (6.22)$$

We are now in a position to define two additional effects:

(a) a mobile factor reallocation effect:

$$q[x^S(q, v^S + \Delta v^S) - x^S(q, v^S)] + q[x^D(p, v^D - \Delta v^S) - x^D(p, v^D)], \qquad (6.23)$$

and

(b) a gains from factor trade effect:

$$(\tilde{r}^S - r^*)v^F. \qquad (6.24)$$

Whilst the mobile factor reallocation effect in the form of equation (6.23) cannot be signed in this very general model, it follows from equation (6.21) that the gains from factor trade effect must be positive (or at least non-negative). The factor gains from trade effect may be interpreted in terms of an increase in producer surplus resulting from the occurrence of foreign investment.

It is very straightforward to reinterpret the gains from factor trade effect if foreign-owned factors are rewarded according to the factor prices in the special economic zone after the inflow of foreign-owned factors. The relevant factor price vector is r^S and has been defined above. Therefore in this case the gains from factor trade effect have to be redefined as $(\tilde{r}^S - r^S)v^F$. The factor gains from trade effect is still positive even if the foreign-owned factors are rewarded according to the factor prices in the special economic zone. This follows from equation (6.21) after setting $r^S = r^*$. As before, the rationale for this is an increase in producer surplus. An interesting special case arises if foreign-owned factors are rewarded according to the factor prices in the special economic zone and the changes in the factor supplies brought about by foreign investment do not change factor prices but only outputs. In this case the gains from factor trade effect vanish.[12]

Dévereux and Chen (1995) focus in their analysis on the gains from factor trade effect. In their analysis foreign investment changes the factor prices in the special economic zone and the foreign factors are rewarded according to the factor prices in the special economic zone. Whilst the gains from the factor trade effect are non-negative, the mobile factor reallocation effect can be positive, zero or negative. More discussion on this is provided in section 4 below.

To conclude this section I add equations (6.22) and (6.6) to obtain $F^2 - F^0$. This yields Proposition 2.

Proposition 2: *Let a special economic zone be established and assumptions* (6.1) *to* (6.5) *be satisfied. Then, subject to Hatta normality, the setting up of the special economic zone is desirable if and only if the sum of the following four effects is positive: (a) the partition gain (loss), (b) the production gain, (c) the mobile factor reallocation effect and (d) the gains from factor trade effects. (For definitions of these effects, see Proposition 1 and equations* (6.12) *and* (6.13)*).*

As explained before, the received literature making use of a local (calculus) approach ignores the partition gain and the production gain. Also the mobile factor reallocation effect and the gains from factor trade effect have only been analysed using local methods. It is therefore high time to consider each of these effects in some detail.

3. THE EFFECTS OF THE PARTITION

Whilst the production gain is necessarily non-negative it may be shown that the partition gain may be positive, zero or negative. In order to understand the economic meaning of Propositions 1 and 2 it is essential to work out conditions under which the partition gain is positive, negative or zero.

To this end I proceed to make use of two sets defined over the partitions $v^D, v^S \geq 0$. These are

$$S^1 = \{v^D, v^S \mid v^D + v^S = v,\ w^D = w(p,v^S) = w(p,v^D);\ v^D, v^S \geq 0\} \quad (6.25)$$

and

$$S^2 = \left\{v^D, v^S \mid v^D + v^S = v;\ \frac{\partial R^D}{\partial v_i^D} = \frac{\partial R^S}{\partial v_i^S};\ i = 1,\ldots,l;\ v^D, v^S \geq 0\right\}. \quad (6.26)$$

S^1 represents the set of all partitions which imply that the factor prices in the domestic zone in the new equilibrium are equal to the factor prices in the whole economy in the original equilibrium. It should be noted that the functions $w^D = w^D(p,v)$ exist for any number of factors and goods. S^2 represents the set of all partitions which imply that in the new equilibrium the prices of all factors, $i = 1,\ldots,l$, which are mobile between the domestic and the special economic zone are equalised.[13]

What can be said about the set S^1? In defining the set S^1 I am applying a very well-known theorem of factor price equalisation between countries to the theory of special economic zones. If two countries have the same production functions and both their factor endowments lie within the same diversification cone (set of factor endowments which are consistent with the same specialisation pattern in production) then (subject to standard assumptions) one may decompose the closed world economy into two countries which have equal factor prices in a free trade equilibrium.

The application of the factor price equalisation theorem to special economic zones seems of considerable interest because its key assumptions, namely identical production functions and comparable factors, are much more likely to be satisfied within a country than between countries.

As with factor price equalisation we have to distinguish three different cases.

Case A: The number of factors is equal to the number of goods and the Jacobian determinant of the unit cost functions is non-vanishing. In this case there exists a diversification cone which is more than a ray.

Case B: The number of factors falls short of the number of produced goods. In this case, generally speaking, the same holds as in case A.

Case C: The number of factors exceeds the number of produced goods. In this case the set S^1 is much smaller. Not all the partitions of the economy factor endowments can be chosen independently. The simplest case is that v^S is collinear with v. There are many other possibilities as well. For more detail, see e.g. Woodland (1982).[14]

If there are no further constraints on the partition and the partition actually undertaken belongs to S^1 then we know that the partition gain, expression (6.13), is equal to zero, because $x(p,v^D) + x(p,v^S) = x(p,v)$. This is a very important and interesting benchmark case. If there are mobile factors, as there usually are, the set S^2 is relevant too. The set of partitions that implies that the benchmark case is relevant in the presence of mobile factors is $S^1 \cap S^2$. This set may well be empty; that is why the following analysis of the partition effect is important.

The key idea underlying the following analysis is simple yet very general. Assume that the establishment of the special economic zone takes place in several stages. In stage 1 the government assigns v^D and v^S to the domestic and special economic zone respectively keeping the prices faced by producers and consumers unchanged. At unchanged prices this implies that

$$p[x(p,v^D)+x(p,v^S)]-px(p,v)\leq 0\,. \tag{6.27}$$

This follows simply from the definition of the revenue function $R(p,v)$. If the partition results in a fall of all outputs then the partition gain (see equation (6.13)) is negative. But this is clearly a special case. All we know from (6.27) is that the output of at least one good must fall if (6.27) is satisfied as a strict inequality. Generally the partition may have a pro- or an anti-protectionist bias.[15]

Before providing a formal definition of the pro- or anti-protectionist bias of the said partition, the reader's attention is drawn to Figure 6.1. Point C denotes the free trade production point. If the whole economy is a special economic zone C would be attained. Actually in the original equilibrium production is taking place at D. There is an import tax on good 2. At D the economy is integrated. As a result of the partition I assume that we move from D to E. Factor prices change and production takes place outside the diversification cone of the original equilibrium. There is specialisation of production in the domestic and in the special economic zone (at unchanged goods prices).

An inspection of Figure 6.1 shows that, the move from D to E can be decomposed into two moves: one from D to F and another from F to E. Let output changes on the production possibility locus of the integrated economy be denoted by Δx^I. We say that the partition has an anti-protectionist bias if for any movement on the production possibility locus of the integrated economy $(p-q)\Delta x^I < 0$. Alternatively, if for any movement on the production possibility locus of the integrated economy $(p-q)\Delta x^I > 0$, we say that the partition has a pro-protectionist bias. Clearly the movement from D to F on Figure 6.1 represents a partition with an anti-protectionist bias. The move from F to E is referred to as the disintegration effect. The outputs of all goods fall equiproportionately and therefore the value of output at world market prices falls equiproportionately too. It is easy to show that the partition gain is negative if the partition has a pro-protectionist bias. It also follows that the partition gain is positive only if the partition has an anti-protectionist bias.

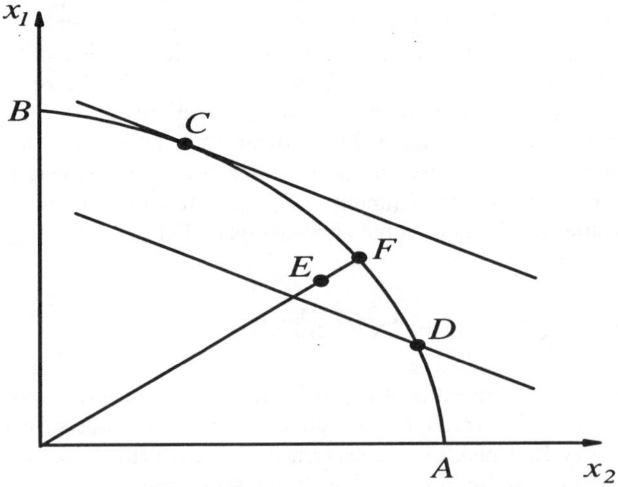

Figure 6.1 Production Possibility Frontier and Production Equilibria

Returning to the interpretation of Proposition 1, it is important to note that one of its key advantages is that it formalises the intuition of many politicians: the establishment of special economic zones is beneficial (even in the absence of foreign investment) because it yields production gains and, if a judicious choice of factors to be used in the special economic zone (paying due attention to factor mobility) is made, one may generate additional efficiency gains. Essentially the partition itself may be used as an instrument of second best policy. The pessimism of some of the received literature on the benefits of special economic zones results mainly from the possible immiserisation effects of foreign investment (the best known example is Hamada 1974).

The main message of this section and the chapter is that even if foreign investment per se has an immiserisation effect because the sum of the mobile factor reallocation effect and the gains from factor trade effect (for definitions see equations (6.23) and (6.24)) is negative, this negative effect may well be offset by the positive production and partition gains (see equations (6.12) and (6.13)).

Finally, the relevance of the global approach put forward in this section may be highlighted by a simple example drawn from recent literature. In an interesting article, Dévereux and Chen (1995) have argued that the received literature on the welfare effects of the establishment of special economic zones has ignored an important effect: the so-called factor terms of trade effect (see page 708, their equation (8)). This is a very useful contribution but, since they apply only a local analysis, there are some considerable problems of interpretation. Note that in their modelling the special economic zone is created by the inflow of foreign investment. This entails that in the original equilibrium there is no foreign investment and therefore no special economic zone. The amount of labour (the mobile factor) used in the special economic zone must therefore be zero in the original equilibrium. This means that the factor terms of trade effect, as defined in their analysis, must be zero. On the other hand one may, of course, assume that in the original equilibrium some foreign investment has already taken place. Then their analysis yields the welfare effects of a small increase in foreign investment. However, it ignores the welfare effects of the establishment of the special economic zone. To overcome these problems clearly a global approach is called for.

4. THE EFFECTS OF FOREIGN INVESTMENT

The welfare effects of foreign investment are reflected in the mobile factor reallocation effect (see equation (6.24)) and a gains from factor trade effect (see equation (6.23)). My first task in this section is to transform these two effects in order to relate them to the results of the received literature.[16]

Going back to equations (6.16) and (6.20), we can rewrite equation (6.20) as

$$\begin{aligned} F^2 - F^1 = {} & R^S(q, v^S + \Delta v^S) - R(q, v^S) + R^D(p, v^D - \Delta v^S) - R^D(p, v^D) \\ & -(p-q)[x^D(p, v^D - \Delta v^S) - x^D(p, v^D)] + (\tilde{r}^S - r^*)v^F. \end{aligned} \tag{6.28}$$

We now derive a sufficient condition for foreign investment to raise welfare. From the concavity of $R^S(\cdot)$ and $R^D(\cdot)$ in factor endowments we know that

$$R^S(q, v^S) < R^S(q, v^S + \Delta v^S) - w^2 \Delta v^S \tag{6.29}$$

$$R^D(p, v^D) < R^D(p, v^D - \Delta v^S) + w^2 \Delta v^S, \tag{6.30}$$

where w^2 stands for the vector of the factor prices of the mobile factors in the new equilibrium. From equations (6.29) and (6.30) it follows that

$$R^S(q, v^S + \Delta v^S) - R^S(q, v^S) + R^D(p, v^D - \Delta v^S) - R^D(p, v^D) > 0. \tag{6.31}$$

Equation (6.28) can therefore be rewritten as

$$F^2 - F^1 > (\tilde{r}^S - r^*)v^F - (p-q)[x^D(p, v^D - \Delta v^S) - x^D(p, v^D)]. \tag{6.32}$$

Definition: *Foreign investment is said to have a pro-protectionist bias if and only if*

$$(p-q)[x^D(p,v^D-\Delta v^S)-x^D(p,v^D)]>0\,.$$

In the Hamada (1974) model foreign investment has a pro-protectionist bias. Also in the Hamada model the gains from factor trade effect is zero because changes in foreign investment have only output effects and no effects on factor prices.

It is also straightforward to derive a necessary and sufficient condition for foreign investment to raise welfare. Rewriting equations (6.29) and (6.30) and making use of the mean value theorem, we have that

$$R^S(q,v^S)=R^S(q,v^S+\Delta v^S)-\tilde{w}^S\Delta v^S \tag{6.33}$$

and

$$R^D(p,v^D)=R^D(p,v^D-\Delta v^S)+\tilde{w}^D\Delta v^S\,, \tag{6.34}$$

where $\tilde{w}^S$ denotes the gradient vector of $R^S(\cdot)$ between v^S and $v^S+\Delta v^S$ and $\tilde{w}^D$ stands for the gradient vector of $R^D(\cdot)$ between v^D and $v^D-\Delta v^S$. Proceeding as before we now obtain

$$F^2-F^1=(\tilde{w}^S-\tilde{w}^D)\Delta v^S+(\tilde{r}^S-r^*)v^F-(p-q)[x^D(p,v^D-\Delta v^S)-x^D(p,v^D)]\,. \tag{6.35}$$

Equation (6.35) gives rise to the following Proposition 3.

Proposition 3: *Subject to Hatta normality, foreign investment in the special economic zone raises welfare if and only if the sum of the mobile factor reallocation effect, defined as*

$$(\tilde{w}^S-\tilde{w}^D)\Delta v^S-(p-q)[x^D(p,v^D-\Delta v^S)-x^D(p,v^D)]\,,$$

and the gains from factor trade effect $(\tilde{r}^S-r^*)v^F$ *is positve.*

Proof. Proposition 3 follows directly from equation (6.35). □

The main interest of Proposition 3 lies in the novel definition of the mobile factor reallocation effect. We know from equations (6.29), (6.30), (6.33) and (6.34) that $(\tilde{w}^S-\tilde{w}^D)\Delta v^S$ must be positive. We also know that the gains from factor trade effect must be positive. Therefore one can define an upper bound to $(p-q)[x^D(p,v^D-\Delta v^S)-x^D(p,v^D)]$ that is just consistent with foreign investment being welfare increasing. Note also very carefully that throughout the analysis there is no presumption that the same set of goods is produced in the special and domestic zones. This applies before and after the introduction of foreign investment. Dévereux and Chen (1995) have put forward a strong and valid argument for taking into account the gains from factor trade effect. The traditional analysis focuses exclusively on

$$(p-q)x^D[(p,v^D-\Delta v^S)-x^D(p,v^D)],$$

the second term in the mobile factor reallocation effect. The reason for this is clear: the local factor price equalisation property is assumed in Hamada (1974). However, due to their local analysis, Dévereux and Chen overlook the first term of the mobile factor reallocation effect: $(\tilde{w}^S-\tilde{w}^D)\Delta v^S$. This effect has been shown to be positive. It can be interpreted as the gains from internal factor trade: a rise in producer surplus due to changes in the prices of the mobile factors. There is no reason on a priori grounds why this effect should not be more important than the effects emphasised in the received literature.

5. CONCLUSIONS AND EXTENSIONS

Our focus in this chapter has been on the efficiency effects of the establishment of production special economic zones. I have developed a very general framework that is suitable for a global analysis. Many of the effects identified and defined in this chapter have been overlooked in the received literature because of its insistence on a local analysis. Moreover, all the effects have been stated in a way that should make them readily communicable to policy makers. As noted before, it seems a great pity that the literature on special economic zones to date apparently had little or no influence on policy making.

It cannot be emphasised strongly enough that it would be very straightforward to extend the modelling framework of this chapter in many directions. First and foremost, one could introduce intermediate inputs which are subject to quotas in the original equilibrium. In the final equilibrium no quotas apply to imports into the special economic zone. Secondly, one should incorporate into the analysis non-traded goods and variable factor supplies. A simple approach in this context is to assume that the number of traded goods is at least equal to the number of primary factors in fixed and in variable supply. In this case it can be shown that the prices of the variable factors are determined from the zero profitability conditions. The same holds for the prices of the non-traded goods. Subject to reasonable assumptions, the prices of the non-traded goods and the factors in variable supply are then determined in the domestic zone. The special economic zone may be regarded as a 'small country' relative to the domestic zone. Again a major advantage of this approach is that the application of the factor price equalisation theorem yields a benchmark case.

It is also straightforward to extend the framework to allow for multi-household economies. Note that, if the value of output measured at international prices rises as a result of the creation of the special zone, we should be able to distribute the resulting gain in a Pareto improving fashion. To achieve this, impose employment taxes and subsidies on the factors that are used in the special economic zone so that the factor prices received by the households are the same independently of where the factors are used. However, firms in the special economic zones face the factor prices implied by the world market prices for goods. In this case the establishment of special economic zones should yield additional revenue for the government, which can be used to produce more public goods.

Finally, various distortions such as increasing returns to scale and imperfect competition or involuntary unemployment may be introduced.[17] The global method put forward in this chapter works provided that factor markets are perfectly competitive, as they apparently are in many developing countries.

NOTES

1. It will be shown that the global approach put forward in this chapter can also be applied to quantity constraints on trade, as will be explained briefly in the conclusion.
2. It may be shown that conditions which are necessary and sufficient for the setting up of a welfare-raising production special economic zone are also sufficient for the creation of a welfare-raising production and consumption special economic zone.
3. The received literature on special economic zones may be regarded as an application of the large and time-honoured literature on partial tariff reform. Recent contributions to this literature include Anderson (1995), Turunen-Red and Woodland (1991) and Diewert, Turunen-Red and Woodland (1991).
4. I show briefly in the conclusion how several of the assumptions can be relaxed. Many extensions and generalisations of my approach are possible, e.g. the introduction of transaction costs, multi-household economies and the production of public goods.
5. Again I show in the conclusion how the assumption can be relaxed.
6. A complete analysis of special economic zones would include an analysis of smuggling and cheating. This is beyond the scope of this chapter.
7. Throughout the chapter I allow for the fact that the equilibrium output vectors in the domestic or special economic zones may be non-unique. However, since all production possibility sets are convex all equilibrium output vectors belong to a convex and compact set. The revenue or national product functions are always well defined (see also Schweinberger 1989).
8. To understand the part played by the global approach, consider the following limit:

$$\lim_{v^s \to 0} : q[x(p, v - v^s) + x(p, v^s)] - qx(p, v) \; .$$

Clearly this limit is equal to zero. That is why the partition gain (or loss) is an effect that fails to show up in a local analysis.

9. In some of the literature it is emphasised that mobile labour used in the special economic zone is more highly skilled than the labour used in the domestic zone. Therefore, the wages of labour in the special economic zone are higher than in the domestic zone. This can easily be incorporated into my model if the transformation of low-skilled into high-skilled labour can be described by well-behaved production functions. Only a reinterpretation of the production gain in terms of a reduced form is required.
10. One may assume that foreign factors are rewarded according to world market or domestic prices. I cover both cases in the following analysis.
11. The mean value theorem is frequently used in global analysis; see, for example, Ethier (1984).
12. It should be carefully noted that the two approaches to the modelling of foreign investment outlined in the text are very different from a normative point of view. If demand for foreign factors is rationed and the foreign factors are rewarded according to the given world market prices the equilibrium is second best or constrained Pareto-efficient. This is not the case if the foreign factors receive the factor prices ruling in the special economic zone.
13. I shall explain below that my novel approach remains fully applicable even if all factors are mobile between the two zones. The latter is an assumption that can sometimes be found in the literature. In my view it is not a satisfactory assumption because geographic entities are defined by immobile factors.
14. It is well known that the so-called Ricardo-Viner or sector specific factor model belongs to this category; see also the papers by Copeland (1994) and Dévereux and Chen (1995).
15. This implies that the creation of a special economic zone, per se, may have a pro- or anti-protectionist bias. This has to be distinguished from the pro- or anti-protectionist bias of foreign investment, which is a centrepiece of a considerable part of the welfare analysis of the received literature.
16. A problem with much of the received literature is that it is not clear at all why foreign-owned factors should be attracted to the special economic zone. It is a fact that in the case of the People's Republic of China never more that thirty percent of total direct foreign investment was allocated to special economic zones; see Knoth (2000).
17. It is indeed very surprising to note that none of the insights of the 'New Trade Theory' has found its way into the literature on special economic zones.

REFERENCES

Anderson, J.E. (1995), 'Tariff index theory', *Review of International Economics,* **3**, 156-73.

Anderson, J.E. and J.P. Neary (1992), 'Trade reform with quotas, partial retention, and tariffs', *Econometrica,* **60**, 57-76.

Copeland, B.R. (1994), 'The welfare effects of a duty free zone: tariffs versus quotas', *Working Paper,* University of British Columbia.

Dévereux, J. and L. L. Chen (1995), 'Export zones and welfare: another look', *Oxford Economic Papers,* **47**, 705-13.

Diewert, W.E., Turunen-Red, A.H. and A.D. Woodland (1991), 'Tariff reform in a small open multi-household economy with domestic distortions and nontraded goods', *International Economic Review,* **32**, 937-57.

Ethier, W.J. (1984), 'Higher dimensional issues in trade theory', in Jones, R.W. and P.B. Kenen (eds), *Handbook of International Economics*, vol. 1, Amsterdam: North Holland, pp. 131-84.

Grubel, H. (1982), 'Towards a theory of free economic zones', *Weltwirtschaftliches Archiv,* **118**, 39-61.

Hamada, K. (1974): 'An economic analysis of the duty free zone', *Journal of International Economics,* **4**, 225-41.
Hamilton, C. and L.E.O. Svensson (1982), 'On the welfare effects of a 'duty free zone'', *Journal of International Economics,* **13**, 45-64.
Hatta, T. (1977), 'A recommendation for a better tariff structure', *Econometrica,* **45**, 1859-69.
Knoth, C. (2000), 'Special economic zones and economic transformation - the case of the People's Republic of China', Ph.D. Thesis, University of Konstanz.
Rodriguez, C.A. (1976), 'A note on the economics of the duty free zone', *Journal of International Economics,* **6**, 385-88.
Schweinberger, A.G. (1989), 'Foreign capital flows, tariffs and welfare: a global analysis', *Canadian Journal of Economics,* **2**, 310-27.
Schweinberger, A.G. and P.J. Lloyd (1988), 'Trade expenditure functions and the gains from trade', *Journal of International Economics,* **24**, 275-97.
Turunen-Red, A.H. and A.D. Woodland (1991), 'Strict Pareto-improving multilateral reforms of tariffs', *Econometrica,* **59**, 1127-52.
Woodland, A.D. (1982), *International Trade and Resource Allocation*, Amsterdam: North Holland.
Wong, K.-Y. (1986), 'International factor movements, repatriation and welfare', *Journal of International Economics,* **21**, 327-35.
Young, L. (1987), 'Intermediate goods and the formation of duty free zones', *Journal of Development Economics,* **25**, 369- 84.
Young, L. and K.F. Miyagiwa (1987), 'Unemployment and the formation of duty free zones', *Journal of Development Economics,* **26**, 397-405.

7. Redistributive Taxation in Closed and Open Economies

Ngo Van Long and Koji Shimomura

1. INTRODUCTION

The dynamics of redistributive taxation has received a great deal of interest among theorists. Quite often, the government is modelled as a Stackelberg leader in the sense that it announces, at the beginning of the game, a time path of tax rates, and other economic agents such as workers and capitalists are modelled as followers that maximise their intertemporal utility, taking the announced time path of tax rates as given. One criticism that has been raised against this approach is that the government's solution is generally time-inconsistent, because at some stage in the future, it will have an incentive to renege on its promises (Kydland and Prescott 1977). This criticism has turned out to be somewhat exaggerated, because recently it has been discovered that, depending on the specific structure of the model under consideration, an open-loop Stackelberg equilibrium may have the desired time-consistency property.[1] Another criticism of some analysis of open-loop Stackelberg redistributive taxation game is that the stability of steady-state equilibria is often assumed. Kemp et al. (1993, Section 3) have shown that around a steady state there may exist cycles, and cyclical redistributive taxation may be optimal.

In this chapter, we raise a third point concerning the standard analysis of models of redistributive taxation. It is about the assumption that at a steady-state equilibrium of a redistributive game, all quantity variables *and all shadow prices* are stationary. This assumption has led to the claim that at a steady-state equilibrium, the tax rate on capital income must be zero, regardless of the elasticity of intertemporal substitution (see, for example, Judd 1985). Our chapter offers a counter-example which shows that (i) a steady-state equilibrium (in quantities) exists while the shadow prices are not stationary (we call this a *'semi-stationary' steady state*), (ii) at this steady-state equilibrium the tax rate on capital income is non-zero, and (iii) in our example, there is no other steady-state equilibrium in quantities. Our counter-example, valid for open economies as well as closed economies, is important because it indicates that the standard short-cut of setting all equations of motions to zero can lead to incorrect conclusion about optimal tax in a steady state.

The implications of our chapter can be important, both in the context of public finance theory and in the context of optimisation theory, in particular optimal control theory and the theory of differential games. In the public finance literature, there seems to be a widespread belief that if capitalists are intertemporal maximisers, then the redistributive power of the government is very limited: in the long run, an optimising government should not tax capital income. This result has been reported in a number of different models, of which the best known are Judd (1985) and Chamley (1986).[2] In their models, the government is assumed to care about income distribution (in the sense of giving different weights to the welfare of different social classes). They interpret their result as confirming that efficiency must predominate, at least in the long run. According to them, capital income tax, being non-lump-sum, creates inefficiency, and must be avoided. Our model, by showing that the optimal tax on capital income can be non-zero, even in the long run, suggests that there is a long-term trade-off between efficiency and equity.[3] It indicates that the results of Judd and Chamley are, at best, model-specific. In fact, Judd (1985) assumes convergence to steady states, and Chamley (1986) proves local convergence only under the strong assumption of identical utility functions. In the models of Judd and Chamley, the government is assumed to be able to commit to a time path of tax rates. The same assumption is made in our model. This feature distinguishes these models from a different class of models in which the governments cannot commit to a preannounced tax path, and where, as a result, only time-independent feedback strategies are permitted. (See Kemp et al. (1993, Section 4), and Shimomura (1991) for equilibrium with time-independent feedback strategies.) In this second class of models, the typical result is that the tax on capital income is non-zero in the long run.

The implications of our results concerning semi-stationary states for optimal control theory and differential games can be far reaching. Normally, steady states are obtained by setting all motions of stock variables (such as capital stocks) and of shadow prices to zero. Our analysis shows that there are cases where doing so would give rise to a set of simultaneous equations that has no solution (except when parameters happen to permit a solution, a non-generic result). In such cases, one should try to look for a semi-stationary state, where quantities are stationary but shadow prices are not. One should of course check that the sufficiency conditions, including the transversality conditions, are satisfied. As far as we know, our results on semi-stationary states are new. An important question is, when shadow prices are not stationary, would this not mean that the 'implicit market' is sending signals to the optimising agents that they should re-allocate resources? The answer is: not necessarily. This will become clear when the model has been studied in detail, and an intuitive explanation, in terms of joint-products, will be given after that stage (see Section 3.1).

The plan of our chapter is as follows. In Section 2, we consider a model of redistributive taxation in a closed economy, and prove our basic results. Section 3 is reserved for discussion of some economic implications in the contexts of closed and open economies, and of some technical matters. Section 4 provides an intuitive explanation of our results. Some concluding remarks are offered in Section 5. Technical appendices are available upon requests to the authors.[4]

2. REDISTRIBUTIVE TAXATION IN A CLOSED ECONOMY

We consider a model introduced by Judd (1985) in which there exist a government and two types of infinitely-lived individuals, called workers and capitalists respectively. The government wishes to maximise a social welfare function and its only policy instrument is a tax on capital income, generating government revenue that is distributed as lump-sum payments to workers. We begin by stating the basic assumptions, then proceed to solve for the optimal redistributive taxation, and prove our results concerning semi-stationary steady states.

2.1 The basic assumptions

Each worker supplies one unit of labour, independently of the wage rate. They neither borrow nor lend. They consume all their current income, as if they were disciples of Polonius.[5] Capitalists do not work. They own capital, which they lend to competitive firms at the market interest rate $r(t)$. There is no depreciation. Firms use capital and labour to produce a final good that can be either consumed or invested. We assume constant returns to scale. Let k denote the capital-labour ratio. Output per worker is $f(k)$. For notational simplicity, the numbers of capitalists and workers are both set at unity, without loss of generality. Under competitive conditions and given the assumption that there is no depreciation, the interest rate is the same as the marginal product of capital, $f'(k)$. The wage rate is $w(t) = f(k) - r(t)k(t)$.

The gross income earned by the representative capitalist is $r(t)k(t)$ where $k(t) \geq 0$ is his stock of capital. His net income is $[1-\tau(t)]r(t)k(t)$ where $\tau(t)$ is the tax rate on capital income and $1 \geq \tau(t) \geq 0$. Let $c(t)$ denote his rate of consumption, and let $z(t) = [1-\tau(t)]r(t)$ denote his after-tax income per unit of capital. His stock of capital accumulates according to the equation

$$\dot{k}(t) = z(t)k(t) - c(t)\,. \tag{7.1}$$

Thus $\dot{k}(t)$ is positive (respectively, negative) if consumption is less than (respectively, exceeds) net income.

The government's role is assumed to be purely redistributive: the capital income tax revenue $\tau(t)r(t)k(t)$ is given in a lump sum to the representative worker, who consumes both $\tau(t)r(t)k(t)$ and his wage income $w(t)$. Since $\tau(t)r(t)k(t) = r(t)k(t) - z(t)k(t) = [f(k(t)) - w(t)] - z(t)k(t)$ the consumption of the representative worker is

$$c_w(t) = f(k(t)) - z(t)k(t) . \tag{7.2}$$

The utility of the worker is $v(c_w)$ where $v(\cdot)$ is strictly concave and increasing.

The capitalist has the utility function $u(c)$ which is increasing and strictly concave. We also assume that $\lim_{c \to 0} u'(c) = \infty$ and $\lim_{c \to \infty} u'(c) = 0$. These assumptions ensure that it is never optimal to set $c = 0$. The capitalist takes the time path of $r(t)$ and $\tau(t)$ as given, and his optimisation problem is to choose a time path $c(t)$ to maximise the integral of his stream of discounted utility

$$\int_0^\infty e^{-\rho t} u(c(t))dt$$

subject to (7.1) and $k(0) = k_0 > 0$ (given), where $\rho > 0$ is the rate at which utility is discounted. It is also understood that if $k(t) = 0$ then $c(t) = 0$. We impose either the constraint that, for all t

$$k(t) \geq 0 \tag{7.3}$$

or the constraint that

$$\lim_{t \to \infty} k(t) \exp[-\int_0^t z(\tau)d\tau] = 0 . \tag{7.4}$$

The capitalist thus faces an optimal control problem.[6] Under our assumption about $u(t)$, if $\tau(t) < 1$ and $r(t) > 0$ then $k(t)$ will always be positive along the optimal path.

Remark 1: It is useful to point out that instead of (7.1) and (7.3) we may write the following intertemporal budget constraint

$$\int_{t_0}^{\infty} c(t)\exp[-\int_{t_0}^{t} z(\tau)d\tau]dt = k(t_0), \tag{7.5}$$

where $t_0 = 0$, but clearly t_0 can be any point of time. Note that we can integrate (7.1) to get

$$k(t_0) - \lim_{t\to\infty} k(t)\exp[-\int_{t_0}^{t} z(\tau)d\tau] = \lim_{t\to\infty} \int_{t_0}^{t} c(s)\exp[-\int_{t_0}^{s} z(\tau)d\tau]ds.$$

Thus (7.1) and (7.4) imply (7.5). Conversely, one can show that (7.5) implies (7.1) and (7.4).

2.2 The capitalist's consumption decision

The Hamiltonian for the capitalist's optimisation problem is

$$H^c = u(c) + \psi[zk - c]. \tag{7.6}$$

From this we obtain the necessary conditions

$$\frac{\partial H^c}{\partial c} = u'(c) - \psi = 0 \tag{7.7}$$

$$\dot{\psi} = \rho\psi - \frac{\partial H^c}{\partial k} = \psi(\rho - z) \tag{7.8}$$

$$\dot{k} = \frac{\partial H^c}{\partial \psi} = zk - c \tag{7.9}$$

and the transversality condition is

$$\lim_{t\to\infty} e^{-\rho t} u'(c(t))k(t) = 0. \tag{7.10}$$

Differentiating (7.7) with respect to t we get

$$u''(c)\dot{c} = \dot{\psi} = \psi(\rho - z) = u'(c)(\rho - z). \tag{7.11}$$

Therefore conditions (7.7) and (7.8) can be combined into a single condition

$$\dot{c} = \frac{c}{\beta(c)}(z - \rho),$$

where by definition $\beta(c) = -u''(c)c / u'(c) > 0$ is the elasticity of marginal utility. The intertemporal elasticity of substitution is defined as $1/\beta(c)$. In what follows, we assume that $\beta(c)$ is a constant, denoted by β.

Remark 2: Under the assumption that β is a constant, we can integrate (7.11) to get

$$c(t) = c(t_0)\exp[\beta^{-1}\int_{t_0}^{t}(z(\tau) - \rho)d\tau]. \tag{7.12}$$

Substituting (7.12) into (7.5), we get

$$c(t_0) = \frac{k(t_0)}{\int_{t_0}^{\infty}\exp[\int_{t_0}^{\tau}\{z(s)(\beta^{-1} - 1) - (\rho/\beta)\}ds]d\tau} \tag{7.13}$$

Thus, current consumption depends on future tax rates. However, if $\beta = 1$, which is the case of a logarithmic utility function, then (7.13) becomes

$$c(t_0) = \rho k(t_0), \tag{7.14}$$

which indicates that current consumption is independent of future tax rates. Furthermore, since t_0 is arbitrary, it follows that, given $\beta = 1$,

$$c(t) = \rho k(t). \tag{7.15}$$

2.3 The government's optimisation problem

The government takes the pair of differential equations (7.9) and (7.11), together with the initial condition $k(0) = k_0$ and the transversality condition (7.10), as the representative capitalist's 'reaction function' to the government's announced time path $z(t)$. The government's optimisation problem consists of choosing a time path $z(t)$ to maximise the integral of discounted flow of the weighted sum of utility $\gamma v(c_w(t)) + u(c(t))$:

$$\max \int_0^\infty e^{-\rho t}\{\gamma v(c_w(t)) + u(c(t))\}dt \tag{7.16}$$

subject to (7.2) and

$$\dot{k}(t) = z(t)k(t) - c(t) \tag{7.17}$$

$$\dot{c}(t) = (z(t) - \rho)c(t) / \beta \tag{7.18}$$

$$k(0) = k_0 \tag{7.19}$$

$$\lim_{t\to\infty} e^{-\rho t}u'(c(t))k(t) = 0\,, \tag{7.20}$$

where γ is the weight given to the utility of the worker.

Notice that in this formulation, the capital stock is not the only state variable: we treat c as a state variable, too. (This is the standard approach, see Judd (1985), Kemp, Long and Shimomura (1993), among others.) The Hamiltonian for this problem is

$$H = \gamma v(f(k) - zk) + u(c) + p[zk - c] + qc(z - \rho) / \beta \tag{7.21}$$

and the necessary conditions are

$$\frac{\partial H}{\partial z} = -\gamma kv' + pk + qc / \beta = 0 \tag{7.22}$$

$$\dot{p} = \rho p - \frac{\partial H}{\partial k} = \rho p - zp - \gamma(f' - z)v' \tag{7.23}$$

$$\dot{q} = \rho q - \frac{\partial H}{\partial c} = \rho q - q(z - \rho) / \beta - u'(c) + p \tag{7.24}$$

together with (7.17), (7.18), (7.19), (7.20), and the transversality conditions

$$\lim_{t\to\infty} e^{-\rho t} pk = \lim_{t\to\infty} e^{-\rho t} qc = 0\,. \tag{7.25}$$

2.4 The optimal capital income tax rate

We want to find the optimal capital income tax rate in a steady state, defined as the situation where the state variables remain constant forever, i.e., $\dot{c} = \dot{k} = 0$ for all t. For the moment, let us follow the standard procedure of finding a steady state by equating to zero the time derivatives of (i) all the state variables and (ii) all the associated shadow prices. The steady state condition $\dot{c} = 0$ implies $z = \rho$ in the steady state. Using this result to simplify (7.23) and then equating $\dot{p}$ to zero, we get $f' = z$. Since $f' = r$, it follows that $z = r$, implying that in a steady state, where the time derivatives of all shadow prices are equated to zero, the tax rate on capital income is zero, and the steady state capital stock k^* satisfies the modified golden rule property

$$f'(k^*) = \rho . \qquad (7.26)$$

Since $\dot{k} = 0$, we obtain $c^* = \rho k^*$. Substitute this into (7.22) to get

$$k^*[p^* + \rho(q^* / \beta) - \gamma v'(f(k^*) - \rho k^*)] = 0 . \qquad (7.27)$$

Since we have set $\dot{p} = 0$, equation (7.27) holds at a steady state only if $\dot{q} = 0$ too. This in turn implies, via (7.24), that

$$\rho q^* + p^* = u'(\rho k^*) . \qquad (7.28)$$

Since k^* has been determined by (7.26), the two equations (7.27) and (7.28) determine the pair (q^*, p^*). It can be easily verified that q^* satisfies the condition

$$u'(\rho k^*) - \gamma v'(f(k^*) - \rho k^*) = \rho q^*[1/\beta - 1] . \qquad (7.29)$$

This indicates that the two weighted marginal utilities are generally not equalised. This reflects the fact that the government has only one policy instrument to do two jobs: redistributing income and influencing capital accumulation.

It is tempting to conclude that in this model, at the optimal steady state, the optimal tax rate on capital income is zero for all $\beta > 0$. However, such a conclusion seems to be too hasty. Let us consider the case where the utility function $u(\cdot)$ is logarithmic: $u(c) = \ln c$. In this case, $\beta = 1$ and $u'(\rho k^*) = 1/(\rho k^*)$ and hence we can substitute (7.28) into (7.27) to get

$$k^*[\{1/(\rho k^*)\} - \gamma v'(f(k^*) - \rho k^*)] = 0 . \tag{7.30}$$

In general it is not possible for k^* to satisfy both this equation and equation (7.26). It follows that if $u(c) = \ln c$ then a steady state where all shadow prices are stationary does not exist (generically). This is not a negative result, however, for, as will be shown below, there exists a steady state $(\hat{k}, \hat{c})$ where all state variables are stationary while the shadow prices are not stationary. We will call such a steady state a *semi-stationary equilibrium.* At this steady state, the capital stock does not satisfy the modified golden rule and the optimal tax on capital income is non-zero.

First, setting $\dot{c} = 0$, we get

$$z = \rho . \tag{7.31}$$

Next, setting $\dot{k} = 0$, we get

$$\hat{c} = \rho \hat{k} . \tag{7.32}$$

Substituting these results into (7.22), with $\beta = 1$, we get

$$\hat{k}[p(t) + \rho q(t) - \gamma v'(f(\hat{k}) - \rho \hat{k})] = 0 . \tag{7.33}$$

Since we seek a $\hat{k}$ that is positive and stationary, (7.33) implies

$$p(t) + \rho q(t) = \gamma v'[f(\hat{k}) - \rho \hat{k}] \tag{7.34}$$

and it follows that $\dot{p}(t) + \rho \dot{q}(t) = 0$. That is, the weighted sum of shadow prices $p(t) + \rho q(t)$ is stationary at the semi-stationary steady state. Multiplying equation (7.24) by ρ, adding it to equation (7.23), and equating the result to zero, we get

$$\dot{p}(t) + \rho \dot{q}(t) = \gamma[2\rho - f'(\hat{k})]v'(f(\hat{k}) - \rho \hat{k}) - (1/\hat{k}) = 0 . \tag{7.35}$$

This equation determines $\hat{k}$.

To summarise, when the utility function $u(c)$ is logarithmic, there exists a steady state pair $(\hat{k}, \hat{c})$ with non-stationary shadow prices $(p(t), q(t))$ where $\hat{k}$ is determined by

$$\gamma[2\rho - f'(\hat{k})]v'(f(\hat{k}) - \rho\hat{k}) - (1/\hat{k}) = 0 \tag{7.36}$$

and $\hat{c} = \rho\hat{k}$, while $p(t) + \rho q(t)$ is a *constant* given by (7.34). (If the system begins at $(\hat{k}, \hat{c})$ then it will remain there, while the shadow prices will be changing continuously, with $p(t) = p(0) - \gamma[f'(\hat{k}) - \rho]v'[f(\hat{k}) - \rho\hat{k}]t$ where $p(0)$ is arbitrary.) Note that equation (7.36) can be written as

$$u'(\rho\hat{k}) - \gamma v'(f(\hat{k}) - \rho\hat{k}) = \rho^{-1}[\rho - f'(\hat{k})]\gamma v'(f(\hat{k}) - \rho\hat{k}). \tag{7.37}$$

This shows that the gap between the two weighted marginal utilities is generally non-zero. It is positive if and only if $f'(\hat{k}) < \rho$.

When the utility function $u(c)$ is logarithmic, the optimal tax on capital in the steady state is

$$\hat{\tau} = f'(\hat{k}) - z = f'(\hat{k}) - \rho = \rho - \frac{1}{\gamma\hat{k}v'(f(\hat{k}) - \rho\hat{k})}, \tag{7.38}$$

which can be positive or negative. From (7.38) and (7.37), $\hat{\tau}$ is negative if and only if $u'(\rho\hat{k})$ exceeds $\gamma v'(f(k) - \rho\hat{k})$.

3. DISCUSSION

In this section, we will discuss four issues concerning the results established in Section 2. First, we will explain why the non-stationarity of shadow prices need not indicate that the planner must adjust stocks. Secondly, we will show that, with $\beta = 1$, one can reformulate the government's problem in such a way that there is only one state variable, not two. This new method of solution is clearly related to the linear dependence between the two shadow prices that we observed in the preceding section. Thirdly, we will indicate that the non-stationarity of shadow prices is not specific to our continuous time approach: the same result is obtained in discrete time. Fourthly, we will demonstrate that our result holds also for open economies.

3.1 Stationary stocks with non-stationary shadow prices

In the preceding section, we found that if the utility function of capitalists is logarithmic, then there does not exist a full steady state where all shadow prices are stationary. We also found that there exists a semi-stationary steady state, at which the tax on capital income is non-zero. This raises an important issue about the optimality (or otherwise) of a semi-stationary steady state. As is well known, shadow prices are normally interpreted as marginal values of state variables (or 'stocks' for short); if their values are changing, would this not indicate that the planner ought to adjust stock levels? Upon reflection, the answer to this question is 'not necessarily'. Recall that, for $\beta = 1$, equation (7.15) indicates that the state variables k and c are linearly dependent; $c = \rho k$. So it is the weighted sum of shadow prices, $p(t) + \rho q(t)$, that matters, not the individual shadow prices. Perhaps the following parallel between, on the one hand, linearly dependent stocks in a dynamic optimisation model, and, on the other hand, *joint-products* in elementary textbooks, may shed some light. A sheep farmer gets income from selling wool and mutton. One sheep supplies one unit of wool and ρ units of mutton. The total cost of raising x sheep is $\phi(x)$, a strictly convex and increasing function. The price of wool is p and the price of mutton is q. Then the value of a sheep is $p + \rho q$. If this sum is constant, then the farmer's decision on the number of sheep he wants to keep is given by $\phi'(x) = p + \rho q$, hence x is a constant. As a result, the quantities of wool and mutton that the farmer supplies will remain constant if $p + \rho q$ is constant, even when the individual terms p and q change over time.

We have not, however, verified that the sufficient conditions are satisfied at a semi-stationary steady state. It turns out that sufficiency can be proven indirectly, as follows. In the following subsection, we reformulate the government's problem and obtain both necessary and sufficient conditions. At the steady state of this reformulated problem, all real variables are identical to those obtained at the semi-stationary steady state of the original problem. This implies that the semi-stationary steady state in Section 2 is truly optimal.

3.2 A reformulation

In Section 2, we showed that when the capitalist's utility function is $u(c) = \ln c$, then a steady state with stationary shadow prices (in addition to stationary state variables) does not exist (generically), and that there exists a steady state with non-stationary shadow prices. At this steady state, the optimal tax on capital is non-zero. In deriving those conclusions, we made use of the standard formulation of the government's optimisation problem: we introduced $c(t)$ as an additional state variable. In the present subsection, we show that the same results can be obtained using an alternative formulation. This approach consists of representing the capitalist's optimal consumption rule in the feedback form, which is possible when $u(c) = \ln c$.[7]

Instead of representing the capitalist's optimal paths by the pair of differential equations (7.9) and (7.11), we note that in the case $\beta = 1$ (i.e., utility is logarithmic), we can represent these paths by the following pair of equations[8]

$$c(t) = \rho k(t) \tag{7.39}$$

$$\dot{c}(t) = \rho\dot{k}(t) = \rho[z(t)k(t) - \rho k(t)] = \rho[z(t)k(t) - c(t)], \tag{7.40}$$

the latter being (7.11) with $\beta = 1$.

The representation (7.39)–(7.40) highlights the fact that when $\beta = 1$, the capitalist's current consumption $c(t)$ depends only on his current capital stock $k(t)$, and is independent of current and future tax rates. His current saving, $z(t)k(t) - c(t)$, does depend on the current tax rate. This fact is only implicit in (7.9) and (7.11).

Remark 3: There is an alternative way of showing $c = \rho k$ when $\beta = 1$. With $\beta = 1$, we get from (7.11) that

$$z(t) = \rho + \dot{c}(t)/c(t)$$

and hence (7.9) yields

$$\frac{\dot{k}(t)}{k(t)} = \rho + \frac{\dot{c}(t)}{c(t)} - \frac{c(t)}{k(t)}.$$

Define $\theta(t) = k(t)/c(t)$. Then

$$\frac{\dot{\theta}(t)}{\theta(t)} = \rho - \frac{1}{\theta(t)}. \tag{7.41}$$

This equation, and the condition

$$\lim_{t\to\infty} \theta(t)e^{-\rho t} = 0, \tag{7.42}$$

which is obtained from (7.10), give $\theta(t) = \rho$ as the only solution that satisfies (7.42).

Using (7.39)–(7.40), the optimisation problem of the government can be re-written as

$$\max \int_0^\infty e^{-\rho t}\{\gamma v(f(k(t)) - z(t)k(t)) + \ln(\rho k(t))\}dt$$

subject to (7.40) and $k(0) = k_0$. The Hamiltonian is

$$\tilde{H} = \gamma v(f(k(t)) - z(t)k(t)) + \ln(\rho k(t)) + \psi[z(t)k(t) - \rho k(t)], \quad (7.43)$$

from which we obtain the optimality conditions

$$\frac{\partial \tilde{H}}{\partial z} = -\gamma k v' + \psi k = 0 \quad (7.44)$$

$$\dot{\psi} = \rho\psi - \frac{\partial \tilde{H}}{\partial k} = z\psi - \frac{1}{k} - \gamma[f'(k) - z]v'. \quad (7.45)$$

At a steady state with $\dot{k} = \dot{\psi} = 0$, we have $z = \rho$ and

$$2\rho - f'(k) = 1/\gamma k v'. \quad (7.46)$$

Equation (7.46) is identical to (7.35). It follows that the steady state of this problem is identical to that given by (7.35).

The approach taken in this subsection, while confirming our results found in the Section 2, has several advantages: (i) simplicity, (ii) sufficiency is ensured because the maximised Hamiltonian is concave in the state variable,[9] and (iii) it is transparent that the solution is time-consistent.

3.3 Semi-stationary equilibria in discrete time

It can be shown that our results apply also in discrete time formulation. Here we just sketch the main points. Capitalists maximise

$$\sum_{t=0}^{\infty} \delta^t u(c_t) \quad (7.47)$$

subject to

$$c_t + k_{t+1} = (1 - \tau_t) r_t k_t \quad (7.48)$$

where r_t is the gross rate of return, $0 < \delta < 1$ is the discount factor, and k_0 is given. This gives the Euler equation

$$u'(c_t) = \delta u'(c_{t+1})(1 - \tau_{t+1}) r_{t+1} \quad (7.49)$$

and the usual transversality condition. Workers consume

$$c_{wt} = w_t + \tau_t r_t k_t \,. \tag{7.50}$$

The resource constraint is

$$c_t + c_{wt} + k_{t+1} = F(k_t)\,, \tag{7.51}$$

where $F(k)$ is the gross output (i.e., output plus the depreciated stock of capital). Multiplying (7.48) by $\delta^t u'(c_t)$, then summing from $t=0$ to ∞, and using (7.49) and the transversality condition, we get the implementability condition:

$$\sum_{t=0}^{\infty} \delta^t u'(c_0)(1-\tau_0)F'(k_0)k_0 \,. \tag{7.52}$$

From (7.49) and (7.48),

$$c_t + k_{t+1} = k_t u'(c_{t-1}) / \delta u'(c_t)\,. \tag{7.53}$$

The government seeks to maximise

$$\sum_{t=0}^{\infty} \delta^t [u(c_t) + \gamma v(c_{wt})] \tag{7.54}$$

subject to (7.51), (7.52) and (7.53). We form the Lagrangean and let μ_t, θ_t, and λ_t be the Lagrangean multipliers corresponding to (7.51), (7.52) and (7.53). Differentiating the Lagrangean with respect to k_{t+1}, c_t and c_{wt}, we obtain the following first order conditions

$$\lambda_t - \mu_t = \lambda_{t+1}\left[\frac{u'(c_t)}{\delta u'(c_{t+1})}\right] - \mu_{t+1}F'(k_{t+1}) \tag{7.55}$$

$$\delta^t u'(c_t) = \theta\delta^t [c_t u''(c_t) + u'(c_t)] - \lambda_t + \mu_t - \frac{\lambda_t k_t u'(c_{t-1}) u''(c_t)}{\delta [u'(c_t)]^2} + \frac{\lambda_{t+1} k_{t+1} u''(c_{t+1})}{\delta u'(c_{t+2})} \tag{7.56}$$

$$\delta^t \gamma v'(c_{wt}) = \mu_t \, . \tag{7.57}$$

Now let us consider a semi-stationary state. That is, we let $c_t = \overline{c}$, $c_{wt} = \overline{c}_w$ and $k_t = \overline{k}$. From (7.48) we have

$$\frac{\mu_t}{\delta^t} = \mu_0 = \gamma v'(\overline{c}_w) \, . \tag{7.58}$$

Notice that while μ_t / δ^t is a constant, it is *not true* that λ_t / δ^t must also be a constant. Equation (7.55) yields, in a semi-stationary state, a first order difference equation in the discounted multiplier λ_t / δ^t :

$$\frac{\lambda_{tt+1}}{\delta^{t+1}} - \frac{\lambda_t}{\delta^t} = \mu_0 [\delta F'(\overline{k}) - 1] \, . \tag{7.59}$$

In the case where $u(c)$ is logarithmic, we can show that a full stationary equilibrium does not exist, and we can only have a semi-stationary equilibrium, with capital stock $\hat{k}$ that satisfies a condition analogous to its continuous time counterpart (see Long and Shimomura 2000).

3.4 Redistributive taxation in an open economy

It is clear that the basic results of Section 2 also apply to open economies. To do this in the simplest way we consider a small open economy producing two goods: good 1, which is an investment good, and good 2, which is a consumption good. Their outputs are denoted by X_1 and X_2 respectively. The production functions are $X_i = F_i(K_i, L_i)$, $i = 1,2$, where each $F_i(K_i, L_i)$ is homogeneous of degree one, strictly quasi-concave and increasing in each argument. To fix ideas, assume that good 1 is labour intensive, though this is not essential for our argument. Let π denote the (time-independent) price of the consumption good in terms of the investment good, which serves as the numeraire. The small open economy takes π as exogenously given. Perfect competition is assumed to prevail in the product markets and factor markets.

It is well known that the above assumptions allow us to obtain the GNP function $y = g(k, \pi)$, where y is aggregate output in terms of the numeraire good and $k(t)$ is the economy's stock of capital per worker. Let us list below the properties of the function $g(k, \pi)$. Given π, there exist two positive numbers $k_A(\pi)$ and $k_B(\pi)$, where $k_A(\pi) < k_B(\pi)$, such that (i) if $k \le k_A(\pi)$, then the economy specialises in the production of good 1, and

$g(k,\pi) = f_1(k)(\equiv F_1(k,1))$; (ii) if $k \geq k_B(\pi)$, then the economy specialises in the production of good 2, and $g(k,\pi) = \pi f_2(k)(\equiv \pi F_2(k,1))$; (iii) if $k_A(\pi) < k < k_B(\pi)$, then the economy produces both goods, and aggregate output is $g(k,\pi) = f_1(k_A(\pi)) + (k - k_A(\pi)) f_1'(k_A(\pi))$. Over the range of diversification described in (iii), the marginal product of capital is constant, and given by

$$\partial g / \partial k = f_1'(k_A(\pi)).$$

Since π is assumed to be constant, we can suppress the dependence of y on π and write $f(k)$ as a shorthand expression for $g(k,\pi)$. Note that the function $f(k)$ is continuous, increasing, and concave, with strict concavity holding for $k \leq k_A(\pi)$, and for $k \geq k_B(\pi)$. For $k_A(\pi) < k < k_B(\pi)$, the function $f(k)$ is linear.

It is clear that the model and the analysis in Section 2 can be adapted to our open economy, with only a few minor changes. The results of Section 2 apply to this model.

4. AN INTUITIVE EXPLANATION

While the main purpose of this chapter is to show that, in some model formulations, the unique steady state in quantities can be obtained only by allowing shadow prices to be non-stationary, we feel that it may be useful to provide some economic explanation. Why is it that, if the representative capitalist's utility function is logarithmic ($\beta = 1$), the optimal tax on capital income in the steady state is non-zero, while if their utility function has an elasticity of marginal utility $\beta \neq 1$, the optimal tax is zero in the steady state?

The reason is that, if $\beta = 1$ (i.e., if the representative capitalist has a logarithmic utility function), then the income effect and the substitution effect of a change in capital income tax on his current consumption cancel each other out, and his optimal current consumption is simply $\rho a(t)$, where $a(t)$ denotes the current level of his wealth (which, in our model, is the same as his capital stock $k(t)$). This means that $c(t)$ and $k(t)$ cannot be separated by the only policy instrument that we assume is available to the government, i.e., the time path of the tax rate $\tau(.)$. The government can use this policy instrument to influence the time path $k(.)$ but it cannot break the relationship $c(t) = \rho k(t)$. If $\beta \neq 1$, the situation is quite different: there is no such fixed, tax-independent relationship. Thus, if $\beta = 1$, the government is much handicapped, and it is no longer optimal to try to achieve the golden rule $f'(k) = \rho$ in the long run.

The above explanation raises an interesting question: given $\beta = 1$, what additional policy instrument would ensure that the optimal redistributive taxation implies a zero tax rate on capital income in the steady state? The key to the answer is that the nexus $c = \rho k$ must be broken. And this can be done if another asset is introduced into the economy, say government bonds, denoted by b. (If b is negative, this means the government is the net creditor.) For then, the representative capitalist's wealth, denoted by a, is the sum of k and b, and his optimal consumption rule is $c(t) = \rho[k(t) + b(t)]$, and it is no longer true that $c(t) = \rho k(t)$. It can be shown that, with this additional policy instrument, in the long run, the optimal tax on capital income is zero, and the golden rule $f'(k) = \rho$ is restored. (If $b < 0$ in the steady state, which is the case if the weight γ is sufficiently great, this means the government in effect owns part of the capital stock, and the rental income on that part is distributed to the workers.) Because of space constraint, we only offer an outline of the proof below.[10]

Let $b(t)$ denote the stock of government bonds. A government bond is a piece of paper that entitles its holder to earn the market interest rate $r(t)$, and to exchange it, whenever he wishes to, for a unit of capital. Initially $b(0) = 0$. Let $T(t)$ be the lump-sum transfer to workers. The government's budget constraint is $\dot{b}(t) + \tau(t)[r(t)k(t) + r(t)b(t)] = r(t)b(t) + T(t)$. (The right-hand side is the government disbursements, and the left-hand side is the government receipts, which consist of tax revenue and proceeds from the sale of additional bonds.) Let $a(t) \equiv k(t) + b(t)$ be the total wealth of the representative capitalist. He is indifferent between using his savings to acquire additional government bonds and using them to build up his stock of capital goods. His optimal consumption strategy must solve

$$\max_{c} \int_0^{\infty} e^{-\rho t} \ln(c) dt$$

subject to

$$\dot{a}(t) = z(t)a(t) - c(t) \text{ and } a(0) = a_0 = k_0 .$$

This yields the optimal consumption rule $c(t) = \rho k(t)$. It follows that $\dot{a}(t) = [z(t) - \rho]a(t) = [z(t) - \rho][k(t) + b(t)]$. The consumption of the representative worker is $c_w(t) = w(t) + T(t) = f(k(t)) - r(t)k(t) + T(t)$. Using the government budget constraint, we can write

$$c_w(t) = f(k(t)) - z(t)[k(t) + b(t)] + \dot{b}(t).$$

Let $x(t) \equiv \dot{b}(t)$ be a control variable for the government. We can write the optimisation problem for the government as

$$\max \int_0^\infty e^{-\rho t} \{\gamma v\left(f(k) - z(k+b) + x\right) + \ln[\rho(k+b)]\} dt$$

subject to $\dot{b} = x$, $\dot{k} = \dot{a} - \dot{b} = (z-\rho)(k+b) - x$, $k(0) = k_0 > 0$ and $b(0) = 0$. It is straightforward to show that at a full steady state we must have $z = \rho = f'(k^*)$, and b^* is given by

$$\gamma v'\left(f(k^*) - \rho(k^* + b^*)\right) = 1/\rho(k^* + b^*). \tag{7.60}$$

Thus, in the presence of government bonds, the optimal tax on capital income is zero at the steady state. Notice that from (7.60), if γ is sufficiently great then b^* is negative, implying that the government is a net creditor. One can consider, as an illustration, the following scenario: suppose that initially the economy has the capital stock $k(0) = k*$ where $f'(k*) = \rho$ and $b(0) = 0$. Then the government imposes a tax $\tau > 0$ so that the after-tax income of the representative capitalist is less than $\rho k*$. Since the capitalist's optimal consumption rule is $c = \rho k$, to satisfy this consumption and to pay the income tax, he must 'eat up' part of his capital stock, if the government cannot be a creditor. But since we allow b to be negative, the government can offer the capitalist the choice to pay part of his tax in the form issuing IOUs to the government, and there need not be any fall in k. This means that part of the physical capital stock k becomes effectively owned by the government. At a steady state with a negative b^*, even though the tax rate is zero, the government is able to make lump-sum payments to the workers, financed by the interest income it received from the capitalists.

5. CONCLUDING REMARKS

We have shown that it may be incorrect to characterise the properties of a steady state by setting the motion of all shadow prices equal to zero. Such a procedure can lead to policy recommendations that are unwarranted. Using the standard representation of the representative capitalist's 'reaction function', we have also demonstrated that, in the case where the capitalist's utility function is logarithmic, the optimal tax on capital income in a steady state (with non-stationary shadow prices) is not zero, and there does not exist a steady state with stationary shadow prices. The steady state we found can also be obtained using a feedback representation of the capitalist's optimal consumption rule. Our results apply to both closed and open economies.

Another related issue in the taxation literature is whether government policies, obtained by solving an optimal control problem, are time-inconsistent. Xie (1997) has shown that if the production function is linear in capital and the utility function is logarithmic, then the optimal tax path is time-consistent. In our model, even though the production function is not linear, the solution is also time-consistent as long as the utility function is logarithmic.

ACKNOWLEDGEMENTS

We would like to thank Murray C. Kemp, Gerhard Sorger, Alan Woodland and an anonymous referee for helpful comments.

NOTES

1. See Xie (1997). The basic point in Xie's article is that a so-called 'transversality condition' at the initial time of the control problem of the Stackelberg leader may turn out not to be a necessary condition, as was commonly claimed. For a more detailed discussion of this point, see Dockner et al. (2000, Chapter 5), who also provide examples of the non-applicability of such 'transversality conditions' in finite horizon and infinite horizon open-loop Stackelberg games.
2. Roberts (1984) also argues that the redistributive power of governments is limited, but for a different reason: individuals have an incentive to misrepresent their personal characteristics. We do not deal with this issue here.
3. This result was first reported in Kemp et al. (1993) for general utility function. A special case was reported in Lansing (1999), with a logarithmic utility function. Our semi-stationarity property is a new discovery.
4. Alternatively, readers may refer to a closely related paper, Long and Shimomura (2000).
5. Polonius gave the following advice to his son: 'Neither a borrower, nor a lender be; For loans oft loses itself and friend, And borrowing dulls the edge of husbandry.' (Hamlet, Act I, scene iii.)
6. See, for example, Leonard and Long (1992).
7. The Hamilton-Jacobi-Bellman equation for the capitalist's optimisation problem is
$$\rho V(t,a) - V_t(t,a) = \max[\ln c + V_a(t,a)\{z(t)a - c\}]$$
and it can be verified that the function
$$V(t,a) = \int_t^{\infty} [e^{-\rho(s-t)} \int_t^s \{z(\tau) - \rho\} d\tau] ds + \ln(\rho a)/\rho$$
satisfies the above functional equation and that the optimal control rule is $c(t) = \rho a(t)$.
8. The first equation was derived in Remark 2 of Section 2. The second is obtained by differentiating the first, (7.39), with respect to t.
9. See Long and Shimomura (2000).
10. Lansing (1999) independently discovered the same result on the usefulness of the bond

market in breaking the consumption-capital nexus.

REFERENCES

Chamley, C. (1986), 'Optimal taxation of capital income in general equilibrium with infinite lives', *Econometrica*, **54**, 607-22.

Dockner, E., Jorgensen, S., Long, N.V. and Sorger, G. (2000) *Differential Games in Economics and Management Sciences*, Cambridge, UK: Cambridge University Press.

Judd, Kenneth L. (1985), 'Redistributive taxation in a simple perfect foresight model', *Journal of Public Economics*, **28**, 59-83.

Kemp, M.C., Long, N.V. and Shimomura, K. (1993), 'Cyclical and non-cyclical redistributive taxation', *International Economic Review*, **34**, 415-30.

Kydland, F., and E. Prescott (1977), 'Rules rather than discretion: the inconsistency of optimal plan', *Journal of Political Economy*, **85**, 473-92.

Lansing, K. (1999), 'Optimal redistributive capital taxation in a neoclassical growth model', *Journal of Public Economics*, **73**, 423-53.

Leonard, Daniel, and Ngo Van Long (1992), *Optimal Control Theory and Static Optimization in Economics*, Cambridge, UK: Cambridge University Press.

Long, Ngo Van, and Koji Shimomura (2000), 'Semi-stationary equilibria in leader-follower games', *CIRANO Working Papers*, **2000-s8**.

Roberts, K. (1984), 'The theoretical limits to redistribution', *Review of Economic Studies*, **51**, 177-95.

Shimomura, K. (1991), 'The feedback equilibrium of a differential game of capitalism', *Journal of Economic Dynamics and Control*, **15**, 317-35.

Xie, Danyang (1997), 'On time inconsistency: a technical issue in Stackelberg differential games', *Journal of Economic Theory*, **76**, 412-30.

8. Unilateral Reforms of Trade and Environmental Policy

Arja H. Turunen-Red and Alan D. Woodland

1. INTRODUCTION

Examples of the perceived close relationship between countries' policies toward international trade and the quality of their domestic environment are easily found in both academic and policy-oriented literature.[1] Environmental restrictions are sometimes regarded as implicit non-tariff barriers against foreign imports; on the other hand, lax environmental standards have been cited as a substitute for export subsidies. Trade policies that reallocate a country's resources may, on the one hand, promote waste production or, if the favoured industries happen to be relatively clean, may also lead to environmental gains.

In the present chapter, we choose to study the interaction of environmental and trade policy by concentrating only on one central goal of policy, which, for us, is the home country's welfare. We therefore assume that all policy reforms are judged on the basis of their impact on domestic aggregate utility; export promotion or subsidisation of domestic industry (in order to attain some redistribution or employment related goals) are not our focus. Since our model involves only one small economy and excludes transboundary environmental effects, we do not consider international environmental agreements or concerns that the small country may have regarding polluting output elsewhere.

We study the nexus of trade and environmental policy from the *second best point of view*, attempting to design reforms in the home country's existing trade barriers and pollution levies that are guaranteed to result in welfare gains, once all consequences of reforms are taken into account. As it turns out, even in a relatively uncomplicated model such as ours, keeping track of all repercussions of policy changes is a complex task. This is because our description of the home economy includes two economic distortions; any adjustment of policy will therefore set off a chain of repercussions. For example, direct effects of changes in tariffs on the country's net trade will be combined with indirect (spill-over) effects on the polluting emissions (reallocation of the country's net output of traded goods will automatically alter the net output of pollutants) and changes in the country's environmental taxes will not only affect the output of pollutants but will also impact the net output of private goods. Careful evaluation of all of these effects is our first task. Applying the resulting welfare criteria (which are derived in Section 3), we then derive some suggestions for efficiency and welfare improving reforms.

We apply a straightforward dual model of a small open economy. The model (given in Section 2) involves a competitive production sector, an aggregate consumer and a policy setting government. The activities of the national production sector are assumed to result in environmental damage, which is represented by a vector of pollutants. The ensuing environmental damage is measured using a number of environmental quality indicators (e.g., air or water quality measures), which directly impact aggregate welfare but bear no external effect on the production technology. The country's trade policy instruments are represented by tariffs, while environmental policy is described by taxes on polluting emissions.

We consider three alternative policy setting scenarios (in Section 4). First, we assume that the domestic government can only alter one subset of policy instruments (either trade tariffs or environmental taxes) while the remaining policy variables are kept fixed. Starting from an arbitrary initial equilibrium, we show that differential reforms of the variable policy instruments toward their conditionally optimal levels (which take into account the presence of the fixed distortions) are welfare improving, assuming that an intuitive correlation condition on the country's environmental and trade distortions is satisfied. The role of the correlation condition is to ensure that the indirect effects of a policy change are not large enough to overwhelm the welfare gains that arise from the change in the primary policy variables. According to the condition, polluting emissions that are lightly taxed (relatively to their welfare impact) are, on average, positively correlated with products that are highly protected by tariffs.[2]

Contrasting with our discussion in Section 4.1, where a subset of policy variables is kept fixed while other policies are altered, in Section 4.2 we assume that the secondary policy instruments are adjusted *optimally* when the primary policy reform is undertaken. We show that the optimal adjustment of the secondary policy instruments suitably minimises the indirect (spill-over) effects of the primary reform. This implies that many familiar directions of policy reform (e.g., proportional reductions of distortions), which originally were discussed using models containing only one economic distortion, remain welfare improving also in our two-distortion model. No additional conditions (such as the correlation condition of Section 4.1) need to be imposed for welfare gains to be attained.

Finally, in Section 4.3, we bridge the two opposite cases of Sections 4.1 and 4.2 and assume that the home government can adjust the secondary policy instruments but that the adjustment is merely an automatically derived reaction, determined by a *functional* relationship between the primary and secondary reforms. For example, we consider the case in which the change of tariffs is directly tied, via a linear function, to the chosen change of pollution levies. We show that, irrespective of its simple form, the linear adjustment function for tariffs and environmental tax reforms is sufficiently powerful to reduce the indirect impact of the primary policy reform. In particular, we obtain that *all* primary reforms that are welfare improving when the secondary policy instruments are optimally adjusted are also welfare improving under the automatic linear adjustment rule. The advantage of this automatic adjustment rule is that no time-consuming and laborious econometric calculations need to be performed in order to find the suitable ways of adjusting the secondary policy variables in order to make sure that their values are optimal in the new equilibrium; given a change which is of primary interest, a simple linear function, which is obtained using information regarding the initial equilibrium only, yields the convenient policy response.

The present model is a small open economy version of the many country trade model of Turunen-Red and Woodland (1999), which includes transboundary environmental effects. Our current recommendations are much affected by the work of Copeland (1994), who offered some examples of welfare improving policy reforms in the small open economy context. We expand on Copeland's results, offering additional directional results, while also reformulating some of his conditions as suitably defined correlations.

2. THE MODEL

We consider a small open home economy that interacts with the rest of the world by trading in N commodities. The (fixed) world market prices of tradable goods and services are given by the vector $p^T \equiv (1, w^T)$,[3] and the domestic prices of tradables, denoted by $(p+\tau)$, are assumed to include tariffs denoted by τ. In addition to trade taxes, the home country may impose environmental taxes t on the vector of various environmental pollutants, z.

The home country's aggregate production sector is modelled using the *revenue function* $G(p+\tau, t)$,[4] which we take to be twice continuously differentiable. By Hotelling's Lemma, partial derivatives of the revenue function with respect to the price variables $(p,-t)$ yield the net supply functions for traded commodities, $y=G_p(p+\tau,t)$, and the supply of environmental pollutants,

$$z=-G_t(p+\tau,t). \qquad (8.1)$$

Equation (8.1) implies that the quantity of polluting discharges is chosen by the domestic industry so as to maximise profit. Any pollution abatement activities that the industry may undertake are, therefore, also assumed to be performed according to the profit maximisation principle, taking into account the cost of pollution emitted (the environmental taxes), the technological possibilities for such abatement (described by the aggregate technology) and the world market prices of trade goods.

The matrix $G_{tt} = [-\partial z_n / \partial t_m]$ of second derivatives of the revenue function indicates the sensitivity of the aggregate production sector decision making to changes in environmental taxes. As the matrix G_{tt} is positive semidefinite, an increase in the tax t_m, say, causes the discharges of the mth polluting agent to be reduced. However, the matrix G_{tt} allows for the possibility that, due to technological substitution, policy-induced suppression of some forms of pollution may lead to a worsening of dirty discharges elsewhere (i.e., off-diagonal elements of G_{tt} may be negative). The matrices

$$-G_{tp} = \left[\partial z_n^k / \partial p_m \right] \text{ and } -G_{pt} = \left[\partial y_m / \partial t_n \right]$$

indicate the degree of substitutability and/or complementarity among various pollutants and the N traded commodities. Hence, if the nth element of the pollution vector refers to CO_2-emissions (say), then $\partial z_n / \partial p_m > 0$ is interpreted to mean that an increase in the price of the mth product reduces the emissions of CO_2, i.e., carbon dioxide and the mth traded commodity are technological substitutes.

We assume that industrial pollution affects the home country's welfare by altering environmental quality indicators, which are denoted by the vector q. These indicators may include, for example, various air and water quality measures and the area of forests damaged by acid rain. The environmental quality variables, q, are determined by the polluting discharges according to the ecological 'damage function'

$$q = f(z). \tag{8.2}$$

The specification (8.2) allows for an arbitrary number of environmental quality indicators and places no restrictions on the interactions of the polluting mechanisms across the relevant measures. However, equation (8.2) only considers environmental damage arising from the country's own polluting emissions. Cross-border effects are excluded in the current analysis.

We model the home country's consumption sector using the (twice continuously differentiable) *restricted expenditure function*, $E(p+\tau, q, u)$, where u denotes aggregate welfare. Given the domestic prices of tradables and the quality of the environment, the value of the function E gives the minimum cost for attaining a specific level of welfare and this explicitly depends on the state of the domestic environment. In particular, we assume that E is increasing in the indices q, i.e., worsening of environmental quality results in a higher cost for any given u. According to Shephard's Lemma, the gradient vector $E_p(p+\tau,q,u)$ yields the aggregate net demand for traded goods. The matrix E_{pp} then gives the corresponding consumption substitution effects, and the partial derivatives $r \equiv E_q(p+\tau,q,u)$ represent the aggregate consumer's shadow evaluations for improvements in environmental quality (i.e., reductions of q). Sensitivity of consumption demand to environmental quality is represented by the matrix E_{pq}.[5]

For the convenience of notation, we define the *maximal net revenue function*

$$S(p+\tau,t,\ q,u) \equiv G(p+\tau,t) - E(p+\tau,\ q,u)\ . \tag{8.3}$$

The home country's net export functions can then be compactly expressed as the derivatives of the maximal net revenue function with respect to domestic prices, S_p, and the net output of pollutants is obtained as $z = -S_t = -G_t$. The matrix S_{pp} yields the pure substitution effects in the country's (compensated) net exports in response to changes in domestic relative prices.

Using the net revenue function, the equilibrium conditions for our small open home economy can be expressed as

$$p^T S_p(p+\tau,t,q,u) = 0, \tag{8.4}$$

$$q = f(z), \tag{8.5}$$

$$z = -S_t\,(p+\tau,t,q,u). \tag{8.6}$$

Equations (8.5) and (8.6) determine the country's pollution output, z, and the resulting state of the environment, q, as we have already discussed. Equation (8.4) states the home country's trade balance condition and given the environmental variables, the home country taxes and tariffs (t and τ) and the world prices (p), (8.4) can be solved for the aggregate welfare, which we take to be the primary endogenous variable of the model.[6] We assume that the model possesses sufficient regularity so as to determine home welfare as a once continuously differentiable function of the exogenous prices $(p+\tau,t)$.

Welfare effects of changes in these variables are the focus of the subsequent sections.

3. DIRECT AND INDIRECT IMPACT OF POLICY CHANGES

We assume that the goal of any changes in the trade and/or environmental policies of the home country is an improvement in the aggregate welfare.[7] In order to develop conditions that characterise the existence and directions of such policy reforms it is necessary to correctly evaluate and identify all effects of exogenous policy changes.

For this purpose, we totally differentiate the balance of trade condition (8.4), while taking into account the differentials of the environmental variables of interest, given in (8.5) and (8.6). Simple calculations yield the welfare change as

$$-p^T S_{pu} du = (p^T S_{pp} + \tilde{t}^T G_{tp})d\tau + (p^T G_{pt} + \tilde{t}^T G_{tt})dt \tag{8.7}$$

$$= (-\tau^T S_{pp} + \delta^T G_{tp})d\tau + (\delta^T G_{tt} - \tau^T G_{pt})dt, \tag{8.8}$$

where

$$\begin{aligned} &\delta^T \equiv \tilde{t}^T - t^T \equiv p^T E_{pq} f_z - t^T = r^T f_z - \tau^T E_{pq} f_z - t^T, \\ &f_z \equiv \partial f(z) / \partial z. \end{aligned} \tag{8.9}$$

Equations (8.7) and (8.8) bring together all direct and indirect effects of changes in the environmental and trade policies of the home country. On the right-hand side of each equation, changes in both types of policy variables are associated with (in the bracketed terms) corresponding changes in the country's trade balance, at the initial level of welfare. If these changes in potential consumption are positive, they can be converted into welfare gains, given that the multiplier

$$-p^T S_{pu} = p^T E_{pu}$$

on the left-hand side of (8.7) and (8.8) is also positive. Following the standard practice of policy reform literature (which serves to fix the direction of welfare improving reforms), we assume that this multiplier is indeed positive. Consequently, a tariff and/or tax reform is welfare improving if and only if the right-hand side of (8.7) is positive.[8]

The effect of policy reform on the home country's constant utility trade balance is given two equivalent expressions in (8.7) and (8.8). Both combine the *direct* and *indirect effects* of reforms. The terms involving the matrices G_{tt} and S_{pp} represent the direct impact of changes in environmental taxes on the aggregate production sector's polluting emissions and the direct effect changes in the country's tariffs on the net output of traded commodities, respectively. Since the diagonal elements of G_{tt} are non-negative, an increase in the *m*th environmental tax, say, will directly reduce the output of the *m*th industrial pollutant. There may be additional production substitution effects arising from the change in the *m*th pollutant tax; if so, these effects are taken into account by the (non-zero) off-diagonal elements in G_{tt}. Analogously, as the matrix S_{pp} is positive semidefinite, a reduction in one tariff will directly reduce domestic output of the corresponding commodity and may cause changes in the net output of other goods and services (given by the off-diagonal elements of S_{pp}). The terms involving the matrices G_{pt} and G_{tp} in (8.7) and (8.8) represent the indirect adjustments in the country's net output of tradables and industrial pollutants arising from changes in environmental taxes and tariffs. The term $\tilde{t}^T G_{tp}$ in (8.7), for instance, quantifies changes in polluting discharges that are caused by a tariff-induced reallocation of the country's output of private goods. Analogous indirect substitution effects arising from changes in environmental taxes are given in (8.7) and (8.8) by the terms involving the matrix G_{pt}.

The two expressions given in (8.7) and (8.8) for the effects of exogenous changes in the country's policy variables differ by the means by which these effects are evaluated and aggregated across private goods and industrial pollutants. In (8.7), changes in net output are evaluated by *shadow prices*, which equal the world prices (p) for traded commodities and are defined by the marginal changes in the (constant utility) consumer expenditure ($\tilde{t}^T \equiv p^T E_{pq} f_z$) for polluting discharges. In (8.8), relative evaluations of changes in net output are accomplished using the relevant *price distortions*, which are defined by the tariffs τ and the vector δ.[9] As noted in (8.9), the environmental distortion vector, δ, is defined as the difference between the true marginal damage of pollution on consumers, $\tilde{t}$, and the actual environmental taxes imposed at the initial equilibrium, t, and is therefore non-zero whenever the cost of pollution imposed on industry deviates from its real cost on society.

4. WELFARE IMPROVING REFORM

Formulae (8.7) and (8.8), which quantify the welfare impact of changes in the home country's environmental and trade policies, clearly indicate that the direct and indirect effects of an arbitrary policy change do not have to be positive (efficiency and welfare improving) and that these effects do not need to augment each other (i.e., they do not have to have the same sign). Furthermore, if environmental policy changes are combined with simultaneous changes in the country's trade policy, there is no guarantee that the combined welfare impact is positive even if, in isolation, a change in one set of policy variables would be welfare improving.

In order to sort out the complex interactions, we begin in this section by considering changes in one set of policy variables only. In other words, we assume that the domestic government can only adjust its environmental taxes (or, tariffs) while having to maintain tariffs (or, environmental taxes) fixed.

4.1 Reform with additional fixed distortions

Using formulae (8.7) and (8.8), we easily obtain the following characterisations of all welfare improving reform directions for tariffs and environmental taxes.

Theorem 1: *(i) If the environmental taxes, t, are kept fixed, a differential tariff reform in the direction* $d\tau$ *is welfare improving if and only if*

$$(p^T S_{pp} + \tilde{t}^T G_{tp})d\tau \;=\; (-\tau^T S_{pp} + \delta^T G_{tp})d\tau > 0; \qquad (8.10)$$

(ii) If the trade tariffs, τ*, are kept fixed, a differential reform in environmental taxes in the direction dt is welfare improving if and only if*

$$(p^T G_{pt} + \tilde{t}^T G_{tt})dt \;=\; (-\tau^T G_{pt} + \delta^T G_{tt})dt > 0. \qquad (8.11)$$

Condition (8.10) for a tariff reform simply requires that the sum of the direct and indirect (spill-over) effects of the reform be positive. Given sufficient normality of consumer demand (so that $-p^T S_{pu}$ in (8.7) and (8.8) is positive), this guarantees that welfare gains are attained. According to (8.10), the extent to which the interaction of the direct and indirect effects of tariff reform pose a problem depends on the impact of the resulting production reallocation for private goods on the net output of pollutants (given by the matrix G_{tp}), and the effect of this on consumers (evaluated by the shadow prices $\tilde{t}$).

Conditions (8.10) and (8.11) can be used to check whether an arbitrary direction of reform in tariffs or taxes is a potential improvement. However, in order to develop some concrete suggestions for policy reforms, basic intuition of the initial situation is useful. Since we have assumed that one set of policy variables is constrained to remain fixed, it seems that one useful general direction of reform would be one that moves the other (variable) policy instruments toward levels that would be optimal in the presence of the fixed distortions. We state the ensuing results and their implications for each set of policy instruments in turn.

Corollary 1.1: *Let the environmental taxes, t, be fixed and let τ^{opt} denote the corresponding (second best) optimal tariffs in the home country. Then, a differential tariff reform in the direction $d\tau = (\tau^{opt} - \tau)$ is welfare improving if and only if*

$$\delta^T G_{tp}\tau \equiv (\tilde{t} - t)^T G_{tp}\tau = \sum_i (\tilde{t}_i - t_i) \sum_j \left(-\frac{\partial z_i}{\partial p_j}\right)\tau_j < 0. \tag{8.12}$$

Proof. Using (8.8) and setting the bracketed multiplier of the tariff reform term equal to zero, we obtain that the (second best) optimal tariffs of the home country are characterised by the equation

$$\tau^{(opt)T} = \delta^T G_{tp}(S_{pp})^{-1}. \tag{8.13}$$

Therefore, substituting $d\tau = (\tau^{opt} - \tau)$ and (8.12) into (8.10), we obtain that the expression (8.10) is positive given (8.12), as is required for a welfare improvement to exist. □

The tariff reform considered in Corollary 1.1 changes the home country's initial tariffs toward levels that are optimal, given that the environmental policy measures cannot be altered.[10] Condition (8.12), which is sufficient for this reform to be welfare improving, is a correlation condition on the country's trade distortions (as indicated by tariffs) and the environmental effects generated by changes of tariffs (as indicated by the term $\delta^T G_{tp}$). Given that most elements of the matrix G_{tp} are negative, the condition will hold if pollutants that are lightly taxed and most damaging (so that $(\tilde{t}_m - t_m) > 0$) are emitted in production of goods that are highly protected. In this case, it makes sense to reduce the high tariffs (this would be the likely direction of the tariff reform in question); doing so would yield the usual efficiency gains in the country's trade and, in addition, reductions in polluting discharges associated with the lower levels of domestic production of the most polluting private goods would yield further welfare gains.[11]

Slightly modifying the proof of Corollary 1.1 we obtain that an entire family of tariff reforms of the form $d\tau = \alpha\tau^{opt} - \beta\tau$, $(\alpha, \beta) > 0_2$, is welfare improving, given (8.12). Choosing $\alpha = 1$ and $\beta = 0$, we then obtain that a tariff reform proportional to what the tariffs ought to be (given the fixed environmental taxes) is one feasible direction of change as is a proportional reduction of tariffs (choosing $\alpha = 0$ and $\beta = 1$). The latter observation conveniently generalises one of the standard results of tariff reform theory (proportional reductions of tariffs are welfare improving in a small country) to our case, which involves domestically generated environmental distortions.[12]

For reforms of environmental taxes when the country's tariffs are kept fixed, we obtain the following recommendation.

Corollary 1.2: *Let the tariffs,* τ, *be fixed and let* t^{opt} *denote the corresponding (second best) optimal levels of environmental taxes in the home country. Then, a differential tax reform in the direction* $dt = (t^{opt} - t)$ *is welfare improving if and only if condition* (8.12) *is satisfied.*

Proof. Using (8.8) and setting the bracketed multiplier of the tax reform term equal to zero, we obtain that the (second best) optimal tariffs of the home country are characterised by the equation

$$t^{(opt)T} = \tilde{t}^T - \tau^T G_{pt}(G_{tt})^{-1}. \tag{8.14}$$

Therefore, substituting $dt = (t^{opt} - t)$ and (8.14) into (8.11), we obtain that the expression (8.11) is positive, given (8.12). □

Analogously to Corollary 1.1, a movement in environmental taxes toward their conditionally optimal levels is welfare improving, given the correlation condition (8.12) for the country's trade and environmental distortions.[13] Simple modifications of the proof of Corollary 1.2 further yield that a tax increase proportional to the environmental distortions ($dt = \delta \equiv \tilde{t} - t$) and a tax reform of the form $dt = (t^{opt} - \tilde{t})$ will result in welfare gains under the same correlation condition.[14]

4.2 Reform with optimal adjustment

The results of the previous subsection were derived assuming that one set of policy variables cannot be altered. In another extreme, one could assume that the domestic government is, in fact, able to *optimally* adjust either its trade or environmental policy, given any reform in the other. Intuition suggests that this quite demanding supposition should provide a significant simplification of analysis; it should also provide further insight into the structure of the policy spill-overs that are present in our two-distortion model.

Conditions under which welfare improvements will now exist are given in our next theorem. Directional recommendations are then discussed.[15]

Theorem 2: (*i*) *Let the environmental taxes t be chosen optimally, given the trade tariffs, and assume that the pollution substitution matrix* G_{tt} *is invertible. Then, a differential tariff reform* $d\tau$ *is welfare improving if and only if*

$$-\tau^T \tilde{S}_{pp}\, d\tau > 0, \quad \tilde{S}_{pp} \equiv (S_{pp} - G_{pt}(G_{tt})^{-1} G_{tp}); \qquad (8.15)$$

(*ii*) *Let the tariffs* τ *be chosen optimally, given the environmental taxes, and assume that the net trade substitution matrix* S_{pp} *is invertible. Then, a differential tax reform dt is welfare improving if and only if*

$$\delta^T \tilde{G}_{tt}\, dt > 0, \quad \tilde{G}_{tt} \equiv (G_{tt} - G_{tp}(S_{pp})^{-1} G_{pt}). \qquad (8.16)$$

According to Theorem 2, assuming optimal adjustment, the existence and directions of welfare improving tariff and environmental tax reforms are determined by the revised net substitution matrices $\tilde{S}_{pp}$ and $\tilde{G}_{tt}$, respectively, as stated in (8.15) and (8.16). Two useful observations can be made regarding these conditions. First, by comparing (8.15) and (8.16) to (8.7) and (8.8), which apply when only a subset of policy instruments can be altered at a time, it can be seen that the criteria (8.15) and (8.16) subsume both the direct and spill-over effects of reforms into single net substitution matrices $\tilde{S}_{pp}$ and $\tilde{G}_{tt}$. These matrices therefore determine the entire impact of all changes in tariffs and taxes.

Secondly, as is evident from (8.7) and (8.8), the positive semidefinite net substitution matrices S_{pp} and G_{tt} determine the effects of changes in tariffs and in environmental taxes, respectively, if the domestic economy contains only *one* (either tariffs or taxes) type of distortion. In the present case, in which secondary distortions exist but are adjusted optimally, the welfare consequences of tariff and tax reforms can also be expressed in terms of single net substitution matrices, namely $\tilde{S}_{pp}$ and $\tilde{G}_{tt}$. Furthermore, these matrices share the positive semidefiniteness of S_{pp} and G_{tt}, which means that the indirect welfare effects which do arise due to the presence of the additional distortions in the current case are sufficiently minimised by the optimal adjustment of the alternative policy instruments so as to maintain the definiteness properties of the way in which the economy responds to the primary changes in tariffs or taxes.

Since the fundamental nature of the economy's response to policy reforms is similar in this case to that in standard models containing only single distortions, familiar suggestions as to directions of these reforms can be reinstated. For example, it is easy to show that all tariff reforms that belong to the linear family

$$d\tau = (\rho p - \varepsilon\tau),\ (\rho,\varepsilon) > 0_2, \qquad (8.17)$$

are welfare improving in the current context.[16] Hence, irrespective of the presence of environmental distortions, *a proportional reduction of tariffs* $d\tau = -\tau$ remains a welfare improving choice for tariff reform in a small country. Furthermore, using (8.15), if all tariffs are positive and all traded commodities are net substitutes according to the revised net substitution matrix $\tilde{S}_{pp}$, Vanek's (1964) *concertina theorem* for tariff reform can be extended to a small open economy with environmental distortions. According to the concertina theorem, a reduction in the country's highest *ad valorem* tariff rate is welfare enhancing.

Analogously, for reforms of environmental taxes, we obtain, using (8.16) and by taking advantage of the definiteness of the matrix $\tilde{G}_{tt}$, that the linear family

$$dt = (\alpha\tilde{t} + \phi\delta),\ (\alpha,\phi) > 0_2, \qquad (8.18)$$

of reforms in pollution taxes is welfare improving, assuming that trade tariffs can be optimally adjusted. This family includes, as special cases, reforms proportional to the initial environmental distortions ($dt = \delta$) and reforms proportional to the actual marginal damage arising from pollution ($dt = \tilde{t}$).

4.3 Tied reforms of tariffs and taxes

We have shown that the spill-over effects of tariff or environmental tax reform can be conveniently minimised if one set of the policy instruments is adjusted optimally as other policy variables are changed. In practice, however, such a continuously optimising process of adjustment (which requires repeated detailed estimation and calculation of relevant response matrices) is not likely to be feasible. Still, optimal adjustment in response to a change in one set of policies is only one possible, extremely demanding, form of tying together two subsets of policy instruments. Another, less stringent, approach is to specify a functional relationship between the reforms of taxes and tariffs. Such tying of directions of separate reforms could perhaps restore the convenient directional recommendations that we obtained under optimal adjustment.

In this section, we demonstrate that simple *linear* functions yield the most convenient means of tying together reforms of tariffs and taxes in our context. These functions define an automatic adjustment process, which, for any given reform in one set of policy variables, defines a convenient change in other policy instruments. We first consider the possibility of adjusting the country's tariffs in order to compensate for the spill-over effects arising from environmental policy. The following theorem identifies the functional form for the policy tie.

Theorem 3: *Let the net substitution matrix* S_{pp} *be invertible and let the tariff reform be defined by the equation*

$$d\tau = -(S_{pp})^{-1} G_{pt}\, dt\ , \tag{8.19}$$

where dt is the differential reform in environmental taxes. Then, all tax reforms for which condition (8.16) *holds are welfare improving.*

Equation (8.19) defines a linear adjustment formula for tariffs that can be applied to determine a response to *any* proposed change in the country's environmental taxes. Consequently, according to Theorem 3, the directions of environmental tax reforms that are welfare improving are identified by the condition (8.16). This implies, in particular, that all directions of environmental tax reform that are welfare improving under optimal adjustment of tariffs are also welfare improving under the adjustment rule (8.19). That the directions of changes in environmental taxes can be chosen as if the trade tariffs were optimally adjusted follows because the tariff reform (8.19) suitably 'neutralises' the spill-over effects of an environmental tax reform. The positive definiteness of the 'reduced form' substitution matrix, $\tilde{G}_{tt}$, then follows and ensures, for example, that familiar proportional tax changes (e.g., $dt = \delta$ and $dt = \tilde{t}$) remain welfare improving under the linear adjustment mechanism.[17]

Equation (8.19) bears a striking superficial resemblance to the optimal tariff formula in (8.13). The important conceptual difference of the two formulae is, however, that (8.19) relates *changes* in tariffs to changes in environmental taxes, whereas (8.13) is a relationship between *levels* of tariffs and taxes and defines the conditionally optimal elements of τ. Furthermore, while the coefficient matrices in (8.13) and (8.19) have the same form, the reform (8.19) in tariffs is in no sense optimal. The numerical values in the coefficient matrices in (8.13) and (8.19) can only coincide if, at the initial equilibrium, the tariffs have already been chosen optimally corresponding to the given environmental taxes.

An analogous automatic adjustment process can be defined for the case in which reforms of tariffs take the role of the primary policy tool. This case would apply when the country's trade policy is constrained or directed by international agreements. The convenient linear tax reform formula now becomes

$$dt = -(G_{tt})^{-1} G_{tp}\, d\tau\,, \tag{8.20}$$

given the reform $d\tau$ in tariffs. This reform of pollution taxes removes the environmental spill-over effects that arise from tariff reform and guarantees that any change of tariffs that is welfare improving when environmental taxes can be optimally adjusted (e.g., a proportional reduction of tariffs) remains welfare improving also under (8.20).

Assuming that the elements in the matrix G_{pt} are mainly negative (reflecting reductions in net outputs in response to increases in pollution taxes) and that the matrices $(S_{pp})^{-1}$ and $(G_{tt})^{-1}$ are mostly positive, formulae (8.19) and (8.20) suggest that the two sets of policy instruments should be altered in a (broadly) similar fashion. According to (8.19), a rise in the level of environmental taxes ought to be combined with a rise of tariffs and, by (8.20), trade liberalisation ought to be combined with a reduction of pollution levies. While these general directions of changes may appear counter-intuitive, our results show that they can nevertheless make economic sense. The goal of our secondary adjustments in policy is to eliminate or reduce the spill-over effects of the primary policy reforms. It is these spill-over effects of reforms that may become counter-productive if they are not explicitly taken into account in welfare calculations. As shown by Theorem 3, however, suitable linearly determined adjustments in secondary policy instruments can eliminate the possibility of negative welfare consequences arising from indirect effects; given this, directions of changes in primary policy variables can be chosen, in an easy manner, based on their direct effects.

5. CONCLUSIONS

Our goal in the present paper has been to clarify the complex interactions of trade and environmental policies by studying a fairly simple but general model of a small open economy. Within this model, we derived welfare criteria that carefully quantify and separate direct and indirect (spill-over) effects of policy reforms when more than one type of economic distortion are present. Using these criteria, three policy analyses were conducted.

Perhaps not surprisingly, we obtained that the most familiar and intuitively attractive results regarding policy reforms are available if it is assumed that secondary policy instruments can be optimally adjusted once a reform of primary interest has been undertaken. The optimal adjustment minimises the indirect impact of the primary reform and therefore guarantees that, e.g., proportional reductions of distortions yield welfare gains. The practical shortcoming of this policy advice is, however, that the directions of the optimal adjustment must be estimated after each step of change in the primary policy variables so as to make sure the secondary policy variables attain their optimal values at the new equilibrium (after the primary change).

Interestingly, we were able to show that the intuitively appealing policy recommendation directions can be sustained also without the use of the optimal adjustment. A simple linear, automatic, adjustment rule, which we characterised in Section 3, was shown to be sufficiently powerful in reducing the welfare impact of the indirect effects of policy reform. The exact form of this simple adjustment function can be evaluated using information pertaining to the initial equilibrium only.

For the perhaps most practical case in which the domestic government is constrained to alter only one subset of its policy variables we formulated correlation conditions for the country's environmental and trade distortions which, if satisfied, again imply that intuitively attractive policy proposals can be made.

Our model of a small open economy could be used as a platform for rigorous econometric studies. By embedding environmental distortions in a general economic model we have derived welfare criteria and policy suggestions, which apply economic information in forms that are available from econometric studies of established type.

NOTES

1. For a survey of recent theoretical results on trade and environment, see Copeland and Taylor (1995). For a policy-oriented treatment, see Esty (1994).
2. Under this same correlation condition, other intuitively appealing reform directions (such as proportional changes in distortions) are also shown to be welfare enhancing.
3. Notation: p^T refers to the transpose of the (column) vector p.
4. The revenue function is defined as

$$G(p+\tau,t) \equiv \max_{y,z}\left\{(p+\tau)^T y - t^T z : (y,z)\in T\right\},$$

where T is the home country's aggregate technology set (including any pollution abatement technology) and y denotes the net output of traded goods. The function G gives the maximal (net) value of the country's traded goods output, while taking into account the (tax) cost of polluting discharges. We assume that the problem is well defined even when some (or all) environmental taxes are zero. The definition of the revenue function suppresses the home country's (fixed and non-polluting) factor endowment. The properties of the function G are analogous to those of the GNP-function (discussed, e.g., in Woodland (1982, Ch. 5)). In particular, the revenue function is convex and linearly homogeneous in all domestic prices and pollution taxes.
5. If demand for private goods happens to be (weakly) separable from the environment, as is often assumed in the literature, we may set $E_{pq} = 0$.
6. Equation (8.4) is equivalent to the aggregate consumer's budget constraint, which we

assume to include all tariff and tax income as lump sum income.

7. We will not considering other possible goals of policy. One such goal, suggested by the referee, is revenue-neutrality of changes in tariffs and taxes.
8. The multiplier $-p^T S_{pu}$ is a price-weighted sum of income effects in consumption (since $S_{pu} = -E_{pu}$). This sum is positive if all commodities are normal in consumption.
9. Equation (8.8) is analogous to Copeland's (1994: equation (7)).
10. As may be expected, the optimal tariff formula (8.13) implies that free trade is optimal in our small open economy only when environmental tax distortions have been removed ($\delta \equiv \tilde{t} - t = 0$) or if production activities have no polluting effects ($G_{tp} = 0$).
11. Copeland (1994) used a condition closely related to (8.12). He defined the concept of *damage intensity with respect to pollutants* for individual private goods by requiring that $\delta^T G_{tp_n} < 0$ for the *n*th traded good (say). Using Copeland's concept, condition (8.12) could be replaced by the requirement that all traded goods with positive tariffs are damage intensive with respect to pollutants.
12. Analogously to Corollary 1.1, we also obtain that a reform of tariffs proportional to world prices ($d\tau = p$) and a reform of tariffs in the direction defined by the expression $d\tau = (S_{pp})^{-1} G_{pt} \tilde{t}$ are welfare improving if the correlation condition $\tilde{t}^T G_{tp} p > 0$ is satisfied. Any positive linear combination of these reforms is also welfare improving under the same condition. These reform directions can be obtained by considering the alternative characterisation of (second best) optimal tariffs, which requires that, in (8.7), $(p^T S_{pp} + \tilde{t}^T G_{tp}) = 0^T$.
13. Formula (8.14) implies that the optimal pollution levies are equal to the shadow prices of pollutants ($t_{opt} = \tilde{t}$) only if trade is non-distorted ($\tau = 0$) or if pollution taxes can have no impact upon production decisions ($G_{pt} = 0$).
14. A tax increase proportional to the consumer shadow evaluations of the pollutants ($dt = \tilde{t}$) and a tax increase proportional to the optimal taxes ($dt = t^{opt}$) will be welfare improving, given the correlation condition stated in note 12.
15. Theorem 2 is obtained by substituting the optimal tariff and tax expressions (8.13) and (8.14) into (8.7) and (8.8).
16. Diewert et al. (1989) considered this family of tariff reforms in a small open economy model that did not include environmental externalities.
17. Theorem 3 is proven by substituting (8.19) into (8.7) and, after a cancellation of expressions of opposite signs, by combining the remaining terms that involve the tax reform dt.

REFERENCES

Copeland, B. (1994), 'International trade and the environment: policy reform in a polluted small open economy', *Journal of Environmental Economics and Management,* **26**, 44-65.

Copeland, B. and S. Taylor (1995), 'Trade and the environment: a partial synthesis', *American Journal of Agricultural Economics*, **77**, 765-771.

Diewert, W.E., Turunen-Red, A.H. and A.D. Woodland (1989), 'Productivity and Pareto improving changes in taxes and tariffs', *Review of Economic Studies,* **56**, 199-216.

Esty, D. (1994), *Greening of GATT: Trade, Environment, and the Future*, Washington, D.C.: Institute for International Economics.

Turunen-Red, A.H. and A.D. Woodland (1999), 'Multilateral reforms of trade and environmental policy', Department of Economics and Finance, University of New Orleans, revised.

Vanek, J. (1964), 'Unilateral trade liberalization and global world income', *Quarterly Journal of Economics*, **78**, 139-47.

Woodland, A.D. (1982), *International Trade and Resource Allocation*, Amsterdam: North-Holland Publishing Company.

9. Quotas, Voluntary Export Restraints and Welfare

Masayuki Okawa

1. INTRODUCTION

Quotas and voluntary export restraints (VERs) are the main non-tariff trade barriers that directly limit the quantities of commodities brought into an importing country, and have been widely adopted as blunt protectionist policies. Thus many trade theorists have focused their attention on these trade instruments mainly in imperfectly competitive market frameworks.

Back in the 1960s, Bhagwati (1965, p. 68) initiated the discussion concerning the equivalence of quotas and tariffs in the case of domestic monopoly and showed that the output of the monopolist is smaller under a quota than an equivalent tariff. This non-equivalence problem was subsequently considered by, among others, Itoh and Ono (1982) and Hwang and Mai (1988) in a variety of imperfectly competitive market structures. However, under the GATT trading system the opportunity for the industrialised countries to use a quota as a protectionist instrument is restricted to some special groups of commodities.

Instead, in the last two or three decades VERs based on the agreements with both the exporting firms and the government of the exporting country have been frequently adopted by the industrialised countries. Therefore the attention of trade theorists was initially directed to exploring theoretically whether VERs can be really voluntary or not, or under what economic circumstances VERs can be accepted voluntarily by exporting countries. For example, among others, Harris (1985) and Krishna (1989) set up a two-country, duopoly trading model in which firms produce differentiated goods and compete in their prices. They showed that a VER increases the profits of both exporting and importing firms and explained why the exporting firms voluntarily accept a VER. Mai and Hwang (1988) demonstrated, by taking a conjectural variations approach, that the profits of both exporting and importing firms can be increased by an imposition of a VER if and only if the free trade equilibrium is more collusive than the Cournot equilibrium. On the other hand, Suzumura and Ishikawa (1997) and Kemp et al. (1997) focused on the effects of a VER on the welfare of the importing country and on the profits of the firms. They showed that the national welfare of the importing country could increase only if a VER reduces the profit of the exporting firm. This implies that when the importing country aiming for higher national welfare imposes a VER, a VER cannot be a voluntarily agreeable policy for the exporting firms.

In all the literature cited above the scope of the analysis has been restricted to the market of the importing country and it has been assumed that the market is segmented: the duopoly firms compete in the domestic market only, both before and after quotas or VERs are enforced. That a market is segmented implies that a change in the trading system from free trade to restriction by a quota or a VER does not affect the supply behaviour of the exporting firm in its home market.

However, in current trading circumstances, it seems more realistic to assume that, if the market concerned is internationally oligopolistic, the firms compete in an integrated world market under free trade and that, after a quota or a VER is imposed, the integrated market must be segmented in multiple (two in the two-country model) domestic markets. In this setting, the behaviour of the exporting firms in their home markets would be affected by a change in the trading regime.

Therefore, this chapter studies and compares the effects of quotas and VERs in the setting of an integrated world market. To that end, I set up a simple two-country, two-good and one-factor model in which one of the markets is internationally duopolistic. Each of the two goods is produced and consumed in each country. Thus under free trade the market is a single integrated international market. The difference between quotas and VERs in this study is as follows. Under a quota the government of an importing country buys imports at the level of imports at the equilibrium price under free trade and supplies them in the domestic market. The government redistributes the quota revenue to the domestic agents in a lump-sum fashion. On the other hand, under a VER set at the free trade level of imports the rent accrues to the exporting firm. Evidently we will see that the difference in the distribution of the rent caused by the two policies will affect the behaviour of the duopolists and the welfare of the trading countries. I take a conjectural variations approach only to make my results comparable with those of my predecessors. We will see that in the integrated world framework the conjecture of a firm is just one of several factors that affect the results.

2. THE MODEL

Let us consider a two-country, two-good and one-factor model of trade. Each country produces both goods (good 1 and 2) by employing one primary factor (labour). In each of two countries, α and β, good 1 is produced under conditions of constant returns to scale, free entry and perfect competition. I choose good 1 as the numeraire. A monopoly firm in each of the countries produces good 2. I assume that in each country fixed amounts of labour are needed to produce good 2. Thus the total cost of producing good 2 consists of a constant marginal cost and a fixed cost: the average cost is decreasing and the marginal cost is constant. Thus, from the profit maximisation condition of the first industry, the wage rate is constant in each country. Labour is inelastically supplied, can move freely between the industries and is fully employed in each country.

There are two classes of economic agents in each country, the class of households and the monopolist (the producer of good 2). All households are identical in all respects: they are endowed with identical preferences and identical amounts of labour. The households supply their labour to firms and consume both goods. I normalise, without loss, the number of households in each country to one. On the other hand, the monopolist owns his firm and does not supply labour. Thus, his source of income is monopoly profit. He consumes good 1 only and maximises his utility by maximising his monopoly profit. Under free trade, the monopolist in each country competes in quantities and is a price-taker in the factor market.

I assume that country α exports good 1 to country β and imports good 2 from country β. I further assume that country α imposes a quota or a VER at the level of imports of good 2 under free trade.

3. THE ANALYSIS

This section studies the effects of a quota and a VER on the behaviour of the monopoly firms and on the welfare of the importing and exporting countries. To that end I first consider a free trade equilibrium between country α and country β. First consider the optimal behaviour of monopolist i $(i=\alpha,\beta)$ under free trade. The profit of the monopolist is

$$\pi^i = px^i - C^i(x^i), \tag{9.1}$$

where p is the world price of good 2 under free trade, x^i is the output of the i-th monopolist and $C^i(x^i)$ is the total cost of producing x^i. A simple form of the first-order profit maximisation condition for monopolist i is

$$p + x^i(dp/dx^i) = c^i, \tag{9.2}$$

where c^i is the constant marginal cost of monopolist i. To elucidate the feedback term (dp/dx^i), I resort to the market-clearing condition for good 2 under free trade:

$$\sum_{i=\alpha,\beta} D^i(p,F^i) = \sum_{i=\alpha,\beta} x^i , \tag{9.3}$$

where $D^i(\cdot)$ is the Marshallian demand function of country i for good 2, and F^i is the factor income of a household and is constant. Differentiating (9.3) with respect to x^i, taking account of the response of monopolist j ($j \neq i$), I obtain the first-order profit maximisation condition for monopolist i under free trade as

$$p[1 - x^i(1+\lambda^i)(\sum D^i\eta^i)^{-1}] = c^i , \tag{9.4}$$

where $\eta^i \equiv -(p/D^i)(dD^i/dp) > 0$ is the price elasticity of demand of country i for good 2 and $\lambda^i \equiv dx^j/dx^i$ ($i \neq j$; $i, j = \alpha, \beta$) is a conjectural variations term. The conjectural variations term describes the change in the output of the monopolist j anticipated by monopolist i in response to a unit change in the latter's output. I assume that the term is constant and symmetric: $\lambda^\alpha = \lambda^\beta = \lambda$. The three equations in (9.3) and (9.4) determine three endogenous variables x^α, x^β and p. I assume that there exists a unique stable equilibrium under free trade.

I first consider the effects of a quota imposed at the level of imports of good 2 under free trade. I assume that the α-government imposes quotas equal to the free level of imports of good 2 from country β: $Q = x^{\beta F} - D^{\beta F}$, where the variables with superscript F denote that those variables are evaluated at the equilibrium under free trade. I assume that the α-government buys Q of good 2 from monopolist β at the equilibrium price under free trade and supplies them tó the domestic market. Thus, as the export earnings of the β monopolist are the same as those under free trade, I assume that the β monopolist accepts the quota. The α monopolist behaves as a pure monopoly firm under the quota and maximises his profits under the following market-clearing condition

$$D^\alpha(p, y^\alpha) = x^\alpha + Q , \tag{9.5}$$

where $y^\alpha = F^\alpha + (p - p^F)Q$ is the income of a typical household consisting of both constant factor income (F^α) and the quota-revenue of the α-government redistributed to the households in country α, $(p - p^F)Q$. p^F is the equilibrium price of good 2 under free trade. The first-order condition for the maximisation of profit is

$$p[1 - x^\alpha (D^\alpha \eta^\alpha - \phi^\alpha Q)^{-1}] = c^\alpha, \tag{9.6}$$

where ϕ^α is the marginal propensity of the households in α to consume good 2. When good 2 is inferior and ϕ^α is negative, the term $(D^\alpha \eta^\alpha - \phi^\alpha Q)$ is positive and, even when good 2 is normal and ϕ^α is positive, we see that $D^\alpha \eta^\alpha - \phi^\alpha Q = D^\alpha \overline{\eta}^\alpha + \phi^\alpha x^\alpha > 0$, where $\overline{\eta}^\alpha$ is the Slutsky compensated price elasticity of demand for good 2 in α.

I now compare the optimal output of the α monopolist under a quota and under free trade. To that end, let us introduce the marginal profit function of the α monopolist under a quota:

$$\begin{aligned} J(x^\alpha) &\equiv d\pi^\alpha / dx^\alpha \\ &= p(x^\alpha)\{1 - x^\alpha [D^\alpha (x^\alpha)\eta^\alpha (x^\alpha) - \phi^\alpha (x^\alpha) Q]^{-1}\} - c^\alpha. \end{aligned} \tag{9.7}$$

We easily see that $J(x^{\alpha Q}) = 0$, where $x^{\alpha Q}$ is the unique optimal output of the α monopolist under the quota. I also assume that the following second-order optimality condition is satisfied:

$$dJ(x^\alpha)/dx^\alpha < 0$$

It follows that $x^{\alpha Q} \lesseqgtr x^{\alpha F}$ if and only if $J(x^{\alpha F}) \lesseqgtr 0$. Evaluating the marginal profit function in (9.7) at $x^\alpha = x^{\alpha F}$, we see from (9.4) that

$$J(x^{\alpha F}) = p^F x^{\alpha F} \left(\sum D^{iF} \eta^{iF} \right)^{-1} (\lambda - \Phi^F), \tag{9.8}$$

where $\Phi \equiv (D^\beta \eta^\beta + \phi^\alpha Q)(D^\alpha \eta^\alpha - \phi^\alpha Q)^{-1} > 0$. Therefore

$$x^{\alpha Q} \lesseqgtr x^{\alpha F} \Leftrightarrow \lambda - \Phi^F \lesseqgtr 0. \tag{9.9}$$

Let us look at a special case first. In a segmented domestic market setting based on partial equilibrium approach, the income effect of the quota-revenue does not appear (i.e., $\phi^{\alpha} = 0$) and good 2 is sold and consumed only in country α (i.e., $D^{\beta} = 0$). Thus, in that case we find that $\Phi^{F} = 0$ and

$$x^{\alpha Q} \lesseqgtr x^{\alpha F} \Leftrightarrow \lambda \lesseqgtr 0 .$$

On the other hand, in our setting we note the following. First, when the monopoly firms' conjectures are less cooperative than a particular level ($\lambda < \Phi^{F}$), including both non-cooperative conjecture ($\lambda < 0$) and the Cournot conjecture ($\lambda = 0$), the optimal output of monopolist α is smaller under a quota than under free trade. Secondly, when the monopoly firms' conjectures are more cooperative than the critical level ($\lambda > \Phi^{F}$), the optimal output of the α monopolist is larger under a quota than under free trade.

However, I do not look at the role of the conjecture of the monopoly firms only: it is just one factor that affects the results. In our integrated world market framework, the effect of a quota set at the level of imports under free trade on the behaviour of the monopolist in the importing country is regarded as a composite of the following three different effects. These are (a) the effect of a change in the market regime from an integrated world market to a segmented domestic market, (b) the change in the conjecture of monopolist α from a non-Cournot type under free trade to the Cournot type ($\lambda = 0$) under a quota and (c) the income effects of the quota-revenue. The first effect of the change in the market regime is caused by a contraction of the market-size from an integrated world market to a domestic one. This effect is captured by the changes in the second term of the marginal revenue from $x^{\alpha}\left(\sum D^{i}\eta^{i}\right)^{-1}$ in (9.4) to $x^{\alpha}(D^{\alpha}\eta^{\alpha})^{-1}$ in (9.6). This effect works to reduce the marginal revenue and decrease the monopolist's output under a quota. The second effect of the change in the domestic monopolist's conjecture appears when the firm's conjecture under free trade is of a non-Cournot type. The effects are extensively studied in the literature on the conjectural variations approach (see, among others, Mai and Hwang 1988). Finally, the income effect of the quota revenue appears in the term, $-\phi^{\alpha}Q$, in (9.6). One can see that if good 2 is normal (inferior), the income effect works to decrease (increase) the marginal revenue. The economic intuition is as follows. In maximising his profit under a quota regime, the monopolist recognises that he can control the quota-revenue by controlling the price of good 2. Suppose that the monopolist increases his output under a quota. The increase in the supply of good 2 decreases the price of good 2 and thus reduces the quota-revenue redistributed to the households as well. If good 2 is normal (inferior), this reduction of households' income decreases (increases) the demand for good 2 and thus decreases (increases) the price of good 2. Therefore, if good 2 is normal (inferior), the income effect of quota-revenue will reduce (increase) the marginal revenue of the monopolist and decrease (increase) his optimal output.

Let us turn to the welfare effects of the quotas in country α. To that end, I introduce the maximum bonus, which is defined as the difference between maximum income and the income needed to maintain given utility levels of the economic agents (see Wan 1965). Given the utility levels of α-factor owners and the α monopolist under free trade, i.e., $u^{\alpha F}$ and $\pi^{\alpha F}$, the maximum bonus of country α under a quota is

$$B^{\alpha}(x^{\alpha}) \equiv y^{\alpha}(x^{\alpha}) + px^{\alpha} - C^{\alpha}(x^{\alpha}) - e^{\alpha}(p, u^{\alpha F}) - \pi^{\alpha F}, \qquad (9.10)$$

where $e^{\alpha}(\cdot)$ is the expenditure function of the α-households. Then we see that

$$dB^{\alpha} / dx^{\alpha} = p - c^{\alpha} > 0. \qquad (9.11)$$

I assume there is a scheme of lump-sum compensation, which ensures that, after the change in the regime, either all agents are not worse off or all agents are not better off. Therefore, country α is potentially worse off (better off) under a quota than under free trade if the output of the α monopolist is smaller (greater) under a quota than under free trade. We arrive at our first proposition.

Proposition 1: *(i) If the inequality $\lambda - \Phi^F < 0$ is satisfied, the equilibrium output of the α monopolist is smaller under a quota than under free trade. Moreover country α is potentially worse off under a quota than under free trade. (ii) If the inequality $\lambda - \Phi^F > 0$ is satisfied, the equilibrium output of the α monopolist is greater under a quota than under free trade. Moreover country α is potentially better off under a quota than under free trade.*

Let us now turn to the effects of a quota on the optimal behaviour of the β monopolist and on the welfare of country β. Under the quota, as the export revenue of the exporting firm β is restricted to the constant $p^F Q$, the purpose of the monopolist is to maximise the profit from the domestic sales in country β. The profit of the β monopolist under the quota is

$$\pi^{\beta} = p^F Q + p^{\beta}(x^{\beta} - Q) - C^{\beta}(x^{\beta}), \qquad (9.12)$$

where p^F is the price of good 2 in country β and x^β is the total output of monopolist β under the quota. I define the marginal profit function of the β monopolist under the quota as

$$G^\beta(x^\beta) \equiv d\pi^\beta / dx^\beta = p^\beta\left[1-\left(x^\beta - Q\right)/ D^\beta \eta^\beta\right] - c^\beta . \qquad (9.13)$$

Evidently the optimal output of monopolist β ($x^{\beta Q}$) satisfies $G(x^{\beta Q}) = 0$. I assume that $G(\cdot)$ is strictly concave and the second-order condition for the maximum is satisfied. Then we see that

$$x^{\beta Q} \lesseqgtr x^{\beta F} \text{ if and only if } G(x^{\beta F}) \lesseqgtr 0 .$$

Evaluating (9.13) at $x^\beta = x^{\beta F}$, we find from (9.4) that

$$G(x^{\beta F}) = p^F x^{\beta F} \left(\sum D^{iF} \eta^{iF}\right)^{-1} (\lambda - \Psi^F), \qquad (9.14)$$

where

$$\Psi \equiv \frac{D^\alpha \eta^\alpha}{D^\beta \eta^\beta}\left(\frac{x^\beta - Q}{x^\beta}\right) - \frac{Q}{x^\beta} .$$

The sign of Ψ is ambiguous. Thus, let us here assume that the share of the exports of good 2 to the total output of the β monopolist is small enough and that $\Psi > 0$. Therefore, we find that

$$x^{\beta Q} \lesseqgtr x^{\beta F} \quad \Leftrightarrow \quad \lambda - \Psi^F \lesseqgtr 0 .$$

In view of equations (9.4) and (9.13), we can see that the effect of a quota on the behaviour of the β monopolist is similar to that to the monopolist α: a composite of a change in regime from an integrated world market to a domestic market and a change in the conjectural variations from a non-Cournot value to the Cournot one.

I turn next to the effects of a quota on the welfare of country β. To that end, let us here again introduce the maximum bonus of β:

$$B(x^\beta) \equiv F^\beta + p^\beta (x^\beta - Q) - C(x^\beta) - e^\beta (p^\beta, u^{\beta F}) - \pi^{\beta F} .$$

It follows that

$$dB^{\beta} / dx^{\beta} = p^{\beta} - c^{\beta} > 0 .$$

We therefore obtain our second proposition.

Proposition 2: *If the inequality $\lambda - \Psi^{F} < 0$ ($\lambda - \Psi^{F} > 0$) is satisfied, the equilibrium output of the β monopolist is smaller (larger) under a quota than under a free trade. Moreover country β is potentially worse off (better off) under a quota than under free trade.*

I now assume that the government of the importing country α imposes a VER instead of a quota at the level of imports under free trade. In this study, the difference between the two policies that directly control the quantity of imports is only that the quota revenue is redistributed to the domestic agents under a quota, while the rent accrues to the exporting firm. I assume that the VER is always binding. Therefore, after the VER is imposed, the domestic monopolist α turns out to be a Stackelberg leader and the exporting monopolist β turns to be a price-taking follower whose supply is strictly restricted to the VER level. Thus the export revenue of the monopolist β depends on the equilibrium price of good 2 in country α.

Let us first consider the behaviour of monopolist α. The analysis will proceed very similarly to the preceding analysis of a VER. Thus, to avoid tedious repetition of the argument, let us simply state the results. The marginal profit of the monopolist under a VER is

$$H^{\alpha}(x^{\alpha}) \equiv d\pi^{VER} / dx^{\alpha} = p^{\alpha}(1 - x^{\alpha} / D^{\alpha}\eta^{\alpha}) - c^{\alpha} .$$

The optimal output of the monopolist α is obtained as a unique solution of $H^{\alpha}(x^{\alpha}) = 0$. I assume again that the second-order condition for a maximum is satisfied. Evaluating $H^{\alpha}(\cdot)$ at $x^{\alpha} = x^{\alpha F}$, we find from (9.4) that $x^{\alpha V} \lesseqgtr x^{\alpha F}$ if and only if $\lambda - \Theta^{F} \lesseqgtr 0$, where $x^{\alpha V}$ is the optimal output of the α monopolist under a VER and $\Theta \equiv D^{\beta}\eta^{\beta} / D^{\alpha}\eta^{\alpha} > 0$. It is also seen that the welfare of country α is lower (higher) if $x^{\alpha V}$ is smaller (larger) than $x^{\alpha F}$. One can see that the effect of the VER is a composite of the two effects. Firstly, there is the effect of a contraction of the market size from an integrated world market to a domestic market. This effect is captured by Θ^{F} and works to reduce the output of the monopolist under a VER. Secondly, there is the effect of a change in the game structure from a non-Cournot one to a Cournot game. The conjectural variations term, λ, reflects this effect.

Let us here compare the effects of a VER with those of a quota. It is, however, difficult to obtain crisp results in our integrated world market framework. Thus, let us restrict attention to a special case in which good 2 is sold and consumed in country α only (i.e., $D^{\beta}=0$ and $\Theta=0$), a case already studied in the preceding literature. Consider here the Cournot case only. Under a VER regime the output of monopolist α and the welfare of the importing country are the same as under free trade. On the other hand, one can see, by setting $D^{\beta}=0$ and $\lambda=0$ in (9.9), that the output of the monopolist of the importing country α is smaller and the welfare of that country lower under a quota than under free trade. Thus, the output of the monopolist α is smaller and the welfare of the importing country is lower under a quota than both under a VER and free trade. This difference in the effects is due to whether the rent caused by the policies accrues to domestic consumers under a quota or to the exporting firm. Let us add this result to our third proposition.

Proposition 3: *Suppose that good 2 is sold and consumed in the importing country only and firms compete in the Cournot fashion. Then the optimal output of the monopolist is smaller and the welfare of the importing country is lower under a quota than both under a VER and free trade.*

Let us finally turn to the response of the β monopolist and the welfare of country β. The world market is segmented into two markets, α and β, and the β monopolist operates in the two markets. Thus the profit of the β monopolist under the VER is $\pi^{\beta V}=p^{\alpha}V+p^{\beta}(x^{\beta}-V)-C^{\beta}(x^{\beta})$, where V is the level of exports under the VER and p^{i} $(i=\alpha,\beta)$ is the price of good 2 under a VER. I have assumed that the β monopolist behaves as a price-taking follower in the α-market under a VER. Thus, the export revenue of the monopolist depends on the behaviour of monopolist α in the α-market. I assume therefore that the β monopolist concentrates on maximising his profit from the sales in his home market β. Thus provided that $p^{\alpha}V$ is sufficiently small, we will obtain the same results as those in Proposition 2 except for the replacement of a quota by a VER.

It is shown in the domestic market framework that country α benefits potentially from a VER if and only if the β monopolist is harmed by the VER (see Suzumura and Ishikawa 1997 and Kemp et al. 1997). However, in our integrated market context we find that it is neither necessary nor sufficient for country α to benefit potentially from the VER in order that the β monopolist be harmed by the VER.

4. CONCLUDING REMARKS

I have examined the welfare effects of quotas and VERs set at the level of imports under free trade in a two-country integrated market framework. The difference between the two quantitative policies in this study is as follows. In a quota regime, the government of the importing country buys the imported good at the equilibrium price of the good under free trade and the quota-revenue is redistributed to the domestic consumers. On the other hand, under a binding VER monopolist α turns out to be a Stackelberg leader and the exporting firm turns to be a price-taking follower. The rent accrues to the exporting firm under a VER.

The preceding literature is based on a domestic market setting. We have seen that the preceding literature's main conclusions are included as special cases of our results and that its results do not carry over to our integrated world market framework. It is emphasised that VERs are inherently discriminative: both quotas and tariffs are imposed on imports from all sources, while VERs are usually negotiated with only the most important exporting countries leaving minor suppliers free of restrictions. It is easily seen that, even if we introduce the third minor price-taking exporter that is free of restriction under a VER, our basic results will not be reversed.

The analyses cited above and this study assume that a VER is set at the level of free trade equilibrium. A merit of this assumption is that, even in a general equilibrium setting, we can drive fruitful results on the effects of a quota or a VER. On the other hand, Ishikawa (1998), Yoshida (1999) and Okawa (2000) have performed comparative static analyses and examined the effects of a reduction of a VER.

Finally, it is noted that the welfare implications of voluntary import expansion (VIE), with foreign firms' exports set at their free-trade equilibrium level, can be handled by the analysis of Section 3. Hence, the results with VER replaced by a VIE remain valid.

ACKNOWLEDGEMENTS

I would like to thank Murray C. Kemp, Koji Shimomura, Alan Woodland and a referee for their valuable comments and suggestions. This research was supported in part by the Ministry of Education, Science and Culture in Japan (Grant-in-aid No. 11630022).

REFERENCES

Bhagwati, J. (1965), 'On the equivalence of tariffs and quotas', in R.E. Baldwin et al. (eds), *Trade, Growth and the Balance of Payments: Essays in Honor of G. Haberler,* Chicago, IL: Rand McNally.

Bhagwati, J. (1968), 'More on the equivalence of tariffs and quotas', *American Economic Review,* **58**, 142-46.

Harris, R. (1985), 'Why voluntary export restraints are 'voluntary'', *Canadian Journal of Economics,* **58** (4), 799-809.

Hwang, H. and C. Mai (1988), 'On the equivalence of tariffs and quotas under duopoly: a conjectural variation approach', *Journal of International Economics,* **24**, 373-80.

Ishikawa, J. (1998), 'Who benefits from voluntary export restraints?', *Review of International Economics,* **6**, 129-41.

Ito, M. and Y. Ono (1982), 'Tariffs, quotas and market structure', *Quarterly Journal of Economics,* **97**, 295-305.

Kemp, M.C., Shimomura, K. and M. Okawa (1997), 'Voluntary export restraints and economic welfare', *Japanese Economic Review*, **48**, 187-98.

Krishna, K. (1989), 'Trade restriction as facilitating practices', *Journal of International Economics,* **26**, 250-70.

Mai, C.C. and H. Hwang (1988), 'Why voluntary export restraints are voluntary: an extension', *Canadian Journal of Economics*, **21**, 877-82.

Okawa, M. (2000), 'On the effects of voluntary export restraints under imperfect competition', unpublished paper, Ritsumeikan University.

Suzumura, K. and J. Ishikawa (1997), 'Voluntary export restraints and economic welfare', *Japanese Economic Review*, **48**, 176-86.

Wan, H.Y. (1965), 'Maximum bonus - an alternative measure for trading gains', *Review of Economic Studies,* **32**, 49-58.

Yoshida, C. (1999), 'The welfare effects of voluntary exports restraints', *Seoul Journal of Economics*, **12**, 43-155.

PART THREE

Market Structure

10. International Joint Ventures, Moral Hazards and Technology Spillovers

Kar-yiu Wong and Wing-fai Leung

1. INTRODUCTION

There are many reasons why two (or more) firms choose to form a joint venture to produce a commodity. To increase the monopoly power is one reason often suggested. Another interesting reason is that a joint venture allows the partners to combine some of their advantages that are complementary to each other, including financial capital and technological knowledge.[1] Of all the forms of joint ventures, those formed by firms in different countries, which are commonly called international joint ventures (IJVs), receive special attention.

For an IJV, the difference between a multinational corporation (MNC) and a local firm is often emphasised. According to the ownership-location-internalisation (OLI) literature, a MNC that chooses to supply to a foreign market through direct investment rather than exports must possess some ownership advantages in order to overcome the obvious disadvantages of its unfamiliarity local cultures and systems.[2] We follow the approach of this literature, but focus instead on an option of a MNC that has not been covered in the OLI literature: the formation of an IJV with a local firm. Many studies have pointed out that, in forming an IJV, a MNC contributes some of its ownership advantages while a local firm will make use of its knowledge and familiarity of the local market and domestic cultures and systems.[3]

One feature of IJVs that has captured the attention of many people is that the life of a typical IJV seems to be short, in fact, much shorter than the life of a typical and comparable wholly-owned subsidiary of a MNC (Beamish 1985, Franko 1971, Kogut 1988a and 1988b, Geringer and Hebert 1991 and Li and Guisinger 1991). In particular, Gomes-Casseres (1987) finds that, although the liquidation of joint ventures is not very different from wholly-owned subsidiaries (WOSs), the sellout rate of joint ventures (to one of the partners or outsiders) is higher than WOSs. The paper is based on a sample of over 5000 subsidiaries (either joint-ventured or wholly-owned) of USA MNCs established between 1900 and 1975.[4] It shows the share of subsidiaries (of either form) that may be sold or liquidated by 1975, and any change in ownership structure (from joint-ventured to wholly-owned or vice versa) between date of entry and the date of liquidation or sale, or between date of entry and 1975. On the whole, the termination rate of IJVs is about 30% while that of WOSs is only about 15% (Gomes-Casseres 1987).[5] Chowdhury (1992) further breaks down the termination rates between joint ventures and WOSs into several periods instead of the lump-sum data in Gomes-Casseres (1987). His findings suggest that the average life of both IJVs and WOSs had consistently declined from 1951 to 1975. Leung (1997) applies the proportional hazard model to study the duration of IJVs and WOSs by using a different data set of USA MNCs. The results suggest that the IJVs have significant shorter life span than WOSs.

Why does the life of a typical IJV seem to be short? If a MNC and a local firm agree to form a joint venture in the first place, why would they want to dissolve it in the future? That the average life of IJVs is shorter than that of WOSs suggests that the structure of IJV may be part of the reason. In fact, since the two firms choose to dissolve a joint venture that they formed sometime previously implies that something must have happened after the formation of the joint venture.

The objective of this chapter is to explain why two firms choose to form an international joint venture and decide to dissolve it later. There are several features of our model: moral hazard, cooperation costs and technology spillovers. The presence of moral hazard means that one of the firms may choose to provide insufficient effort to make an IJV attractive to the other firm.[6] The cooperation cost, as suggested by Leung (1998), is another factor that may encourage firms to break away an existing IJV. If an IJV is formed, both firms may learn from each other through technology spillovers and, with such technology improvement, one or both of the firms may choose to break away from the joint venture in the future. (See Benito and Gripsrud 1992 and Parkhe 1991, among others, for technology spillovers.[7]) An implication of the present theory is that an IJV can be formed and dissolved later even in the absence of uncertainty or imperfect information.

Sections 2 to 4 of this chapter develop the model. For simplicity, we begin with a single-period model. Section 2 focuses on a single firm, whereas Section 3 turns to the case of duopoly with a MNC and a local firm competing in a Cournot fashion. Section 4 examines the formation of an IJV. How the local firm chooses its effort in different cases is explained. Section 5 explains how the two firms decide between forming a joint venture and producing separately. Section 6 looks at a two-period model, which is used to explain technology spillover between the two firms when an IJV has been formed, and to analyse the conditions under which the firms would choose to break up the joint venture later. The last section provides some concluding comments.

2. THE MODEL: SINGLE FIRM AND SINGLE PERIOD

We first introduce a one-period model, which will later be extended to two periods to analyse intertemporal choice. Consider a homogeneous product and its market in an economy called 'home'. The inverse demand for the product in the market is described by $p = p(q)$, where p is the market price and q the demand. It is assumed that $p'(q) < 0$ and that p'' is either negative or not too positive, where a prime denotes a derivative.[8] The market is big enough to support the two firms to be introduced below.

There is a single home firm in the economy. Before the entry of the foreign firm, the home firm is a monopolist. Its cost of production includes two components: a variable cost that depends on the level of production, cx, where c is a positive constant and x is the level of production, and a 'fixed' cost which is independent of the level of output, f. This means that c is a constant marginal cost. The 'fixed' cost of production, which is fixed in the production process, can indeed be changed by the firm by spending different levels of effort. Examples of 'fixed' cost are the costs of establishing good relations with the suppliers of inputs (factor owners and suppliers of intermediate inputs, for example) and purchasers of its output (such as wholesalers and retailers), the costs of marketing and advertisement, and the costs of getting familiar with the local political, social, economic, and legal systems. If we denote the effort made by the firm by e, we can write the 'fixed' cost of production as $f = f(e)$, which satisfies the following properties:

$$f(e) > 0, f'(e) < 0, f''(e) > 0. \tag{10.1}$$

Based on condition (10.1), the value of $-f'(e)$ can be illustrated by schedule FF in Figure 10.1. Note that $-f'(e)$ is positive, but declining.

Since making efforts is costly, we denote the cost of providing a level of effort e by $g = g(e)$, which has the following properties:

$$g(e) > 0, g'(e) > 0, g''(e) > 0. \tag{10.2}$$

The first derivative of the function, $g'(e)$, can be illustrated by a schedule like GG in Figure 10.1. Condition (10.2) implies that the schedule is rising.

For the sake of analysis, we assume that the home firm takes two stages to maximise its profit. First, it chooses the optimal effort, e, and pays a cost of $g(e)$. The effort then gives a certain 'fixed' cost of production, $f(e)$. Second, it chooses the optimal output level, x.

We first describe the second stage. In this stage, both the effort e and the 'fixed' cost $f(e)$ are taken as given. The firm chooses the output to maximise its nominal profit given by

$$\theta(x,e) = p(x)x - cx - f(e), \tag{10.3}$$

where the market equilibrium $q = x$ has been used. Note that the nominal profit does not include the cost of effort, which is paid for in stage 1. The first-order condition is[9]

$$p + p'x = c. \tag{10.4}$$

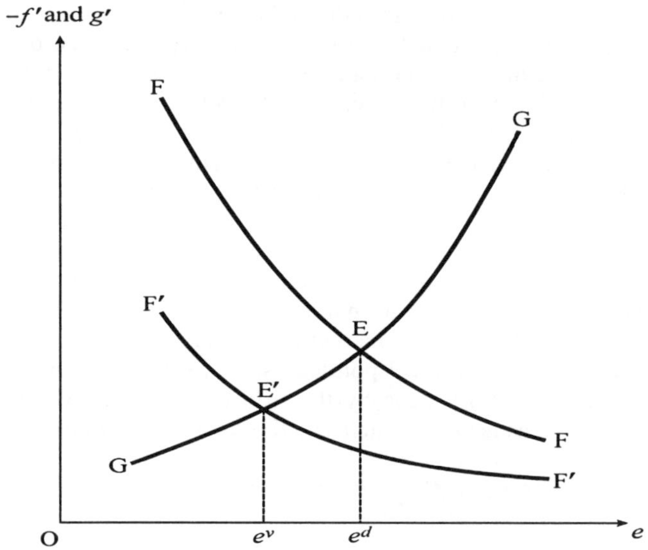

Figure 10.1 Determination of Optimal Effort

Note that the first-order condition and thus the optimal output do not depend on the effort, since effort is assumed to affect the 'fixed' cost of production only.[10] Let us use a superscript m to represent the equilibrium value of a variable when the home firm is a monopolist; for example, x^m is the optimal output chosen by the firm and p^m is the resulting market price. The corresponding nominal profit of the firm is equal to

$$\theta(x^m;e) = p(x^m)x^m - cx^m - f(e). \tag{10.5}$$

In stage 1, the firm chooses the level of effort to maximise its net profit, which is the nominal profit minus the cost of effort:

$$\pi(e) = \theta(x^m,e) - g(e).$$

The first-order condition is

$$-f'(e) = g'(e), \tag{10.6}$$

where condition (10.5) has been used. Note that the output does not appear in condition (10.6), meaning that the optimal level of effort is independent of the output. Denote the optimal effort by e^m. The second-order condition is

$$-f''(e^m) - g''(e^m) < 0,$$

which is satisfied because of conditions (10.1) and (10.2).

Condition (10.6) and the optimal effort can be illustrated graphically. As explained earlier, schedules *FF* and *GG* in Figure 10.1 represent $-f'(e)$ and $g'(e)$ respectively. This means that the optimal effort is obtained from the intersecting point *E* between schedules *FF* and *GG*.

3. RIVALRY BETWEEN TWO FIRMS

We now introduce a foreign firm to the above model. Suppose that there exists a foreign firm, which is capable of producing the same product in the local economy and supplying it to the local market. For simplicity we assume that the foreign firm has no production in its own country.[11] For the time being we consider the case of duopoly, with the foreign firm and the local firm producing and competing in a Cournot fashion. An asterisk distinguishes variables of the foreign firm. In particular it is facing a constant marginal cost c^* and a 'fixed' cost of production $f^*(e^*)$ after spending an effort of e^* and paying a cost of $g^*(e^*)$.

The two firms, however, have asymmetric positions. The foreign firm, being a newcomer in the local market, is in a disadvantageous position as compared with the home firm: it lacks good knowledge of the local political, economic, social and legal systems and, as compared with a home firm, usually has a less developed relationship with local suppliers and possibly wholesalers and retailers, and could have a cultural gap in the production process. Therefore a foreign firm producing in another country must have some ownership advantages such as a more advanced technology over the home firms. To capture these two features, we make the following assumptions.

Assumption I: $f^*(e^*) > f(e^d)$, *where* e^* *and* e^d *(to be determined later) are the efforts chosen by the foreign and local firms when competing in a Cournot way respectively.*

Assumption II: $c^* < c$.

The first assumption is to capture the fact that the foreign firm is in a disadvantageous position in producing the good in the local economy, while the second assumption represents the superior technology the foreign firm has with respect to the home firm.

To analyse the present case of rivalry between the firms, we first have to find out how the entry of the foreign firm may affect the home firm's 'fixed' cost. The answer is nothing, which means that the effort chosen by the home firm is not affected by the presence of the foreign firm. The reason, as shown by condition (10.6), is that the home firm's choice of effort is not affected by its output.

As in the previous section, the competition between both firms can be analysed in two separate stages. In the first stage, they choose the level of efforts, thus fixing the 'fixed' cost of production. They then compete in output. Let us analyse the second stage first. With the levels of effort chosen, their nominal profit can be written as

$$\theta(x, x^*; e) = p(x + x^*)x - cx - f(e) \tag{10.7}$$

$$\theta^*(x, x^*; e^*) = p(x + x^*)x^* - c^*x^* - f^*(e^*). \tag{10.8}$$

Assuming Cournot competition, the first-order conditions for profit maximisation are[12]

$$p + p'x = c \tag{10.9}$$

$$p + p'x^* = c^*. \tag{10.10}$$

These are of course the firms' reaction functions, which are illustrated by schedules *HH* and *FF*, respectively, in Figure 10.2. The intersecting point of the two schedules, *N*, is the Nash equilibrium. Let us denote the Nash equilibrium outputs of the home and foreign firms by x^d and x^{*d} respectively. Based on Assumption II and the assumption of a falling marginal revenue curve, the home firm, with a higher marginal cost, has a smaller market share. For a 'stable' equilibrium, it is assumed that schedule *HH* is steeper than schedule *FF* in a region close to point *N*.[13] For a reason to be made clear later, let us treat the home firm's marginal cost c as a parameter and determine the output effects of a change in c. Differentiate (10.9) and (10.10) and rearrange the terms to give

$$\begin{bmatrix} 2p' + p''x & p' + p''x \\ p' + p''x^* & 2p' + p''x^* \end{bmatrix} \begin{bmatrix} dx \\ dx^* \end{bmatrix} = \begin{bmatrix} dc \\ 0 \end{bmatrix}. \tag{10.11}$$

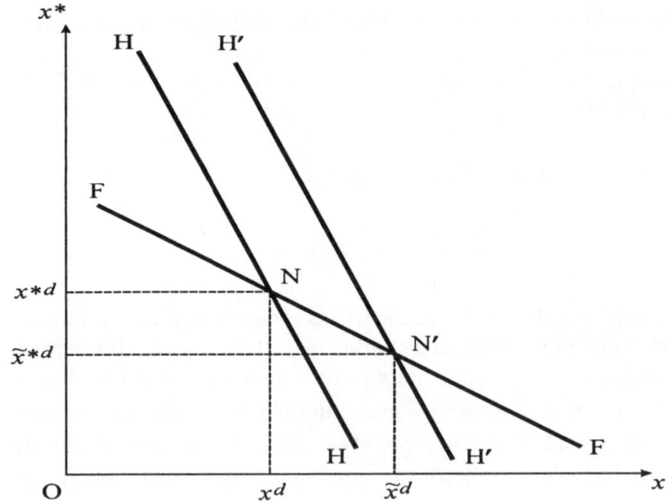

Figure 10.2 Equilibria of the Duopoly Option

Denote the determinant of the matrix in (10.11) by $D=(2p'+p''x)(2p'+p''x^*)-(p'+p''x)(p'+p''x^*)>0$, where the sign comes from the 'stability' condition. Solving (10.11), we have

$$\frac{dx}{dc}=\frac{2p'+p''x^*}{D}<0 \tag{10.12}$$

$$\frac{dx^*}{dc}=-\frac{p'+p''x^*}{D}>0, \tag{10.13}$$

where the sign comes from the assumption that p'' is either negative or sufficiently small in magnitude if positive. Assumptions (10.12) and (10.13) imply that a drop in c will encourage the home firm's production but discourage that of the foreign firm. This result is also shown in Figure 10.2. From (10.11), a drop in c shifts the home firm's reaction curve to the right but the foreign firm's reaction curve remains unchanged. The new Nash equilibrium point, N', represents a higher output of the home firm but a lower output of the foreign firm.

Assumptions (10.12) and (10.13) can be combined to give the effect on the total output

$$\frac{d(x+x^*)}{dc}=\frac{p'}{D}<0, \tag{10.14}$$

which means that a drop in c will encourage a larger aggregate output of the firms.

In the first stage, both firms choose the optimal levels of efforts to maximise their net profits

$$\pi(e) = \theta(x^d, e) - g(e)$$

$$\pi^*(e^*) = \theta^*(x^{*d}, e^*) - g^*(e^*).$$

Based on (10.6), the effort chosen by each firm is independent of the output. Therefore the first-order conditions are similar to (10.6). As we did earlier, we use the superscript d to represent the equilibrium value of a variable in the present case; for example, e^d and e^{*d} are the Nash equilibrium outputs chosen by the firms, with the corresponding costs of efforts given by $g^d \equiv g(e^d)$ and $g^{*d} \equiv g^*(e^{*d})$, and the profits of the firms given by $\theta^d \equiv \theta(x^d, e^d)$, $\theta^{*d} \equiv \theta^*(x^{*d}, e^{*d})$, $\pi^d \equiv \pi(e^d)$ and $\pi^{*d} \equiv \pi^*(e^{*d})$ respectively. Note that, because the chosen effort is independent of the output level, the home firm chooses the same effort in the present duopoly case as in the previous monopoly case, i.e., $e^m = e^d$.

As explained earlier, the disadvantageous position of the foreign firm is represented by a higher 'fixed' cost of production, i.e., $f^*(e^{*d}) > f(e^d)$.

4. A JOINT VENTURE OF THE FIRMS

In this section, we consider an alternative option for the foreign firm to produce the good in the local economy: forming a joint venture with the home firm. It is formed under the following assumptions:

1. In the presence of a joint venture, both firms would not produce separately.
2. The joint venture will have a marginal cost of c^* and a 'fixed' cost of production $f(e) + \phi$, where $\phi > 0$ and e is to be chosen by the home firm.
3. The joint venture chooses an output, X, to maximise the following nominal profit:

$$\Theta(X; e) = p(X)X - c^*X - f(e) - \phi. \tag{10.15}$$

4. The home firm receives a fraction s, $0 \le s \le 1$, of the resulting profit, and the foreign firm receives the rest. The determination of s will be explained later.

Let us explain these assumptions. Assumption 1 is a normal phenomenon. One reason is that both firms are willing to stop producing separately as a goodwill gesture of cooperation. Assumption 2 represents the basis for the two firms to cooperate in the present chapter: the joint venture uses the foreign firm's advanced technology, in terms of a lower marginal cost, and the home firm's better knowledge of the domestic market, leading to a lower 'fixed' cost from effort. The variable ϕ refers to the cost of cooperation, which includes the costs of coordination, communication, and possibly friction between the firms. For simplicity, we assume that ϕ is given exogenously. Assumption 3 seems to be a natural one, but it has two implications. First, the level of effort has yet to be determined. This is left for the home firm to choose. Second, the cost of effort, $g(e)$, has not been included in the nominal profit of the joint venture. These two implications require further explanation.

Since effort is a variable difficult to quantify, measure and verify, the present model involves moral hazard by the home firm.[14] Even if both firms sign an agreement that requires the home firm to spend a particular time on lowering the fixed cost, it is difficult to determine or verify in court how much effort the home firm has actually spent and what the cost of the effort is. In the present model, with perfect information and no uncertainty, the foreign firm can determine how much effort the home firm will choose to spend under the present conditions.[15] It is just that it is difficult to require the home firm to choose a particular level of effort or to verify that the home firm has chosen an effort different from the one stated in an agreement.[16] The foreign firm knows well functions $f(e)$ and $g(e)$, but it is difficult to verify in court what effort the home firm has spent.

Based on the above assumptions and description, we consider the following three-stage game when a joint venture is formed. In the first stage, the home firm chooses the optimal level of effort. This in turn determines the 'fixed' cost of production, $f(e)$. In the second stage, both firms decide how to share the nominal profit of the joint venture and, in the last stage, they choose an output to maximise the nominal profit of the joint venture. In each stage, each firm is aware of what they will choose in later stages.

We first examine the third stage. The joint venture chooses x to maximise the profit defined by (10.15). The first-order condition is

$$p + p'X = c^*. \tag{10.16}$$

Note that this condition is similar to the first-order condition (10.4) for the home firm when it is a monopolist because in both cases there is only one single supplier. Let the optimal output be denoted by X^v, where the superscript v represents a variable in the presence of this joint venture. Furthermore, in both cases, the optimal output is independent of the level of effort chosen by the home firm. There is a difference between the two cases, however, because the marginal cost of the joint venture is lower than that of the home firm, as stated in Assumption 2. Thus (10.16) yields a higher output and a higher profit than does (10.4). Denote the resulting nominal profit of the joint venture by

$$\hat{\Theta}(e) \equiv \Theta(X^v; e) = p(X^v)X^v - c^* X^v - f(e) - \phi. \tag{10.17}$$

Note that even though the optimal output of the joint venture is not a function of the effort chosen by the home firm, $\hat{\Theta}(e)$ is.

In the second stage, the two firms share the nominal profit in a Nash bargaining game. In such a game, we assume that the alternative to a joint venture is a duopolistic situation as described above. In the latter situation, the local and foreign firms will receive nominal profits equal to θ^d and θ^{*d}, respectively. As a result, the home firm's share of the profit of the IJV, s, is chosen to solve the following problem:

$$\max_s \left[s\hat{\Theta}(e) - \theta^d \right] \left[(1-s)\hat{\Theta}(e) - \theta^{*d} \right]. \tag{10.18}$$

The first-order condition is

$$s\hat{\Theta}(e) = \frac{\hat{\Theta}(e) - \theta^{*d} + \theta^d}{2}. \tag{10.19}$$

Note that the left-hand side of (10.19) is the portion of the joint venture's nominal profit the home firm receives, based on the effort chosen by the home firm. Denote the share that satisfies (10.19) by $s(e)$, which is a function of the home firm's effort.

In the first stage of the game, the home firm chooses its effort to maximise its net profit. Its problem is

$$\max_s \pi(e) = s(e)\hat{\Theta}(e) - g(e). \tag{10.20}$$

Making use of (10.19), (10.20) reduces to

$$\max_s \pi(e) = \frac{\hat{\Theta}(e) - \theta^{*d} + \theta^d}{2} - g(e). \tag{10.21}$$

Using condition (10.17), the first-order condition becomes

$$-\frac{1}{2}f'(e) = g'(e). \tag{10.22}$$

The optimal effort can be illustrated in Figure 10.1. Schedule $F'F'$ is constructed so that vertically it is half-way between schedule FF and the horizontal axis. The equilibrium point is the intersecting point E' between schedules $F'F'$ and GG. A comparison between points E and E' shows that, with the formation of the joint venture, the home firm chooses to spend less effort, e^v, which results in a higher 'fixed' cost of production $f(e^v)$ as compared with what it does when it produces alone or as a duopolist, e^d. Denote the resulting profit of the joint venture by $\Theta^v \equiv \hat{\Theta}(e^v)$. Therefore the nominal profits of the home and foreign firms are respectively equal to

$$s\Theta^v = \frac{\Theta^v - \theta^{*d} + \theta^d}{2} \tag{10.23}$$

$$(1-s)\Theta^v = \frac{\Theta^v + \theta^{*d} - \theta^d}{2}. \tag{10.24}$$

The net profit of the home firm is $\pi^v = s\Theta^v - g(e^v)$. Because the foreign firm does not have to spend any effort in forming the joint venture, its nominal profit is the same as its net profit, i.e., $\pi^{*v} = (1-s)\Theta^v$.

5. CHOOSING BETWEEN JOINT VENTURE AND SEPARATE PRODUCTION

After explaining how a joint venture can be formed, the next question is whether the firms prefer to have a joint venture or to produce the good separately as duopolists. Each firm chooses the option that produces a higher profit. Let us denote the outcome joint venture by V and the outcome of separate production by D. We then say that $V \succ D$ if *both* firms prefer a joint venture with each other to separate production, and that $D \succ V$ if at least one firm prefers separate production to a joint venture.

5.1 The home firm

The home firm prefers a joint venture to a duopoly production if and only if it gets a higher net profit:

$$s\Theta^v - g^v > \pi^d = \theta^d - g^d. \qquad (10.25)$$

Making use of condition (10.23) and rearranging terms, (10.25) reduces to

$$\Theta^v > \theta^d + \theta^{*d} - 2(g^d - g^v). \qquad (10.26)$$

Consider the following condition:

Condition A: $\Theta^v > \theta^d + \theta^{*d}$.

Condition A means that the net profit of the joint venture is higher than the total net profits of the firms when producing separately. From (10.22), we know that $g^d > g^v$. Thus Condition A implies (10.26).

5.2 The foreign firm

The foreign firm prefers a joint venture if and only if its profit share is larger than the net profit under duopoly competition:

$$(1-s)\Theta^v > \pi^{*d} = \theta^{*d} - g^{*d}. \qquad (10.27)$$

Making use of condition (10.24), (10.27) reduces to

$$\Theta^v > \theta^d + \theta^{*d} - 2g^{*d}. \qquad (10.28)$$

It is easy to see that Condition A implies (10.28).

A joint venture will be formed if and only if both firms prefer the joint venture to separate production. Thus we have the following proposition.

Proposition 1: *(a)* $V \succ D$ *if and only if conditions* (10.26) *and* (10.28) *are satisfied. (b)* $V \succ D$ *if Condition A is satisfied.*

Since Condition A is a sufficient condition for the formation of a joint venture, let us analyse it more carefully. It states that the nominal profit of the joint venture is greater than the sum of the nominal profits of the firms when producing separately as Cournot duopolists. Using the definitions of these nominal profits, we have

$$\begin{aligned}\Theta^v-\theta^d-\theta^{*d} &= \left[p(X^v)X^v-c^*X^v-f(e^v)-\phi\right]-\left[p(q^d)x^d-cx^d-f(e^d)\right]\\ &-\left[p(q^d)x^{*d}-c^*x^{*d}-f^*(e^{*d})\right]\\ &=\left[p(X^v)X^v-c^*X^v-f(e^d)\right]-\left[p(q^d)x^d-c^*x^d-f(e^d)\right]\\ &-\left[p(q^d)x^{*d}-c^*x^{*d}-f(e^d)\right]+(c-c^*)x^d\\ &+\left[f^*(e^{*d})-f(e^d)\right]+\left[f(e^d)-f(e^v)\right]-\phi.\end{aligned} \tag{10.29}$$

Let us analyse condition (10.29). The individual terms on its RHS have the following signs:

(a) $\left[p(X^v)X^v-c^*X^v-f(e^d)\right]-\left[p(q^d)x^d-c^*x^d-f(e^d)\right]$
$-\left[p(q^d)x^{*d}-c^*x^{*d}-f(e^d)\right]>0$;

(b) $(c-c^*)x^d>0$;

(c) $\left[f^*(e^{*d})-f(e^d)\right]>0$; and

(d) $\left[f(e^d)-f(e^v)\right]<0$.

The term in (a) represents the difference between the maximum profit when two identical firms produce jointly and the sum of their profits when they produce non-cooperatively, which is positive because a joint venture can better exploit the monopoly power. The signs of the terms in (b) and (c) are due to Assumptions 2 and 1, respectively. The term in (d) is negative due to the moral hazard problem as explained before. As a result, Condition A is not necessarily satisfied.

Proposition 2: *If the cooperation cost is sufficiently small, the home firm always prefers an IJV to separate production. If the cooperation cost is sufficiently small and if the drop in the home firm's effort will be sufficiently small, then Condition A is satisfied and* $V \succ D$.

Proof. To see the first statement, assume that the home firm chooses the same effort e^m when cooperating with the foreign firm as it does as a monopolist (or duopolist). Then the joint profit of both firms must be higher because both firms act as a single monopolist and because both firms have complementary technologies. Consequently the home firm must get a higher profit. If the home firm chooses the effort it supplies optimally, its profit will be higher, or not lower. To see the second statement note that, under the given conditions, term (d) and ϕ in (10.29) are sufficiently small and the RHS is positive, implying Condition A. By Proposition 1, $V \succ D$.

Proposition 3: *$V \succ D$ if (i) condition* (10.28) *is satisfied and (ii)* $g^{*d} < (g^d - g^v)$.

Proof. Conditions (i) and (ii) imply condition (10.26), so both firms prefer an IJV.

6. TECHNOLOGY SPILLOVER AND BREAK-UP OF A JOINT VENTURE

So far we have been focusing on a one-period model. Although the joint venture makes use of the advantages of both firms, the technology of each firm remains unchanged. We now turn to a two-period model to analyse why in some cases a joint venture is formed but breaks up in the future.

We assume that in each of the two periods, the firms have the option of forming a joint venture (*V*) and the option of producing separately as duopolists (*D*). To represent different outcomes in these two periods, we use a duplet (*i*, *j*), where *i*, *j* = *V*, *D*. In general, there are altogether four possible outcomes: (*V*, *V*), (*V*, *D*), (*D*, *V*) and (*D*, *D*).

The main feature of the present two-period model is that, when the firms form a joint venture, both are able to learn from each other. This leads to a change in the technology they use in the second period, thus affecting their choice between a joint venture and separate production.

We now analyse more carefully the decisions of the firms. First, let us be more explicit about how firms learn from each other. Recalling that the home firm is more efficient in terms of the 'fixed' cost of production but less efficient in terms of the marginal cost, we make the following simple assumptions:

(i) In the first period, both firms have the technology described in previous sections.
(ii) In the second period, the home firm has a marginal cost equal to δc^*, and the foreign firm faces a 'fixed' cost function of $\delta^* f(e)$ and has to pay an effort cost of $\delta^* g(e)$ if it spends an effort of e^*, where for all relevant values of *e*, δ and δ^* are positive constants, satisfying $1 < \delta < c / c^*$ and $1 < \delta^* < [f^*(e) + g^*(e)]/[f(e) + g(e)]$.
(iii) Learning is free.

Assumption (ii) means that the home firm learns from the foreign firm through a joint venture, and is able to reduce its marginal cost although the marginal cost is still greater than that of the foreign firm. Similarly, the foreign firm reduces its 'fixed' cost of production although the latter is greater than what the home firm has. The foreign firm learns not only how to change its 'fixed' cost but also the cost of its effort. Assumption (iii) is made to simplify our analysis.

Before we analyse the two-period model, let us examine how the technology spillovers may affect the two firms. Suppose that, after one period of cooperation in the form of a joint venture, both firms now want to compete as Cournot duopolists. This case can easily be compared with the one described in Section 3, except that the firms' technologies are different than before. Our main focus is how the profits may change after the firms have learned from each other.

We can again conceptually assume that the firms compete in two separate stages: in stage one they choose the level of effort and in stage two they compete in a Cournot way. Our analysis is simplified by the fact that the effort they choose is independent of the output. We thus can immediately get the following results. Since the home firm maintains the same 'fixed' cost of production and the same effort cost function as before, the home firm chooses the same effort as before, i.e., e^d. Since the foreign firm learns from the home firm in terms of the latter's 'fixed' cost and effort cost, the first-order condition of an optimal effort as expressed in (10.6) also applies to the foreign firm. This means that the foreign firm will also choose the same effort as the home firm, e^d.

As a result, the marginal cost and fixed cost of the home firm in the present case are δc^* ($< c$) and $f(e^d)$ respectively and those of the foreign firm are c^* and $\delta^* f(e^d)$ $\left[< f^*(e^d)\right]$. The Nash equilibrium can be derived using the technique described in Section 3 and can be compared with the Cournot equilibrium before the technology spillover. Because the marginal cost of the foreign firm is unchanged, its reaction function will remain the same as before, which is illustrated by *FF* in Figure 10.2. For the home firm, the reduction in marginal cost will encourage it to produce more for each production level of the foreign firm, meaning that its new reaction curve, such as $H'H'$ in Figure 10.2, is on the right of the original reaction curve, *HH*. Schedule $H'H'$ cuts schedule *FF* at the new Nash equilibrium point N'. Using a tilde and a superscript *d* to represent variables after technology spillover, let us denote the new equilibrium output of the home firm by $\tilde{x}^d$ and that of the foreign firm by $\tilde{x}^{*d}$. Comparing the new and initial Nash equilibrium points, we get $\tilde{x}^d > x^d$ and $\tilde{x}^{*d} < x^{*d}$. This confirms conditions (10.12) and (10.13).

How are the profits of the two firms affected by the technology spillovers? Let us consider first the home firm. Because the effort it chooses is independent of output level and thus is not affected by the spillover effect, the change in its net profit is equal to

$$\tilde{\pi}^d - \pi^d = \left[\tilde{p}^d \tilde{x}^d - \delta c^* \tilde{x}^d - f^d - g^d\right] - \left[p^d x^d - cx^d - f^d - g^d\right]$$
$$= \left[\left(\tilde{p}^d \tilde{x}^d - c\tilde{x}^d - f^d\right) - \left(p^d x^d - cx^d - f^d\right)\right] + \left(c - \delta c^*\right)\tilde{x}^d > 0 \qquad (10.30)$$

where the sign is due to the following factors:

(a) $\left[\left(\tilde{p}^d \tilde{x}^d - c\tilde{x}^d - f^d\right) - \left(p^d x^d - cx^d - f^d\right)\right] + \left(c - \delta c^*\right)\tilde{x}^d > 0$ because of a drop in the output of its rival; and

(b) $(c - \delta c^*)\tilde{x}^d > 0$ because of the spillover effect.

We now turn to the foreign firm. The change in its profit is equal to

$$\tilde{\pi}^{*d} - \pi^{*d} = \left[\tilde{p}^d \tilde{x}^{*d} - c^* \tilde{x}^{*d} - \tilde{f}^{*d} - \tilde{g}^{*d}\right] - \left[p^d x^{*d} - c^* x^{*d} - f^{*d} - g^{*d}\right]$$
$$= \left(\tilde{p}^d \tilde{x}^{*d} - c^* \tilde{x}^{*d}\right) - \left(p^d x^{*d} - c^* x^{*d}\right) + \left(-\tilde{f}^{*d} - \tilde{g}^{*d}\right) \qquad (10.31)$$
$$- \left(-f^{*d} - g^{*d}\right),$$

where $\tilde{f}^{*d} = \delta^* f(e^d)$ and $\tilde{g}^{*d} = \delta^* g(e^d)$. In analysing (10.31), note that we have

$$\left(-\tilde{f}^{*d} - \tilde{g}^{*d}\right) - \left(-f^{*d} - g^{*d}\right)$$
$$= \left[-\delta^* f(e^d) - \delta^* g(e^d)\right] - \left[-f^*(e^{*d}) - g(e^{*d})\right]$$
$$= \left\{\left[-\delta^* f(e^d) - \delta^* g(e^d)\right] - \left[-\delta^* f(e^{*d}) - \delta^* g(e^{*d})\right]\right\}$$
$$+ \left\{\left[-\delta^* f(e^{*d}) - \delta^* g(e^{*d})\right] - \left[-f^*(e^{*d}) - g^*(e^{*d})\right]\right\}.$$

To determine the sign of the change in profit given in (10.31), let us note the following factors:

(a) $\left(\tilde{p}^d \tilde{x}^{*d} - c^* \tilde{x}^{*d}\right) - \left(p^d x^{*d} - c^* x^{*d}\right) < 0$ because of an increase in the home firm's output;

(b) $\left\{\left[-\delta^* f(e^d) - \delta^* g(e^d)\right] - \left[-\delta^* f(e^{*d}) - \delta^* g(e^{*d})\right]\right\} > 0$ due to profit maximisation after the spillover; and

(c) $\left\{\left[-\delta^* f(e^{*d}) - \delta^* g(e^{*d})\right] - \left[-f^*(e^{*d}) - g^*(e^{*d})\right]\right\} > 0$ due to technology spillover.

Combining these factors together, we note that the sign of the change in profit given by (10.31) is ambiguous.

We now turn to the case in which the two firms choose to produce separately as duopolists in period 1. In this case there is no technology transfer, meaning that technologies of the firms remain the same in period 2. This means that (*D*, *V*) will not be an outcome in the present model. The reason is that if $D \succ V$ in period 1 then the firm(s) that prefers separate production will still prefer separate production in period 2. Thus we are left with three possible outcomes.

In the present two-period model, denote the sum of the discounted profits of the home firm by W_{ij} and that of the foreign firms by W_{ij}^*, where $i = d, v$ for the duopolist or joint venture outcome in period 1, respectively, and $j = d, v$ for those in period 2, respectively. Also denote the discount rates of the home and foreign firms by ρ and ρ^*, respectively. Therefore the two-period profits of the firms in the following three cases are as follows.

1. Outcome (*D*, *D*):

$$W_{dd} = (1+\rho)\pi^d \tag{10.32}$$

$$W_{dd}^* = (1+\rho^*)\pi^{*d}. \tag{10.33}$$

2. Outcome (*V*, *V*):

$$W_{vv} = (1+\rho)\pi^v \tag{10.34}$$

$$W_{vv}^* = (1+\rho^*)\pi^{*v}. \tag{10.35}$$

3. Outcome (*V*, *D*):

$$W_{vd} = \pi^v + \rho\tilde{\pi}^d \tag{10.36}$$

$$W_{vd}^* = \pi^{*v} + \rho^*\tilde{\pi}^{*d}. \tag{10.37}$$

It should be noted that if the firms form a joint venture in period 1 and if in period 2 the joint venture stays, the technology spillover will have no impacts on the firms' profits because the joint venture will still be using the marginal cost supplied by the foreign firm and the 'fixed' cost supplied by the home firm. Let us now compare these three outcomes. Our comparison can be divided into three parts.

6.1 (*V*, *V*) versus (*D*, *D*)

Conditions (10.32) and (10.33) indicate that the two-period profit of each firm is directly proportional to its profit in one period. Therefore $(V, V) \succ (D, D)$ if and only if $V \succ D$. See Propositions 1 and 2.

The options of the home firm can be illustrated in Figure 10.3, where the horizontal axis represents its (current value) net profit in period 1, π_1, and the vertical axis stands for its net profit in period 2, π_2. Different combinations of π_1 and π_2 that yield the same two-period profit of the home firm, $W_{dd} = \pi_1 + \rho\pi_2$, can be represented by one of the parallel iso-profit lines, each with a slope of $-1/\rho$. Line *AB* is an iso-profit line passing through the point (π^d, π^d). This line stands for the two-period profit with outcome (*D*, *D*). The net profits of the home firm under outcome (*V*, *V*) can be represented by a point on the 45°-line *OHK*. Therefore the home firm prefers (*V*, *V*) to (*D*, *D*) if and only if its net profits under outcome (*V*, *V*) is on the line segment *HK* above *H*.

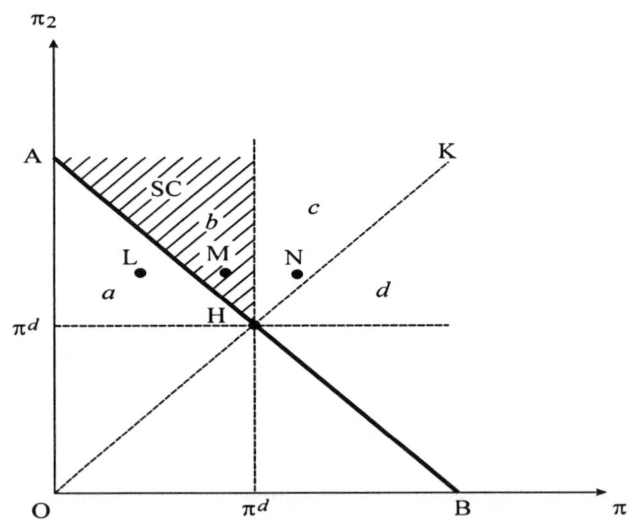

Figure 10.3 Options of the Home Firm

The choice of the foreign firm can be illustrated in the same way. Figure 10.4 represents the firm's period-1 net profit π_1^* (horizontal axis) and period 2 net profit π_2^* (vertical axis). *CD* is the iso-profit line with a slope of $-1/\rho^*$ and passing through point *F* (π^{*d}, π^{*d}). *OFG* is the 45°-line from the origin.

Consequently the foreign firm prefers (*V*, *V*) to (*D*, *D*) if and only if its net profit under outcome (*V*, *V*) is on the line segment *FG* above *F*.

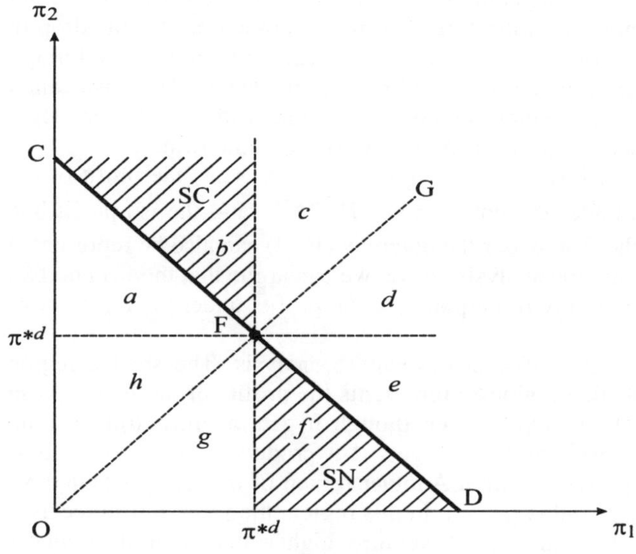

Figure 10.4 Options of the Foreign Firm

6.2 (*V*, *D*) versus (*D*, *D*)

The question now is, if the firms are going to produce separately as duopolists in the second period, does it make any sense to form a joint venture in the first period? To answer this question, let us recall that in the presence of a joint venture, both firms learn from each other and are able to reduce their costs. However, the two firms are affected differently by the technology spillovers. As explained earlier, the joint venture allows the home firm to achieve a higher profit in the second period, but the foreign firm may be hurt by the joint venture. The impacts of the joint venture have to be taken into account when comparing between these two outcomes.

The profit of the home firm, when a joint venture is formed in the first period, can be represented by a point (π^v, $\tilde{\pi}^d$) in Figure 10.3. As explained earlier, $\tilde{\pi}^d > \pi^d$. Three possible points representing possible profits of the home firm are shown in the diagram: *L*, *M* and *N*, all of which depict a higher second-period profit than π^d. Point *L* represents a lower two-period profit for the home firm than under (*D*, *D*). Thus (*V*, *D*) is dominated by (*D*, *D*). At point *N*, the home firm gets a higher profit in each of the period under the outcome (*V*, *D*) and thus prefers it to the outcome (*D*, *D*). Point *M* shows an interesting case. This point means that the formation of a joint venture lowers the current value of the home firm's profit, $\pi^v < \pi^d$. However, because point *M* is above line *AB*, the home firm is able to gain enough in the second period through learning from the foreign firm to compensate for the drop in its profit in the first period. We call this type of cooperation with the foreign firm a *strategic cooperation*. The shaded region labelled *SC* (and also called region *b*) in Figure 10.3 represents possible profits with which a strategic cooperation with the foreign firm is preferred by the home firm.

We now turn to the foreign firm. Figure 10.4 represents the profit of the firm in each period under the outcome (*D*, *D*), π^{*d}, and the iso-profit line *CD*. The profits of the firm under the outcome (*V*, *D*) can also be represented in the figure. Following the analysis above, we can argue that the firm prefers (*V*, *D*) to (*D*, *D*) if and only if the point for the profits under (*V*, *D*) is above line *CD*.

Two regions in Figure 10.4 deserve more analysis. The shaded region labelled *SC* (also labelled region *b*) represents the profits of the foreign firm that it prefers (*V*, *D*) to (*D*, *D*) even though it gets a profit from a joint venture in period 1 less than what it gets if it produces separately. This is what we call *strategic cooperation*. Another region of interest is labelled *SN* (also labelled region *f*) and is shaded. In this region, the foreign firm receives a profit in period 1 from a joint venture higher than that it produces separately as a duopolist. However forming a joint venture causes a big drop in the profit in period 2 when both firms compete in separate production as compared with what it can get in the same period should there be no cooperation. The cooperation in period 1 is thus too costly to the foreign firm, which then prefers not to cooperate. We call this case *strategic non-cooperation*.

6.3 (*V*, *V*) versus (*V*, *D*)

We now turn to another case: both firms cooperate in period 1 but in period 2 they have the option of continuing the cooperation or breaking up the joint venture. For this case, the choice boils down to what the firms can get in period 2 in these two options: joint venture and duopolistic production. Such comparison has been done earlier, except that the two firms have improved their technologies. For example, in period 2 the home firm chooses to keep the joint venture if and only if the condition

$$\pi^v > \tilde{\pi}^d \tag{10.38}$$

holds or, applying condition (10.26), if and only if

$$\Theta^v > \tilde{\theta}^d + \tilde{\theta}^{*d} - 2(\tilde{g}^d - g^v). \tag{10.39}$$

The decision criterion for the home firm can also be illustrated in Figure 10.3. Note that its net profits in the two periods under outcome (*V*, *V*) are represented by a point on line *OHK*. Therefore condition (10.38) means that the net profits (π^v, $\tilde{\pi}^d$) under outcome (*V*, *D*) are depicted by a point below line *OHK*.

Similarly, in period 2 the foreign firm prefers to keep the joint venture if and only if

$$\pi^{*v} > \tilde{\pi}^{*d}, \tag{10.40}$$

or, applying condition (10.28), if and only if

$$\Theta^v > \tilde{\theta}^d + \tilde{\theta}^{*d} - 2\tilde{g}^{*d}. \tag{10.41}$$

Using the same argument as for the home firm, we can conclude that the foreign firm chooses to keep the joint venture if its net profits (π^{*v}, $\tilde{\pi}^{*d}$) under outcome (*V*, *D*) is represented by a point below line *OFG* in Figure 10.4.

6.4 The optimal choice

So far we have been comparing only any two of the outcomes. We now consider these three options together. We first consider the home firm and summarise its decisions by the following rules:

(i) The home firm prefers (*V*, *V*) to (*D*, *D*) if and only if (π^v, π^v) is on line segment *HK* and above *H*.

(ii) The home firm prefers (*V*, *D*) to (*D*, *D*) if and only if (π^v, $\tilde{\pi}^d$) is above *AB*.

(iii) The home firm prefers (*V*, *V*) to (*V*, *D*) if and only if (π^v, $\tilde{\pi}^d$) is below *OHK*.

In Figure 10.3 we identify four regions *a*, *b*, *c* and *d* and try to determine how the decision of the home firm will be affected if (π^v, $\tilde{\pi}^d$) is represented by a point in one of these regions. Note that we neglect the area below a horizontal line passing through point *H* because, if a joint venture is formed in period 1, the profit of the home firm in period 2 will be higher than π^d through technology spillover. Based on the three points in the above summary, we can make the following conclusions concerning the choice of the firm:

(a) The home firm will choose (*V*, *D*) if (π^v, $\tilde{\pi}^d$) is in region *b* or *c*. To see why, note that in one of these regions, (π^v, $\tilde{\pi}^d$) is above *AB* and *OHK*.

So by rules (ii) and (iii), (*V*, *D*) dominates. Note that region *b* is the region of strategic cooperation.

(b) The home firm will choose (*V*, *V*) if $(\pi^v, \tilde{\pi}^d)$ is in region *d*. In this case, (π^v, π^v) is on line segment *HK* and above *H* and $(\pi^v, \tilde{\pi}^d)$ is below *OHK*. The result follows from rules (i) and (iii).

(c) The home firm will choose (*D*, *D*) if $(\pi^v, \tilde{\pi}^d)$ is in region *a*. In this case, (π^v, π^v) is not on line segment *HK* and $(\pi^v, \tilde{\pi}^d)$ is below *AB*. The result follows from rules (i) and (ii).

The above results mean that if $(\pi^v, \tilde{\pi}^d)$ is in region *b*, *c* or *d*, the home firm prefers to have a joint venture in period 1. If it is in region *b* or *c*, then the firm prefers to break away from the joint venture in period 2.

We can now turn to the foreign firm. Rules similar to rules (i) to (iii) given above can be stated for the firm in its decision. The decision criterion can also be stated in terms of the location of the net profit point $(\pi^{*v}, \tilde{\pi}^{*d})$. One difference between these two firms is that, with duopolistic production in period 2, the foreign firm may experience a drop in its net profit if a joint venture is formed in period 1. As a result, the region below a horizontal line through point *F* cannot be excluded for a point representing $(\pi^{*v}, \tilde{\pi}^{*d})$. In Figure 10.4, regions *a* to *h* can be identified.

(a) The foreign firm will choose (*V*, *D*) if $(\pi^{*v}, \tilde{\pi}^{*d})$ is in region *b* or *c*. In one of these regions, $(\pi^{*v}, \tilde{\pi}^{*d})$ is above *CD* and *OFG*. Note that region *b* is the region of strategic cooperation.

(b) The foreign firm will choose (*V*, *V*) if $(\pi^{*v}, \tilde{\pi}^{*d})$ is in region *d* or *e*. (π^{*v}, π^{*v}) is on line segment *FG* and above *F* and $(\pi^{*v}, \tilde{\pi}^{*d})$ is below *OFG*.

(c) The foreign firm will choose (*D*, *D*) if $(\pi^{*v}, \tilde{\pi}^{*d})$ is in regions *a*, *f*, *g* or *h*. In this case, (π^{*v}, π^{*v}) is not on line segment *FG* and $(\pi^{*v}, \tilde{\pi}^{*d})$ is below *CD*. Note that region *f* is the region of strategic non-cooperation. This means that in this region the foreign firm will not choose to have a joint venture and then a break-up in period 2, but it will prefer to maintain separate production throughout the two periods.

Let us now bring both firms together and find out the actual outcome in different cases. The following rules can be used to determine the outcome:

(a) If both firms prefer the same outcome, that outcome will happen.

(b) If any one of the firms prefers (*D*, *D*), a joint venture will not be formed and (*D*, *D*) must be the outcome.

(c) If a firm prefers (*V*, *V*) while the other firm wants (*V*, *D*), then (*V*, *V*) will not be formed and the former firm will choose between (*V*, *D*) and (*D*, *D*). Such decision of the former firm will dominate and it will become the actual outcome.

Using the above the rules, the outcomes are given in Table 10.1.

Table 10.1 Outcomes in Different Cases

	Home Firm H		
Foreign Firm F	(*V*, *V*)	(*V*, *D*)	(*D*, *D*)
(*V*, *V*)	(*V*, *V*)	?	(*D*, *D*)
(*V*, *D*)	(*V*, *D*)	(*V*, *D*)	(*D*, *D*)
(*D*, *D*)	(*D*, *D*)	(*D*, *D*)	(*D*, *D*)

Note: The entry '?' means that the outcome is (*V*, *D*) if $(\pi^{*v}, \tilde{\pi}^{*d})$ is in region *e* in Figure 10.4 or is (*D*, *D*) if $(\pi^{*v}, \tilde{\pi}^{*d})$ is in region *f*.

In Table 10.1, the first row shows different options of the home firm (H) while the first column gives the options of the foreign firm (F). The other cells show the outcomes based on the preferences of the two firms and rules (i) to (iii). Note that, if the foreign firm prefers (*V*, *V*) while the home firm wants (*V*, *D*), the foreign firm is left with the options of (*V*, *D*) and (*D*, *D*). What it chooses depends on the location of $(\pi^{*v}, \tilde{\pi}^{*d})$ in Figure 10.4. If, on the other hand, the home firm prefers (*V*, *V*) while the foreign firm wants (*V*, *D*), the home firm will choose (*V*, *D*) from the remaining options because, if a joint venture is formed in period 1, it can have a higher profit when producing as a duopolist in period 2 than what it can have in the same period if no joint venture is formed.

7. CONCLUDING REMARKS

In this chapter we provided a theory to explain why a MNC and a local firm choose to form an IJV and why they decide to dissolve it sometime later. Our theory has two important features: moral hazard and technology spillover. The presence of moral hazard means that an IJV may not be beneficial to both firms and so there are cases in which at least one of the firms prefers not to have a joint venture. Technology spillover means that in the presence of a joint venture the firms learn from each other and are able to improve their technology. It is the technology spillover that is the key in our theory to the formation of an IJV and its break-up in the future.

In this chapter we introduced the concepts of *strategic cooperation* and *strategic non-cooperation*. Strategic cooperation exists if one of the firms is willing to sacrifice in the short run in forming a joint venture if the joint venture can bring a bigger future gain. Strategic non-cooperation, on the other hand, is the case when a firm chooses not to form a joint venture even though it will bring a short-term benefit. This chapter shows that the usual one-period analysis of joint ventures may give misleading results.

ACKNOWLEDGEMENTS

Thanks are due to an anonymous reviewer and the participants at the workshop on 'International Economics and Asia' held on July 19 – 21, 2000 at City University of Hong Kong. This project is partially supported by the Competitive Earmarked Grant for Research (No. 9040320).

NOTES

1. See, for example, Beamish (1985), Benito and Gripsrud (1992), Blodgett (1991), Gomes-Casseres (1989), Hennart (1988), Kogut, (1988b), Lee and Beamish, (1995), Perlmutter and Heenan (1986) and Reynolds (1984).
2. See Wong (1995, Chapter 13) for a recent survey of the literature.
3. See, for example, Blodgett (1991), Kogut (1988b), Kogut and Singh (1988) and Leung (1998).
4. Harvard Multinational Enterprise Project.
5. Termination is called 'instability' in Franko (1971) and Gomes-Casseres (1987). Following Franko (1971), there are three reasons why an international joint venture would terminate: (a) The joint venture is totally liquidated, i.e., the operation is terminated or all the assets are sold or scrapped; (b) The ownership changes even though the joint venture is still operating, e.g., the joint venture is sold to the local partner or a third party; (c) The foreign firm (i.e., the MNC) may buy out the joint venture from the local partner and create a wholly-owned subsidiary. Gomes-Casseres (1987) points out that a wholly-owned subsidiary can terminate if it is liquidated or sold to local firms, or if the MNC sells part of the equity of the wholly-owned subsidiary and changes the venture form to a joint venture. The termination rate of international joint ventures is the number of joint ventures terminated as a percentage of the total number of joint ventures. The termination rate of wholly-owned subsidiaries is defined in a similar way.
6. For example, it was reported that Krohne, a German manufacturer of electromagnetic flow meters, complained that its China partner in a joint venture was not working hard enough (Vanhonacker 1997).
7. In fact, technology spillover is often regarded as one of the major reasons for many developing countries to attract foreign investment and joint venture between local and foreign firms. See, for example, Miller et al. (1997).
8. The latter assumption implies that the demand curve is concave or not too convex to the origin so that the marginal revenue curve is downward sloping.
9. Note that an interior solution is assumed because the case with no output is not interesting in the present chapter. The second-order condition is assumed to hold.
10. The result will be different if the effort affects the marginal cost. For simplicity, this case is not considered in the present chapter.
11. It may be due to, for example, prohibitive transport costs or a prohibitive tariff.
12. This chapter ignores the uninteresting case in which one or both firms are not producing.
13. See Wong (1995). The 'stability' condition is satisfied if the demand curve is not too curved toward the origin.
14. Note that we assume that only the local firm is responsible for the 'fixed' cost, and thus moral hazard occurs in that firm only. Double moral hazard exists when both firms supply effort, but it is not needed for the results in the present chapter.
15. In the moral hazard literature, uncertainty is usually assumed. Effort is what an agent spends on improving the probability of a good state. By observing what state is going to happen, it is difficult to verify what effort an agent has chosen. However, if the preferences of the

agent are known publicly, other agents know what the amount of effort the agent will choose. In the present chapter, we avoid assuming uncertainty because we want to simplify our analysis and because including uncertainty will not change the results qualitatively. See Bruce and Wong (1996) for a model of moral hazard and insurance.

16. In the present model without uncertainty, the agreement between the two firms may include a requirement concerning the level of fixed cost, which is measurable and requires a certain effort made by the local firm. We do not consider this option in the present chapter because it is not the focus here. Rather, we want to examine how moral hazard may affect the formation of a joint venture.

REFERENCES

Beamish, Paul W. (1985), 'The characteristics of joint ventures in developed and developing countries', *Columbia Journal of World Business*, Fall, 13-19.

Benito, Gabriel R.G. and Geir Gripsrud (1992), 'The expansion of foreign direct investments: discrete rational location choices or a cultural learning process?', *Journal of International Business Studies*, Third Quarter, 461-76.

Blodgett, Linda Longfellow (1991), 'Partner contributions as predictors of equity share in international joint ventures', *Journal of International Business Studies*, First Quarter, 63-79.

Bruce, Neil and Kar-yiu Wong (1996), 'Moral hazard, monitoring costs, and optimal government intervention', *Journal of Risk and Uncertainty*, **12**, 77-90.

Chowdhury, Jafor (1992), 'Performance of international joint ventures and wholly owned foreign subsidiaries: a comparative perspective', *Management International Review*, **32**, 115-33.

Franko, Lawrence G. (1971), *Joint Venture Survival in Multinational Corporations*, New York: Praeger Publishing.

Geringer, J. Michael and Louis Hebert (1991), 'Measuring performance of international joint ventures', *Journal of International Business Studies*, **22**, 249-63.

Gomes-Casseres, Benjamin (1987), 'Joint venture instability: is it a problem?', *Columbia Journal of World Business*, Summer, 97-102.

Gomes-Casseres, Benjamin (1989), 'Joint ventures in the face of global competition', *Sloan Management Review*, Spring, 17-26.

Hennart, Jean-Francois (1988), 'A transaction costs theory of equity joint ventures', *Strategic Management Journal*, **9**, 361-74.

Kogut, Bruce (1988a), 'Joint ventures: theoretical and empirical perspectives', *Strategic Management Journal*, **9**, 319-32.

Kogut, Bruce (1988b), 'A study of the life cycle of joint ventures', *Management International Review*, Special Issue, 39-52.

Kogut, Bruce and Harbir Singh (1988), 'The effect of national culture on the choice of entry mode', *Journal of International Business Studies*, **19**, 411-32.

Lee, Chol and Paul W. Beamish, (1995), 'The characteristics and performance of Korean joint ventures in LDCs', *Journal of International Business Studies*, Third Quarter, 637-54.

Leung, Wing-fai (1997), 'The duration times of international joint ventures and foreign wholly-owned subsidiaries', *Applied Economics*, **29**, 1255-69.

Leung, Wing-fai (1998), 'A model of coexistence of international joint ventures and

foreign wholly-owned subsidiaries', *Japan and the World Economy*, 10, 233-52.
Li, J. and S. Guisinger (1992), 'The globalization of service multinationals in the "Triad" regions: Japan, Western Europe and North America', *Journal of International Business Studies*, **23**, 675-96.
Miller, R., Glen, J., Jaspersen, F. and Y. Karmokolias (1997). 'International joint ventures in developing countries', *Finance & Development*, **34**, 26-29.
Parkhe, Arvind (1991), 'Interfirm diversity, organizational learning, and longevity in global strategic alliance', *Journal of International Business Studies*, Fourth Quarter, 579-601.
Perlmutter, Howard V. and David A. Heenan (1986), 'Cooperate to compete globally', *Harvard Business Review*, March-April, 136-52.
Reynolds, John I. (1984), 'The 'pinched shoe' effect of international joint ventures', *Columbia Journal of World Business*, Summer, 23-29.
Vanhonacker, Wilfred (1997), 'Entering in China: an unconventional approach', *Harvard Business Review*, March-April, 130-40.
Wong, Kar-yiu (1995), *International Trade in Goods and Factor Mobility*, Cambridge, Mass.: MIT Press.

11. The Innovation and Market Structure in General Equilibrium

Joshua S. Gans and Robin Stonecash

1. INTRODUCTION

Theoretical studies of the interdependency between market structure and innovation fall into two classes. The first is the partial equilibrium analyses that view innovation as generated by in-house research and development (R&D) expenditures. A seminal paper in this literature is Dasgupta and Stiglitz (1980). The second class is associated with endogenous growth theory. This literature considers the general equilibrium implications of innovations when knowledge spillovers between firms are important (Romer 1990 and Barro and Sala-i-Martin 1994). This literature often neglects the strategic implications of firm interaction that arise from an in-house R&D perspective.

There have been a few attempts to integrate the strategic implications of in-house R&D into general equilibrium models. The work of Van De Klundert and Smulders (1995, 1993) and Perotti (1995) represent examples of this. They confirm the general conclusion of the industrial organisation and growth literature that *average* innovation is too low and concentration too high relative to the social optimum. However, each of these papers generates this result assuming a very specific form of R&D technology – the production of in-house knowledge is purely labour intensive.

In this chapter, we show that this conclusion is not robust. Using a static general equilibrium model, it is shown that *the average level of innovation can exceed the social optimum.* This is because we assume that R&D uses final goods rather than labour. This is the 'lab-equipment' specification of Rivera-Batiz and Romer (1991). This assumption means that greater R&D, rather than depleting the resources available for final good production and, therefore, reducing effective market size, stimulates demand. Hence, it is possible that even the duplication of R&D expenditures under competitive situations can raise the incentives of firms to conduct R&D. This, however, represents a situation in which the private returns to entry exceed the social returns and, hence, the average as well as the total level of innovation can exceed socially optimal levels.

2. BASIC MODEL

This section presents the basic set-up and notation for the analysis to follow. Note the specific sectoral structure assumed here could easily be manipulated without altering the results to follow. We choose this specification, as we believe it to be the simplest form to capture the interactions between innovation, competition and labour or resource market equilibria.

2.1 Sectoral structure and technology

We model a closed economy that consists of two production sectors – an upstream and a downstream sector. Since our focus is on the market structure implications of innovation, we assume (as does Arrow 1962), that the downstream sector is perfectly competitive with all firms being price takers. These firms produce a homogeneous final good denoted *Y*, using a Cobb-Douglas technology, employing both labour, L_Y, and a composite of intermediate inputs, *X*:

$$Y = X^{\alpha} L_Y^{1-\alpha}, \quad 1 \geq \alpha \geq 0.$$

This production function exhibits constant returns to scale.[1] In addition, it is assumed that the downstream sector is competitive with all firms being price takers. This final good is assumed to be the numeraire.

Households consume final goods not used in production and supply one unit of labour inelastically for which they receive a competitive wage, *w*. The total labour endowment is $\overline{L}$. The existence of this labour constraint means that the parameter, $\overline{L}$, is a useful proxy for examining market size effects.

Intermediate inputs are produced in the upstream sector. In this chapter, we assume that these inputs are homogeneous. The total level of intermediate inputs produced is:

$$X = \sum_{i=1}^{N} x_i ,$$

where *i* indexes a firm and *N* is the total number of upstream producers.

Profit-maximising final goods producers will choose their labour and intermediate input demands to satisfy the following condition (using the Cobb-Douglas assumption):

$$wL_Y / pX = (1-\alpha)/\alpha , \tag{11.1}$$

where *p* is the per unit price of *X* (or, given the homogeneity assumption, x_i).

2.2 Research technology

Firms in the upstream sector are potential innovators. They produce goods using only labour according to a simple linear production function:

$$\hat{x}_i = \hat{l}_i / \Psi(\hat{F}_i).$$

F_i represents the level of process technology for firm *i*. The choice of F_i itself, is assumed to be endogenous. Higher choices of F_i mean a lower labour requirement; that is, $\Psi'(F_i) < 0$ with a choice of zero fixed costs making production prohibitively costly, i.e.,[2]

$$\Psi(F_i) \to \infty \text{ as } F_i \to 0.$$

We follow the assumptions of Dasgupta and Stiglitz (1980) and Gans (1998a, 1998b) by having a rich technology space, with $F_i \in \Re^+$.[3]

By choosing higher levels of F_i, firms raise the fixed cost incurred. We assume that innovating to a level, F_i, requires the use of F_i units of the final good. Thus, the research technology assumed here is akin to Rivera-Batiz and Romer's (1991) 'lab-equipment' model – the production of technology uses inputs with the same intensity as final good production.[4]

It is convenient to specify a functional form for Ψ:

$$\Psi(F_i) = F_i^{-\theta}.$$

This is the form used by Dasgupta and Stiglitz (1980), which is convenient because θ describes the elasticity of unit cost reductions with respect to research expenditures.

An alternative specification for modelling the impact of research and development would be to consider product innovation. This would be done by assuming that research resulted in products of higher quality (Grossman and Helpman 1991 and Sutton 1998). Such a specification is equivalent to the process innovation story here and so it simplifies matters to focus on one dimension exclusively.[5]

The presence of fixed costs, while being endogenous, means that the upstream sector cannot be perfectly competitive. That said, the competitiveness of that sector is potentially diverse. Therefore, below we consider a range of market structures ranging from those with exogenous entry barriers to those with no entry barriers. Using the common framework here we can then analyse the welfare implications of alternative structures in a general equilibrium setting.

3. EQUILIBRIA

We begin our discussion of the alternative implications of market structure by looking at the case of homogeneous products. Intermediate inputs are perfect substitutes for one another. Because of this, to simplify matters, we will assume that there are no (explicit) start-up costs to entry by any firm. In this setting, we can contrast the Cournot (with and without entry barriers) and Bertrand (contestable natural monopoly) outcomes.

3.1 Cournot conjectures (fixed *N*)

We begin with the situation in which N is fixed. Since the final good sector is perfectly competitive, factor allocations in this sector must satisfy the Cobb-Douglas optimising condition above. Given the labour market clearing condition

$$\bar{L} = L_Y + L_X ,$$

and the fact that wages equal the marginal product of labour in final good production, then

$$w = (1-\alpha) X^{\alpha} L_Y^{1-\alpha} .$$

From this (and (11.1)) we can obtain the allocations of labour and intermediate inputs in the final sector in terms of an aggregate of upstream innovation choices,

$$L_Y = \bar{L}\left((1-\alpha)/\alpha + \Im\right)^{-1} (1-\alpha)/\alpha , \quad X = \bar{L}\left((1-\alpha)/\alpha + \Im\right)^{-1} ,$$

and

$$L_X = \bar{L}\left((1-\alpha)/\alpha + \Im\right)^{-1} \Im ,$$

where

$$\Im = \sum_{i=1}^{N} \Psi(F_i) .$$

Suppose that both potential entrants and incumbent firms hold Cournot conjectures regarding the behaviour of others. They determine their quantity and innovation decisions simultaneously holding those of others as given.

Utilising the fact (from (11.1)) that $p = wL_Y X^{-1}\alpha/(1-\alpha)$, the profit function of firm i can be written as

$$\pi_i = \left(p - w\Psi(F_i)\right)x_i - F_i = \left(L_Y\left(\tfrac{1-\alpha}{\alpha}\right)\left(x_i + \sum_{j\neq i} x_j\right)^{-1} - \Psi(F_i)\right)wx_i - F_i.$$

When firm i makes its choices, in addition to holding fixed the quantities and innovation levels of other firms $j \neq i$, it holds wages and labour demand in the final good sector as fixed. Under these assumptions, as in Dasgupta and Stiglitz (1980), the optimal quantity and innovation levels are determined by

$$p = (1-\varepsilon x_i / X)^{-1} w\Psi(F_i) - w\Psi'(F_i)x_i = 1.$$

Note that the sectoral inverse elasticity of demand, ε, is

$$\varepsilon(X) \equiv -X\, p'(X)/\, p(X) = 1.$$

Moreover, suppose (following Dasgupta and Stiglitz 1980) that the equilibrium is symmetric. In this case, $X = Nx$, where x is the symmetric individual firm quantity produced. In this case therefore

$$p = \left(\tfrac{N}{N-1}\right) w\Psi(F),$$

where F is the symmetric choice of innovation.

Using this (in conjunction with labour market clearing) we find that

$$L_Y = \bar{L}\left(\tfrac{N}{N-1}\right)\left(\tfrac{1-\alpha}{\alpha}\right)\left(\left(\tfrac{N}{N-1}\right)\left(\tfrac{1-\alpha}{\alpha}\right)+1\right)^{-1} \text{ and } X = \bar{L}\Psi(F)^{-1}\left(\left(\tfrac{N}{N-1}\right)\left(\tfrac{1-\alpha}{\alpha}\right)+1\right)^{-1}.$$

From this we can find equilibrium wages as a function of the innovation level and industry concentration, N:

$$w = \alpha^{\alpha}(1-\alpha)^{1-\alpha}\left(\tfrac{N-1}{N}\right)^{\alpha}\Psi(F)^{-\alpha}.$$

Observe that wages rise with the average level of innovation among firms and with the number of firms in the industry. This is because both of these raise the demand for labour by intermediate input firms.

Once again, in order to obtain comparable results it helps to use a functional form. Using the functional form for Ψ above, firms choose the level of innovation given by

$$F_i = \left(\alpha^{\alpha}(1-\alpha)^{1-\alpha}\left(\left(\tfrac{N}{N-1}\right)\left(\tfrac{1-\alpha}{\alpha}\right)+1\right)^{-1}\left(\tfrac{N}{N-1}\right)^{\alpha}\tfrac{\theta}{N}\bar{L}F^{\theta(1+\alpha)}\right)^{1/(1+\theta)},$$

where it should be recalled that F is the symmetric choice of innovation by all firms. Interestingly, maximising out for price-quantity choices, individual innovation levels are increasing in the level of innovation chosen by other firms (F) and the market size ($\bar{L}$). This strategic complementarity comes from the fact that wages and the industry demand curve are determined endogenously. When wages and the industry demand curve are fixed (i.e., industry production does not have economy-wide resource effects), then the first-order effects of other firms' innovation level on the returns to own innovation are zero. However, to the extent that a decision to raise own innovation is complementary with raising output, since output decisions are strategic substitutes, this indirectly reduces the returns to innovation. When wages and industry demand are endogenous, the demand-creation effects of innovation outweigh these Cournot effects. Ultimately, greater innovation raises the incentives for further innovation.

On the other hand, increased competition lowers the returns to innovation. This is because new entrants take market share from incumbents and this is not compensated for by the increase in wages and, hence, industry demand that competition stimulates. This can be more clearly seen by looking at the equilibrium innovation level

$$F^C = \left(\alpha^{\alpha}(1-\alpha)^{1-\alpha}\left(\left(\tfrac{N}{N-1}\right)\left(\tfrac{1-\alpha}{\alpha}\right)+1\right)^{-1}\left(\tfrac{N}{N-1}\right)^{\alpha}\tfrac{\theta}{N}\bar{L}\right)^{1/(1-\theta\alpha)}.$$

It is quite easy to show that if $N > 2$, as N rises, the equilibrium amount spent on research falls (regardless of the other parameter values). Therefore, despite the additional wage effect, the conclusions of Dasgupta and Stiglitz (1980) regarding the negative effects of competition on average innovation remain.

In a homogeneous product industry it is socially optimal to have low concentration given the increasing returns associated with innovation. Nonetheless, we can respect the entry barriers implicit in the fixed N assumption and suppose that the planner chooses the level of innovation subject to those constraints. In this case, consumption is

$$C(N,F) = \bar{L}\left(\left(\tfrac{N}{N-1}\right)\left(\tfrac{1-\alpha}{\alpha}\right)+1\right)^{-1}\Psi(F)^{-\alpha}\left(\left(\tfrac{N}{N-1}\right)\left(\tfrac{1-\alpha}{\alpha}\right)+1\right)^{1-\alpha} - NF.$$

The socially optimal level of innovation is determined by the first order condition

$$F^{SOC}(N) = \left(\alpha^{\alpha}(1-\alpha)^{1-\alpha}\left(\left(\tfrac{N}{N-1}\right)\left(\tfrac{1-\alpha}{\alpha}\right)+1\right)^{-1}\left(\tfrac{N}{N-1}\right)^{1-\alpha}\tfrac{\theta}{N}\overline{L}\right)^{1/(1-\theta\alpha)}.$$

It is very easy to see that $F^{SOC}(N) > F^{C}(N)$ for all $N > 1$. Hence, there is under-investment in innovation.

3.2 Cournot conjectures (free entry)

What happens when N is determined endogenously by allowing for free entry and exit of firms? Observe that in the previous case equilibrium profits are

$$\begin{aligned}\pi(N) &= \left(P - w\Psi\left(F^{C}\right)\right)x - F^{C} \\ &= \left(\tfrac{1}{N-1}\right)\alpha^{\alpha}(1-\alpha)^{1-\alpha}\left(\tfrac{N-1}{N}\right)^{\alpha}\Psi\left(F^{C}\right)^{-\alpha}\tfrac{1}{N}\overline{L}\left(\left(\tfrac{N}{N-1}\right)\left(\tfrac{1-\alpha}{\alpha}\right)+1\right)^{-1} - F^{C}.\end{aligned}$$

Setting this equal to zero, we can determine the equilibrium N as

$$N^{C} = (1+\theta)/\theta.$$

This result is exactly the same as the partial equilibrium result of Dasgupta and Stiglitz (1980). They show that, when θ and ε depend on industry output X,

$$N^{C} = \varepsilon\left(X^{C}\right)\left(1+\theta\left(X^{C}\right)\right)/\theta\left(X^{C}\right),$$

where ε is the elasticity of industry demand. This is a general phenomenon in models with endogenous sunk costs: that firms will 'escalate' research in order to forestall entry (Sutton 1998). Concentration is higher, the more efficient is the research technology. Moreover, equilibrium concentration is independent of industry demand and factor price considerations. As such, it is clear why, by making these endogenous in a general equilibrium setting, this independence result is preserved. Nonetheless, observe that the size of the market ($\overline{L}$) and the efficiency of the research technology, θ, both raise the equilibrium average level of innovation

$$F^{C}(N) = \left(\alpha^{\alpha}(1-\alpha)^{1-\alpha}\left(\left(\tfrac{1+\theta}{\theta}\right)\left(\tfrac{1-\alpha}{\alpha}\right)+1\right)^{-1}\left(\tfrac{\theta}{1+\theta}\right)^{\alpha}\tfrac{1}{1+\theta}\overline{L}\right)^{1/(1-\theta\alpha)}.$$

Dasgupta and Stiglitz (1980) found that under free entry, average innovation was less than the social optimum but that industry research expenditures could exceed the optimal level. This is because average innovation mattered for efficiency and this expenditure was duplicated among firms. This latter effect was a social cost. In our model, if $\alpha = 1$ and labour is not used in final good production then it is easy to show that average innovation in equilibrium is less than the social optimum. That is,

$$F^{SOC} = \left(\theta\bar{L}\right)^{1/(1-\theta)} > \left(\bar{L}\theta/(1+\theta)^2\right)^{1/(1-\theta\alpha)} = F^C.$$

However, when $\alpha < 1$, it is possible that the *average* level of innovation as well as the total research expenditure could *exceed* the socially optimal level. By putting F^C into the first order condition for a social optimum and examining when this value is negative, we can determine the range of parameters for which there is average over-investment in innovation. Based on numerical results this range of parameters is depicted in Figure 11.1.

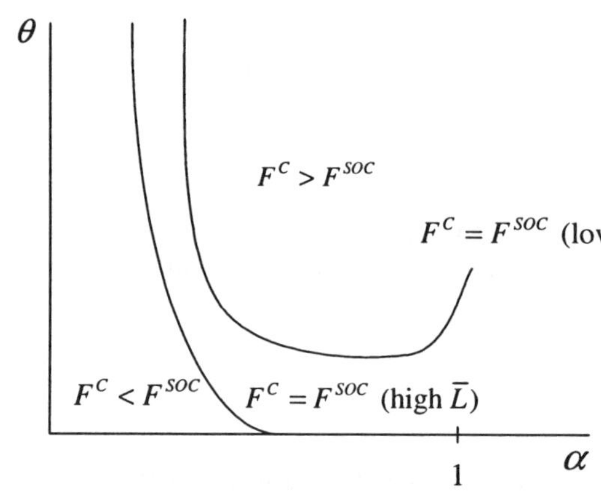

Figure 11.1 Socially Optimal versus Equilibrium R&D

The intuition behind this result is subtle. When $\alpha = 1$, as the market size rises, there are increased incentives to 'escalate' innovation to forestall entry. However, while this does prevent further entry, the desired expansion in output is constrained by the fixed labour supply to the industry. When $\alpha < 1$, this constraint is lifted and firms in the industry are free to compete labour away from the final goods sector in order to raise output and innovation. This allows equilibrium industry demand to exceed its optimal level because of the resulting distortion in factor prices from the competition in the upstream sector. This effect is stronger the more efficient is the research technology allowing for escalation in response to entry. This offsets other effects caused by falling prices and leads to innovation that is greater than the social optimum. To be clear, it is the general equilibrium structure of the model that allows an over-innovation result, so that competition can distort the sectoral allocation of scarce factors.

This result hinges critically on the 'lab-equipment' nature of R&D investment. What this means is that greater total R&D expenditure has a demand increasing effect as opposed to a pure resource depleting effect as would occur if R&D were purely labour intensive. Van De Klundert and Smulders (1993) use this latter formulation and preserve the conventional under-investment result. Given this difference in results, it becomes important to look at a more reasonable specification for R&D investment. In Gans (1997), the choice of inputs into R&D is endogenised and it is shown that, as the market size grows, R&D becomes more final good as opposed to labour intensive. This is because the relative price of final goods to wages falls at larger scales of production. This property would be preserved for the result of this chapter. Therefore, since over-investment is more likely at high market sizes, it can be concluded that this is a robust conclusion.

3.3 Bertrand conjectures (free entry)

When firms hold Bertrand conjectures, because of the increasing returns nature of production, only one firm will survive in a homogeneous product industry. Thus, the outcome is akin to a contestable natural monopoly, so long as there is one potential entrant. In this case, prices are equal to average cost:

$$p = w\Psi(F) + F/X .$$

In this case, the level of innovation will be the same as the social optimum. The reason for this is that the incumbent firm will be forced to raise the level of innovation so long as there are efficiency gains to be had in the downstream sector. This mirrors conclusions of Moriguchi (1994).[6]

4. CONCLUSIONS AND FUTURE DIRECTIONS

There are a number of interesting directions in which this chapter could head. First, as Sutton (1998) notes, industries in which firms have high R&D intensities tend to be characterised by product differentiation. Therefore, a natural extension would be to consider a differentiated products model for intermediate inputs and repeat the exercise conducted in this chapter. Second, the strategic use of innovation to deter entry in a dynamic game could also have interesting general equilibrium effects. Finally, it would be interesting to investigate the possibility that innovation and competition in one sector could distort the level of innovation conducted in other sectors that are perhaps organised with regulated monopolies.

ACKNOWLEDGEMENTS

We thank Maxim Engers, Murray Kemp, Shannon Mitchell, Sjak Smulders and Trevor Stegman for helpful discussions. All errors remain our own.

NOTES

1. The Cobb-Douglas assumption is not critical here. The results could also be presented using a general constant returns to scale production function with the restrictions discussed by Ciccone and Matsuyama (1996).
2. Each result to follow requires only that the marginal labour requirement when $F_i = 0$ be some positive constant.
3. Dasgupta and Stiglitz (1980) and Vassilikas (1989) analyse continuous mechanisms for technological choice but in very different contexts to that used here.
4. The implications of this assumption on the nature of fixed costs is robust to allowing the firm to choose the intensity with which labour and final goods are used in R&D (Gans 1997).
5. Athey and Schmutzler (1995) consider both product and process innovation and find that both types of innovation are complements at a firm decision level.
6. Note, however, the contrary predictions of Gans and Quiggin (2001) when there exists an entrepreneurial fringe.

REFERENCES

Arrow, K.J. (1962), 'Economic welfare and the allocation of resources for invention', in R. Nelson (ed.), *The Rate and Direction of Inventive Activity: Economic and Social Factors*, NBER: Princeton University Press.

Athey, S. and A. Schmutzler (1995), 'Product and process flexibility in an innovative environment', *Rand Journal of Economics*, **26** (4), 557-74.

Barro, R. and X. Sala-i-Martin (1994), 'Quality improvements in models of growth', Yale Economic Growth Center Discussion Paper 715, Yale University.

Ciccone, A., and K. Matsuyama (1996), 'Start-up costs and pecuniary externalities as barriers to economic development', *Journal of Development Economics,* **49** (1), 33-59.

Dasgupta, P. and J.E. Stiglitz (1980), 'Industrial structure and the nature of innovative activity', *Economic Journal*, **90** (358), 266-93.

Gans, J.S. (1997), 'Fixed cost assumptions in industrialisation theories', *Economic Letters*, **56** (1), 111-19.

Gans, J.S. (1998a), 'Time lags and indicative planning in a dynamic model of industrialisation', *Journal of the Japanese and International Economies*, **12** (2), 103-30.

Gans, J.S. (1998b), 'Industrialization with a menu of technologies: appropriate technologies and the big push', *Structural Change and Economic Dynamics*, **9** (3), 333-48.

Gans, J.S. and J. Quiggin (2001), 'A technological and organisation explanation of the size distribution of firms', *Small Business Economics*, (forthcoming).

Grossman, G.M. and E. Helpman (1991), *Innovation and Growth in the Global Economy*, MIT Press: Cambridge.

Moriguchi, C. (1994), 'Marginal cost pricing in a pure fixed cost economy', *Journal of Mathematical Economics*, **26** (3), 363-85.

Perotti, P. (1995), 'Sunk costs, market structure and growth', mimeo, Duke University.

Rivera-Batiz, L. and P.M. Romer (1991), 'Economic integration and endogenous growth', *Quarterly Journal of Economics*, **106** (2), 531-55.

Romer, P.M. (1990), 'Endogenous technological change', *Journal of Political Economy*, **98** (5) Supplement, S71-102.

Smulders, J. and T. Van De Klundert (1995), 'Imperfect competition, concentration and growth with firm-specific R&D', *European Economic Review*, **3** (1), 139-60.

Sutton, J. (1998), *Technology and Market Structure*, MIT Press: Cambridge.

Van De Klundert, T. and J. Smulders (1993), 'Imperfect competition and technological change: a general equilibrium analysis', *Revista Internazionale di Scienze Sociali*, **101** (3), 321-50.

Vassilakis, S. (1989), 'Increasing returns and strategic behavior: the worker-firm ratio', *Rand Journal of Economics*, **20** (4), 622-36.

12. Imperfect Substitutes and Strategic Trade Policies under Cournot Duopoly

Yasuo Uekawa, Seiichi Katayama and Hiroshi Ohta

1. INTRODUCTION

The purpose of this study is to build a general reciprocal market model of the strategic trade policy and to explore the welfare consequence of the policy. We will show that under certain conditions an export subsidy improves world welfare.

Strategic trade policy has been extensively studied for nearly two decades. The issues and the results of strategic trade policy are broad, and they have been surveyed by, for example, Brander (1995) and Chang and Katayama (1995) among others.

Krugman (1984) analysed an export subsidy in the reciprocal-market model. As the title of his paper indicates, an import protection policy works as an export promotion in the international competition in the presence of oligopoly and economies of scale. Indeed, Brander and Spencer (1985) have shown that, in a Cournot duopoly setting, an export subsidy to a home firm is desirable because it raises the firm's market share and profit at the expense of its foreign competitor. This finding has generated a great deal of controversy, and the consequence for export subsidies is subject to qualifications. (See, for example, Eaton and Grossman 1986, Cheng 1988 and Dixit 1984.)

In the present chapter we re-examine the issues of the appropriately chosen pattern of tariffs and, more importantly, of subsidies by focusing on two vital and hitherto relatively neglected discussions on the cost asymmetry and the differentiated goods in international trade. It seems that Krugman's (1984) analysis is not made in a rigorous model. In fact, the previous models focusing on cost differences are based on the assumption of constant marginal cost and, in the end, the production scale effect is insulated from vigorous scrutiny when discussing the optimality of subsidy (for example, Neary 1994). It is thus found in Uekawa (1994) that the effect of scale economies is treated properly under the assumption of more general nonlinear cost functions. This is one line of generalisation that we try to follow in this chapter.

The other type of asymmetry is found in traded goods themselves. Most existing studies of strategic trade policy within the framework of oligopolistic competition have assumed homogeneous goods. The assumption yields by itself an analytical simplicity. However, as is well known, product differentiation is one of the significant features in oligopolistic markets. To understand the importance of non-homogeneity among the commodities in the duopoly market, let us take an example of the aircraft construction industry. Airbus and Boeing are mutually competing, and EU has a preference to the former and the US to the latter. In addition to preferences, other factors such as national prestige might be rather relevant for demand. When outputs of the foreign and the domestic firms are not homogeneous, but only imperfectly substitutable for each other, an interesting set of questions is raised concerning how the degree of substitutability between them affects the structure of optimum trade policies. The model presented in this chapter considers the point by assuming imperfect substitutes produced by duopolists.

A model of product differentiation is presented to show, first of all, the uniqueness of the oligopolistic equilibrium. To perform the comparative static analysis, it is necessary to secure the uniqueness as the first step, although the existing literature has not paid attention to this point.

After proving the uniqueness of equilibrium, we examine another issue that also seems to be paid less attention in the literature: the policy effect on world welfare. Many studies have already considered the optimal subsidy and its welfare implication. However its implication for world welfare is rarely analysed. We will present the conditions under which a strategic subsidy improves world welfare. Our analysis shows that, contrary to the homogeneous goods case, the degree of substitutability among the differentiated products plays the decisive role for the welfare result.

2. THE MODEL

Consider a two-country trade model as follows. There are three goods (Z, X and Y). Good Z is competitively produced in the two countries under constant returns to scale and is taken as the numeraire in both countries. Good X is produced by one imperfectly competitive domestic firm and good Y by another imperfectly competitive firm in the foreign country. They behave in a Cournot fashion.[1]

Cost functions of good X, denoted by $c(X)$ and $c^*(Y)$, are characterised by

$$c'(X) > 0, \;\; c''(X) \leq 0 \;\text{ and }\; c^{*\prime}(Y) > 0, \;\; c^{*\prime\prime}(Y) \leq 0\,, \qquad (12.1)$$

where $X = x + x^*$ is the total output of good X, and x and x^* are domestic and foreign sales, respectively, by the domestic firm. Throughout, a starred variable denotes the entity in the foreign market. Similarly, $Y = y + y^*$ is the total output of good Y produced by the foreign firm, and y and y^* are its sales to the home and foreign markets, respectively. Note that we presume in condition (12.1) increasing returns to scale in production for some reason, for example, sufficiently large fixed costs for both firms.

The social utility functions for the two countries are assumed to take the quasi-linear forms

$$\begin{aligned} U(x, y, z) &= u(x, y) + z \\ U(x^*, y^*, z^*) &= u^*(x^*, y^*) + z^*, \end{aligned} \tag{12.2}$$

where x, y and z are consumption levels of goods X, Y and Z in the domestic country and those with stars correspond to the foreign entities.

Assume that the sub-utilities in (12.2), namely, $u(x, y)$ and $u^*(x^*, y^*)$ are increasing and strictly concave such that for i, j=1,2,

$$u_i > 0, \quad u_i^* > 0 \quad \text{and} \quad u_{ii} < u_{ij} < 0, \quad u_{ii}^* < u_{ij}^* < 0, \tag{12.3}$$

where u_i is the partial derivative of $u(x, y)$ with respective to its i-th argument, i=1,2 : for example, $u_1 = \partial u / \partial x$ and $u_{12} = \partial^2 u / \partial y \partial x$. Since good Z is taken as the numeraire in both countries, $P^Z = P^{Z*} \equiv 1$, where P^Z (respectively, P^{Z*}) is the price of good Z in the home (foreign) country.

We see from the above assumptions on the social utility functions that the inverse demand functions of goods X and Y are obtained as

$$\begin{aligned} P^X(x, y) &= u_1, & P^Y(x, y) &= u_2, \\ P^{X*}(x^*, y^*) &= u_1^*, & P^{Y*}(x^*, y^*) &= u_2^*. \end{aligned} \tag{12.4}$$

From (12.3) and (12.4), it is readily seen that

$$\begin{aligned} P_1^X &= u_{11} < P_2^X = u_{12} = P_1^Y < 0, & P_2^Y &= u_{22} < P_1^Y = u_{12} = P_2^X < 0, \\ P_1^{X*} &= u_{11}^* < P_2^{X*} = u_{12}^* = P_1^{Y*} < 0, & P_2^{Y*} &= u_{22}^* < P_1^{Y*} = u_{12}^* = P_2^{X*} < 0. \end{aligned} \tag{12.5}$$

Consider domestic import tariffs and export subsidies as the trade policy instruments. For simplicity we assume that the foreign country imposes neither import tariffs nor export subsidies under any circumstances. In other words, the foreign country is passive in its trade policies. Let the domestic import tariff be denoted by t and the domestic export subsidy by s.

Thus, the profit of domestic and foreign firms are expressed, respectively, by

$$\begin{aligned} V(x,x^*,y^*,y) &= xP^X + x^*P^{X^*} - c(x+x^*) + sx^* \\ V^*(x,x^*,y^*,y) &= y^*P^{Y^*} + yP^X - c^*(y+y^*) - ty. \end{aligned} \tag{12.6}$$

Accordingly, the first order conditions for the profit-maximising problem faced by each firm are

$$\begin{aligned} V_1 &= P^X + xP_1^X - c' = 0 \\ V_2 &= P^{X^*} + x^*P_1^{X^*} - c' + s = 0 \\ V_3^* &= P^{Y^*} + y^*P_2^{Y^*} - c^{*\prime} = 0 \\ V_4^* &= P^Y + yP_2^Y - c^{*\prime} - t = 0 \end{aligned} \tag{12.7}$$

for any given t and given s.

Partial derivatives of the second order in the system of equation (12.7) are thus

$$\begin{aligned} V_{11} &= 2P_1^X + xP_{11}^X - c'' \equiv q_{11} - c'' + P_1^X \\ V_{22} &= 2P_1^{X^*} + x^*P_{11}^{X^*} - c'' \equiv q_{11}^* - c'' + P_1^{X^*} \\ V_{33}^* &= 2P_2^{Y^*} + y^*P_{22}^{Y^*} - c^{*''} \equiv q_{22}^* - c^{*''} + P_2^{Y^*} \\ V_{44}^* &= 2P_2^Y + yP_{22}^Y - c^{*''} \equiv q_{22} - c^{*''} + P_2^Y \\ V_{12} &= V_{21} = -c'' \\ V_{13} &= V_{24} = V_{42}^* = V_{31}^* = 0 \\ V_{14} &= P_2^X + xP_{12}^X \\ V_{23} &= P_2^{X^*} + xP_{12}^{X^*} \\ V_{41}^* &= P_1^Y + yP_{21}^Y \\ V_{32}^* &= P_1^{Y^*} + y^*P_{21}^{Y^*} \\ V_{34}^* &= V_{43}^* = -c^{*''}. \end{aligned} \tag{12.8}$$

To ensure for the stability of the Cournot competition in the home and foreign markets, we assume throughout the chapter that the following conditions hold (see, Dixit 1986):

$$V_{14} < 0; \quad V_{23} < 0, \quad \text{and} \quad V_{32}^* < 0; \quad V_{41}^* < 0. \tag{12.9}$$

Also, we assume that

$$q_{11} - 2c'' < 0;\ q^*_{11} - 2c'' < 0, \text{ and } q^*_{22} - 2c^{*''} < 0;\ \ q_{22} - 2c^{*''} < 0\,. \quad (12.10)$$

Condition (12.9) implies the strategic substitutability of goods X and Y in the both domestic and foreign markets, while condition (12.10) implies that the marginal costs are decreasing because of the sufficiently large fixed costs of the firms.

Thus we see from (12.1), (12.8) and (12.10) that the second order conditions in the profit maximising problems for the two firms are all satisfied:

$$\begin{aligned} &V_{11} = q_{11} - c'' + P_1^X < 0 \\ &V_{22} = q^*_{11} - c'' + P_1^{X*} < 0 \\ &V_{11}V_{22} - V_{12}V_{21} > 0 \\ &V^*_{33} = q^*_{22} - c^{*''} + P_2^{Y*} < 0 \\ &V^*_{44} = q_{22} - c^{*''} + P_2^{Y} < 0 \\ &V^*_{33}V^*_{44} - V^*_{34}V^*_{43} > 0 \end{aligned} \quad (12.11)$$

Examining the principal minors of the Jacobian matrix of the equation system (12.7), we can readily prove the following proposition.

Proposition 1: *The Jacobian matrix of the equation system* (12.7) *is an N-P matrix where all the principal minors of odd orders are negative and those of even orders positive. Therefore, the solution, if any, to the system* (12.7) *is unique.*

The proof of this proposition is provided in Appendix 1.[2] See Nikaido (1968, 371) for the definition of N-P matrices and their relationship with uniqueness.

The next task is to obtain the comparative statics result on the Cournot equilibrium with respect to the home country policy variables, tariffs and subsidies. For the comparative statics to be meaningful, the uniqueness of the equilibrium solution is vital but we do not find a counterpart to the above proposition in the previous literature.

Note that the solution to the system of equation (12.7) depends on the values of t and s, since x, x^*, y^* and y are all responding to them. The total differentiation of (12.7) produces

$$\begin{bmatrix} dx \\ dx^* \\ dy^* \\ dy \end{bmatrix} = |A|^{-1} \begin{bmatrix} A_{11} & A_{21} & A_{31} & A_{41} \\ A_{12} & A_{22} & A_{32} & A_{42} \\ A_{13} & A_{23} & A_{33} & A_{43} \\ A_{14} & A_{24} & A_{34} & A_{44} \end{bmatrix} \begin{bmatrix} 0 \\ -ds \\ 0 \\ dt \end{bmatrix}, \quad (12.12)$$

where $|A|$ is the determinant of the Jacobian matrix of (12.7) and A_{ij} $(i, j = 1, ..., 4)$ is a co-factor of the (i, j)-th element of the matrix.

3. THE EFFECTS OF TARIFFS AND SUBSIDIES

3.1 The impact of a change in an import tariff

This subsection examines the effects of a change in the domestic import tariff on consumption and production of goods X and Y in both countries.

In order to determine the comparative static effects, we assume the following.

Assumption 1: $P_1^{X*} < V_{23}$ *and* $P_2^{Y*} < V_{32}^*$.

The values of the left hand side in both inequalities are the changes in marginal utilities, while those in the right are the changes in the marginal profit of the firms. (See, conditions (12.9) and (12.10).) Assumption 1 implies that the marginal utilities of consumers are declining faster than the marginal profits when the amount of sales increases.

Expressing the partial derivatives with respect to the i-th argument by subscript i, i=1,2, we calculate the effects of changes in t and s upon consumption levels from (12.12). These effects are

$$x_t(t,s) = A_{41}/|A| = -[V_{14}(V_{22}V_{33}^* - V_{23}V_{32}^*) + c''c^{*\prime\prime}V_{23}]/|A| > 0, \quad (12.13)$$

$$x_t^*(t,s) = A_{42}/|A| = -[V_{11}V_{23}c^{*\prime\prime} + c''V_{14}V_{33}^*]/|A| \geq 0, \quad (12.14)$$

with equality only if $c'' = c^{*\prime\prime} = 0$,

$$y_t^*(t,s) = A_{43}/|A| = [c^{*\prime\prime}(V_{11}V_{22} - V_{12}V_{21}) + c''V_{32}^*V_{14}]/|A| \leq 0 \quad (12.15)$$

with equality only if $c'' = c^{*\prime\prime} = 0$,

$$y_t(t,s) = A_{44}/|A| = \begin{vmatrix} V_{11} & V_{12} & 0 \\ V_{21} & V_{22} & V_{23} \\ 0 & V_{32}^* & V_{33}^* \end{vmatrix} /|A| < 0, \quad (12.16)$$

since

$$V_{ii} < c'' \leq 0 \ \ (i = 1,2), \ \ V_{23} < 0, \ \ V_{32}^* < 0, \ \ q_{11}^* - 2c'' < 0$$

and $q_{22}^* - 2c^{*\prime\prime} < 0$ from (12.9) and (12.10). Then, it is readily seen that the effects upon production are

$$\partial X / \partial t \equiv X_t = x_t + x_t^* > 0 \quad \text{and} \quad \partial Y / \partial t \equiv Y_t = y_t^* + y_t < 0 \,. \quad (12.17)$$

Furthermore, we can determine the effects of tariffs on the total values of sales by the home and foreign firms, respectively, using the first-order conditions, as follows.

$$\partial[P^X(x,y)x + P^{X*}(x^*,y^*)x^*]/\partial t = x_t c' + xP_2^X y_t + x_t^*(c' - s) + x^* P_2^X y_t^* \quad (12.18)$$

$$\partial[P^Y(x,y)y + P^{Y*}(x^*,y^*)y^*]/\partial t = y_t(c^{*\prime} + t) + yP_1^Y x_t + y_t^* c^{*\prime} + y^* P_1^{Y*} x_t^* \,. \quad (12.19)$$

Supposing that the initial rate of export subsidy is lower than the marginal cost for the domestic firm and the initial tariff is non-negative, the sign of equation (12.18) is positive and that of (12.19) negative from (12.5) and (12.13)–(12.16).

The results are formulated in the following proposition.

Proposition 2: *Suppose that either c" or c*" is negative and Assumption 1 is satisfied. Then a rise in the domestic import tariff increases the consumption of good X in both countries and its output by the domestic firm, and reduces the consumption of good Y in both countries and its output by the foreign firm. Also, the tariff increase raises the sales revenue of the domestic firm and reduces that of the foreign firm.*

Proposition 2 implies that the domestic tariff induces a rent shifting from the foreign to the domestic firm.

3.2 The impact of a change in an export subsidy

The effects of a change in the domestic export subsidy on the consumption and production pattern are obtained similarly as in the case of tariffs, except that the Assumption 1 is now to be replaced by

Assumption 2: $P_1^X < V_{14}$ *and* $P_2^Y < V_{14}^*$.

The assumption implies that the marginal utilities change more than the marginal profits when the firms increase sales. Relegating the entire calculation to Appendix 2, we summarise the results in the following proposition.

Proposition 3: *Suppose that either c'' or $c^{*''}$ is negative and Assumption 2 is satisfied. Then an increase in the domestic export subsidy increases the consumption of good X in both countries and its output by the domestic firm, and reduces the consumption of good Y in both countries and its output of the foreign firm. Also, the increase in the subsidy raises the total sales revenue of the domestic firm and decreases that of the foreign firm.*

As in the case of domestic tariff, a subsidy induces rent shifting between the two firms.

4. TRADE POLICY AND WELFARE

Now, we move on to welfare analysis. The national welfare in each country in this model is calculated as the sum of consumer's surplus, producer's surplus and the net government revenue for the country:

$$\begin{aligned} W(t,s) &= \{u(x,y) - xP^X - yP^Y\} \\ &\quad + \{xP^X + x^* P^{X^*} - c(x+x^*) + sx^*\} + (ty - sx^*) \qquad (12.20) \\ &= u(x,y) - yP^Y + x^* P^{X^*} - c(x+x^*) + ty \end{aligned}$$

and

$$W^*(t,s) = u^*(x^*,y^*) - x^* P^{X^*} + yP^Y - c^*(y^*+y) - ty. \qquad (12.21)$$

4.1 The full optimum

If the home government can use tariffs and subsidies simultaneously to maximise its national welfare, a full optimum for the home country is obtained. Our interest is to know which signs the solution to the optimisation problem denoted by (t^0, s^0) can take. In other words, it is of interest to know if the home government should fully utilise these protective measures. If the tariffs and subsidies are both positive at the full optimum, we can argue that the home government has a strong tendency towards protection. Unfortunately, the signs turn out to be indeterminate in general. If we confine to the case of linear costs, where $c''(X) = c^{*''}(Y) = 0$, they are revealed to be positive in sign (see, Appendix 3).

Proposition 4: *In the case where the cost functions are linear in the global sense, a full optimum calls for positive t^0 and s^0.*

4.2 The sole use of an import tariff

In this subsection we analyse the effects of a change in the import tariff on the home and the foreign country's welfare in the absence of export subsidy. In this case, (12.20) and (12.21) become

$$W(t,0) = u(x,y) - yP^Y + x^* P^{X*} - c(x+x^*) + ty \qquad (12.22)$$

$$W^*(t,0) = u^*(x^*,y^*) - x^* P^{X*} + yP^Y - c(y^* + y) - ty. \qquad (12.23)$$

Consider first the effect of a change in the import tariff on the home country's welfare. Using (12.22), we have that the derivative of home welfare with respect to the tariff rate is

$$W_t(t,0) = M + ty_t, \qquad (12.24)$$

where

$$M \equiv \left(P^X - c'\right)x_t + y\left\{1 - \left(P_1^Y x_t + P_2^Y y_t\right)\right\} + x^* P_2^{X*} y_t^*.$$

Since M>0 from Appendix 4 and $y_t < 0$ from (12.16), we immediately assert that the optimal tariff t^{00} turns out to be $t^{00} = -M / y_t > 0$. Thus, we obtain the following proposition.

Proposition 5: *Assume that the export subsidy rate is zero. An increase in the home country's import tariff raises its welfare if initially t is sufficiently small. Thus the optimal tariff rate is positive.*

In the perfect substitute case treated by Brander and Spencer (1985) and Uekawa (1994), one sufficient condition is given to prove the same proposition. The condition is that the foreign firm's net export price does not increase when there is an increase in the domestic import tariff. Here we can see that the same conclusion holds *without* such condition and under very general cost conditions.

Consider next the effect of a change in the domestic import tariff on the foreign welfare. Differentiating W^* with respect to *t*, we obtain

$$W_t^*(t,0) = y\left(P_1^Y x_t - 1\right) + y_t{*}\left(P^{Y*} - c{*'}\right) - x{*}\left(P_1^{X*} x_t{*} + P_2^{X*} y_t{*}\right). \qquad (12.25)$$

When both countries' cost functions are linear as in Dixit (1988),

$$c'' = c^{*''} = 0, \;\; x_t^* = y_t^* = 0 \quad \text{and} \quad W_t^*(t,0) < 0 \,,$$

since Appendix 5 shows that the sum of the first two terms of the right-hand side of (12.25) is negative. Otherwise it is not easy to see the sign of $W_t^*(t,0)$. The result in this case is summarised in the following proposition.

Proposition 6: *Assume that the export subsidy rate is zero. The impact effect of an increase in the home country's import tariff on the foreign welfare is generally indeterminate. If the cost functions are linear in both countries, the effect works to reduce the foreign welfare.*

4.3 The sole use of an export subsidy

The effects of a change in the export subsidy on the domestic and the foreign welfare are obtained by the similar procedure for tariffs. Let us simply list the results here (see Appendix 6 for details).

Proposition 7: *Assume that the import tariff is zero. An increase in the home country's export subsidy raises its welfare if initially s is sufficiently small. Thus the optimal subsidy rate is positive.*

Proposition 8: *Assume that the import tariff is zero. The effect of an increase in the home country's export subsidy on the foreign welfare is in general indeterminate.*

The indeterminacy in Proposition 8 arises from the fact that the output of the foreign firm reduces (Proposition 3) but there is an increase in the consumption of good *X*, which substitutes the decline of consumption of good *Y*. Hence the total effect is not determined.

5. WORLD WELFARE

In this section, we examine the policy effect on world welfare. World welfare is written as a simple sum of welfares of the two countries. From (12.20) and (12.21), we therefore have that world welfare is given by

$$\begin{aligned} U^W &\equiv W(t,s) + W^*(t,s) \\ &= u(x,y) + u^*(x^*,y^*) - c(x+x^*) - c^*(y^*+y). \end{aligned} \tag{12.26}$$

Consider first the effect of an import tariff, starting from free trade. From (12.26), when $s = 0$, we have

$$U^W(t,0) = W(t,0) + W^*(t,0). \tag{12.27}$$

Differentiating $U^W(t,\ 0)$ with respect to t yields

$$\begin{aligned} U_t^W(t,0) &= W_t(t,0) + W_t^*(t,0) \\ &= \{(P^X - c')x_t + (P^Y - c^{*\prime})y_t\} + \{(P^{X*} - c')x_t^* + (P^{Y*} - c^{*\prime})y_t^*\}. \end{aligned} \tag{12.28}$$

To see the sign of $U_t^W(t,0)$, first we define c_0 such that

$$(x_t + x_t^*)c' + (y_t + y_t^*)c^{*\prime} = (x_t + x_t^*)c_0 + (y_t + y_t^*)c_0. \tag{12.29}$$

From (12.17), $X_t > 0$ and $Y_t < 0$, and from Appendix 7, if $c^{*\prime\prime} \le c'' < 0$ and $u_{11}^* < u_{22}^* < 0$, then $X_t + Y_t < 0$. As shown in Appendix 8, we can prove that when $c' \ge c^{*\prime} \ge 0$ and $c'' \ge c^{*\prime\prime}$,

$$c' \ge c^{*\prime} \ge c_0. \tag{12.30}$$

Therefore, using the first-order profit maximisation condition (12.7), we obtain

$$P^X > c_0 \text{ and } P^{Y*} > c_0. \tag{12.31}$$

In addition, since we consider here $s = 0$ and start from free trade ($t = s = 0$), condition (12.7) implies that

$$P^{X*} > c' > c_0 \text{ and } P^Y > c^{*\prime} > c_0. \tag{12.32}$$

Therefore,

$$P^X, P^{X*}, P^Y, P^{Y*} > c_0. \tag{12.33}$$

Further, we can define $\overline{P}^X, \overline{P}^Y$ and $\tilde{P}$ by

$$\max\{P^X, P^{X*}\} \ge \overline{P}^X \ge \min\{P^X, P^{X*}\} \tag{12.34}$$

$$\max\left\{P^Y, P^{Y*}\right\} \geq \overline{P}^Y \geq \min\left\{P^Y, P^{Y*}\right\} \tag{12.35}$$

and

$$P^X x_t + P^{X*} x_t^* = \overline{P}^X \left(x_t + x_t^*\right) = \overline{P}^X X_t \tag{12.36}$$

$$P^Y y_t + P^{Y*} y_t^* = \overline{P}^Y \left(y_t + y_t^*\right) = \overline{P}^Y Y_t \tag{12.37}$$

and

$$\overline{P}^X X_t + \overline{P}^Y Y_t = \tilde{P}\left(X_t + Y_t\right). \tag{12.38}$$

From the definition of $\tilde{P}$ in (12.38), we can see from Appendix 9 that if $\overline{P}^X < \overline{P}^Y$, then $\tilde{P} > c_0$.

From the above arguments, we have

$$\begin{aligned} &U_t^W(t,0) = (\tilde{P} - c_0)(X_t + Y_t) < 0 \\ &\text{if } c' \geq c^{*\prime} \geq 0,\ c'' \geq c^{*\prime\prime},\ u_{11}^* \leq u_{22}^* \text{ and } \overline{P}^X < \overline{P}^Y, \end{aligned} \tag{12.39}$$

and hence we obtain the following proposition.

Proposition 9: *If $c' \geq c^{*\prime} \geq 0$, $c'' \geq c^{*\prime\prime}$, $u_{11}^* \leq u_{22}^*$ and $\overline{P}^X < \overline{P}^Y$, a rise in the domestic import tariff, starting from free trade, reduces world welfare.*

Under the above assumptions, an increase in the domestic import tariff reduces world welfare. Intuitively, cost conditions $c' \geq c^{*\prime} \geq 0$ and $c'' \geq c^{*\prime\prime}$ imply that the domestic cost structure is weakly inferior to the foreign one. The condition that $u_{11}^* < u_{22}^*$ implies that the marginal utility of the foreign consumers decreases less rapidly when they increase the consumption of their own national products than the products imported from the home country. In other words, the foreign consumers' marginal utility of their national product falls more rapidly as the consumption level of that product decreases as the result of tariff. They may be attached to their national brand. Here we have to notice the significance of the assumption. The heterogeneity among goods and the preference structure play decisive roles. An introduction of a tariff to Cournot markets affects the equilibrium solution via production as well as consumer surplus changes.

The condition that $\overline{P}^X < \overline{P}^Y$ implies the situation where on average the price that the foreign firm faces is higher than that faced by the domestic firm throughout the markets in both countries. In other words, total sales and total production by the foreign firm may not be large enough. Therefore, it is not wise from the world point of view under these conditions to protect the home firm, which is inferior in production to the foreign firm.

Consider next the effect of an export subsidy on world welfare starting from free trade. Differentiating $U^W(0,s)$ with respect to s yields

$$\begin{aligned} U_s^W(0,s) &= W_s(0,s) + W_s^*(0,s) \\ &= P^X x_s + P^Y y_s + P^{X*} x_s^* + P^{Y*} y_s^* - (x_s + x_s^*)c' - (y_s^* + y_s)c^{*\prime}. \end{aligned} \tag{12.40}$$

The analysis follows the same way as that leading to Proposition 9. Let c^0 satisfy

$$\left(x_s + x_s^*\right)c' + \left(y_s + y_s^*\right)c^{*\prime} = \left(x_s + x_s^*\right)c^0 + \left(y_s + y_s^*\right)c^0. \tag{12.41}$$

It is shown in Appendix 10 that if $c' \le c^{*\prime}$, $c'' < 0$ and $c^{*\prime\prime} \cong 0$ then

$$c^{*\prime} \ge c' \ge c^0. \tag{12.42}$$

Following the same process as above and carefully formulating $\hat{P}^X, \hat{P}^Y$ and $\breve{P}$ with similar definitions as in the tariff case, we can also show that

$$\breve{P} > c^0 \quad \text{if} \quad \hat{P}^X > \hat{P}^Y. \tag{12.43}$$

Therefore,

$$U_s^W(0,s) = (\breve{P} - c^0)(X_s + Y_s) > 0 \text{ if } c' \le c^{*\prime}, c'' \le 0, c^{*\prime\prime} \cong 0 \text{ and } \hat{P}^X > \hat{P}^Y$$

(see Appendix 11). We therefore have the following proposition.

Proposition 10: *If $c' \le c^{*\prime}, c'' < 0, c^{*\prime\prime} \cong 0$ and $\hat{P}^X > \hat{P}^Y$, then an increase in the domestic export subsidy, starting from free trade, increases world welfare.*

The sufficient conditions in the above proposition imply that the domestic cost condition is superior to the foreign one and the sales and production levels by the domestic firm are not large enough on average. In other words, if it is the case that the production level on average of the cost-superior home firm is less than that of the foreign firm at the market equilibrium, a domestic subsidy is effective for an increase in world welfare.

We may interpret the result as a pro-competitive proposition. A subsidy to the cost effective firm brings prices down overall, not just the prices of the product of the cost effective firm but those of the cost ineffective firm as well. Consumer surpluses are raised and world welfare is affected favorably. Because of this price reduction effect, a subsidy is regarded as pro-competitive.

However, Proposition 10 also shows that the desirability of a subsidy is subject to a reservation. Contrary to the existing literature, it restricts the applicability of subsidy to the case where subsidy recipients are suffering from smaller market shares than their competitors.

It is known in the closed-economy oligopoly model that promoting a less (more) efficient firm's production reduces (raises) total welfare (see, for example, Lahiri and Ono 1988). Our result in the subsidy case is an extension of the argument to the international oligopoly case. However, in our model, we have to notice the difference between tariffs and subsidies in their effect on world welfare. Under the tariff regime the heterogeneous character of goods and national preference does matter, while the heterogeneity of goods in preference does not affect the result under the subsidy regime. Therefore, the production or cost effectiveness can be thought of as of first-order significance in the determination of the welfare effect under a subsidy.

6. CONCLUDING REMARKS

The present chapter examines a duopoly model of intra-industry trade in a general equilibrium setting. We have considered a general cost structure that is a generalisation of the linear cost case analysed everywhere in the literature. In addition, we have allowed for duopolists to produce imperfect substitutes. Such generalisations as the non-linearity of cost functions, imperfect substitutes and the use of an export subsidy in addition to an import tariff have yielded a number of new results in the theory of trade with imperfect competition.

We have established the conditions for the uniqueness of solution in the model for any given tariff and subsidy structure. We have also examined the effects of a home country's import tariff and export subsidy on the outputs of both firms and the consumption in home and foreign countries. The policy effects on the welfare of both countries and world welfare are also examined.

Special attention should be paid to the fact that if (a) the production conditions in the foreign country are better than that in the home county, (b) the foreign consumers are attached more to their national products than to imported goods, and (c) the output level of the foreign firm is not large enough on average, then a rise in the import tariff lowers world welfare. Conversely, if the home country has better production conditions and if the home firm has not produced much on average, then an increase in the export subsidy raises world welfare. In other words, for raising world welfare through trade policies by the home country, the home government should observe what the markets are telling us, not just the cost conditions of the firms that are sufficient for the same result in the case of homogeneous products.

ACKNOWLEDGEMENTS

We are indebted to J. Feeney, M.C. Kemp, H. Kim, N.V. Long, Y. Ono, K. Miyagiwa, M.S. Tayor and the anonymous referees for their comments. Especially, C. Kowalczyk carefully read the original manuscript and gave us valuable comments.

The early version of this chapter was presented at an international conference on 'Recent Developments in International Economics', Aix en Provence, June 1995, and seminars at the universities of McGill, Korea and Kwansei Gakuin. This research was partly conducted at Harvard University to which the second author is grateful for the kind hospitality. The research by Katayama and Ohta is partly funded by the Grant-in-Aid for Scientific Research of the Ministry of Education.

This research was started as 'Imperfect Substitutes, Intra-Industry Trade and Policy under Cournot Duopolistic Competition' by the late Professor Y. Uekawa who passed away in October 1993. It is very regrettable that he died before the completion of this article. However, the second and the third authors are solely responsible for any remaining errors.

NOTES

1. When imperfectly competitive firms are producing imperfect substitutes, Bertrand competition is a possible mode of oligopolistic competition. However, it is argued that the mode of competition is determined endogenously rather than exogenously. See, for example, Kreps and Scheinkman (1983) and Maggi (1996). Here we assume Cournot competition. Cournot behaviour does not lose its significance when we consider market share competition as quantity competition.
2. The Appendix (Katayama and Ohta 2000), comprising Appendices 1-11 and containing the proofs of propositions, is available to readers upon request to the authors.

REFERENCES

Brander, J.A. (1995), 'Strategic Trade Policy', in G. Grossman and K. Rogoff (eds), *Handbook of International Economics,* Amsterdam: North Holland, pp. 395-1455.

Brander, J.A. and B.J. Spencer (1985), 'Export subsidies and international market share rivalry', *Journal of International Economics,* **18**, 83-100.

Chang,W.W. and S. Katayama (1995), 'Theory and policy of trade with imperfect competition', in W.W. Chang and S. Katayama (eds), *Imperfect Competition in International Trade,* Boston, Mass.: Kluwer Academic Publishers, pp. 15-52.

Cheng, L.K. (1988) 'Assisting domestic industries under international oligopoly, the relevance of competition to optimal policies', *American Economic Review*, **78**, 746-56.

Dixit, A. (1984), 'International trade policies for oligopolistic industries', *Economic Journal*, **94**, 1-16.

Dixit, A. (1986), 'Comparative statics for oligopoly', *International Economic Review,* **27**, 107-22.

Dixit, A. (1988), 'Anti-dumping and countervailing duties under oligopoly', *European Economic Review,* 32, 55-68.

Eaton, J. and G.M. Grossman (1986), 'Optimal trade and industrial policy under oligopoly', *Quarterly Journal of Economics*, **51**, 383-406.

Katayama, S. and H. Ohta (2000), 'Imperfect substitutes and strategic trade policies under Cournot duopoly: mathematical note'', *Kobe Economic and Business Review,* **45**, 1-13.

Kreps, D.M. and J.A. Scheinkman (1983), 'Quantity precommitment and Bertrand competition yield Cournot outcomes', *Bell Journal of Economics,* **14**, 326-37.

Krugman, P.R. (1984), 'Imperfect competition as export promotion: international competition in the presence of oligopoly and economies of scale', in H. Kerzkowski (ed.), *Monopolistic Competition and International Trade*, Oxford: Clarendon Press, pp. 180-93.

Lahiri, S. and Y. Ono (1988), 'Helping minor firms reduces welfare', *Economic Journal,* **98**, 1199-202.

Maggi, G. (1996), 'Strategic trade policies with endogenous mode of competition', *American Economic Review,* **86**, 237-58.

Neary, J.P. (1994), 'Cost asymmetries in international subsidy games: should government help winners or losers?', *Journal of International Economics,* **37**, 197-218.

Nikaido, F. (1968), *Convex Structures and Economic Theory,* New York: Academic Press.

Uekawa,Y. (1994), 'Imperfect competition, intra-industry trade and trade policy', *Economic Studies Quarterly*, **45**, 1-13.

13. Comparative Static Analysis for Cournot Oligopoly

Koji Okuguchi

1. INTRODUCTION

Cournot oligopoly can be formulated for a closed economy without international trade as well as for an open economy allowing for international trade. There are several papers on the existence of the Cournot oligopoly. The classical proof of the existence of equilibrium is based on the fixed point theorem for functions of several variables, while the stability analysis relies on ad hoc adjustment system for individual firms. Krugman (1984) has formulated international Cournot duopoly with several markets and has derived the export promoting effects of import protection under decreasing marginal costs.

Very often the equilibrium condition for an individual agent in an economy contains only its variable, say x_i, an aggregate variable for all agents

$$X \equiv \sum_i x_i$$

and a parameter α. That is, the equilibrium condition is of the form

$$g_i(x_i, X; \alpha) = 0 .$$

If g_i satisfies the condition for the validity of the implicit function theorem, x_i becomes solvable as a unique function of X and α as $x_i = h_i(X, \alpha)$. Hence the equilibrium aggregate value is characterised as a unique solution of

$$X = \sum_i h_i(X, \alpha) .$$

We can use this remarkable fact to prove the existence of Cournot oligopoly equilibrium more easily than the classical one based on the fixed point theorem for functions of several variables (see Okuguchi 1993 for details; also see Szidarovszky and Yakowitz 1977). Moreover, if this fact is taken into consideration, we can perform comparative static analysis for Cournot oligopoly more easily without appealing to the stability condition, which, as Dixit (1986) points out, is ad hoc, and also without doing much complicated computation.

The plan of this chapter is as follows. In Section 2 dealing with Cournot oligopoly in a closed economy, I will conduct comparative static analysis of a change in the firm's cost function caused by a change in its cost function parameter. In so doing I will take advantage of the fact that the individual firm's equilibrium condition contains its output, on the one hand, and the aggregate (industry) output and the parameter affecting its cost function on the other. In Section 3 I perform a comparative static analysis for international Cournot duopoly with several markets à la Krugman, also taking into account the relationships existing between individual variables and aggregate ones. Since international duopoly is considered, there are two aggregate variables, one for the domestic country and the other for the foreign country. The main purpose of the chapter, however, is not to derive many new results but to demonstrate the superiority and simplicity of my general comparative static methodology as compared with others based on the stability condition and involving complicated computation.

2. COURNOT OLIGOPOLY IN A CLOSED ECONOMY

Consider Cournot oligopoly in a closed economy with n firms and without product differentiation. Let x_i, $C_i(x_i,\alpha)$ and π_i be output, cost and profit of firm i, respectively, and let $P = f(X), f' < 0,$ be the inverse demand function, where α is a parameter common to all cost functions, P is the price of the good produced by the firms and

$$X \equiv \sum_{i=1}^{n} x_i$$

is aggregate industry output. The parameter α may refer to the production technology in the industry, the price of a factor of production or the pollution tax rate. In the case of commercial fishing from a common property fishing ground, it represents the inverse of the stock level of the fish. By definition, profit for firm i is expressed as

$$\pi_i \equiv x_i f(X) - C_i(x_i,\alpha), \; i = 1,2,...,n. \tag{13.1}$$

I now introduce the following assumptions.

Assumption 1: *The cost function satisfies the inequalities*

$$C_{i\alpha} \equiv \partial C_i/\partial\alpha \geq 0,\ C_{i\alpha}' \equiv \partial(\partial C_i/\partial x_i)/\partial\alpha \geq 0\,,$$

where the inequality is strict for at least one $i = 1, 2, ..., n$.

Assumption 2: $f' + x_i f'' < 0,\ i = 1, 2, ..., n.$

Assumption 3: $f' < C_i'',\ i = 1, 2, ..., n.$

The first assumption requires that total and marginal costs are non-decreasing in α for all firms and they both increase with an increase in α for at least one firm. Under the second assumption, any firm's marginal revenue with respect to a change in its own output decreases if any other firm's output increases. This means that any two firms' outputs are strategic substitutes for each other in the sense of Bulow et al. (1985). The assumption holds if f is concave. It holds also even if f is convex provided the degree of convexity is sufficiently small. The third assumption holds if the marginal cost is non-decreasing. It may hold also even if marginal cost is decreasing, the case analysed in Section 3. Under Assumptions 2 and 3 any firm's profit function is a concave function of its own output, which ensures that the second-order condition for profit maximisation is satisfied.

Assuming away corner solutions, the first order condition for profit maximisation is given by

$$\partial\pi_i/\partial x_i = f(x) + x_i f'(X) - C_i'(x_i, \alpha) = 0,\ i = 1, 2, ..., n, \tag{13.2}$$

where X is the industry total output. Applying the general method for comparative statics referred to in Section 1, I solve for the individual variable x_i in (13.2) as a function of the aggregate variable X and the parameter α to get

$$x_i \equiv \varphi_i(X, \alpha),\ i = 1, 2, ..., n, \tag{13.3}$$

where, by Assumptions 1–3,

$$\begin{aligned} \partial\varphi_i/\partial X &= -(f' + x_i f'')/(f' - C_i'') < 0, \\ \partial\varphi_i/\partial\alpha &= C_{i\alpha}'/(f' - C_i'') \leq 0, \end{aligned} \tag{13.4}$$

with strict inequality for at least one i.

The Cournot equilibrium industry output is characterised as a unique solution of the equation containing the aggregate variable and the parameter

$$X = \sum_{i=1}^{n} \varphi_i(X,\alpha) \equiv \varphi(X,\alpha). \tag{13.5}$$

The equilibrium industry output as a function of the parameter has the property

$$dX/d\alpha = (\partial\varphi/\partial\alpha)/(1-\partial\varphi/\partial X) < 0 \tag{13.6}$$

in light of (13.4). Hence the following proposition has been proved.

Proposition 1: *Under Assumptions 1–3, an increase in* α *decreases the Cournot equilibrium industry output.*

Some comments on this proposition are in order. Consider a pollution tax, for example. If the production cost of firm i is $C_{0i}(x_i)$, the firm emits one unit of pollutant per unit of output and α is the pollution tax rate per unit of pollutant, then the total cost for the firm is

$$C_i(x_i,\alpha) = C_{0i}(x_i) + \alpha x_i.$$

In this case an increase in the tax rate leads to a decrease in the equilibrium total output and pollutant. Consider next the example of commercial fishery. Suppose firm i's total fishing cost is

$$C_i(x_i,\alpha) = C_{0i}(x_i)/S \equiv \alpha C_{0i}(x_i),$$

where S is the stock level of the fish in a common fishing ground. An increase in α is equivalent to a decrease in the stock level. Hence, if the level of fish stock decreases, the equilibrium total harvest rate of the fish decreases (see Okuguchi 1996). As a third example, consider the cost function in the form

$$C_i(x_i,\alpha) \equiv c_{i0} + (a_i + \alpha)x_i,$$

where α is a constant component of marginal cost common to all firms (see Kimmel 1992). In this case, an increase in α causes a decrease in the equilibrium industry output.

I next analyse the effects of a change in α on individual firms' outputs. A little calculation yields

$$dx_i/d\alpha = A_i/B_i, \; i = 1,2,\ldots,n, \tag{13.7}$$

where

$$A_i \equiv \sum_{j \neq i} \{(f' + x_i f'')C_{j\alpha}' - (f' + x_j f'')C_{i\alpha}'\}/(f' - C_j'') - C_{i\alpha}'$$

$$B_i \equiv (C_i'' - f')\left(1 - \sum_j (f' + x_j f'')/(C_j'' - f')\right) > 0.$$

The following proposition emerges from (13.7).

Proposition 2: U*nder Assumptions 1–3, firm i' s output increases if and only if* A_i *is positive.*

As it stands, the sign of A_i is indeterminate in general. However, if the inverse demand function is linear and if, in addition,

$$C_{1\alpha}' < C_{i\alpha}', \; i = 2,\ldots,n,$$

i.e., the marginal cost of firm 1 is least affected by a change in α, then the first expression on the right-hand side of A_1 becomes positive. If $C_{1\alpha}'$ is sufficiently small, A_1 takes a positive value.

Taking into account the fact that the equilibrium value of π_i is a function of α, differentiating it with respect to α and using (13.2), I derive

$$d\pi_i/d\alpha = x_i \, dP/d\alpha - x_i f' dx_i/d\alpha - C_{i\alpha}, \; i = 1,2,\ldots,n. \tag{13.8}$$

This yields the following proposition.

Proposition 3: *Under Assumptions 1–3, the profit of firm i,* π_i*, increases if and only if*

$$dP/d\alpha > f' dx_i/d\alpha + C_{i\alpha}/x_i.$$

A special example will help to illustrate the applicability of Propositions 2 and 3. Let only firm 1's cost function be affected by a change in α. Since, in this case $A_i > 0,\ i = 2,...,n$, outputs of all firms other than firm 1 increase with an increase in α by virtue of Proposition 2. On the other hand, firm 1's output decreases in view of Proposition 1. Clearly the condition for Proposition 3 holds for all firms other than firm 1. Hence profits of firms other than firm 1 increase. Since the condition in Proposition 3 is not satisfied for firm 1, its profit decreases in the event of an increase in α. Note that linearity of the inverse demand function has not been assumed in this example.

3. INTERNATIONAL DUOPOLY

Krugman (1984) was the first to formulate a model of international Cournot duopoly with several markets. In this section I adapt comparative static analysis of Section 2 to deal with Krugman's model (see Okuguchi 1990 and Okuguchi and Serizawa 1996 for earlier analyses).

Let there be two countries (home and foreign) producing identical goods or substitutes that are marketed to several markets, possibly including the home and/or foreign countries. I assume, for the sake of analytical simplicity, that only the home country's cost function is influenced by a change in parameter α. Let countries 1 and 2 be the home and foreign countries, respectively. Let x_{ki}, $R^{ki}(x_{1i}, x_{2i})$, $C_k(X_k, \alpha)$ and π_k be country k's supply to market i, revenue from market i, cost function and total profits, respectively, where

$$X_k \equiv \sum_{i=1}^{n} x_{ki},\ k = 1,2.$$

Note that C_2 is independent of α. By definition, aggregate profit for country k is

$$\pi_k \equiv \sum_{i=1}^{n} R^{ki}(x_{1i}, x_{2i}) - C_k(X_k, \alpha),\ k = 1,2. \tag{13.9}$$

I now introduce the following fundamental assumptions.

Assumption 4a:

$$\partial C_k / \partial X_k \equiv C_k' > 0,\ \partial^2 C_k / \partial X_k^2 \equiv C_k'' < 0,\ k = 1,2;$$
$$\partial C_1 / \partial \alpha \equiv C_{1\alpha} > 0,\ \partial C_1' / \partial \alpha \equiv C_{1\alpha}' > 0.$$

Assumption 4b:

$$R_k^{ki} \equiv \partial R^{ki}/\partial x_{ki} > 0,\ k=1,2;\ i=1,2,\dots,n,$$
$$R_{kk}^{ki} \equiv \partial^2 R^{ki}/\partial x_{ki}^2 < C_{kk}'',\ k,j=1,2;\ k \neq j;\ i=1,2,\dots,n,$$
$$R_{kj}^{ki} \equiv \partial^2 R^{ki}/\partial x_{ki}\partial x_{kj} < 0,\ k,j=1,2;\ k \neq j;\ i=1,2,\dots,n.$$

Assumption 4c: $\Delta_i \equiv R_{11}^{1i}R_{22}^{2i} - R_{12}^{1i}R_{21}^{2i} > 0,\ i=1,2,\dots,n.$

Assuming away corner solutions, the first-order conditions for profit maximisation are

$$R_k^{ki}(x_{1i}, x_{2i}) - C_k'(X_k, \alpha) = 0,\ k=1,2;\ i=1,2,\dots,n. \tag{13.10}$$

The second-order condition holds in light of Assumption 4c. Solving (13.10), the individual variable x_{ki} can be expressed as a function of two aggregate variables, X_1 and X_2, and the parameter α. Hence

$$x_{ki} \equiv \varphi_{ki}(X_1, X_2, \alpha),\ k=1,2;\ i=1,2,\dots,n, \tag{13.11}$$

where in view of Assumptions 4a–4c, the partial derivatives of φ_{ki} are evaluated as

$$\begin{aligned}
&\partial\varphi_{ki}/\partial X_k = R_{jj}^{ji}C_k''/\Delta_i > 0,\\
&\partial\varphi_{ki}/\partial X_j = -R_{12}^{ki}C_j''/\Delta_i < 0,\ k,j=1,2;\ k\neq j,\\
&\partial\varphi_{1i}/\partial\alpha = R_{22}^{2i}C_{1\alpha}'/\Delta_i < 0,\\
&\partial\varphi_{2i}/\partial\alpha = -R_{21}^{2i}C_{1\alpha}'/\Delta_i > 0.
\end{aligned} \tag{13.12}$$

The Cournot equilibrium total outputs of the home and foreign countries are obtained as the solution of the system of two equations given by

$$X_k = \varphi_k(X_1, X_2, \alpha) \equiv \sum_{i=1}^{n}\varphi_{ki}(X_1, X_2, \alpha),\ k=1,2. \tag{13.13}$$

In light of (13.12), the partial derivatives of φ_k have the signs

$$\partial\varphi_k/\partial X_k > 0,\ \partial\varphi_k/\partial X_j < 0,$$
$$\partial\varphi_1/\partial\alpha \equiv \varphi_{1\alpha} < 0,\ \ \partial\varphi_2/\partial\alpha \equiv \varphi_{2\alpha} > 0,\ \ k, j = 1,2;\ \ k \neq j. \tag{13.14}$$

I now introduce an additional assumption.

Assumption 5: $$D = \begin{vmatrix} 1-\partial\varphi_1/\partial X_1 & -\partial\varphi_1/\partial X_2 \\ -\partial\varphi_2/\partial X_1 & 1-\partial\varphi_2/\partial X_2 \end{vmatrix} > 0.$$

I can interpret this assumption as follows. If there is no product differentiation,

$$P_i = f_i(x_{1i}+x_{2i}),\ f' < 0,$$

is the inverse demand function in market i and if, in addition, it is linear for all i, Assumption 5 is shown to be satisfied if

$$C_k'' \sum_{i=1}^{n} (1/f_i') < 3/2,\ \ k = 1,2. \tag{13.15}$$

Ceteris paribus, the smaller is n, the number of markets, the more likely is (13.15) to hold. If there is only one market, (13.15) is satisfied if $f_1' < C_k''$, $k = 1,2$, which corresponds to Assumption 3 in Section 2. In the case of decreasing marginal costs, (13.15) is more likely to hold the smaller the absolute value of C_k''.

Solving (13.13) with respect to X_k, I have

$$X_k \equiv X_k(\alpha),\ \ k = 1,2, \tag{13.16}$$

where, by virtue of Assumption 5 and (13.14),

$$dX_1/d\alpha < 0,\ \ dX_2/d\alpha > 0. \tag{13.17}$$

Taking into account (13.12) and (13.17), I get

$$dx_{1i}/d\alpha < 0,\ \ dx_{2i}/d\alpha > 0,\ \ i = 1,2,\ldots,n. \tag{13.18}$$

Differentiating π_k with respect to α and taking into account (13.10), I obtain that

$$d\pi_1/d\alpha = \sum_{i=1}^{n} R_2^{1i} dx_{2i} / d\alpha - C_{1\alpha} < 0,$$
$$d\pi_2/d\alpha = \sum_{i=1}^{n} R_1^{2i} dx_{1i} / d\alpha > 0. \qquad (13.19)$$

The analysis in this section is summarised in the following proposition. A similar result, derived using a different method of analysis, was obtained by Zhang and Zhang (1998).

Proposition 4: *Under Assumptions 4a-4c and 5, a change that raises (lowers) the home country's total and marginal costs leads to decreases (increases) in the home country's total output and profits as well as to decreases (increases) in its supplies to all markets, while the foreign country's corresponding equilibrium values all increase (decrease).*

4. CONCLUSIONS

Equilibrium conditions for many economic models involve individual firms' variables, the aggregate variable, which is the sum of individual variables, and an exogenous parameter. These equilibrium conditions enable us to express the individual variables as functions of the aggregate variable and the parameter. The equilibrium aggregate value therefore can be solved as a unique function of the parameter. Taking this fact into account, I have conducted comparative static analysis for a model of Cournot oligopoly in a closed economy as well as in a multi-market international context. The analysis has been conducted without use of the stability condition for the equilibrium. I have derived the results much more easily than others, on the basis of some crucial assumptions, and interpreted them from an economic point of view. In this chapter, only the effects of a change in the parameter affecting the cost function have been analysed. An extension would be to adapt the comparative static method to examine the effects of a change in a parameter that affects the demand function.

ACKNOWLEDGEMENTS

I have benefited immensely from comments of an anonymous referee and Alan Woodland in revising this chapter.

REFERENCES

Bulow, J., Jeanakoplos J. and P.D. Klemperer (1985), 'Multimarket oligopoly: strategic substitutes and complements', *Journal of Political Economy*, **93**, 488-511.

Dixit, A. (1986), 'Comparative statics for oligopoly', *International Economic Review*, **27**, 107-22.

Kimmel, S. (1992), 'Effects of cost changes on oligopolist's profits', *Journal of Industrial Economics*, **40**, 441-49.

Krugman, P. (1984), 'Import protection as export promotion', in H. Kierzkowski (ed.), *Monopolistic Competition and International Trade*, Oxford: Clarendon Press, pp. 180-93.

Okuguchi, K. (1990), 'Cournot duopoly with several markets', *Regional Sciences and Urban Economics*, **20**, 305-11.

Okuguchi, K. (1993), 'Unified approach to Cournot models: oligopoly, taxation and aggregate provision of a pure public good', *European Journal of Political Economy*, **9**, 233-45.

Okuguchi, K. (1996), 'Oligopoly in fishery', in D.T. Nguyen (ed.), *Queensland, Australia and the Asia – Pacific Economy*, Brisbane: Griffith University, pp. 523-27.

Okuguchi, K. and N. Serizawa, (1996), 'Effects of trade policy on international duopoly', *Keio Economic Studies*, **33**, 13-22.

Szidarovszky, F. and S. Yakowitz (1977), 'A new proof of the existence and uniqueness of the Cournot oligopoly', *International Economic Review*, **18**, 787-89.

Zhang, A. and Y. Zhang (1998), 'An analysis of import protection as export promotion under economies of scale', *Japan and World Economy*, **10**, 199-219.

14. Endogenous Timing and Welfare in the Game of Trade Policies under International Oligopoly

Takao Ohkawa, Makoto Okamura and Makoto Tawada

1. INTRODUCTION

The most familiar model to tackle the analysis of government intervention in trade under imperfect competition is the 'three-country' model initiated by Brander and Spencer (1985). It consists of two export countries in the absence of consumers, one import country in the absence of producers and international oligopoly arises in the market of the import country. In the 'three-country' framework, many researches adopt the Cournot-Nash equilibrium of bilateral government intervention as a solution concept.[1] In other words, they assume that each government moves simultaneously at the stage of intervention in trade.

Arvan (1991) and Shivakumar (1993) pointed out the possibility of sequential move in the three-country model with incomplete information. Arvan (1991) introduced demand uncertainty into this model and argued for the possibility of sequential play between governments. He identified the degree of demand uncertainty and the number of firms as key elements to determine the type of play. Shivakumar (1993) extended Arvan's model by introducing an export quota as an additional instrument for governments. Then he established the conclusion that sequential play possibly occurs when the export quota is chosen as a policy instrument and the uncertainty is large in degree. In these studies, the decision on the timing of bilateral government intervention is strongly connected with the degree of uncertainty.

In other frameworks dealing with trade policy games, several researches treating the problem of the endogenous timing game between governments also conclude that the simultaneous move setting is not always appropriate. Syropoulos (1994) analysed the endogenous timing of government intervention in the traditional two-country trade model with perfect competition. He established that a sequential move is always the solution in a quota game, and showed the possibility of a sequential move in a tariff game. Collie (1994) examined the theoretical possibility of the usage of countervailing duties by the analysis of endogenous timing on trade policies in the framework that both domestic and foreign firms compete à la Cournot in the domestic market. He concluded that the domestic government sets the level of the tariff first and then the foreign government sets that of the export subsidy, so that any countervailing duty by the domestic government does not arise. We should notice that the model with complete information is used in these researches.

The purpose of this chapter is to examine whether the Cournot-Nash solution concept fits with non-cooperative commercial policy games under the three-country model with complete information. Our conclusions are as follows. (1) If the number of firms in one export country is the same as that in the other, then both governments set the level of export subsidy simultaneously. (2) If the difference in the number of firms between export countries is not less than one, then the sequential move arises. The government of the country with the *smaller* number of firms sets the level of its subsidy, and then the other government imposes an export tax to its firms. (3) If the difference in the number of firms is very small, bilateral government intervention increases the level of welfare of the import country. Otherwise, it is harmful to the import country.

The first result, together with the second, implies that the difference in the number of firms between countries solely becomes a sufficient cause of a sequential play between governments and thus that a Stackelberg game may be more appropriate in the analysis of strategic trade policies.

One implication of the third result is that, as is pointed out in Bliss (1996), industrial or anti-trust policies in the export countries affect the welfare of the third country for these domestic policies influence the market structure (the number of firms) of the export countries. Our results also suggest that, depending on the number of firms, one of the export countries may adopt an export tax rather than a subsidy. Then the third country would be made worse off by the strategic trade policies of the export countries. The World Trade Organisation (WTO) cannot intervene in the content of industrial and anti-trust policies of each member country directly. It prohibits export subsidies but does not prohibit export taxes. These features suggest that each member country should consider policy harmonisation between domestic public policies and trade policies with each other and the WTO needs to discuss restrictions on export taxes as well as subsidies.

The chapter is organised as follows. Section 2 presents a multi-stage game to analyse the timing of policy setting, and solves this game using subgame perfection as a solution concept. In Section 3, we compare the level of each country's welfare in the case of government intervention with that in the case of free trade and derive several implications from this comparison. Conclusions and some directions of further studies are given in Section 4.

2. THE MODEL

Consider a world economy where three countries (called the first, second and third) and one commodity exist. The commodity is produced in the first and second countries and it is exported to the third country. There is no consumption in the producing countries. There are n_i firms located in the i-th country, for $i = 1$ and 2. Each firm has an identical production technology that exhibits constant returns to scale. Its unit cost is denoted by c.

In the third country, there is no production and consumers purchase the commodity imported from the first and second countries. Let the inverse demand function of the third country be $p = P(Q) \equiv A - Q$, where Q is the demand for the commodity, p is the commodity price and A is a positive parameter expressing a market scale and assumed to be greater than c. Each firm competes à la Cournot in the third country market.

The government of each exporting country exercises a subsidising policy to the exporting behaviour of its home firms so as to maximise the country's national welfare. Each government decides not only the level of the subsidy s_i but also the timing of the policy intervention. The government of the third country does not consider any policies on trade.

In order to examine the conventional assumption of a simultaneous move in the game of government intervention, we construct the following multi-stage game. At the first stage, the government of each producing country decides the timing of setting the level of its export subsidy, namely, the first move or the second move. If both governments move first or second, then the timing is said to be simultaneous. Otherwise, it is said to be sequential. At the second stage, each government decides the level of its export subsidy according to the timing.[2] Once each government sets the subsidy levels, all firms produce the commodity and export it to the third country under Cournot competition at the third stage. We introduce the subgame perfect Nash equilibrium as a solution concept to solve the above multi-stage game.

3. THE ANALYSIS

Let us begin with the third stage subgame. We have the semi-symmetric Cournot equilibrium, which means that the levels of output of firms located in the same country are identical. The equilibrium output level of each firm in the i-th country, q_i, is given by

$$q_i = [a - n_i s_j + (n_j + 1)s_i]/N, \quad i, j = 1,2; \quad i \neq j, \tag{14.1}$$

where $N \equiv n_1 + n_2 + 1$ and $a \equiv A - c > 0$.

At the second stage, taking the other country's subsidy as given, the government of the i-th country sets the level of subsidy s_i in order to maximise its national welfare W_i. National welfare is defined as the firm's profit plus the government's net revenue, as given by

$$W_i = n_i(\pi_i - s_i q_i),\ i = 1,2, \tag{14.2}$$

where $\pi_i = P(Q)q_i - (c - s_i)q_i$ and $Q = n_1 q_1 + n_2 q_2$. Substituting (14.1) into (14.2) and maximising (14.2) with respect to s_i yields the first-order conditions for the welfare maximisation problems. Then we rearrange these first-order conditions and obtain

$$s_i = r_i(s_j) \equiv -\frac{n_j(n_j - n_i + 1)}{2n_i(n_j + 1)} s_j + \frac{a(n_j - n_i + 1)}{2n_i(n_j + 1)},\ i,j = 1,2;\quad i \neq j. \tag{14.3}$$

Equations (14.3) are the government reaction functions with respect to export subsidies.

Using (14.3), we can investigate the timing decision at the first stage. According to Hamilton and Slutsky (1990), if we know the slopes of the reaction functions and the shapes of the country iso-welfare curves, we can easily examine the decision of timing. Both the slopes of the reaction functions and the shapes of the iso-welfare curves depend on the difference in the numbers of firms between both export countries. The following lemmas are concerned with the properties of the reaction functions and of the iso-welfare curves, respectively.

Lemma 1: *If* $n_i \geq (<)\, n_j + 1$, *then the slope of i-th country's reaction function is non-positive (positive).*[3] *In particular, it is flat if and only if* $n_i = n_j + 1$.

Proof. The proof is clear from equation (14.3).

Lemma 2: *Suppose that the slope of the i-th country's reaction function is negative (positive). Define the locus of* $\partial W_i / \partial s_j = 0$ *as* $s_i = u_i(s_j)$. *If* $\mathrm{sgn}(s_i - r_i(s_j)) = \mathrm{sgn}(s_i - u_i(s_j))$, *then the i-th country's iso-welfare curve is downward (upward) sloping. If* $\mathrm{sgn}(s_i - r_i(s_j)) \neq \mathrm{sgn}(s_i - u_i(s_j))$, *then the i-th country's iso-welfare curve is upward (downward) sloping.*

Proof. See the Appendix, which is available upon request to the author.

Lemma 1 shows that the slope of the reaction function in each export country depends on the difference in the number of firms between both countries and that all reaction functions are not upward sloping in any case. Lemma 2 implies that the iso-welfare curves of each country are U-shaped. In view of Theorem 5 in Hamilton and Slutsky (1990), our Lemmas 1 and 2 mean that the pure-strategy Nash equilibrium is uniquely determined at the first stage subgame. In other words, a unique subgame perfect Nash equilibrium exists in our multi-stage game.

The following lemma is convenient to seek the Pareto superior set necessary to choose timing of decision.

Lemma 3: *Suppose that the reaction function of the i-th country slopes negatively. Then, the welfare of the i-th country along the reaction function rises (falls) according to an increase in* s_j *if* $s_j > (<)\ a/n_j$. *If the reaction function slopes positively, the result is reversed.*

Proof. See the Appendix.

Taking Lemmas 1-3 into account, we establish the following proposition.

Proposition 1: *(i) If the numbers of firms in both export countries are identical, then the timing of decision is simultaneous. Each government subsidises its home firms. (ii) Suppose that the difference in the number of firms between countries is just one. Then the timing of decision is indecisive in the sense that the government of the country with the larger number of firms does not take any action for any given strategy of the other government. The government of the country with the smaller number of firms subsidises its home firms while the optimal strategy of the other government is non-intervention. (iii) Suppose that the difference in the number of firms between countries is more than one. Then the timing of decision is sequential. The government of the country with the smaller number of firms acts as a leader and subsidises its home firms, while the other government acts as a follower and imposes an export tax on its home firms.*

Proof. (i) As shown in Figure 14.1, the reaction function of each country has a negative slope. The intersection of two reaction curves gives a Cournot-Nash (simultaneous move) equilibrium. The shaded portion shown in Figure 14.1 represents the Pareto superior set. Because neither of the reaction curves passes through the interior of the Pareto superior set, it is clear from Theorem 5 of Hamilton and Slutsky (1990) that both governments intend to be a first mover. So the timing of decision is simultaneous. If we solve (14.3) with the condition that $n \equiv n_1 = n_2$, we can obtain the optimal rate of export subsidy s_i^α as

$$s_i^\alpha = a/n(2n+3) > 0,\ i = 1,2. \qquad (14.4)$$

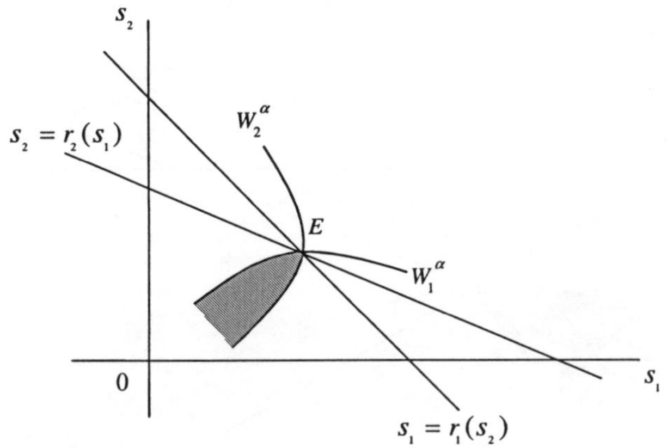

Figure 14.1 Reaction Functions and the Pareto Dominant Set in the Case of $n_1=n_2$

(ii) Without loss of generality, we can suppose that $n_2 = n_1 + 1$. Then it is clear from (14.3) that the reaction function of the second country is reduced to $r_2(s_1) = 0$. Thus the government of the second country sets s_2 to zero irrespective of the level of s_1. Therefore, the optimal subsidy in the first country is $s_1^{\beta} = a / n_1(n_1 + 2) > 0$ and the optimal subsidy of the second country is $s_2^{\beta} = 0$, from which assertion (ii) follows.

(iii) Suppose that $n_2 > n_1 + 1$ without loss of generality. In this case, the slope of the reaction function of the first country is negative, while that of the second country is positive. The reaction curve of the second country passes through the interior of the Pareto superior set as in Figure 14.2, where the Pareto-superior set is indicated as the shaded area. Due to Theorem 5 of Hamilton and Slutsky (1990), we can conclude that the timing of the decision is sequential. The government of the first country behaves as a leader while the other behaves as a follower. Using (14.3), we calculate the Stackelberg equilibrium subsidies, where the governments of the first and the second countries are a leader and a follower, respectively, and obtain the equilibrium subsidies s_1^{γ} and s_2^{γ} as

$$s_1^{\gamma} = a/n_1\left(n_1 + 2\right) > 0\,, \tag{14.5}$$

$$s_2^{\gamma} = \frac{\left(n_1 + 1 - n_2\right)a}{2n_2\left(n_1 + 2\right)} < 0\,. \tag{14.6}$$

This completes the proof.

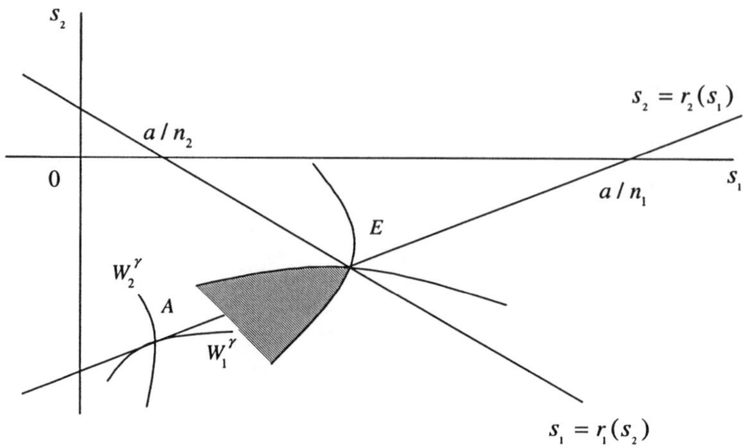

Figure 14.2 Reaction Functions and the Pareto Dominant Set in the Case of $n_2 > n_1 + 1$

Proposition 1 demonstrates that the simultaneous move of the two governments is not general. The only exception is the case where the number of firms is the same in both export countries. This implies that previous research based on the assumption of simultaneous move needs to be re-examined.

The reason why the government of the country with the larger number of firms (the second country) adopts the export tax is as follows.[4] First of all, notice two important assumptions: all firms have identical technologies and behave as Cournot oligopolists. This means that under free trade the outcome (output or profit) of each firm is identical in equilibrium. Under bilateral government intervention, however, strategic trade policies have two effects to improve export countries' welfare. One is to shift a part of the foreign firms' profit to the domestic firms by subsidising the domestic firms. The other is to keep the international market price high enough to earn a profit under imperfect competition. For the latter, the use of an export tax may be effective, because it can control the total supply of the commodity in the international market. The former effect is called the strategic distortion and the latter is called the terms of trade distortion.[5]

The government of the first country (the country with the smaller number of firms) may not have enough power to control the total supply of the commodity because the market share of the first country's firms is small. The first country's government is rather tempted to shift a part of the profit of the second country's firms, which is large enough to attract the first country. Thus, the government of the first country subsidises its home firms. On the other hand, the second country's government may not necessarily subsidise its home firms, because the scale of the rent-shifting effect from the first country's firms is small and because its subsidy policy may cause a drastic price reduction due to the large market share of the second country's firms. Therefore, it may prefer to impose an export tax on its firms so as to maintain the commodity price at a suitable level, countervailing the first country's subsidising policy. Consequently, the strategic distortion dominates in the first country, while the terms of trade distortion dominates in the second country.

In the special case where $n_2 = n_1 + 1$, the second country's government does not have any incentive to intervene. Concerning this case, Dixit (1984) discussed optimal policies from a different point of view. He considered a policy controlling the number of firms in a country and showed that, if the government uses this policy without any intervention in trade, the optimal number of firms in that country must be one more than that of the other country. Our result is, conversely, that, if the number of firms in a country is one more than that of the other country, the optimal trade policy of this country is non-intervention. Therefore, these two results seem to have a dual relationship with each other.

4. THE WELFARE COMPARISON

In this section, we compare the level of each country's welfare under bilateral government intervention with that of free trade. We define the third country's welfare as consumer surplus, so that it is expressed as

$$W_3 \equiv \int_0^Q P(x)dx - P(Q)Q = \frac{1}{2}Q^2. \tag{14.7}$$

We calculate the level of each country's welfare under the free trade by setting $s_1 = s_2 = 0$. From (14.1), (14.2) and (14.7) these are given by

$$W_i^F = n_i a^2 / N^2,\ i = 1,2 \tag{14.8}$$

$$W_3^F = (n_1 + n_2)^2 a^2 / 2N^2, \tag{14.9}$$

where W_i^F stands for the welfare of the i-th country under free trade.

Next, in the case where $n \equiv n_1 = n_2$, we calculate the welfare of the i-th country under trade intervention and obtain

$$W_i^\alpha = (n+1)a^2/(2n+3)^2,\ i=1,2, \tag{14.10}$$

$$W_3^\alpha = 2(n+1)^2 a^2/(2n+3)^2, \tag{14.11}$$

from (14.1), (14.2), (14.4) and (14.7), where W_i^α stands for the welfare of the i-th country in this case.

By a similar manner, we calculate the welfare of each country in the case where $n_2 \geq n_1 + 1$ and obtain

$$W_1^\gamma = a^2/4(n_1+2), \tag{14.12}$$

$$W_2^\gamma = (n_1+1)a^2/4(n_1+2)^2, \tag{14.13}$$

$$W_3^\gamma = (2n_1+3)^2 a^2/8(n_1+2)^2, \tag{14.14}$$

from (14.1), (14.2), (14.5), (14.6) and (14.7), where W_i^γ stands for the welfare of the i-th country in this case. Using (14.8) – (14.14), we can derive the following results about the comparison of the level of welfare between free trade and trade intervention.

Proposition 2: *Suppose that free trade prevails initially. (i) If there is no difference in the number of firms between both export countries, bilateral trade intervention reduces the level of welfare of each export country. If the number of firms differs between export countries, bilateral trade intervention improves the welfare of the country with the smaller number of firms. (ii) There is a critical value δ, which is at least greater than 12, the country with the larger number of firms becomes better off (worse off) by trade intervention if the difference in firm numbers is more (less) than the critical value. (iii) As for the welfare of the third country, there is also a critical value, such that trade intervention is gainful (harmful) to the third country if the difference in firm numbers is less (more) than three. If the difference is just three, then trade intervention does not affect the welfare of the third country.*

Proof. See the Appendix.

Our obtained results are summarised in Table 14.1. As seen in the table, a prisoner's dilemma occurs between the export countries in the case of simultaneous moves: while leadership advantage and followership disadvantage emerge when a small difference in the number of firms exists, both countries' welfare improves when the difference is sufficiently large.

Table 14.1 Summary of the Results

Number of firms	Type of play	Subsidy or tariff		Economic welfare		
		Country		Country		
		1	2	1	2	3
$n_2 = n_1$	Simultaneous	S	S	–	–	+
$n_2 = n_1 + 1$	Indecisive	S	F	+	–	+
$n_2 = n_1 + 2$	Sequential	S	T	+	–	+
$n_2 = n_1 + 3$	Sequential	S	T	+	–	0
$n_1 + \delta > n_2$ $n_2 > n_1 + 3$	Sequential	S	T	+	–	–
$n_2 = n_1 + \delta$	Sequential	S	T	+	0	–
$n_2 = n_1 + \delta$	Sequential	S	T	+	+	–

Notes: S, F, and T stand for subsidy, free trade and tariff, respectively. –, 0, and + mean that a country becomes worse off, indifferent and better off, respectively, by the government intervention. Whenever the policy is sequential, the governments of the first and the second countries act as a leader and a follower, respectively.

These results can be explained as follows. In the choice of a strategic trade policy, our assumptions of linear demands and identical unit costs enable each export country's government to act as if there were a single firm in each country, whatever the actual number of firms. Once the subsidy and the profit of this fictitious firm are set at their optimal levels, then these are equally shared among the actually existing firms in each country.

Now, keeping this in mind, we suppose that the government of the second country acts as a follower while the first one acts as a leader in policy setting. Then, the first country's government can control the level of production in the second country. In doing so, the first country's government acts as if there exists only one firm in the second country. Hence, the total profit of the second country, which is guided by the government of the first country under the supposition that only one firm operates in the second country, is determined by the number of firms in the first country only. So determined is the welfare level of the second country. In the Stackelberg situation, the number of firms in the second country has nothing to do with the determination of the welfare level of that country. This argument is supported by the fact that the number of firms in the second country, n_2, does not appear in (14.12) and (14.13).

On the other hand, without government intervention, the export country's welfare decreases as the number of firms increases. Therefore, welfare in the second country is possibly higher under government intervention than free trade if the number of firms in the second country becomes sufficiently large relative to that in the first country.

We now turn our attention to the third country's welfare. In view of the above discussion, we should notice that each country's welfare is not affected by the number of firms in the second country in the case of sequential play. On the other hand, under free trade, the welfare of each producing country falls and the welfare of the third country rises as the number of firms increases. As a result, an increase in the number of firms in the second country reduces the welfare level of the third country under government intervention, so that, if the increase is sufficiently large, the welfare of the third country tends to be lower than under free trade.

These results give the following implications for the WTO. First, the difference in the number of firms between two export countries influences the welfare of the import country. This means that industrial policies such as an anti-trust policy and entry regulation, which can control the number of firms in an export country, affect the welfare of the import country indirectly through trade. For example, if the anti-trust policy of the first country is not severe on horizontal mergers, while that of the second is quite rigorous, then the number of firms in the first country may be sufficiently smaller than in the second country. As a result, bilateral intervention harms the third country's welfare. Harmonisation of trade policies with domestic public ones is necessary to protect the benefit of consumers in the import country.

The second implication is concerned with export taxes. The WTO does not discuss export taxes rigorously, because it is considered that an export country does not have a strong incentive to use export taxes in the promotion of trade. But our results suggest that it is possible for a country with the larger number of firms to choose an export tax strategically. In our framework, the export tax is detrimental to the third country's welfare. So, in this case, we need to take serious consideration of export taxes in trade negotiations.

Finally, our attention is given to world welfare. World welfare under free trade is defined as the sum of individual countries' welfare, as given by

$$W^F = \sum_{i=1}^{3} W_i^F = \frac{(n_1 + n_2)(n_1 + n_2 + 2)}{2N^2} a^2 .$$

On the other hand, the world welfare under trade intervention is

$$W^S = \sum_{i=1}^{3} W_i^\alpha = \frac{2(n+1)(n+2)a^2}{(2n+3)^3} \qquad \text{if } n = n_1 = n_2,$$

$$W^S = \sum_{i=1}^{3} W_i^\gamma = \frac{(2n_1+3)(2n_1+5)a^2}{8(n_1+3)} \qquad \text{if } n_2 \geq n_1 + 1.$$

Notice that $W^F = W^S$ if $n_2 = n_1 + 3$. This, together with $\partial W^F / \partial n_2 > 0$, brings forth of the following proposition.

Proposition 3: *If the difference in the numbers of firms between export countries is less (more) than three, world welfare is higher (lower) under trade intervention than under free trade. If the difference is just three, world welfare is not affected by trade intervention.*

We derive one implication from this proposition. Though it is believed that for some countries free trade is not preferable under imperfect competition, and that it is reasonable for countries to use strategic trade policies, free trade may be better than trade intervention from the view of the world as a whole. It is particularly true in the case where production scales of export countries differ sufficiently. Therefore, it is important for the WTO to promote free trade on the one hand and to adjust the benefit from free trade among trading countries on the other, even if the market obeys imperfect competition.

5. REMARKS AND CONCLUSIONS

In the present chapter, considering a three-country model where the first and second countries export a commodity to the third country under Cournot competition, we investigated optimal trade policies for the first and second countries in a game of endogenous timing and compared country welfare levels with and without optimal policies. Our conclusion is that the number of firms in each country is essential to the timing of policy-makers' moves and to the welfare consequences of policies. If the number of firms is the same for the two export countries, both governments offer export subsidies simultaneously and both are worse off than they would be under free trade.

However, if $n_2 > n_1 + 1$, it was shown that the government of the second large country would act subsequent to the government of the first country, say a small country. The large country will impose an export tax on its firms and will be worse off than under free trade. The significant exception to this is the case where the difference in the number of firms between two export countries is sufficiently large. In this case, both export countries will be better off than under free trade. The case where $n_2 = n_1 + 1$ yields a critical outcome for the timing and policy decision of the large country, since the large country's best policy is non-intervention in this case. As long as there is a difference in the number of firms, the small country will always offer an export subsidy first and be better off than under free trade. As for the welfare of the third country, if the difference in the number of firms is less (more) than three, trade under export countries' intervention is gainful (harmful) to the third country.

Finally, as for world welfare, free trade is better (worse) than trade intervention in the case where $n_2 > (<)\, n_1 + 3$. If $n_2 = n_1 + 3$, there is no difference in world welfare between free trade and trade intervention.

Several implications are derived from our results. First, as long as the number of firms differs between export countries, the governments move sequentially. Hence we need to investigate rigorously the bilateral intervention described by the Stackelberg game rather than that described by the Cournot game in the analysis of strategic trade policies. Second, the difference in the number of firms is crucial to each export country's policy and welfare. Since domestic public policies can influence the number of the domestic firms, those policies should be taken into account at the negotiating table of the WTO. Third, in our framework, an export tax is a possible choice of a large country. Export taxes are usually considered to harm the consumer surplus of import countries since it raises the international price. Hence careful attention should be paid to export taxes as well as export subsidies in trade negotiations. Finally, free trade is better than trade intervention for world welfare, even under imperfect competition, if the difference in the number of firms between export countries exceeds three. In this case, there is no reason to support strategic trade policies from the world welfare point of view. Hence the WTO should promote free trade even under imperfect competition and adjust each country's gain and loss from free trade by some suitable policy instruments.

We close the chapter with a proposal for a future research topic. Suppose that free trade is chosen by agreement among trading countries at the WTO. As seen in our analysis, it is possible to make this agreement ineffective by the use of domestic industrial policies. Thus we need to investigate to what extent domestic public policies controlling the number of domestic firms can substitute for international trade policies. In other words, the research is to deal with duality in game theoretic optimisation problems between industrial and trade policies.[6]

ACKNOWLEDGEMENTS

An earlier version of this chapter was presented at the IEFS Japan Meeting at Kobe University in 1997 and the annual meeting of Japan Economic Society at Ritsumeikan University in 1998. We thank Yasuharu Furusawa, Shingo Ishiguro, Jota Ishikawa, Murray C. Kemp, Toru Kikuchi, Noritsugu Nakanishi, Koji Shimomura, Yoshimasa Shirai, Shunpei Takemori and Tsuyoshi Toshimitsu for helpful discussions and comments. We also thank Alan Woodland and a referee for helpful comments and suggestions. Financial support by grant-in-aid for scientific research from the Ministry of

Education of Japan (grant no. 11303004) and by the Zengin Foundation for Studies on Economics and Finance are gratefully acknowledged. Of course, all remaining errors are ours.

NOTES

1. See, for example, Krishna and Thursby (1991) in the analysis of optimal subsidy, and Cooper and Riezman (1989) and Hwang and Schulman (1993) in the analysis of the choice of policy instruments.
2. This type of the timing game is called an observable delay. See Hamilton and Slutsky (1990).
3. Arvan (1991) derived the similar result from the model with demand uncertainty.
4. From now, we assume that $n_2 \geq n_1$ as in the proof of Proposition 1.
5. These terms are from Krishna and Thursby (1991).
6. There are a few studies focusing on the optimisation of the number of firms in a different framework from ours. See, for example, Baye et al. (1996), Cowan (1989) and Dixit (1984). However, they do not consider the duality aspect.

REFERENCES

Arvan, L. (1991), 'Flexibility versus commitment in strategic trade policy under uncertainty', *Journal of International Economics,* **31**, 341-55.

Baye, M.R., K.J. Crocker and J. Ju (1996), 'Divisionalization, franchising, and divestiture incentives in oligopoly', *American Economic Review,* **86**, 223-36.

Bliss, C. (1996), 'Trade and competition control', in J. Bhagwati and R.E. Hudec (eds) *Fair Trade and Harmonization*, MIT Press, pp. 313-28.

Brander, J.A. and B.J. Spencer (1985), 'Export subsidies and international market share rivalry', *Journal of International Economics,* **18**, 83-100.

Collie, D.R. (1994), 'Endogenous timing in trade policy games: should governments use countervailing duties?', *Weltwirtschaftliches Archiv.,* **130**, 191-209.

Cooper, R. and R. Riezman (1989), 'Uncertainty and the choice of trade policy in oligopolistic industries', *Review of Economic Studies*, **56**, 129-40.

Cowan, S.G.B. (1989), 'Trade and competition policies for oligopolies', *Weltwirtschaftliches Archiv.,* **125**, 464-83.

Dixit, A. (1984), 'International trade policy for oligopolistic industries', *Economic Journal, **Supplement***, 1-16.

Hamilton, J.H. and S.M. Slutsky (1990), 'Endogenous timing in duopoly games: Stackelberg or Cournot equilibria', *Games and Economic Behavior,* **2**, 29-46.

Hwang, H. and C.T. Schulman (1993), 'Strategic non-intervention and the choice of trade policy for international oligopoly', *Journal of International Economics,* **34**, 73-93.

Krishna, K. and M. Thursby (1991), 'Optimal policies with strategic distortion', *Journal of International Economics,* **31**, 291-308.

Shivakumar, R. (1993), 'Strategic trade policy: choosing between export subsidies and export quotas under uncertainty', *Journal of International Economics,* **35**, 169-83.

Syropoulos, C. (1994), 'Endogenous timing in games of commercial policy', *Canadian Journal of Economics,* **27,** 847-64.

15. Politics and the Nature of Competition in Oligopolistic Markets

Partha Gangopadhyay

1. INTRODUCTION

The strategic trade and investment models attracted serious criticisms on two well-known grounds. First, their conclusions are extremely sensitive to the assumptions about the mode and nature of competition (Krugman 1993, p. 363). Secondly, it is also highlighted that the optimal rent-seeking policy loses much of its gloss once we consider political costs associated with the policy (Dixit and Grossman 1986, p. 234). An important step towards a better understanding of these issues requires us to endogenise the mode of competition and also to introduce explicitly government policy making in this context. This chapter makes both the nature of competition and government policy making endogenous and, thereby, provides a framework in which industrial structures, conduct of firms and political decisions are endogenously determined.

The central concern is to address two critical issues of government involvement in the context of strategic investment models. First, the nature of competition plays an important role in determining whether government policy has the intended and desirable effects. It is also important to model the nature of competition endogenously in this context since government policy can significantly influence the nature of competition through its effect on the firms' costs structure (Dixon 1986). Secondly, the promotion of one set of firms represents a 'taxation' of others. Government policy thus entails a political cost that is an important ingredient for formulating government policy. The existing literature has a gap since it does not make both government policy and the nature of competition endogenous. This is a major difficulty with the rent-extraction argument since political costs constrain government's behaviour whilst the benefits from strategic government policy largely depend on the endogenous degree of competition. An optimal government policy will thus be misconstrued unless we determine these elements endogenously.

I combine two distinct ideas – namely, the probabilistic voting model and the conjectural variations model – to endogenise the nature of competition and the government policy. First of all, the probabilistic voting model is a recent development in political theory to counter the time-honoured predictions of the traditional political theory (Wittman 1989): for centuries social thinkers argued that democratic governments are plagued by the absence of a stable electoral equilibrium and the risk of expropriation of minorities by majorities. The probabilistic voting model, by assuming a universally concave votes-to-offers curve, establishes the existence of a stable voting equilibrium and also that the expropriation argument is 'an optical illusion'. The probabilistic voting model will allow the relevant government policy to be endogenised. Secondly, the conduct of firms has been made endogenous in a very important contribution of Bresnahan (1981) that is popularly known as the conjectural variations model. Laitner (1980), Bresnahan (1981), Kamien and Schwartz (1983) and Perry (1982) questioned the robustness of the Cournot model as an equilibrium concept by using the model of consistent conjectured reactions. A conjectural variation is a conjecture by one firm about how the other firm will adjust its decision variable in response to potential adjustments by the first firm. The consistent conjectural equilibrium is believed to be a rational expectations equilibrium that collectively confirms individual expectations about changes in the decision variables. It is argued that the Cournot equilibrium is not generally a consistent conjectural equilibrium. However, there are problems with this approach: the consistent conjectural equilibrium is not an equilibrium since each firm can unilaterally change its output to make more profits (Bresnahan 1981, p. 937). Experimental evidence indicates that agents do not converge on the consistent conjectural equilibrium (Holt 1982). It is also recognised that the conjectural variations parameter is not observable in principle. It has also been noted that these models lack a game-theoretic foundation (Shapiro 1989). Yet it is widely held that conjectural variation models are still very important in examining scenarios underpinned by complex dynamic processes.

The simplified story of our model subsumes the following. I examine government policy that concerns an allocation of public infrastructure between two industrial locations. It is argued that the location of public infrastructure will determine the short-run cost functions of firms in these locations. These costs of production will, in turn, determine the nature of competition in the product market.[1] As a result, government policy will endogenously determine the degree and nature of competition in the product market. On the other hand, this allocation of public infrastructure also enables us to analyse the political cost: promotion of an industrial location is an implicit taxation of firms in the other location. As the government increases public infrastructure in a location, voters from this constituency increase their political support for the incumbent government whilst this government loses votes from the other location. An allocation of infrastructure thus influences voters' evaluation of the government and this evaluation constrains government policy on infrastructure that, in turn, impinges on voters' evaluation. In the proposed equilibrium of the game, the government chooses the optimal allocation that influences the voters' evaluation that, in turn, maximises the probability of re-election of the incumbent government. The optimal allocation will determine the nature of competition in the product market.

The game unfolds over two stages. In stage I, the government allocates public infrastructure in order to maximise its probability of re-election given the voters' preferences and characteristics. Thus, at stage I, an electoral platform is formed. In stage II, two firms compete for a unified market whilst their production bases are different. At the perfect Nash equilibrium of this sequential game, the government achieves an electoral equilibrium that maximises votes cast in favour of the government. This optimum allocation of infrastructure provides a winning electoral platform to the incumbent government from which the costs of production for firms and the nature of competition in the product market will emerge. Section 2 develops the sequential game and Section 3 offers the link between the proposed electoral equilibrium and the nature of competition in product markets. Section 4 summarises the findings and concludes.

2. THE MODEL

Consider a market that has duopolists who have two distinct production locations. It is assumed that these locational choices have already been made and, hence, the location of a firm is part of history. It is also assumed that the national economy consists of these locations. The government has a given amount of tax revenue that is to be distributed between these locations for creating public infrastructure. The impact of the public infrastructure is to reduce costs of production. Thus, the larger is public infrastructure in location i vis-à-vis j, the lower is the cost of production of the firm at location i. It is further assumed that buyers are located in such a fashion that the cost of transport is zero and, hence, there is a single price that prevails in the market. The market is thus characterised by the following sequential game. At stage I the electoral equilibrium determines the distribution of public infrastructure. The distribution of infrastructure determines the costs of production of the oligopolists in stage II of the game who engage in competition in the product market to capture the largest possible market shares. Table 15.1 summarises the assumed timing of decisions in the model.

The solution to the game is proposed in a recursive fashion. I first determine the market outcome at stage II and then trace back to stage I using what is popularly known as the logic of backward induction. Rationality and complete information dictate that both these firms and the government will form their expectations by looking ahead and foreseeing the product market equilibrium of stage II. If agents behave in this fashion, they are said to have rational expectations. In stage I all these agents adopt their optimal actions based on the rational expectations. The resultant outcome is the *perfect Nash equilibrium* of the proposed game.

Table 15.1 Time Structure of Decisions

Time	Decisions
History	Tax Revenues Location of Firms Location of Voters Characteristics of Voters
Stage I	Government Allocates Public Infrastructure Electoral Equilibrium is Achieved
Stage II	Duopolists Compete in the Product Market Product Market Equilibrium is Achieved

2.1 Stage II: Nature of competition in the product market

I introduce the following assumptions to characterise the product market.

Assumption 1: *Industry demand function (inverse) is of the linear form*

$$p = a - bX, \tag{15.1}$$

where p and X are price and output respectively and a, b > 0.

Assumption 2: *There are two production locations. Firm i is based at location i, for i = 1, 2.*

Assumption 3: *The cost and mariginal cost of production of firm i are*

$$\begin{aligned} c_i &= c_i(X_i, G_i) = mX_i^2 / G_i \\ MC_i &= 2mX_i / G_i, \end{aligned} \tag{15.2}$$

where X_i *is output of firm i, i =1,2,* G_i *is the allocation of public infrastructure to location i, where firm i is located.*

Thus marginal cost is increasing in output given the public infrastructure and decreasing in level of public infrastructure given output as indicated by

$$\partial MC_i / \partial X_i = 2m / G_i > 0$$
$$\partial MC_i / \partial G_i = -2mX_i / G_i^2 < 0. \tag{15.3}$$

The profit function of firm *i* is

$$\Pi_i = X_i(a - bX) - mX_i^2/G_i\,. \tag{15.4}$$

It is assumed that the firms have non-zero conjectural variation and, hence, for firm 1

$$d\Pi_1 / dX_1 = a - 2bX_1 - bX_2 - bX_1(dX_2 / dX_1) - 2mX_1 / G_1\,. \tag{15.5}$$

I define the conjectural variations as

$$\phi_1 = (dX_2 / dX_1), \phi_2 = (dX_1 / dX_2)\,. \tag{15.6}$$

Hence the reaction functions in the quantity decisions of the duopolists are

$$X_1 = (a - bX_2)/(2b + \phi_1 b + 2m / G_1)$$
$$X_2 = (a - bX_1)/(2b + \phi_2 b + 2m / G_2). \tag{15.7}$$

The consistency condition is that the change of X_1 with respect to X_2 in (15.7) must be self-confirming. That is, the slopes of the reaction functions must be equal to the appropriate conjectural variations. Hence

$$\phi_2 = [-b /(2b + b\phi_1 + 2m / G_1)]$$
$$\phi_1 = [-b /(2b + b\phi_2 + 2m / G_2)]. \tag{15.8}$$

These consistency conditions yield

$$2b\phi_2 + \phi_1\phi_2 b + 2m\phi_2 / G_1 + b = 0$$
$$2b\phi_1 + \phi_1\phi_2 b + 2m\phi_1 / G_2 + b = 0. \tag{15.9}$$

Subtraction of the second from the first of these equations yields

$$(\phi_2 / \phi_1) = [b + (m / G_2)]/[b + (m / G_1)]\,. \tag{15.10}$$

The more negative is ϕ_1 the more accommodating firm 2 is according to the belief of firm 1. Thus at the consistent conjectural equilibrium all expectations are *ex post* confirmed and, hence, (ϕ_2 / ϕ_1) is a measure of relative competitiveness of firm 1.

Definition 1: *The degree of competitiveness of firm 1 vis-à-vis firm 2 is defined as* (ϕ_2 / ϕ_1).

The larger is (ϕ_2 / ϕ_1), the more accommodating is firm 1 and vice versa. It is instructive to note that the degree of competition depends on the allocation of public infrastructure G_1 and G_2. I now turn to the explanation of G_1 and G_2 and that will, in turn, determine the degree of competition.

2.2 Stage I: Electoral equilibrium

Citizen voters have two entitlements. As an economic agent, each voter has entitlement to returns from the firm of his location. I assume that the higher the profit of a firm, the larger is the economic return of the citizen residing in the location in which the firm operates. As a voter he has an entitlement to influence the rules of the game, that is, the allocation of infrastructure. This allocation, in turn, affects his economic returns. It is assumed that each citizen exercises the voting rights in one's interests. The rational government chooses the allocation of infrastructure (rules of the game) that will give rise to nominal returns to voters that will, in turn, maximise its votes. The electoral equilibrium is the optimal allocation of infrastructure that maximises the number of votes cast in favour of the incumbent government.

In order to determine the allocation of public infrastructure G_1 and G_2, I now look at the electoral equilibrium of stage I. I apply the probabilistic voting theorem to explain the electoral equilibrium (Wittman 1989). It is assumed that voters are located in two locations of public infrastructure. Within a location, voters have identical preference for the infrastructure. Thus, there are two groups of voters and their preferences are represented by their utility functions $U_1(G_1 - G^a)$ and $U_2(G_2 - G^b)$, where G^a and G^b are respectively the 'ideal points' of voter groups 1 and 2 given their tax burdens. S_1 and S_2 are the sensitivity parameters of these groups of voters. For instance, S_1 represents the extent to which voters from group 1 based at location 1 decrease their support/vote for the political party in response to a divergence between G_2 and these voters' preferred allocation of public infrastructure G^a. I specify the votes-to-public infrastructure function as

$$V_1 = 50 + n_1 S_1 (U_1 (G_1 - G^a))$$
$$V_2 = 50 + n_2 S_2 (U_2 (G_2 - G^b)). \quad (15.11)$$

Suppose G^* is the total tax revenue to be distributed and group i of voters is located at production location i. Each group splits votes equally between two parties when both the parties offer the same infrastructure.[2] Otherwise, a party loses votes as its public infrastructure offer deviates from the 'ideal point' of a group. From Wittman (1989) we know that vote-maximising electoral equilibrium is ensured when the following first order condition is satisfied:[3]

$$n_1 S_1 (\partial U_1 / \partial G_1) = n_2 S_2 (\partial U_2 / \partial G_2). \quad (15.12)$$

Assumption 4: *The utility functions of the two groups of voters are*

$$U_1 (G_1 - G^a) = -(G_1 - G^a)^2$$
$$U_2 (G_2 - G^b) = -(G_2 - G^b)^2. \quad (15.13)$$

The above formulation of the utility function suggests that voters dislike both shortfalls and over-allocation of public infrastructure to their respective localities. The latter needs an explanation: voters may dislike an over-allocation simply to escape from congestion and pollution that an over-allocation brings with it.[4]

Proposition 1: *If equations* (15.13) *capture voters' preferences and equations* (15.11) *are the votes-to-public-infrastructure offer functions, then the optimal allocations* G_1 *and* G_2 *of the public infrastructure that maximise the votes of the incumbent government are given by*

$$G_1 = w_1 (G^* - G^b) + G^a (1 - w_2)$$
$$G_2 = w_2 (G^* - G^a) + G^b (1 - w_2) \quad (15.14)$$

where

$$w_1 = (n_2 S_2)/(n_1 S_1 + n_2 S_2)$$
$$w_2 = (n_1 S_1)/(n_1 S_1 + n_2 S_2). \quad (15.15)$$

Proof. The proof is provided in the Appendix, which is available upon request to the author.

Equations (15.14) establish that the political elements such as n_i, S_1 and S_2 are the critical ingredients in determining G_1 and G_2, given G^*. If the incumbent government wants office and voters want public infrastructure, then the vote-maximising government allocates public infrastructure in an optimal fashion to create an electoral equilibrium platform that is sensitive to voters' characteristics. The vote-maximising allocation of public infrastructure influences the nature of competition due to its effect on costs of production of duopolists. The higher the allocation that a particular location gets, the lower is the cost of production of the firm based there. This firm, due to its lower cost, will be able to extract larger profits from the output market.

3. ELECTORAL EQUILIBRIUM AND THE NATURE OF COMPETITION

From equations (15.14) and (15.15) it is evident that the allocation of government investment in infrastructure depends on w_1 and w_2 given the exogenously determined budget and the 'ideal points' G^a and G^b. It is instructive to note that w_1 and w_2 depend on the sizes n_1 and n_2 of these voter groups and their political sensitivities S_1 and S_2 to the non-fulfilment of their demand for infrastructure. From equation (15.10) we know that the nature of competition in the product market depends on the ratio of G_1 and G_2 given the values of *a* and *b*. Hence, combining (15.10), (15.14) and (15.15), I argue that the political elements, such as the size of the voter groups (n_i) and political sensitivities of these voters, S_1 and S_2, are the main determinants of the degree of competition, ϕ_2 / ϕ_1, in the product market. In order to highlight this finding, consider two special cases.

Assumption 5: *Each group of voters wants all of the available fund* G^* *to be ploughed back into their respective localities. Hence,*

$$G^* = G^a = G^b. \tag{15.16}$$

Proposition 2: *In the perfect Nash equilibrium of the sequential game, the degree of competition* $(\phi_2{}^* / \phi_1{}^*)$ *lies between the Cournot and Bertrand values and is sensitive to the political landscape of the simplified society.*

Proof. In the perfect Nash equilibrium all agents hold rational expectations about the market outcome at stage II that are given by equations (15.7). The rational expectation outcome in turn depends on the allocation of public infrastructure G_1 and G_2 at stage I. Given the rational expectation outcome, the incumbent government chooses G_1 and G_2 at stage I to maximise votes. If voters' ideal points are given by Assumption 5 then we know that

$$\begin{aligned} G_1 &= [(n_1S_1)/(n_1S_1+n_2S_2)]G^* \\ G_2 &= [(n_2S_2)/(n_1S_1+n_2S_2)]G^*. \end{aligned} \tag{15.17}$$

Using (15.17) I get that

$$(\phi_2^*/\phi_1^*) = [bG^* + m(n_1S_1+n_2S_2)/(n_2S_2)]/[bG^* + m(n_1S_1+n_2S_2)/(n_1S_1)]. \tag{15.18}$$

Equation (15.18) establishes that the equilibrium degree of competition, (ϕ_2^*/ϕ_1^*), is determined by the political factors (n_iS_i) of the society – given the cost and demand conditions. It is also evident that the equilibrium values lies between the Cournot and Bertrand values.

Now attention is turned to the comparative static results.

3.1 Comparative statics under Assumption 5

The starting point of this section is that each group of voters would want the whole of public infrastructure G^* (Assumption 5). In this scenario I have the following comparative static results that characterise the proposed perfect Nash equilibrium.

Proposition 3: *As the size of a group of voters increases, ceteris paribus, the degree of competition shifts against the interest of the other group.*

Proof. Differentiating (15.18) with respect to n_2 I get:

$$\begin{aligned} \partial(\phi_2^*/\phi_1^*)/\partial n_2 &< 0 \\ \partial(\phi_2^*/\phi_1^*)/\partial n_1 &> 0. \end{aligned} \tag{15.19}$$

Thus, for example, as n_2 increases given the size of group 1, the competitiveness of firm 1 based at location 1 goes down since the political power of its opponent increases. This completes the proof. Details are in the Appendix, which is available upon request to the author.

Proposition 4: *In the perfect Nash equilibrium, the competitiveness of firm i is an increasing function of* S_i *and a decreasing function of* S_j*. Thus, the voter sensitivity is an important determinant of the degree of competitiveness in the proposed equilibrium.*

Proof. Details are in the Appendix, which is available upon request to the author. It is shown that

$$\begin{aligned} &\partial(\phi_2 * / \phi_1 *) / \partial S_2 < 0 \\ &\partial(\phi_2 * / \phi_1 *) / \partial S_1 > 0, \end{aligned} \tag{15.20}$$

which proves the proposition.

The upshot is that a location gains a larger (smaller) chunk of the public infrastructure if voters residing in this location are more (less) sensitive about the deviation of the actual infrastructure from their desired allocation. Thus if voters of a region are highly committed to the incumbent government, the region will receive a lower share of public infrastructure that will, in turn, impoverish the region and the voters of the region.

3.2 Comparative statics under the alternative assumption

It is presumed that voters want a fixed share of the public infrastructure and any deviation from this share lowers the welfare of the voters. One may rationalise this by assuming a congestion, or pollution, cost. I represent this idea under the following assumption.

Assumption 6: *Each group of voters has the ideal public infrastructure point*

$$G^a = G^b = \lambda G * \tag{15.21}$$

where $0 < \lambda < 1$.

Lemma 1: *Let equation* (15.21) *be the preferences of the voters. The vote maximising allocation of public infrastructure* G_1 *and* G_2 *are given by*

$$\begin{aligned} G_1 &= G*(w_1 + \lambda + 2w_1\lambda) \\ G_2 &= G*(w_2 + \lambda + 2w_2\lambda). \end{aligned} \tag{15.22}$$

As a result, the degree of competition in equilibrium is

$$\frac{\phi_2 *}{\phi_1 *} = \frac{bG * + \dfrac{bm}{w_2(1+2\lambda)+\lambda}}{bG * + \dfrac{bm}{w_1(1+2\lambda)+\lambda}}. \tag{15.23}$$

Proof. Substituting (15.21) into (15.14) yields

$$\begin{aligned} G_1 &= G*(w_1+\lambda+2w_1\lambda) \\ G_2 &= G*(w_2+\lambda+2w_2\lambda). \end{aligned} \tag{15.24}$$

Substituting (15.24) into (15.10) yields the degree of competition in equilibrium, which is given by (15.23).

Lemma 2: *The competitiveness of firm 1 in equilibrium is an increasing function of* w_1 *and a decreasing function of* w_2.

Proof. Straightforward differentiation of (15.23) with respect to w_1 and w_2 yields the above. Details are in the Appendix, which is available upon request to the author.

Lemma 3: *The weight* w_i *is an increasing function of* S_i *and a decreasing function of* S_j.

Proof. Details are in the Appendix, which is available upon request to the author.

Proposition 5: *The competitiveness of firm i in equilibrium is an increasing function of the political sensitivity of voters of group i.*

Proof. Combining Lemma 2 and Lemma 3 I get that

$$\frac{d\left(\dfrac{\phi_2 *}{\phi_1 *}\right)}{dS_1} = \frac{\partial\left(\dfrac{\phi_2 *}{\phi_1 *}\right)}{\partial w_2}\frac{\partial w_2}{\partial S_1} + \frac{\partial\left(\dfrac{\phi_2 *}{\phi_1 *}\right)}{\partial w_1}\frac{\partial w_1}{\partial S_1} > 0. \tag{15.25}$$

Similarly,

$$d(\phi_2 * / \phi_1 *)/dn_1 > 0,\ (d\phi_2 * / \phi_1 *)dn_2 < 0,\ d(\phi_2 * / \phi_1 *)/dS_2 < 0,$$

completing the proof.

The comparative static results show the precise nature of the sensitivity of the degree of competition to changes in political factors. For example, the degree of competition or competitiveness of firm 1 goes up (down) as the number of voters in its production location, n_1, goes up (down) ceteris paribus. The competitiveness of firm 1 goes up (down) as voters in its production location become more (less) sensitive to the non-fulfilment of their demand for infrastructure. That is, the competitiveness of firm 1 goes up (down) as S_1 goes up (down). In an analogous fashion, the competitiveness of firm 1 goes up (down) as n_2 goes down (up) and S_2 goes down (up).

4. DISCUSSION AND CONCLUSION

The Smithian perspective on competition highlights a congruence of interests of market participants. Suppose, for example, a buyer wants some milk and is ready to give some money to the milkmaid for it, and the milkmaid wants money and is, therefore, ready to give a carton of milk in exchange. This exchange allows each to achieve one's goal and they, thereby, help each other. In a complex market mechanism, however, economic problems are often embedded in a conflicting situation. It is recognised that the market mechanism can easily handle congruent interests but may fail to resolve conflicts in a harmonious or fair fashion (Sen 1984). To redress such conflicts the visible hand of government has usually been invoked (Ostorm 1987). In this chapter I highlight two types of conflicts – market conflicts and political conflicts – and, thereby, attempt to weave them together to illuminate an important intersection between the economy and the polity. I introduce conflicts at the market level in the usual fashion as market rivalry – two prototype firms compete against each other for market shares. By applying a simple game-theoretic reasoning, I obtained the equilibrium market outcome. However, the core of the problem remains that the emerging market outcome, conduct of firms, market shares and take-home profits of these rivals critically depend on the choice of their strategic variable and, hence, on the nature of competition.[5] Dixon (1986) introduced consistent conjectural variations to make the degree of competition endogenous. He established that the degree of competition is driven by investment decisions of firms since capital stocks impinge on costs of production. This chapter exploited this intuition of Dixon by focusing on an impact of public infrastructure, as opposed to private capital, on costs of production. The degree of competition in the product market is therefore driven by an allocation of public infrastructure. The introduction of public infrastructure in the model allows us to link the second type of conflict, namely, the political conflict, with the first type. Since, the availability of public infrastructure is fixed, it is modelled such that there is no congruence of interests of agents coming from two distinct locations; as Hirsch (1977) noted, 'what winners win, losers lose'. An allocation of infrastructure will naturally entail political costs and benefits that a self-seeking government – driven by electoral motive – would try to exploit. An incumbent government will naturally choose an allocation to maximise the probability of its re-election. My model of probabilistic voting has antecedents in the literature: Lindbeck and Weibull (1987) and Dixit and Londregan (1994) adapted the probabilistic model to examine public policies that redistribute income to narrow groups of voters. They assume that the various groups differ in their preferences for the political parties and, thereby, identify political characteristics of a group that makes it an ideal candidate for receiving political largesse. The upshot is that these authors mainly study the major determinants of the political success of a special interest group. On the contrary, I start off with the political characteristics of voters and then apply the probabilistic voting theorem to determine the electoral equilibrium that is driven by political largesse in the form of public infrastructure. This is how my model resolves political conflicts.

The resolution of political conflict can have a serious ramification for the product market due to its impact on the allocation of public infrastructure. This is indeed a serious point to consider. The traditional political theory highlights the failure of the majority-rule voting caused by the absence of a stable electoral equilibrium. As a result, political instability can create significant instability in product markets. This is where I apply the probabilistic voting theorem to highlight the existence of a stable voting equilibrium to establish that democratic political markets are well organised to promote the vote-maximising allocation of infrastructure that will, in turn, lend stability to the product markets. The model predicts that the vote-maximising government adopts an optimal allocation of public infrastructure that induces an electoral equilibrium that, in turn, maximises its chances of re-election. In this perspective, the nature of competition, structure of industry and conduct of firms in an oligopolistic market critically depend on this electoral equilibrium and, hence, on voters' preferences and characteristics. The degree of competition is thus identified with the equilibrium allocation of infrastructure and becomes a continuous variable rather than a binary variable. It captures intermediate situations between the pure Bertrand and Cournot cases. I also find important comparative statics results that show that the structure, conduct of firms and nature of competition in oligopolistic markets will be sensitive to political characteristics. Future extensions of the chapter are desired on two fronts. Firstly, voters' preferences should be made dependent on the final good's price and thus on the nature of competition. This extension can enhance our understanding of the nature of equilibrium by providing circular interdependence between government policy and market outcomes. Secondly, an important extension is possible by allowing for voters 'voting with their feet'. This extension will once again introduce the circular interdependence between government policies and market outcomes.

ACKNOWLEDGEMENTS

I thank Alan Woodland and an anonymous referee for their detailed comments. The usual disclaimer strongly applies.

NOTES

1. Arrow and Kurz (1970) and Barro (1990) have stressed the importance of public infrastructure being a substitute for private capital in the production function. Thus, an increase in public infrastructure in an industrial location, ceteris paribus, reduces cost of production of all firms of that location. Alternatively, one may assume that public infrastructure reduces cost due to the 'iceberg' effect of Samuelson (1954): if public infrastructure is inadequate then a large portion of the goods produced will be wasted and will fail to reach the consumers. An increase in public infrastructure therefore reduces cost by facilitating trade. Public infrastructure has assumed significance in Europe as EC-funded infrastructure projects aim to create strategic advantages for the member nations (Martin and Rogers 1995). As examples, the Channel Tunnel, high-speed rail networks and new telecommunication networks have been undertaken in the recent years to boost industrial development and convergence in Europe.
2. Why should voters care for infrastructure? One plausible explanation is that voters are the stakeholders of the firms both as shareholders and employees.
3. It can be checked that the second-order condition is automatically satisfied.
4. It is important to note that a simple concave utility function, where voters are happier the more infrastructure investment they get but decreasingly so, will provide similar results.
5. From an early work of Marshak and Nelson (1962) we know that if the production structure is inflexible, then the Cournot outcome is a natural conclusion. On other hand, if production is completely inflexible, then the Bertrand outcome is the likely candidate. It is argued that production is more flexible – the more steep the MC function. The nature of competition is introduced as an external assumption in Brander and Spencer (1983, 1985), Dixon (1985), Dixit (1984), Eaton and Grossman (1986) and Yarrow (1985).

REFERENCES

Arrow, K. and M. Kurz (1970), *Public Investment, the Rate of Return, and Optimal Fiscal Policy*, Baltimore: Johns Hopkins University Press.

Barro, R. (1990), 'Government spending in a model of endogenous growth', *Journal of Political Economy*, **98**, 103-25.

Brander, J. and B. Spencer (1983), 'Strategic commitment with R&D: the symmetric case', *Bell Journal of Economics*, **14**, 225-35.

Brander, J. and Spencer, B. (1985), 'Export subsidies and international market share rivalry', *Journal of International Economics*, **18**, 83-100.

Bresnahan, T. (1981), 'Duopoly models with consistent conjectures', *American Economic Review*, **71**, 934-45.

Dixit, A. (1984), 'International trade policy for oligopolistic industries', *Economic*

Journal, **94**, Supplement, 1-16.
Dixit, A. and G. Grossman (1986), 'Targeted export promotion with several oligopolistic industries', *Journal of International Economics*, **21**, 233-49.
Dixit, A. and J. Londregan (1994), 'The determinants of success of special interests in redistributive politics', unpublished paper, Princeton University.
Dixon, H. (1985), 'Strategic investment with competitive product markets', *Journal of Industrial Economics*, **33**, 483-500.
Dixon, H. (1986), 'Strategic investment with consistent conjectures', *Oxford Economic Papers*, **38**, Supplement, 111-28.
Eaton, J. and G. Grossman (1986), 'Optimal trade and industrial policy under oligopoly', *Quarterly Journal of Economics*, **101**, 383-406.
Hirsch, F. (1977), *Social Limits to Growth*, London: Routledge.
Holt, C.A. (1982), 'An experimental test of the consistent-conjectures hypothesis', Working Paper, Department of Economics, University of Minnesota, June.
Kamien, M.I. and N.L. Schwartz (1983), 'Conjectural variations', *Canadian Journal of Economics*, **16**, 191-211.
Krugman, P. (1993), 'The narrow and broad arguments for free trade', *American Economic Review*, **83**, 362-66.
Laitner, J. (1980), 'Rational duopoly equilibria', *Quarterly Journal of Economics*, **95**, 641-62.
Lindbeck, A. and J. Weibull (1987), 'Balanced budget redistribution as the outcome of political competition', *Public Choice*, **54**, 273-97.
Marshak, T. and R. Nelson (1962), 'Flexibility, uncertainty, and economic theory', *Metroeconomica*, **14**, 42-60.
Martin, P. and C.A. Rogers (1995), 'Industrial location and public infrastructure', *Journal of International Economics*, **39**, 335-51.
Ostorm, V. (1987), *The Political Theory of Compound Republic*, University of Nebraska Press.
Perry, M.K. (1982), 'Oligopoly and consistent conjectural variations', *Bell Journal of Economics*, **13**, 197-205.
Samuelson, P.A. (1954), 'The transfer problem and transport costs, II: Analysis of effects of trade impediments', *Economic Journal*, **64**, 264-89.
Sen, A.K. (1984), 'The profit motive', in A.K. Sen (ed.), *Resources, Values and Development*, Oxford: Basil Blackwell, pp. 90-110.
Shapiro, C. (1989), 'Theories of oligopoly behavior', in R. Schmalensee and R. Willig (eds), *Handbook of International Organization*, Vol. 1, Amsterdam: North Holland, pp. 329-414.
Wittman, D. (1989), 'Why democracies produce efficient results', *Journal of Political Economy*, **97**, 1395-424.
Yarrow, G. (1985), 'Measures of monopoly welfare loss in markets with differentiated products', *Journal of Industrial Economics*, **33**, 515-30.

PART FOUR

Economic Dynamics

16. Learning in a Generalised Dornbusch Model of Exchange Rate Dynamics

Carl Chiarella and Alexander Khomin

1. INTRODUCTION

The excess volatility of exchange rates has become one of the widely documented and accepted stylised facts of empirical finance and economics; see e.g. Pagan (1996). However, economists are less agreed as to what the possible causes of this phenomenon may be. One possible explanation is that excess volatility is a result of economic agents seeking to learn about their economic environment; see e.g. Tabellini (1988).

The literature on boundedly rational economic agents simultaneously learning about and interacting with their economic environment has grown enormously in recent years. We cite in particular Evans and Honkapohja (1995), Barucci, Bischi and Gardini (1999) and Chiarella and Khomin (1999). This literature has grown out of dissatisfaction with the extreme informational assumptions of the rational expectations literature.

In this chapter we consider the effects of learning within the framework of the now classical Dornbusch (1976) model of exchange rate dynamics in the presence of external random 'market noise' processes. This model still exerts a strong influence on the economics profession's thinking about exchange rate dynamics and, in one form or another, is at the base of many empirical models of exchange rates. A feature of the model is that agents are assumed to have perfect foresight (rational expectations in stochastic versions). It is this extreme informational assumption that we remove from the agents of the model. We assume, instead, the existence of what we call sophisticated agents who are assumed to know the structure of the economic model in which they play out their economic roles, but they do not know and seek to adaptively learn the parameters of the model. This they do using a fairly sophisticated maximum likelihood learning algorithm. These agents could be thought of as the fundamentalists discussed in some literature on exchange rate dynamics, e.g. Frankel and Froot (1986, 1990). We investigate the convergence of the learning scheme and the nature of the exchange rate dynamics in the presence of learning versus the no-learning situation.

The chapter is organised as follows. Section 2 outlines the generalised version of the Dornbusch model we utilise in our analysis, modified to take account of the fact that we do not assume the sophisticated agents have complete knowledge of the model. These modifications are motivated by the fact that without such complete knowledge the agents cannot be assumed to be capable of employing the so-called jump variable technique to place the dynamics on a stable manifold. We employ the model of Chiarella (1990) who introduces non-linear exchange rate adjustment to obtain a stable dynamics in this situation. Section 3 studies the dynamics of the exchange rate when the sophisticated agents employ maximum likelihood learning to learn the unknown parameters of the model and compares the exchange rate dynamics with the no-learning situation. Section 4 draws some conclusions and makes some suggestions for future research.

2. A GENERALISED DORNBUSCH MODEL OF EXCHANGE RATE DYNAMICS

The well-known, over-shooting feature of the Dornbusch model arises from the fact that domestic prices adjust sluggishly whilst exchange rates are able to adjust instantaneously. Furthermore, the model exhibits saddle-path dynamics, but adjusts to the stable branch via the jump variable technique with the exchange rate being the jump variable. An important underpinning of the jump variable methodology is the assumption of perfect foresight (rational expectations) on the part of the economic agents of the model. Their complete knowledge of the model allows them to calculate precisely the required jump in response to unanticipated 'news' events. By assuming (as we do) less than complete knowledge of the model, we remove from the agents the capability of calculating precisely the required jump to put the exchange rate and price dynamics onto a stable path. In order to generate dynamics that can remain stable whilst the agents are trying to learn about their economic environment we need to make some modifications to the original Dornbusch model. We resolve this issue (of obtaining a stable underlying dynamics) by relaxing some of the strict assumptions of the Dornbusch model. In particular, we allow for imperfect substitutability between domestic and foreign interest-bearing assets, lagged non-linear exchange rate adjustment in the foreign exchange market and a kind of adaptively rational expectation with perfect foresight being obtained as a limiting case. Depending on the speed of adjustment of expectations the model is able to generate either convergence to the steady state or self-sustaining cyclical behaviour of the exchange rate and expectations of its change. In the perfect foresight limit (as speed of adjustment of expectations becomes infinite) the cycles become relaxation cycles in which expectations jump in response to news whilst the exchange rate undergoes non-smooth changes. To this underlying model of the exchange rate fundamentals a white noise 'market noise' process is added.

As we have stated above, our basic economic setting is that of Dornbusch (1976). However, in order to introduce the appropriate imperfections (non-substitutability and lagged exchange rate adjustment) into the model we incorporate the portfolio approach into the modelling of the foreign exchange market as developed by Kouri (1983). Our exposition of the model follows the notation and approach of Gray and Turnovsky (1979) that shows very clearly the saddle-point structure of the Dornbusch model under perfect myopic foresight and how the jump variable technique is used to obtain a stable dynamics.

We denote by R^* the foreign (nominal) rate of interest (assumed exogenous), R the domestic (nominal) rate of interest, E the logarithm of the current exchange rate (units of domestic currency per unit of foreign currency), X the expected rate of exchange depreciation, M the logarithm of the domestic nominal money supply (assumed exogenous), P the logarithm of the domestic price level and Y the logarithm of domestic real output (assumed to be fixed). The exchange rate E should be viewed as the exchange rate fundamental. The actually observed exchange rate will fluctuate around this because of day-by-day trading activity, which is driven by a range of short term factors. We do not seek to model this day-by-day activity and below we capture its effect by the addition of a white noise term.

We briefly recall the well-known elements of the Dornbusch model. Firstly, the demand for real balances is given by

$$M - P = \alpha_1 Y + \alpha_2 R \quad (\alpha_1 > 0, \alpha_2 < 0). \tag{16.1}$$

In the goods market, demand D is assumed to be an increasing function of output Y and the relative price $(E - P)$, and a decreasing function of domestic nominal interest rate R, i.e.

$$D = \beta_0 + \beta_1 Y + \beta_2 R + \beta_3 (E - P), \quad (0 < \beta_1 < 1,\ \beta_2 < 0,\ \beta_3 > 0). \tag{16.2}$$

There is sluggish price adjustment in the goods market according to which the domestic price adjusts to excess demand, so that

$$\dot{P} = \rho[\beta_0 + (\beta_1 - 1)Y + \beta_2 R + \beta_3 (E - P)], \quad (\rho > 0). \tag{16.3}$$

The essential feature of our generalised model is the manner in which the foreign exchange market is modelled. We adopt the portfolio approach of Kouri (1983), in which domestic residents hold some fraction of domestic wealth in foreign assets. This fraction depends on the relative expected return and risk characteristics of domestic and foreign assets, which is measured by the real interest rate differential $R^* + X - R$. Thus, taking the prices of foreign assets as exogenous in foreign currency and the stock of domestic wealth as exogenous in domestic currency, the stock demand for foreign assets may be written

$$\tilde{F}^d = \tilde{f}\left(R^* + X - R\right)V / s, \tag{16.4}$$

where V stands for the value of domestic wealth (net outside assets) in domestic currency, s is the exchange rate ($\ln s = E$) and $\tilde{f}(\cdot)$ is the fraction of V that domestic residents desire to hold in foreign assets. We assume that this fraction is an increasing function of the real interest differential $R^* + X - R$ and is bounded above and below as $R^* + X - R$ tends to large positive or negative values, i.e. $\tilde{f}'\left(R^* + X - R\right) > 0$ and $\tilde{f}_l < \tilde{f} < \tilde{f}_u$. The upper and lower limits $\tilde{f}_u$ and $\tilde{f}_l$ arise from the assumption that domestic residents will hold domestic wealth neither entirely in foreign assets nor entirely in domestic assets as the interest differential $R^* + X - R$ assumes large values. Rather, some fixed proportion of wealth will be held in domestic assets and some in foreign assets, perhaps to satisfy transactions demand. It is also possible that the central bank can change the relation between $\tilde{f}_u$ and $\tilde{f}_l$ by intervention in the foreign exchange market. Taking logarithms of (16.4), the log of domestic demand for foreign assets can be written

$$\log \tilde{F}^d = f\left(R^* + X - R\right) - E + \log V, \tag{16.5}$$

where $f = \log \tilde{f}$ and $f_l < f < f_u$ $(f_l = \log \tilde{f}_l, f_u = \log \tilde{f}_u)$.

The general shape of f, displaying the essential features of positive slope and upper and lower bounds, is shown by the solid curve in Figure 16.1. This demand function, unlike the one implicit in the Dornbusch class of models, allows for imperfect substitutability between foreign and domestic interest-bearing assets. The implicit demand function of the Dornbusch model may be thought of as the step-like limiting function obtained when the middle section of the function f tends to infinite slope (see the dotted curves in Figure 16.1). In this limit, the demand for the foreign asset is indeterminate between f_u and f_l, with the uncovered interest parity condition $R^* + X - R = 0$ being satisfied for all time.

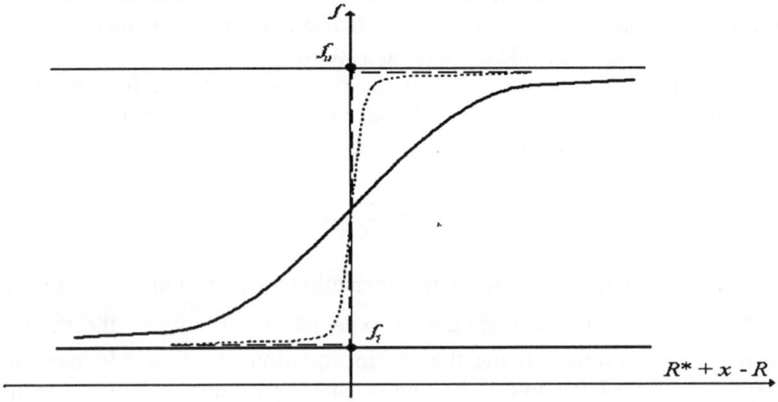

Figure 16.1 The Demand for Foreign Assets

The other element of the foreign exchange market that we include in the model analysed below is the notion that there is gradual adjustment of the exchange rate fundamental E in response to excess demand for foreign assets. Thus we assume that the exchange rate adjusts to excess demand for foreign exchange according to

$$\tau_e \dot{E} = f(R^* + X - R) - E + \log V - \overline{S}, \qquad (16.6)$$

where $\tau_e > 0$ and $\overline{S}$ is the fixed supply of foreign exchange. The parameter τ_e is the time lag with which the exchange rate adjusts to excess demand. In practice we would expect τ_e to be small but not zero. We note that τ_e is related to γ_e, the speed of exchange rate adjustment, via $\gamma_e \equiv 1/\tau_e$. It should be noted that we are concentrating on the special case, also considered by Kouri, in which foreign residents do not hold domestic assets and there is a fixed supply of foreign exchange.[1] The uncovered interest rate parity condition $R^* + X - R = 0$ of the standard Dornbusch model is obtained when the demand function f tends to the perfect substitutability limit discussed earlier (where f becomes a step function).

To give a proper foundation to equation (16.6) we would really need to consider an asset market model with lagged portfolio adjustments; see e.g. Karacaoglu and Ursprung (1988) for a modelling framework and Kearney and MacDonald (1985) and Davis and Lewis (1977) on the empirical relevance. However this would necessarily involve further differential equations for the dynamics of $\tilde{F}^d$ and R and would increase the dimension of the dynamical system we analyse below. We believe that equation (16.6) captures the broad impact of lagged portfolio adjustments whilst at the same time giving us a manageable dynamical system.

The final element of our model is the mechanism for the formation of the expectations variable X. We shall assume that expectations are formed according to the adaptive expectations scheme

$$\tau_X \dot{X} = \dot{E} - X, \tag{16.7}$$

where $\tau_X > 0$ is the time lag in the formation of expectations. Note that γ_X ($=1/\tau_X$) is the speed of adjustment of expectations. To obtain the traditional adaptive expectations scheme the $\dot{E}$ in equation (16.7) would have to be interpreted as the left-hand derivative so that it would be calculated from the most recently observed exchange rate changes. However, we allow our sophisticated agents (who are assumed to know the structure of the model) to use equation (16.6) in calculating $\dot{E}$, in which case it would have to be interpreted as the right-hand derivative. The rationale for assuming $\tau_X > 0$ is the fact that the sophisticated agents do not know all the parameters in equation (16.6) (which they seek to learn) and hence do not wish to over-react in adjusting their expectations. For these reasons we call this expectations scheme adaptively rational. We note that, in the limiting case where $\tau_X \to 0$, the conventional perfect foresight mechanism $X = \dot{E}$ is obtained.

The dynamics of the exchange rate model can be expressed by the differential equations[2]

$$\dot{E} = \gamma_e [f(R^* + X - R) - E + \log V - \overline{S}] \tag{16.8}$$

$$\dot{X} = \gamma_X \left(\dot{E} - X\right) \tag{16.9}$$

$$\dot{P} = \rho\left(\beta_0 + (\beta_1 - 1)Y + \beta_2 R + \beta_3 (E - P)\right), \tag{16.10}$$

with R being determined as a factor of P from the money demand equation (16.1), i.e.

$$R = (M - \alpha_1 Y)/\alpha_2 - P/\alpha_2. \tag{16.11}$$

The steady state point $(\overline{E}, \overline{X}, \overline{P})$ of the dynamical system (16.8)–(16.10) is given by

$$\overline{X} = 0 \tag{16.12}$$

with $\overline{E}$ and $\overline{P}$ being determined by the simultaneous set of equations

$$(\beta_2 + \alpha_2\beta_3)P/\alpha_2 - \beta_3 E = \beta_0 + (\beta_1 - 1)Y + \beta_2(M - \alpha_1 Y)/\alpha_2 \quad (16.13)$$

and

$$f(R^* - (M - \alpha_1 Y)/\alpha_2 + P/\alpha_2) - E = \overline{S}\,. \quad (16.14)$$

The graphical determination of $\overline{P}$ and $\overline{E}$ is shown in Figure 16.2 by the intersection of the curves $\dot{\overline{E}} = 0$ and $\dot{\overline{P}} = 0$. The comparative statics of this steady state point are discussed in Chiarella (1992). We may use (16.11) to calculate $\overline{R}$, which is the corresponding equilibrium value of the domestic interest rate.

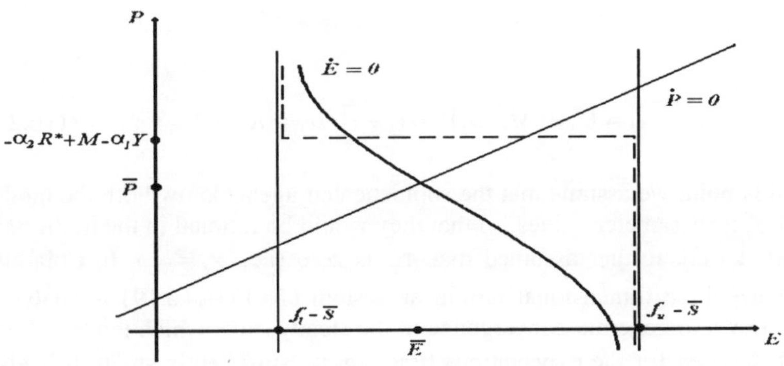

Figure 16.2 Determination of Equilibrium Values $\overline{E}$ and $\overline{P}$

We note that when the limiting case of perfect asset substitutability is approached (i.e. the $\dot{E} = 0$ curve becomes the dotted curve in Figure 16.2) the steady state becomes the steady state of the Dornbusch model in which $\overline{X} = 0$ and $\overline{R} = R^*$ (i.e. uncovered interest parity holds) and (from 16.11)

$$\overline{P} = -\alpha_2 R^* + M - \alpha_1 Y \quad (16.15)$$

and

$$\overline{E} = -\beta_0/\beta_3 - (\alpha_2 + \beta_2/\beta_3)R^* + M - (\alpha_1 + (\beta_1 - 1)/\beta_3)Y\,. \quad (16.16)$$

We define the deviation variables $e = E - \overline{E}$, $x = X - \overline{X}$, $p = P - \overline{P}$ and $r = R - \overline{R}$. In terms of these variables the differential system (16.8)–(16.10) may be written

$$\dot{e} = \gamma_e[\varphi(x + p/\alpha_2) - e] \tag{16.17}$$

$$\dot{x} = \gamma_x[\gamma_e\{\varphi(x + p/\alpha_2) - e\} - x] \tag{16.18}$$

$$\dot{p} = \rho[-(\beta_2 + \alpha_2\beta_3)p/\alpha_2 + \beta_3 e], \tag{16.19}$$

where the function φ is defined according to

$$\varphi(z) = f(n + z) - f(n) \tag{16.20}$$

and

$$n = R^* - (M - \alpha_1 Y)/\alpha_2 + \overline{P}/\alpha_2 = R^* - \overline{R} \tag{16.21}$$

At this point we assume that the sophisticated agents know both the model and all of its parameter values, so that they would be rational in the traditional sense if it were further assumed that τ_X is zero (i.e. $\gamma_x = \infty$). In Chiarella (1990) the three dimensional nonlinear system (16.17)–(16.19) is analysed and is shown to generate convergence to the steady state, which tends to limit cycle behaviour for the expectations time lag τ_X sufficiently small. It is also shown in Chiarella (1990) how the use of the jump variable technique may be avoided, since the limit cycles are stable. Furthermore, when the expectations time lag τ_X tends to zero to yield the perfect foresight limit, the limit cycle is shown to tend to a relaxation cycle.[3] Thus the dynamics of the model under adaptively rational expectations with τ_X close to zero are qualitatively the same as under perfect foresight when τ_X is zero. We believe this fact supports the use of the adaptively rational assumption even in this world where the agents know the model and all of its parameters.

We display in Figure 16.3 the possible types of dynamic behaviour for e generated using the data in Table 16.1 (with the noise term standard deviations set to zero) and the values of τ_x indicated. We stress that these paths should be understood as the trend path or fundamental around which the exchange rate fluctuates due to day-to-day trading activity. The fundamental is moving to a new steady state (in this case lower) value in response to some major 'event', such as a change in monetary policy. Figure 16.3a shows the situation when the new steady state is asymptotically stable. We see clearly the undershooting/overshooting effect (which, in most simulations, becomes more pronounced as the perfect foresight limit $\tau_X = 0$ is approached). However, here the undershooting/overshooting is induced by the imperfect substitutability of assets and lagged nonlinear exchange rate adjustment, rather than by the arbitrary imposition of the jump variable technique of traditional analyses of the Dornbusch model. Figure 16.3b shows the situation when τ_X is very small and hence the steady state is locally unstable and the dynamics tend to the relaxation cycle shown.[4] Figure 16.4 displays the corresponding exchange rate fluctuations when the market noise terms are 'switched on'.

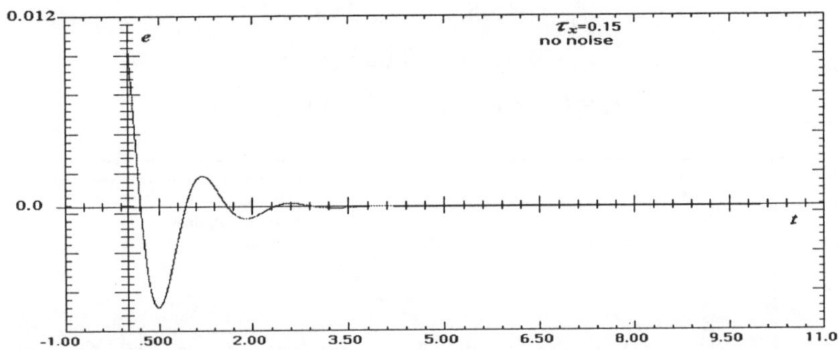

Figure 16.3a Local Stability with No Market Noise

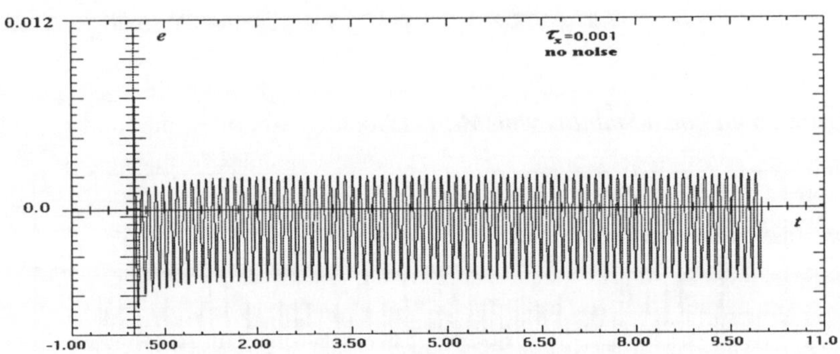

Figure 16.3b Local Instability with No Market Noise

In our study of the effects of agent learning in this model, we consider only the parameter set for which the steady state is locally asymptotically stable. We wish to see to what extent learning in this stable case (which in a sense is the economic theorists' ideal situation) can be a source of excess volatility. We leave for future research a study of learning in situations where the steady state is locally unstable as in Figure 16.3b. At first glance, it seems almost certain that any excess volatility would be amplified in this situation.

Table 16.1 The Parameter Set

$$\alpha_2 = -3, \beta_2 = -1, \beta_3 = 0.35$$
$$\gamma_e = 3.33, \gamma_x = 6.67, \rho = 2.5$$
$$h = 0.001, \sigma_e = 0.3, \sigma_p = 0.2$$
$$f_u = -1.05, f_l = -1.35, a = 2.1$$
$$n^* = 0.05, n_0 = 0.055, \gamma_{e,0} = 3.1$$
$$f(x) = (f_u + f_l)/2 + \tanh(ax)(f_u - f_l)/2$$

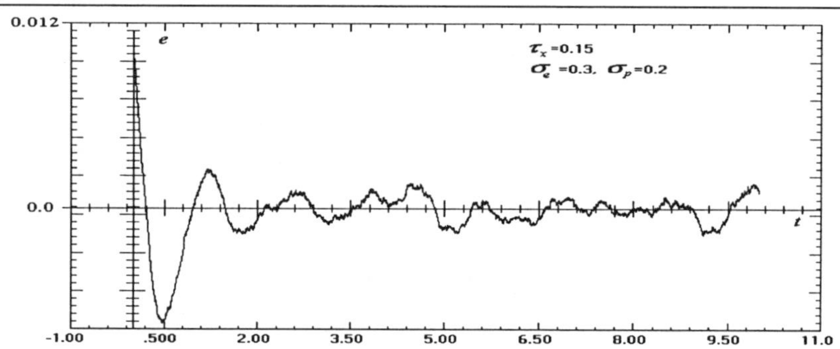

Figure 16.4a Local Stability with Market Noise

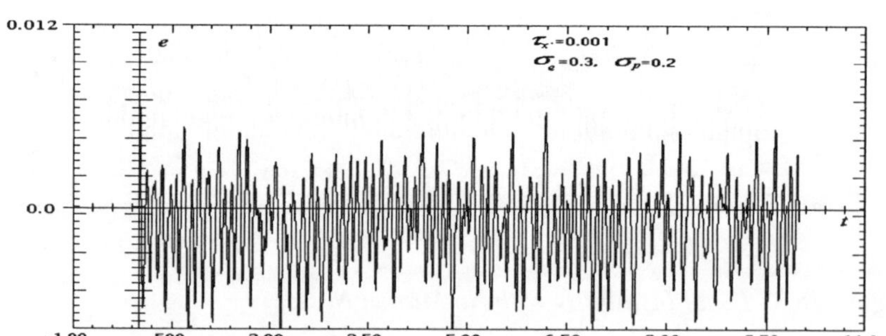

Figure 16.4b Local Instability with Market Noise

3. MAXIMUM LIKELIHOOD LEARNING BY SOPHISTICATED AGENTS

In this section we continue to assume that the sophisticated agents know the structure of the model. However, they do not know all of its parameters and they seek to learn the unknown parameters from observations of the evolution of the exchange rate and the price. The parameters of the model may be broadly categorised as being of two types, fundamental parameters (i.e. the αs, βs and n) and market parameters (the speeds of adjustment i.e. the γs and ρ). We thus consider two learning scenarios, one in which all except one of the fundamental parameters (here n) is known, the other in which all except one of the market parameters (here γ_e) is known.

It is both conceptually and technically more convenient to adopt a discrete time formulation of the model in order to implement the maximum likelihood learning algorithm. Thus, approximating the continuous time derivatives by first differences, we write the model in the form[5]

$$e_{t+h} = e_t + \gamma_e[\phi(x_t + p_t / \alpha_2) - e_t] \tag{16.22}$$

$$x_{t+h} = x_t + h\gamma_x\{\gamma_e[\phi(x_t + p_t / \alpha_2) - e_t] - x_t\} \tag{16.23}$$

$$p_{t+h} = p_t + h\,\rho[-(\beta_2 + \alpha_2\beta_3)p_t / \alpha_2 + \beta_3 e_t]. \tag{16.24}$$

As we have stated, we assume that the sophisticated economic agents do not have full knowledge of all parameters and seek to learn them from observations of the evolution of the system. However, these observations (i.e. of e_t, p_t) are assumed to be noisy[6] due to the incessant arrival of market noise and day-to-day trading activity that cause the market-observed values to fluctuate around the fundamental values e and p. Thus, observed values for e_t and p_t are written

$$\tilde{e}_t = e_t + \sigma_e \sqrt{h}\, \xi_t^{(e)} \tag{16.25}$$

$$\tilde{p}_t = p_t + \sigma_p \sqrt{h}\, \xi_t^{(p)}, \tag{16.26}$$

where the

$$\xi_t^{(i)} \sim N(0,1)$$

are independent standard normal variables that capture the effect of market noise and day-to-day trading activity. Note that we write $\sqrt{h}$ so that in the limit $h \to 0$ we would obtain properly defined stochastic differential equations.

We shall assume, in turn, that the economic agents seek to learn n (which amounts to learning the equilibrium of the system) and γ_e (which amounts to learning the market's speed of adjustment to equilibrium).

Consider the case when the economic agents seek to learn the parameter n. Let n^* be the 'true' value of n (i.e. this is the value of n used by the foreign exchange market in calculating the excess demand function ϕ in equation (16.22)), and n_t the forecast of n used by agents in period t in forming their expectations in equation (16.23). Thus the evolution of market prices is given by

$$\tilde{e}_{t+h} = \tilde{e}_t + h\,\gamma_e\left[\,\phi(x_t + \tilde{p}_t/\alpha_2; n^*) - \tilde{e}_t\right] + \sigma_e\sqrt{h}\,\xi_t^{(e)} \tag{16.27}$$

$$x_{t+h} = x_t + h\gamma_x\left\{\gamma_e\,\left[\,\phi(x_t + \tilde{p}_t/\alpha_2; n_t) - \tilde{e}_t\right] - x_t\right\} \tag{16.28}$$

$$\tilde{p}_{t+h} = \tilde{p}_t + h\,\rho\left[-(\beta_2 + \alpha_2\beta_3)\tilde{p}_t/\alpha_2 + \beta_3\tilde{e}_t\right] + \sigma_p\sqrt{h}\,\xi_t^{(p)}. \tag{16.29}$$

We need to indicate the dependence of the function ϕ on n, so it is now written as $\phi(z;n)$. We place ~ above e and p to indicate that these have now become stochastic variables. We note that the agents' learning affects the market prices via their expectations x_t which are based on the correct model, but calculated with their most recent estimate of n rather than the true value n^*. This has the potential to drive the dynamics away from the steady state and so amplify the effect of the σ_e and σ_p. In order to update their estimate of n_t, the economic agents must estimate the evolution of e_t, p_t. This they do using the estimated system

$$e_{t+h}^{(est)} = \tilde{e}_t + h\,\gamma_e\left[\,\phi(x_t + \tilde{p}_t/\alpha_2; n_t) - \tilde{e}_t\right] \tag{16.30}$$

$$x_{t+h} = x_t + h\gamma_x\left\{\gamma_e\,\left[\,\phi(x_t + \tilde{p}_t/\alpha_2; n_t) - \tilde{e}_t\right] - x_t\right\} \tag{16.31}$$

$$\tilde{p}_{t+h\;t+h}^{(est)} = \tilde{p}_t + h\,\rho\left[-(\beta_2 + \alpha_2\beta_3)\tilde{p}_t/\alpha_2 + \beta_3\tilde{e}_t\right] \tag{16.32}$$

At time t the economic agents are able to form their time t estimation error vector

$$\eta_t = \begin{bmatrix} \tilde{e}_t \\ \tilde{p}_t \end{bmatrix} - \begin{bmatrix} e_t^{(est)} \\ p_t^{(est)} \end{bmatrix} \tag{16.33}$$

that they then use to update their estimate of n_t. In calculating these updates we have assumed that the agents use the maximum likelihood learning algorithm proposed by Sidar (1976) and outlined in the Appendix.[7] We chose this recursive scheme because it satisfies several guidelines: it provides estimates of, and tracks, the unknown parameter value in multi-parameter linear and nonlinear systems and it is computationally simple. The algorithm employs a maximum likelihood approach and updates n_t, which is then used to estimate the state variables at time $(t + h)$, according to

$$n_t = n_{t-h} + A^{-1}B\eta_t , \tag{16.34}$$

where the matrices A and B are generated recursively as outlined in the Appendix. In Figure 16.5 we give a flow-chart representation of the learning algorithm.

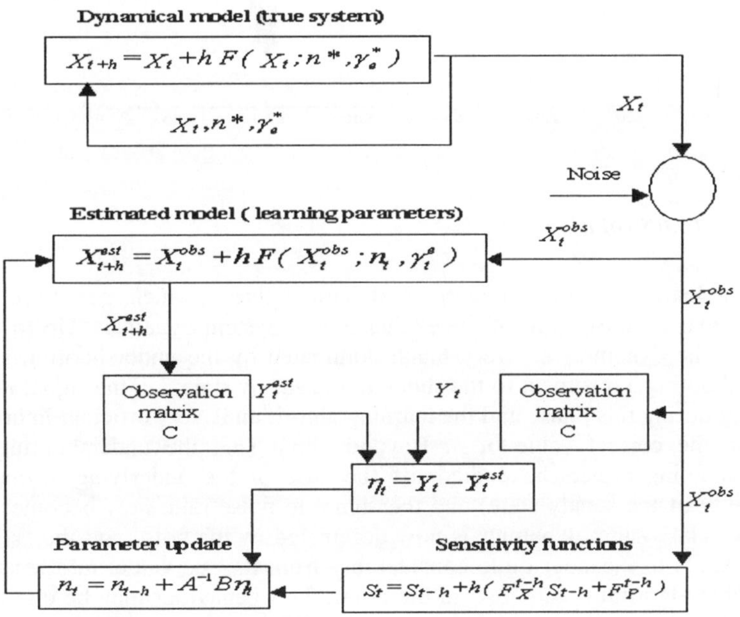

Figure 16.5 Flow Diagram of the Recursive Learning Algorithm

In the simulations reported below we have used the basic parameter values in Table 16.1.[8] For this set of parameter values the model with no noise and no learning exhibits the stable behaviour shown in Figure 16.3a, whilst Figure 16.4a shows no learning with noise. Figure 16.6 shows the evolution of n_t from an initial value within 10% of the true value (i.e. $n_0 = 0.055$), over a time interval which is 10 years on the time-scale of the model. We have used the same sequence of random numbers that was used to generate Figure 16.4a so as to isolate any dynamic effects on the exchange rate dynamics due solely to learning.

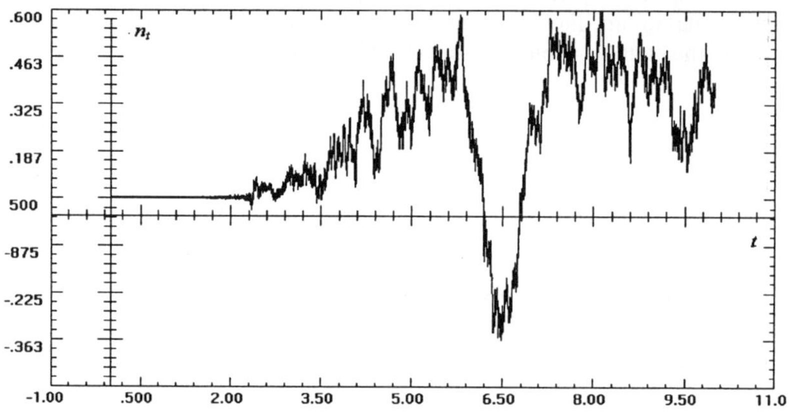

Figure 16.6 Evolution of n_t

The learning seems to undergo two distinct phases, which seem to relate to the signal to noise ratio of the exchange rate system dynamics. Up to about t=2.5, the dynamics are very much dominated by the undershooting and/or overshooting adjustment to the shock to the steady state, i.e. the signal is very strong during this phase and the learning algorithm is very efficient in homing in on the correct value of n. Beyond about t=3, the undershooting and overshooting effects have died off (because of the underlying asymptotic stability of the steady state) and the signal to noise ratio now becomes very weak. The system dynamics is now dominated by the noise and the estimate of n starts to meander quite considerably from its true value; in a sense the learning algorithm 'gets lost' in the noise. This behaviour may be due to the fact that the changing values of n in the difference equation for x_t tend to make the learning system's equilibrium point shift around so that the economic agents end up forever chasing a moving target.

Figure 16.7 shows the corresponding evolution of the exchange rate over the same period. The exchange rate behaviour also reflects two distinct phases. In the first phase, up to about t=3.0, the dynamics is dominated by the adjustment to the new steady state. In the second, beyond t=3.5, the dynamics seem basically to be dominated by the white noise. Whilst it is beyond the scope of this chapter to perform any formal statistical tests, visual inspection does not seem to indicate any greater volatility in Figure 16.7 than in Figure 16.4a. We have made similar observations from reproduction of Figures 16.4a and 16.7 for several different sequences of random numbers.

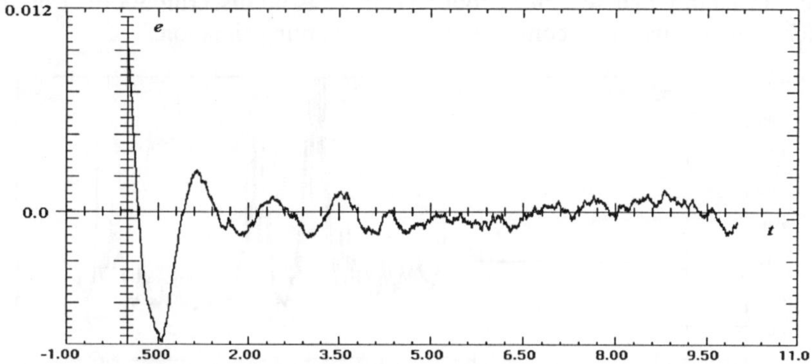

Figure 16.7 Exchange Rate Dynamics – Learning n^*

Our tentative conclusion, at least on the basis of a small number of simulations, is that agents' learning of the fundamental parameters does not create volatility that could be considered excessive with respect to the background market white noise processes. In this stable framework, any excess volatility that empiricists may observe is more likely due to the noisy overshooting and undershooting in response to exogenous, Poisson-jump type 'news' events that cause adjustments to the parameters determining the steady state. It is also possible that excess volatility is due to local instability of the steady state and/or the effect of learning in such an unstable environment. However, we leave investigation of this issue to future research.

Now suppose that the economic agents do not know γ_e and seek to learn it by the adaptive learning algorithm described in the Appendix. We now use the same basic parameter values as in the simulations for the learning of n. Figure 16.8 shows the evolution of γ_e^t, the economic agents' estimate of γ_e. Here also we see that the learning algorithm tends to 'get lost' in the noise once the signal to noise ratio diminishes (i.e. beyond about t=3.5). However, this may now affect the exchange rate dynamics as the parameter γ_e affects the local stability of the steady state. Indeed, we see that between t=6 and t=7 the agents' estimate (or rather mis-estimate) of γ_e becomes quite large. Larger values of γ_e drive the steady state towards local instability and, as a result, we see in Figure 16.9 what may be termed an exchange rate 'bubble' between about t=6 and t=7. Perhaps as a consequence of the resulting higher signal to noise ratio, the learning algorithm brings the estimate of γ_e closer to its true value and, more importantly, to values for which the steady state is locally asymptotically stable. We note that the estimate of γ_e becomes large again towards the end of the simulation, but not sufficiently large to bring about local instability and so, after about t=7, there is no discernible effect on the exchange rate dynamics compared to the no-learning situation.

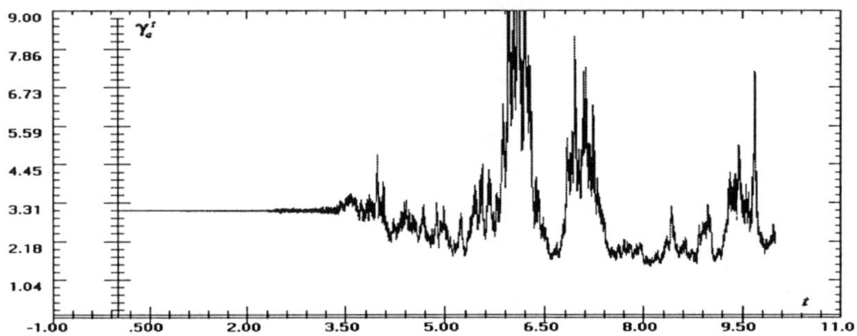

Figure 16.8 Evolution of γ_t^e

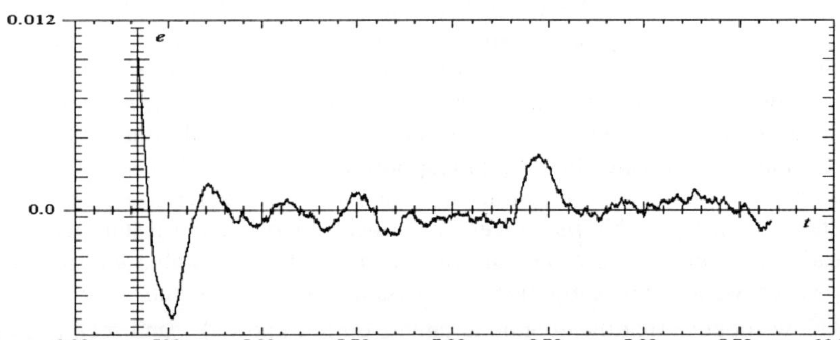

Figure 16.9 Exchange Rate Dynamics – Learning γ_e

We have observed in a number of simulations that the learning of γ_e can cause large exchange rate movements (or bubbles) because of the effect of this parameter on the local stability of the steady state. We should also stress that many other simulations (from different initial values of γ_e) resulted in estimates of γ_e that kept the dynamics in the region of local stability for the entire simulation periods and the dynamics for *e* always converged to paths very close to those of the no-learning situation.

4. CONCLUSION

We have introduced a generalised Dornbusch model of exchange rate dynamics whose particular features are imperfect substitutability between domestic and foreign assets, lagged nonlinear portfolio adjustment and what we term an adaptively rational expectations scheme that has the usual perfect myopic foresight as a limit case. The dynamics of the model are always stable, either to the steady state or to a limit cycle, depending on the parameter configuration. One consequence of this stability is that there is no need to impose the jump variable technique in response to a shock that moves the steady state to a new position.

The economic world of this model is inhabited by sophisticated agents who know the model structure, but not all of its parameter values, and hence would not in any event be able to carry out the calculations required by the jump variable technique of the traditional Dornbusch model.

The agents seek to learn the unknown parameter by using a maximum-likelihood learning algorithm. We use simulation methods to study the evolution of the exchange rate in the case when the steady state is locally asymptotically stable. The types of parameters to be learned fall into two broad categories, those (fundamental parameters) that determine the steady state and those (market parameters) that are the speeds of adjustment to changes in market conditions. The learning of the fundamental parameters does not seem to have any effect on the exchange rate dynamics compared to the situation in which agents are assumed to know the model parameters. This is because these parameters do not affect the stability properties of the equilibrium.

Learning the market parameters can have an effect on the exchange rate dynamics, leading to speculative bubbles because these parameters do affect the stability of the steady state. In this framework, the speculative bubbles come to an end because they generate a higher signal to noise ratio that the learning algorithm can lock onto and so bring the parameter estimate back into the region of local asymptotic stability.

In contrast to our analysis, Tabellini (1988) finds unambiguously that learning does increase exchange rate volatility. He assumes that the agents do know the model and its parameters and seek to learn about the parameters of the external noise processes.

Our conclusions are based on a very small number of simulations and this study needs to be followed by a more thorough Monte Carlo style of analysis to determine the robustness of our tentative conclusions. We see the main contribution of this chapter as suggesting an approach to the study of the impact of agent learning on the dynamics of exchange rates. An issue that needs to be considered in future research is the effect of learning when the steady state is locally unstable.

ACKNOWLEDGEMENTS

We thank an anonymous referee for useful insights and suggestions. The usual caveat applies.

NOTES

1. The assumption of fixed supply of foreign exchange is not as restrictive as it may appear. It is equally possible to model the demand of foreign residents for domestic interest bearing assets as a function of the interest differential. This function will also have upper and lower bounds for similar reasons that the function $\tilde{f}$ does. When the resulting supply function is introduced into equation (16.6) the term $f(\cdot)-\overline{S}$ is replaced by an aggregate excess demand function (depending on the difference of the demand functions of domestic and foreign residents) still having the same shape as f .
2. Note that we now write the differential equations for E and X in terms of the speeds of adjustment γ_e and γ_x .
3. A relaxation cycle is a limiting limit cycle on which periods of slow and infinitely fast motion alternate. In our model, periods of slow movements of exchange rate and expectations and infinitely fast movements of expectations alternate. See Chiarella (1992) for more details and economic interpretations.
4. The amplitude of the relaxation cycles fluctuations is rather large. This is due to the choice of f_u and f_l, which reflect perhaps unrealistic fluctuations in the holdings of foreign wealth. Numerical experiments with other values of f_u and f_l do yield much smaller amplitudes. However, we do not pursue this issue further here as our focus is on the case of local stability.
5. It may be worth noting that if the agents were employing what we term traditional adaptive expectations then the bracket on the right hand side of the (16.23) would become $[(e_t - e_{t-h})/h - x_t]$ as the agents would then not be assumed to know the model.
6. The noise terms in equations (16.26)–(16.27) could also be thought of as allowing for a bid-ask spread.
7. The Appendix is available upon request to the authors.
8. The values of f_u and f_l reflect a variation of the amount of domestic wealth held in foreign assets between 25% and 35%.

REFERENCES

Barucci, E., Bischi, G.I. and L. Gardini (1999), 'Endogenous fluctuations in a bounded rationality economy: learning non perfect foresight equilibria', *Journal of Economic Theory*, **87**, 243-53.

Chiarella, C. (1990), 'Excessive exchange rate variability: a possible explanation using nonlinear economic dynamics', *European Journal of Political Economy*, **6**, 315-53.

Chiarella, C. (1992), 'Monetary and fiscal Policy under non-linear exchange rate dynamics', in G. Feichtinger (ed.), *Dynamic Economic Models and Optimal Control*, Elsevier, pp. 527-46.

Chiarella, C. and A. Khomin (1999), 'Adaptively evolving expectations in models of monetary dynamics: the fundamentalists forward looking', *Annals of Operations Research*, **89**, 21-43.

Davis, K.T. and M.K. Lewis (1977), 'Monetary dynamics and the monetary sector of RBA76', *Conference in Applied Economic Research* (Reserve Bank of Australia, Canberra, Australia).

Dornbusch, R. (1976), 'Expectations and exchange rate dynamics', *Journal of Political Economy*, **84**, 1161-76.

Evans, G.W. and S. Honkapohja (1995), 'Adaptive learning and expectational stability: an introduction', in A. Kirman and M. Salmon (eds), *Learning and Rationality in Economics*, Oxford: Basil Blackwell, pp. 102-26.

Frankel, J.A. and K. Froot (1986), 'Understanding the U.S. Dollar in the eighties: the expectations of chartists and fundamentalists', *Economic Record*, **Supplement,** 24-38.

Frankel, J.A. and K. Froot (1990), 'Chartists, fundamentalists and trading in the foreign exchange market', *American Economic Review*, **80**, 181-85.

Gray, M. and S.J. Turnovsky (1979), 'The stability of exchange rate dynamics under perfect myopic foresight', *International Economic Review*, **20**, 643-60.

Karacaoglu, G. and H.W. Ursprung (1988), 'Exchange rate dynamics under gradual portfolio adjustment', *Journal of Macroeconomics*, **10**, 565-89.

Kearney, C. and R. MacDonald (1985), 'Asset markets and the exchange rate: a structural model of the sterling-dollar rate, 1972-1982', *Journal of Economic Studies*, **12**, 3-20.

Kouri, P.J.F. (1983), 'Balance of payments and the foreign exchange market: a dynamic partial equilibrium model', in J. Bhandari and B.H. Putnam (eds), *Economic Interdependence and Flexible Exchange Rates,* Cambridge, Mass.: MIT Press.

Pagan, A. (1996), 'The econometrics of financial markets', *Journal of Empirical Finance*, **3**, 15-102.

Sidar, M. (1976), 'Recursive identification and tracking of parameters for linear and non-linear multivariate systems', *International Journal of Control*, **24** (3), 361-78.

Tabellini, G. (1988), 'Learning and the volatility of exchange rates', *Journal of International Money and Finance*, **7**, 243-50.

17. International Immigration, Non-Traded Goods and Economic Welfare in an Overlapping Generations Model

Kenji Kondoh

1. INTRODUCTION

Among the accumulated studies of international migration, there is a series of papers adopting two-factor and two-good models where one of the goods is non-traded.[1] The pioneering work of Rivera-Batiz (1982) suggests that immigration to a small country is gainful for the inhabitants in the host country regardless of the relative factor intensities of the two goods. (Rivera-Batiz's analysis concerns the effect of the outflow of labour, but can be easily adapted to yield the above conclusion.) Wong's (1995) extension shows that the conclusion of Rivera-Batiz is valid even in the n-goods and m-factors model. Kondoh (1999) showed how the welfare gain of native inhabitants depends on the nature of the migration (permanent, temporary or repeated). These models assume that the stock of capital is fixed and remittance is achieved by exporting the traded goods. The possibility that the remittance may affect the quantity of the capital stock is ignored.

There is also a series of studies that adopts the overlapping generations model, in which the capital stock changes over time.[2] Concerning the welfare aspects of immigration, Galor (1986) concludes that the inflow of labour is harmful if the immigrants' time preference is different from that of the natives. Here, I draw attention to two important implications of his analysis. First, since Galor adopts a one-good model, there is no trade and no remittance. Second, the crucial reason for the welfare loss is the international difference between the rates of time preference. If there is no difference between the rates of time preferences of the natives and immigrants, and the utility functions are the same in both countries, there is no incentive for migration. Hence, immigration will not cause any change in the welfare of the native inhabitants. Moreover, in Galor's model, a higher saving rate means a larger capital stock in the next period whereas, in reality, the saving rate depends on the amount of the remittance. Finally, remittance is one of the main reasons for trade between the home and host countries, but a one-good model ignores this possibility.

Thus, it is worth studying the economic effects of immigration in an overlapping generations model, in which two factors produce two goods (one of which is the non-traded good).

2. THE MODEL

Consider a small country in which there are two goods and two factors. One good is tradable (T) and the other non-tradable (N). Let the two factors be labour (L) and capital (K). Moreover, it is assumed that there is an inflow of immigrants (L_M) to this country, but that capital is internationally immobile.

The production functions, which are assumed to be linearly homogeneous and strictly quasi concave, can be expressed as

$$T = T(K_T, L_T) = L_T f(k_T) \tag{17.1}$$

$$N = N(K_N, L_N) = L_N g(k_N), \tag{17.2}$$

where K_i and L_i ($i = T, N$) denote the capital and labour inputs for the production of good i, $k_T = K_T / L_T$ and $k_N = K_N / L_N$.

Under the assumption of perfect competition, profit maximisation implies that

$$w = T^L = p_N N^L \tag{17.3}$$

$$r = T^K = p_N N^K, \tag{17.4}$$

where $T^L \equiv \partial T / \partial L_T$ and T^K, N^L, N^K are defined in a similar way. Taking the traded good as the numeraire, we denote the price of the non-traded good, the wage rate and the rental price by $p_N, w,$ and r, respectively. Combining (17.1) and (17.2), we can rewrite (17.3) and (17.4) as

$$w = f(k_T) - k_T f'(k_T) = p_N (g(k_N) - k_N g'(k_N)) \tag{17.5}$$

$$r = f'(k_T) = p_N g'(k_N). \tag{17.6}$$

The full-employment conditions are

$$K_T + K_N = K, \tag{17.7}$$

$$L_T + L_N = L + L_M . \tag{17.8}$$

Let us assume that during each period L individuals are born, so that there is no population growth in the host country. Individuals live in two periods. In the first period they supply their endowment of labour inelastically, earning the competitive market wage, and allocate their income between first-period consumption $c_{1T} + p_N c_{1N}$ and saving s, where c_{ij} $(i = 1,2;\ j = T,N)$ denotes the consumption of good j in period i, and $s \equiv w - c_{1T} - p_N c_{1N}$ constitutes the supply of capital. Capital depreciates completely within one period. Their second-period consumption, $c_{2T} + p_N c_{2N}$, is equal to rs.

Immigrants differ from natives in two respects. First, they make it a rule to remit β $(0 < \beta < w)$ to their family in the home country from their first-period income. Second, they migrate permanently at the beginning of their life; that is, they do not return to their homeland in retirement. As their family remains in the home country, their migration does not affect the number of the next generation in the host country. In view of the above assumptions, the optimal consumption and saving of an immigrant must be different from those of a native inhabitant. We make a distinction by attaching an asterisk to the immigrant's variables. The amount of capital in period $t+1$ is decided by the savings of the two types of labour in period t:

$$K_T^{t+1} + K_N^{t+1} = s^t L + s^{*t} L_M^t . \tag{17.9}$$

We denote the utility function of a native inhabitant born in period t by U^t. He solves the problem of maximising the utility function

$$U(c_{1T}^t, c_{1N}^t, c_{2T}^{t+1}, c_{2N}^{t+1}) \tag{17.10}$$

subject to the intertemporal budget constraint

$$c_{1T}^t + p_N^t c_{1N}^t + \frac{c_{2T}^{t+1}}{r^{t+1}} + \frac{p_N^{t+1} c_{2N}^{t+1}}{r^{t+1}} = w^t . \tag{17.11}$$

An immigrant's utility function is assumed the same as that of a native. Hence the immigrant's problem differs only in the budget constraint (17.9). As the remittance must be taken into consideration, (17.9) should be rewritten for the immigrant as

$$c_{1T}^{*t} + p_N^t c_{1N}^{*t} + \frac{c_{2T}^{*t+1}}{r^{t+1}} + \frac{p_N^{t+1} c_{2N}^{*t+1}}{r^{t+1}} = w^t - \beta. \qquad (17.12)$$

The saving variables s^t and s^{*t} are expressed as

$$s^t = w^t - (c_{1T}^t + p_N^t c_{1N}^t) = \frac{c_{2T}^{t+1} + p_N^{t+1} c_{2N}^{t+1}}{r^{t+1}} \qquad (17.13)$$

$$s^{*t} = w^t - \beta - (c_{1T}^{*t} + p_N^t c_{1N}^{*t}) = \frac{c_{2T}^{*t+1} + p_N^{t+1} c_{2N}^{*t+1}}{r^{t+1}}. \qquad (17.14)$$

It is easy to conclude that $s^t > s^{*t}$.

The purpose of our analysis is to investigate the effects of immigration on the host country by comparing the steady state equilibria.[3] In the steady state, the relative price in each period is constant, that is, $p_N^{t+1} = p_N^t \equiv p_N$. To simplify our analysis, we assume that U is the sum of the sub-utilities for the two periods, denoted as C_1 and C_2 and that both sub-utilities are of the same Cobb-Douglas type, namely

$$U = C_1 + C_2 / r = c_{1T}^{\alpha} c_{1N}^{1-\alpha} + c_{2T}^{\alpha} c_{2N}^{1-\alpha} / r.$$

Following Galor, because consumption is optimal, then

$$\frac{\partial U / \partial C_1}{\partial U / \partial C_2} = r$$

and therefore the rate of time preference is equal to r. Then we can rewrite the consumer's problem as the choice of $c_{1T}, c_{1N}, c_{2T}, c_{2N}$ to maximise the utility function

$$U = c_{1T}^{\alpha} c_{1N}^{1-\alpha} + c_{2T}^{\alpha} c_{2N}^{1-\alpha} / r \qquad (17.15)$$

subject to the inter-temporal budget constraint

$$c_{1T} + p_N c_{1N} + (c_{2T} + p_N c_{2N}) / r = w. \qquad (17.16)$$

The first-order conditions for a solution are

$$\alpha c_{1T}^{\alpha-1} c_{1N}^{1-\alpha} = \alpha c_{2T}^{\alpha-1} c_{2N}^{1-\alpha} = \lambda, \qquad (17.17)$$

$$(1-\alpha)c_{1T}^{\alpha}c_{1N}^{1-\alpha} = (1-\alpha)c_{2T}^{\alpha}c_{2N}^{1-\alpha} = \lambda p_N \,, \tag{17.18}$$

where λ denotes the Lagrangian multiplier associated with (17.16). Remembering that $p_N^{t+1} = p_N^t \equiv p_N$ in the steady rate and that the sub-utility functions are homothetic, we may conclude that $c_{1j} = c_{2j}$, $j = N, T$. Therefore, (17.16) can be rewritten as

$$(1+1/r)(c_{1T} + p_N c_{1N}) = w \,. \tag{17.19}$$

The multiplier λ can be eliminated from (17.17) and (17.18) to obtain

$$\alpha p_N c_{1N} = (1-\alpha)c_{1T} \,. \tag{17.20}$$

By solving the similar optimisation problem, we find that, for an immigrant,

$$(1+1/r)(c_{1T}^* + p_N c_{1N}^*) = w - \beta \tag{17.21}$$

$$\alpha p_N c_{1N}^* = (1-\alpha)c_{1T}^* \,. \tag{17.22}$$

In a steady state, we may rewrite (17.9) as

$$K_T + K_N = (w - c_{1T} - p_N c_{1N})L + (w - \beta - c_{1T}^* - p_N c_{1N}^*)L_M \,. \tag{17.23}$$

From the full-employment conditions, it is also easy to obtain

$$K_T/k_T + K_N/k_N = L + L_M \,. \tag{17.24}$$

Finally, we introduce the market-clearing condition for the non-traded good market. In the steady state,

$$S_N(p_N, L + L_M, K) = D_N(p_N, Y) \,, \tag{17.25}$$

where S_N and D_N denote the supply and demand for the non-traded good, respectively, and Y denotes the total amount that can be spent in this period by (young and old) native inhabitants and immigrants, that is,

$$Y = (w - s + rs)L + (w - \beta - s^* + rs^*)L_M \,.$$

By Walras' Law, the equilibrium condition for the traded good can be ignored.

Thus, we finally have 11 equations (17.5), (17.6), (17.19), (17.20), (17.21), (17.22), (17.23), (17.24) and (17.25). If the exogenous variables L_M and β are given, the 11 unknowns, $p_N, k_T, k_N, w, r, c_{1T}, c_{1N}, c_{1T}^*, c_{1N}^*, K_T$ and K_N will be determined.

For the stability of this equation system, the following two conditions are assumed to hold.

Assumption A: *Equation* (17.25) *satisfies the Walrasian price adjustment process.*

Assumption B: $|dk_{t+1}/dk_t| < 1$, where $k \equiv K/(L+L_M)$.

Assumption A guarantees that the equilibrium price of the non-traded good is stable. Assumption B is the local stability condition of the steady state, as in Galor's (1986) Lemma 1.

3. ANALYSIS

Differentiating the 11 equations (17.5), (17.6), (17.19), (17.20), (17.21), (17.22), (17.23), (17.24) and (17.25) we obtain, after some calculation, that

$$\begin{aligned}\frac{dU}{dL_M} &= \frac{\alpha U}{c_{1T}}\left(\frac{dc_{1T}}{dL_M} + p_N \frac{dc_{1N}}{dL_M}\right) \\ &= \frac{\alpha U}{c_{1T}}\frac{1}{\Delta} p_N^2 (B + k_N N^K) f'' g'' [(1+\frac{1}{r}) c_{1N}(k_N - k_T) + g(k_T - s)],\end{aligned} \tag{17.26}$$

where

$$B \equiv N^M - D_N^Y (w - \beta - s^* + s^* r) L_M$$

and Δ, the determinant of the matrix defined in the Appendix, is negative by the stability Assumption A.[4]

First consider the case $\beta = 0$. Without remittance, the economic effects of increasing the number of immigrants in each period are essentially the same as the effects of increasing the number of native inhabitants. Neither of these affects the capital-labour ratio; nor do they affect the relative prices of the non-traded goods or factor prices. The market for the non-traded good is in equilibrium both before and after immigration. Hence $B=0$, and this yields $dU/dL_M=0$.

Now consider the case in which $L_M=0$, so that there are no immigrants in the host country initially. Since the square-bracketed term in (17.26) becomes zero in this case, we also have $dU/dL_M=0$.[5]

Thus, we have established the following theorem.

Theorem 1: *If $\beta=0$ or $L_M=0$, then $dU/dL_M=0$.*

The next task is to investigate the economic effects of immigration when $\beta>0$. If β is large enough to satisfy $\beta>(r-1)s^*$ and $s>k_T>k_N$, then $k_N>s^*$.[6] We notice that the inflow of migrants raises the capital stock in the host country by their savings. We introduce the superscript $M+K$ to indicate changes caused by immigration, where account is taken of the increase in the capital stock. An illustration of this notation is provided by the definition $K_T^{M+K}\equiv dK_T/dL_M+(dK_T/dK)\cdot(dK/dL_M)$. If $k_T>k_N$ and if $k_N>s^*$, $K_T^{M+K}<0, K_N^{M+K}>0, L_T^{M+K}<0$, and $L_N^{M+K}>0$, then $T^{M+K}<0$ and $N^{M+K}>0$. Applying the above results, $K_N^{M+K}>0, L_N^{M+K}>1$[7] and, recalling that both goods are normal in consumption, so that $0<p_N D_N^Y<1$,

$$N^M+s^*N^K=N^{M+K}=N^L L_N^{M+K}+N^K K_N^{M+K}>N^L L_N^{M+K}$$
$$>p_N D_N^Y N^L=D_N^Y w>D_N^Y\left(1-\frac{1}{w}(\beta-(r-1)s^*)\right)w=D_N^M.$$

Therefore we may conclude that $B+s^*N^K>0$ and, since the square-bracketed term of (17.26) is negative under the above conditions, that $dU/dL_M<0$.[8] In summary, we assert the result of the following theorem.

Theorem 2: *If β and L_M are large enough to satisfy both $\beta>(r-1)s^*$ and $s>k_T>k_N(>s^*)$ then $dU/dL_M<0$.*

This theorem implies that if the host country has already accepted a great number of immigrants, who remit most of their earnings, then an additional inflow of immigrants reduces the economic welfare of the native inhabitants in the host country. If L_M is not large enough then $k_T>s>k_N$, no matter how small is s^*.

4. DISCUSSION

Rivera-Batiz (1982) and Kondoh (1999) concluded that immigrants are gainful to the host country. In this chapter immigrants are harmful under the conditions of Theorem 2. The reasons for these different conclusions can be summarised as follows. In the present model, quite a few immigrants are already in the host country and their lower savings have caused the per capita capital stocks to become relatively low in spite of the higher savings of the native inhabitants. The additional inflow of immigrants further reduces the per capita capital stocks. Therefore, because of the shortage of capital, the production of the capital-intensive good decreases. If $k_T > k_N$, that is, if the traded good is capital-intensive then, since the remittance is achieved by the outflow of the traded good, the shortage of the traded good in the host country is much more serious. However, if the utility function of the native inhabitants is strictly quasi-concave, as when the utility function is Cobb-Douglas, economic welfare is considerably reduced if people lose their well-balanced consumption. To maintain the balance of their consumption, it may be necessary to mainly produce the capital-intensive good, even in the labour-abundant country. As a result, this type of distortion causes an economic loss.

There are some noteworthy relations between Galor (1986) and the present chapter. Galor concludes that one way immigration reduces economic welfare in the host country is if the rate of time preference of immigrants is different from that of the natives. However, we assume that people in each country have the same utility function, so that there is no difference in their rates of time preference. The case where $\beta > 0$, which implies that $s \neq s^*$, is connected with Galor's case of different rates of time preference. However, since we adopt a two-good model, we can conclude that immigration causes an economic loss only when β and L_M are large enough to ensure that $s > k_T > k_N > s^*$. On the other hand, Galor adopts a one-good model and so $s > k > s^* (s < k < s^*)$ is guaranteed in any case.

Finally, Theorem 1 states that if $L_M = 0$ then $dU/dL_M = 0$. We may interpret this to mean that the effects caused by immigration are quite minute at the beginning. Therefore, contrary to Galor, we do not have to reject a slight inflow of one-way immigrants. Theorem 1 also concludes that if $\beta = 0$, then $dU/dL_M = 0$. This implies that immigrants accompanied by their families, namely, permanent migrants, have no influence on the host country.

5. CONCLUDING REMARKS

This chapter reports on an investigation of the economic effects of immigration in an overlapping-generations model where two-factors produce two-goods, one of which is non-tradable. It has been shown that if there are no immigrants in the host country initially, or if immigrants do not remit any part of their income to the home country, immigration does not affect the well-being of native inhabitants. However, if there are many immigrants who remit part of their earnings, their presence may be harmful to the natives.

Because of the property of the Cobb-Douglas utility function, both goods are consumed by the same amount in each period in the steady state regardless of rental price. To avoid this special result, a more general functional form should be adopted. This is a subject for future research.

ACKNOWLEDGEMENTS

This study was assisted by a research grant from Chukyo University. I am very grateful to anonymous referees, Professor Ngo Van Long of McGill University, Professor Makoto Tawada of Nagoya University and Professor Murray C. Kemp of the University of New South Wales for their useful comments. Remaining errors are my own.

NOTES

1. See Rivera-Batiz (1983a, 1983b, 1984, 1986, 1989), Lundahl (1985), Djajić (1986), Quibria (1988, 1989, 1993) and Thompson (1984) for extended analyses in this framework.
2. The pioneer work is Rodriguez (1975). Karayalcin (1994), Kemp and Kondo (1989), Galor and Stark (1990) and Schaeffer (1995) are extensions of Galor (1986).
3. The welfare comparison of steady states is not informative in the general case because it omits transitional utilities. However, one of my main purposes is to compare my results with the static results of Rivera-Batiz (1982). For that particular purpose, the present approach is suitable.
4. The Appendix is available upon request.
5. If $L_M = 0$, making use of $L_T + L_N = L$ and $g = N/L_N$, the square-bracketed term of (17.26) yields

$$p_N f'' g'' N\left(\frac{k_N - k_T}{L} + \frac{k_T - s}{L_N}\right) = \frac{1}{LL_N}(L_N k_N + L_T k_T - sL) = \frac{1}{LL_N}(K_N + K_T - K) = 0.$$

6. Under the condition $s > k_T > k_N$ we obtain

$$s^* - k_N = \frac{K - sL}{L_M} - k_N < \frac{K - k_T L}{L_M} - k_N = \frac{KL_T - K_T L}{L_M L_T} - k_N = \frac{L_N}{L_M}(k_N - k_T) - k_N < 0.$$

7. See Lundahl (1985) and Kondoh (1999) for the derivation.
8. In this case, we also can assert that $dw/dL_M < 0$ and $dr/dL_M > 0$.

REFERENCES

Djajić, S. (1986), 'International migration, remittances and welfare in a development economy', *Journal of Development Economics*, **21,** 229-34.

Galor, O. (1986), 'Time preference and international labour migration', *Journal of Economic Theory*, **38,** 1-20.

Galor, O. and O. Stark (1990), 'Migrants' savings, the probability of return migration and migrants' performance', *International Economic Review*, **31,** 463-67.

Karayalcin, C. (1994), 'Temporary and permanent migration with and without an immobile factor', *Journal of Development Economics*, **43,** 197-215.

Kemp, M.C. and H. Kondo (1989), 'An analysis of international migration: the unilateral case', in K.F. Zimmermann (eds), *Economic Theory of Optimal Population*, Berlin Heidelberg: Springer-Verlag, pp.153-65.

Kondoh, K. (1999), 'Permanent migrants and cross-border workers', *Journal of Regional Science*, **39**, 467-78.

Lundahl, M. (1985), 'International migration, remittances and real income: effects on the source country', *Scandinavian Journal of Economics*, **87,** 647-57.

Quibria, M.G. (1988), 'A note on international migration, non-traded goods and economic welfare in the source country', *Journal of Development Economics*, **28,** 377-87.

Quibria, M.G. (1989), 'International migration and real wages: is there any neo-classical ambiguity?', *Journal of Development Economics*, **28**, 177-83.

Quibria, M.G. (1993), 'International migration, increasing returns, and real wages', *Canadian Journal of Economics*, **26,** 457-68.

Rivera-Batiz, F.L. (1982), 'International migration, non-traded goods and economic welfare in the source country', *Journal of Development Economics*, **11**, 81-90.

Rivera-Batiz, F.L. (1983a), 'The economics of the 'to and fro' migrant: some welfare-theoretical considerations', *Scandinavian Journal of Economics*, **85**, 403-13.

Rivera-Batiz, F.L. (1983b), 'Trade theory, distribution of income, and immigration', *American Economic Review*, **73**, 183-87.

Rivera-Batiz, F.L. (1984), 'International migration, non-traded goods and economic welfare in a two-class economy', *Journal of Development Economics*, **16**, 325-30.

Rivera-Batiz, F.L. (1986), 'International migration, remittances and economic welfare in the source country', *Journal of Economic Studies*, **13**, 3-19.

Rivera-Batiz, F.L. (1989), 'The impact of international migration on real wages', *Journal of Development Economics*, **31,** 185-92.

Rodriguez, C.A. (1975), 'On the welfare aspects of international migration', *Journal of Political Economy*, **83,** 1065-72.

Schaeffer, P.V. (1995), 'The work effort and the consumption of immigrants as a function of their assimilation', *International Economic Review*, **36,** 625-42.

Thompson, H. (1984), 'International migration, non-traded goods and economic welfare in the source country: a comment', *Journal of Development Economics*, **16,** 321-24.

Wong, K.-Y. (1995), '*International Trade in Goods and Factor Mobility*', Cambridge, MA: MIT Press.

18. The Environment, Externalities and Sustainable Growth in an Overlapping Generations Model

Binh Tran-Nam and Cong Nghe Truong

1. INTRODUCTION

It is now generally acknowledged that the aggregate output of an economy and, hence, its economic growth path, depend ultimately on how it makes use of its physical, human, social and environmental capital. The natural capital stock refers to the totality of all ecosystems, which include, for example, water, soil, forest cover, the atmosphere, minerals, ores and fossil fuels. In this sense, the natural environment is fundamental to our well-being and, ultimately, our survival. It is both a source of supply of essential raw materials and energy, and a source of enjoyment.

Contrary to the simple textbook formulation of the production function, natural inputs are not available in fixed quantities. While Hotelling (1931) first formulated a complete theory of the mining firm almost seventy years ago, economists only began constructing general equilibrium models to accommodate resource exhaustibility in the early 1970s. This effort, triggered by the Report for the Club of Rome (see Meadows et al. 1972) and the oil shocks, has resulted in a substantial expansion of the literature on exhaustible resources (see, for example, Kemp and Long 1980; Hartwick and Olewiler 1986). A large part of this vein of literature is concerned with the optimal depletion of nonrenewable resources.

The traditional literature on exhaustible resources has focused on natural capital as an essential factor of production. More recently, research on the environment has focused on biodiversity and renewable natural resources (see, for example, Pearce and Turner 1990, Perrings 1995, Dasgupta 1996). In contrast, following the work of John and Pecchenino (1994) and John et al. (1995), this chapter focuses on the role of the environment as a direct source of pleasure. A recent paper by Bovenberg and Heijdra (1998) analyses environmental tax policy within the framework of continuous overlapping generations.

As a source of enjoyment the environment can directly, or in combination with other leisure goods, provide a flow of utility to human beings. It has been long recognised in economic theory that there is a potential conflict between economic growth and environmental quality. Human activities, through production and consumption, can adversely affect the environment. These externalities and the associated market failure have long been part of standard microeconomic textbooks. The traditional theory of environmental regulation typically recommends the use of Pigouvian taxes or marketable emission permits to restore optimality in the presence of externalities (for a review of environmental economics see Cropper and Oates 1992). This Pigouvian solution has been the subject of repeated attacks based on the now familiar Coasian views (Coase 1960).

There is an illusory distinction between resource and environmental economists. Resource economists, who are interested in population ecology, characterise complex systems by population sizes (or, alternatively tonnage) of different species. Environmental economists, who are interested in systems ecology, typically summarise complex systems in terms of indices of 'quality', such as those of air, soil or water. This chapter combines both approaches and treats environmental capital as a stock measurable in some constant quality units.

The traditional theory of environmental economics tends to ignore the similarity between renewable resources and environmental quality. If the beauty of nature can be thought of as measurable in some constant quality units, then the stock of the environment changes in much the same way as a stock of renewable resources. Undisturbed by human economic activities, the environmental stock grows, remains unchanged or decays autonomously over time. Both productive and consumption activities can degrade the environment (thus depleting its stock of quality units) while collective environmental programs can maintain or even improve the environment.

In assuming that the life spans of economic agents and the economy are the same, the traditional approach fails to address the intergenerational nature of the human impact on the environment: actions taken by the current generation affect the welfare of future generations. This intergenerational issue is in fact one of the central themes of the 1992 Earth Summit. Despite its wide applicability in growth theory, the overlapping generations framework has been surprisingly under-utilised in the fields of exhaustible resources and environmental economics. Some important exceptions are Kemp and Long (1979) who analysed an overlapping generations model of nonrenewable resources, Solow (1986) who studied the intergenerational allocation of natural resources, and John and Pecchenino (1994) and John et al. (1995) who considered economic growth and the environment in an overlapping generations framework. A peculiar assumption of John and Pecchenino (1994) and John et al. (1995) is that the typical person does not consume and enjoy nature when young. More seriously, there is no formal mechanism to explain how the government chooses the environmental tax regime.

The present chapter extends the tradition and analysis of Kemp and Long (1979), John and Pecchenino (1994) and John et al. (1994, 1995). It constructs and investigates a closed aggregative model in which economic agents live for exactly two periods and the long-lived environment is viewed as a nonrivalrous and nonexcludable source of pleasure. Production of the final output (which can be either consumed or saved as capital) generates negative externalities to the environment while taxes are collected to fund environmental maintenance or improvement programs.

The organisation of the remainder of the chapter is as follows. Section 2 states the specific assumptions and formulates the model. The competitive equilibrium of the model is analysed in Section 3. It is shown that there exists a unique solution to a typical person's lifetime utility maximisation problem. The condition for the optimal provision of the environment is derived and some comparative dynamic results established. In Section 4, the concept of sustainability is defined and a necessary condition for long-term sustainability derived. Section 5 examines the steady state of the economy and establishes some comparative static results. Finally, some concluding remarks are given in Section 6.

2. THE MODEL

The model is of a discrete-time, infinite-horizon, closed economy that begins operation in period 1 and continues over periods t = 2, 3,... extending indefinitely into the future. The characteristics of the economy may be summarised as follows.

2.1 Population

At the beginning of period t, a new generation of individuals is born. This generation, called generation t, is distinguished by its date of birth and consists of N_t members. These identical individuals (in terms of resources, endowments and preferences) live for exactly two periods. They are alive in period t (when they are called the young) and in period $t+1$ (when they are called the old); at the end of period $t+1$ they all die. The old people in the initial period 1 (i.e., those individuals who were born in period 0), called generation 0, will all pass away at the end of $t=1$. Thus, at any point in time, the population is composed of two overlapping generations, the young (those born in the current period) and the old (those born in the previous period). A typical person works and saves when young and retires when old. Population size is assumed to change geometrically at the exogenously given, positive constant rate n so that

$$N_{t+1} = (1+n)N_t, \quad t \geq 0, \tag{18.1}$$

where N_0, the number of old people in period 1, is given and positive.

2.2 Firms

The economy produces a single final good, which can be consumed, saved or spent on the environment. The production sector is perfectly competitive. Profit-maximising price-taking firms in the economy produce the final good with the aid of two factors, capital and labour, according to an unchanging constant-returns-to-scale technology F. Let Y_t and K_t denote the aggregate gross output and the capital stock at time t, respectively. The aggregate gross output can be written as

$$Y_t = F(K_t, N_t), \quad t \geq 1, \tag{18.2}$$

where both factors are essential, marginal products are positive but diminishing if both factors are positive, F is concave and satisfies the Inada conditions, and initial capital stock K_1 (> 0) is given. It is further assumed that capital will depreciate by a constant positive fraction δ ($0 < \delta < 1$) after being employed in production.

2.3 The environment

The stock of the environment at time t, measured in some constant quality unit, is denoted by E_t. The change of the environmental stock from one period to the next is determined linearly by three forces. In the absence of human economic activity, the stock of the environment changes naturally over time at the geometrical rate α. (The parameter α may be positive, zero or negative according to whether the environment grows, remains unchanged or decays autonomously over time.) The production of the final good causes external damage to the environment, thus depleting β units of the environmental stock for every unit of the final good produced. Collective environmental expenditures generate γ units of the environmental stock per unit of the final good spent. The evolution of the environment over time can thus be described by

$$E_{t+1} = (1+\alpha)E_t - \beta Y_t + \gamma G_t, \quad t \geq 1, \tag{18.3}$$

where G_t denotes aggregate environmental expenditure at time t, α is assumed to be smaller than n, and E_1 is given and positive. Equation (18.3) implies that human impacts on the ecology (in the aggregate) are assumed to be reversible in the sense that they do not prevent the environment from returning to any previously attained state.

2.4 Households

In each period of his life a typical member of generation t derives satisfaction from the consumption of a final good and the environmental stock. The lifetime welfare of each individual born in period $t \geq 1$ can be summarised by a time separable utility function of the form

$$W_t = U(c_{t,t}, E_t) + (1+\rho)^{-1} U(c_{t,t+1}, E_{t+1}), \quad t \geq 1, \tag{18.4}$$

where $c_{t,i}$ stands for the nonnegative consumption of the time i final good by a typical member of generation t ($i = t, t+1$; $t \geq 1$), $U(x, y)$ is assumed to be twice differentiable, strictly increasing and strictly concave, $U_{12} > 0$,

$$\lim_{x \to 0} U_1 = \lim_{y \to 0} U_2 = \infty,$$

and ρ (> -1) is the constant personal rate of time preference. Implicit in (18.4) is the assumption that the environment is a pure public good. Thus the problems of congestion associated with the environment are assumed away. Equation (18.4) also indicates that an old person receives no utility from bequest.

2.5 The government

Since agents' utilities depend on the environmental stock, which may be damaged by human production activities, there is a need for a collective environmental program to be financed by taxation. To this end it is assumed that there exists a Wicksellian-Lindahlian government during each period in time. At the beginning of each time period t (≥ 1), the population elects a government that accurately reflects the preferences of generation t (since generation t outnumbers generation $t-1$) and legislates policies for the benefits of that generation. This short-lived government levies a proportional environmental tax on the young and guides them in their savings in order to maximise the lifetime welfare of each young person. Since this pure representative democracy's environmental program is also welfare improving for the old, its policy is agreeable to all of its constituents. In particular, the policy of time 1 government is agreeable to generation 0.

Three points deserve further mention. First, strictly speaking, since all the young people are identical and have common knowledge, they will not need government guidance in choosing a level of saving. This point has been forcefully argued in Kemp and Shimomura (1995). In this sense, the government here is simply a social contract that requires the young generation to pay for maintaining the environment. The tax policy is self-enforcing in the sense that each and every young generation understands that if it imposes a tax on the old people then it may suffer the same fate at the hand of the next generation. Thus, there is no need to distinguish between individual and collective decisions in this model.

Second, the tax on the young people has both direct and indirect effects on the environment. Indirectly, it reduces aggregate savings and thus the amount of capital available for production in the next period. In this sense the tax has an effect similar to a Pigouvian tax on output in the conventional literature. Conceptually, the tax paid by a young person can be thought of as her saving on the environment and this reinforces the above argument.

Thirdly, while the environmental tax can be imposed on capital income as well, this will lead to complications in this model. For example, consider the following alternative tax scenarios by the current government:

(a) choose the tax rate on both labour and capital income in the next period, taking the current tax rate as given by the previous government,
(b) taxing both current labour and capital income at the same rate,
(c) taxing current labour income and capital income in the next period at the same rate.

Under regime (a), the time t government has no influence on E_{t+1} (see equation (18.3)). In view of (18.4), such a tax regime is not sensible. Under regime (b), the tax rate in period $t+1$ is unknown at time t so that the maximising problem facing the young generation at time t is indeterminate. If the expected tax rate in period $t+1$ is not equal to the actual in period $t+1$, then the old people in that period will be frustrated. Since the government only stays in office for one period, regime (c) is less plausible than taxing current labour income alone.

2.6 The government's optimising problem

To formulate the problem facing the time t government it is useful to trace out the behaviour of a typical young person in period t. A young person of generation t supplies one unit of labour to competitive firms and receives a wage of w_t units of the final good in return for the labour expended. She is required by law to pay an environment tax at the rate of τ_t per unit of her wage income now ($0 \le \tau_t \le 1$). Her disposable income is then partly consumed and partly saved for her old age.

In period $t+1$, the same person does not work but receives a rental income at the rate of r_{t+1} of the final good per unit of the capital supplied. Since this person does not pay tax and has no bequest motive, she simply consumes her rental income plus her post-production savings. The amount of capital available for production now is simply the amount of saving made by the young generation in the previous period.

At time t ($t \geq 1$) the government takes current capital stock (K_t), labour force (N_t), environmental stock (E_t), current wage rate (w_t) and next period rental rate (r_{t+1}) as given. The government then chooses s_t and τ_t on behalf of each member of generation t to maximise (18.4) subject to (18.3) and

$$\begin{aligned} c_{t,t} + s_t &= (1-\tau_t)w_t \\ c_{t,t+1} &= (1+r_{t+1}-\delta)s_t, \end{aligned} \tag{18.5}$$

where $0 \leq \tau_t \leq 1$ and $0 \leq s_t \leq (1-\tau_t)w_t$.

Thus, taking K_t and E_t as predetermined, the choice of generation t determines K_{t+1} (via saving) and E_{t+1} (via the tax rate). A typical competitive firm in period t takes w_t and r_t as given and hires factor services to maximise profits. Finally, the time t government is required to run a balanced budget. This completes the formal description of the model.

3. ANALYSIS OF THE COMPETITIVE EQUILIBRIUM

We begin with a general definition of the overlapping generations analogue of Walrasian competitive equilibrium for this economy.

3.1 Definition

Definition: *A competitive equilibrium for this economy is an infinite sequence* $\{K_t^*, E_t^*, w_t^*, r_t^*, \tau_t^*, s_t^*, c_{t,t}^*, c_{t,t+1}^* : t \geq 1\}$ *such that* $K_1^* = K_1, E_1^* = E_1$ *and at each date* $t = 1, 2,...$ *(i) all markets clear; (ii) the government budget balances; (iii) every firm maximises its profit subject to the production function* (18.2)*; and (iv) every member of generation t maximises welfare* (18.4) *subject to* (18.3) *and* (18.5).

The equilibrium condition for the goods market requires aggregate income = aggregate expenditure, where aggregate income = aggregate tax + aggregate consumption + aggregate saving and aggregate expenditure =

aggregate consumption + aggregate investment + government expenditure. Combining this equality with the balanced budget condition and keeping in mind that saving (i.e., investment) in the current period is the capital stock available in the next period, we have

$$K_{t+1} = N_t s_t, \ t \geq 1 \tag{18.6}$$

$$G_t = N_t \tau_t w_t, \ t \geq 1, \tag{18.7}$$

where the asterisks are omitted for ease of notation.

The first-order necessary conditions for profit maximisation require firms to hire labour and capital until their marginal products equal their factor prices, i.e.,

$$\begin{aligned} w_t &= f(k_t) - k_t f'(k_t), \ t \geq 1 \\ r_t &= f'(k_t), \ t \geq 1, \end{aligned} \tag{18.8}$$

where $k_t \ (\equiv K_t / N_t)$ is the capital-labour ratio at time t and $f(k_t) = F(K_t / N_t, 1)$ is assumed to satisfy $f(0) = 0, f' > 0, f'' < 0$ and the Inada conditions.

Making use of (18.1) and (18.6), the capital-labour ratio can be expressed as

$$k_t = s_{t-1} / (1+n), \ t \geq 1. \tag{18.9}$$

Equation (18.9) states that capital per worker now is simply per worker saving in the previous period after adjustment for the population growth rate. Similarly, in view of (18.1), (18.7) and (18.8), equation (18.3) can be rewritten in per worker terms as

$$(1+n)e_{t+1} = (1+\alpha)e_t - \beta f(k_t) + \gamma \tau_t [f(k_t) - k_t f'(k_t)], \ t \geq 1, \tag{18.10}$$

where $e_t \ (\equiv E_t / N_t)$ is the environmental stock per worker at time t.

Substituting (18.5) into (18.4), the optimisation problem facing a typical member of generation t ($t \geq 1$) can be expressed in terms of the choice variables τ_t and s_t, and the (given) state variables k_t and e_t as follows. Specifically, the optimisation problem is

$$\begin{aligned} &\underset{\{\tau_t, s_t\}}{\text{Max}} \ W_t \\ &= U[(1-\tau_t)w_t - s_t, N_t e_t] + (1+\rho)^{-1} U[(1+r_{t+1} - \delta)s_t, (1+n)N_t e_{t+1}] \end{aligned} \tag{18.11}$$

subject to (18.8), (18.9), (18.10), $0 \le \tau_t \le 1$ and $0 \le s_t \le (1-\tau_t)w_t$ for $t \ge 1$.

3.2 Existence, uniqueness and characterisation of equilibrium

Now, for any given w_t, since $W_t(\tau_t, s_t)$ is a continuous function defined on the compact set $\{(\tau_t, s_t): 0 \le \tau_t \le 1; 0 \le s_t \le (1-\tau_t)w_t\}$, it must possess a maximum by virtue of the Weierstrass theorem. To demonstrate uniqueness of a solution to (18.11) we first assume that the marginal product of capital is inelastic for all capital-labour ratios, i.e.,

$$-kf''(k)/f'(k) < 1 \text{ for all } k > 0. \tag{18.12}$$

Given (18.12), it can be shown that $W_t(\tau_t, s_t)$ is strictly concave in (τ_t, s_t) (see the Appendix, which is available upon request to the authors). Thus, the solution to (18.11) must be unique and we may state the following proposition.

Proposition 1: *Assuming that* (18.12) *holds, there exists a unique solution* (τ_t^*, s_t^*) *to problem* (18.11).

The optimal pair (τ_t^*, s_t^*) is determined by the first-order necessary (and sufficient) conditions for a solution to problem (18.11)

$$\begin{aligned} \partial W_t / \partial \tau_t &= -w_t U_1 + \gamma N_t w_t U_2 / (1+\rho) = 0, \ t \ge 1 \\ \partial W_t / \partial s_t &= -U_1 + h'(s_t) U_1 / (1+\rho) = 0, \ t \ge 1, \end{aligned} \tag{18.13}$$

where $h(s_t) \equiv (1 + r_{t+1} - \delta)s_t = \{1 + f'[s_t/(1+n)] - \delta\}s_t$ is strictly increasing and concave, and the asterisks in (18.13) are omitted to alleviate notation. In view of Proposition 1, (18.13) yields a unique pair (τ_t^*, s_t^*) to problem (18.11). These two equations can also be manipulated to obtain the Samuelson condition for the optimal provision of the environment for the t generation, which is

$$N_t U_2[h(s_t),(1+n)N_t e_{t+1}] / U_1[h(s_t),(1+n)N_t e_{t+1}] = h'(s_t)/\gamma, \ t \ge 1. \tag{18.14}$$

The left-hand side of (18.14) is the social rate of substitution of the final good for the environment at time $t+1$ (i.e., the sum of the marginal rates of substitution across members of generation t when they are old) whereas the right-hand side of (18.14) is the social rate of transformation (i.e., the 'price' of a unit of the environmental stock in terms of the final good) at time $t+1$.

3.3 Comparative dynamics

A change in any of the model parameters in any time period will alter the time path of the economy. Totally differentiating (18.13), it can be established that $\partial\tau_t/\partial\alpha<0$, $\partial s_t/\partial\alpha>0$, $\partial\tau_t/\partial\beta>0$, $\partial s_t/\partial\beta<0$, $\partial\tau_t/\partial\gamma<0$, $\partial s_t/\partial\gamma>0$, $\partial\tau_t/\partial\delta<0$ and $\partial s_t/\partial\delta>0$ whereas the signs of $\partial\tau_t/\partial\rho$, $\partial s_t/\partial\rho$, $\partial\tau_t/\partial n$ and $\partial s_t/\partial n$ are ambiguous (see the Appendix). Thus, we may now state the following proposition.

Proposition 2:

(i) *The greater the autonomous growth of the environment (higher α), the lower is the equilibrium tax rate and the greater is the equilibrium rate of capital accumulation.*

(ii) *The greater the rate of environmental degradation by productive activities (higher β), the higher is the equilibrium tax rate and the lower is the equilibrium rate of capital accumulation.*

(iii) *The more effective the environmental maintenance technology (higher γ), the lower is the equilibrium tax rate and the greater is the equilibrium rate of capital accumulation.*

(iv) *The greater the rate of capital depreciation (higher δ), the lower is the equilibrium tax rate and the higher is the equilibrium rate of capital accumulation.*

The above results are intuitively appealing. For example, the higher the rate of autonomous growth of the environment (α), the better the environment can withstand the destructive force of human production. In this case, the young generation can afford to allocate less to taxation and more to saving from given aggregate wage income. Similarly, an economy with better environmental maintenance technology (higher γ) has a lower tax rate and saves more. In contrast, an economy in which production causes greater environmental damage (higher β) saves less and has a higher environmental tax rate. To make up for a greater rate of capital depreciation (higher δ), young people will have to spend less on environmental taxation and more on saving.

4. SUSTAINABILITY

4.1 Definition

In the conventional Solow-Swan model of long-run growth, there is no mention of environmental resources. The implicit assumption is that the environmental stock is fixed and does not depend on human activities. Thus an economy is sustainable so long as per capita consumption equals or exceeds some subsistence level.

In the present model, the survival of an economy depends, among other things, on its ability to manage the environment. A necessary condition for the economy to be sustainable in the long run is that its environmental stock never falls below a minimum life-sustaining level. More precisely, the overlapping generations economy is said to be sustainable if $e_t^* \geq \underline{e}$, $c_{t,t}^* \geq \underline{c}$ and $c_{t,t+1}^* \geq \underline{c}$ where $\underline{e}$ (> 0) and $\underline{c}$ (> 0) are arbitrarily small subsistence levels of environment and consumption, respectively, for all $t < \infty$ along a dynamic equilibrium path.

4.2 Sufficient condition for unsustainability

Given that the environment is indispensable to economic agents (in the sense that $\lim_{y \to 0} U_2 = \infty$), the time t government will ensure that $e_{t+1}^* > 0$. While it is possible for the environmental stock to decline over one generation to the next, economic agents cannot keep on damaging the environment forever. Since the net impact of human actions on the environment (in per worker terms) is given by $\gamma\tau_t w_t - \beta f(k_t)$, and since $\tau_t^* \leq 1$ for all $t \geq 1$, it is clear that the maximum net human impact on the environment in each period of time cannot be more than $\gamma w_t - \beta f(k_t)$. This can be expressed in symbols as (see (18.10))

$$e_{t+1} \leq Ae_t + B\Gamma_t, \quad t \geq 1 \tag{18.15}$$

where

$$A \equiv (1+\alpha)/(1+n) < 1, \ B \equiv 1/(1+n) < 1,$$
$$\Gamma_t \equiv (\gamma - \beta)f(k_t) - \gamma k_t f'(k_t).$$

It is shown in the Appendix that if

$$\beta / \gamma \geq -kf''(k)/f'(k) \text{ for all } k, \tag{18.16}$$

then $\Gamma_t \leq 0$ for all $t \geq 1$ and that e_t will approach zero as time grows indefinitely large. The inequality (18.16) means the ratio of the coefficient of environmental damage over that of environmental maintenance exceeds or equals the elasticity of marginal product of capital for all k. If that is true then the economy is doomed in the long run. We may now state the following proposition.

Proposition 3: *If* (18.16) *holds, the economy is unsustainable.*

For the economy to be sustainable, there must be some restrictions on the production technology and model parameters. From Proposition 3 a necessary condition for a sustainable economy is that there is at least one k such that

$$\beta / \gamma < -kf''(k) / f'(k) . \tag{18.17}$$

If a Cobb-Douglas production function is assumed, i.e., $f(k) = k^m$, where $0 < m < 1$, then the sustainability condition simplifies to $\beta / \gamma < 1 - m$, where $1 - m$ is the share of labour income. If this is violated, human activities have a net negative impact on the environment for every period $t \geq 1$. To maintain consumption above the subsistence level, k_t must be kept above a certain positive value, implying that the environmental stock will become zero at some finite time in the future. Alternatively, if a positive environmental stock is to be maintained, the Inada condition (that $f'(k) \to \infty$ as $k \to 0$) implies that the value of k_t will become zero within a finite time horizon. This in turn implies that consumption will eventually fall below the minimum subsistence level. In either case, the economy is doomed for extinction in the long run. It seems reasonable to assume that (18.17) holds as production externalities are typically unintentional whereas collective environmental actions are well planned and executed.

5. STEADY STATE ANALYSIS

5.1 Definition

Definition: *A steady state equilibrium for our economy is a competitive equilibrium in which* $\tau_t^* = \tau^*$, $s_t^* = s^*$, $k_t^* = k^*$ *and* $e_t^* = e^*$ *for all t.*

It is clear that in a steady state both the capital and the environmental stocks grow at the same rate as the population. Such a sustainable steady state, if it exists, can be thought of as a generalisation of the Solow-Swan golden-rule equilibrium. However, it differs from the Solow-Swan equilibrium in the fundamental respect that, since the environment is treated as a pure public good, individual utility increases indefinitely over time in a steady state even though the production technology is unchanging.

5.2 Existence and uniqueness of a steady state

A steady state, if it exists, can be characterised by the timeless version of (18.9), (18.10) and (18.13). There is a complication as the first-order conditions (18.13) generally depend on N_t. Thus, this type of economy may not, in general, possess a steady state equilibrium. In order for a sustainable steady state to exist, further restrictions must be imposed on the model to ensure that conditions (18.13) are independent of the size of the labour force. Two possible alternative assumptions are:

(a) the population growth rate is zero, i.e., $N_t = N_1$ for all $t > 1$,

(b) the utility function $U(x, y)$ is positively homogeneous of degree b ($0 < b < 1$) in y.

In the remainder of this chapter we shall assume (b) to avoid the uninteresting case (a). Under assumption (b), U_1 is positively homogeneous of degree b in y and U_2 is positively homogeneous of degree $(b-1)$ in y so that the first-order optimality conditions (18.13) become independent of N_t.

Now, the timeless version of (18.9) and (18.10) gives

$$s^* = (1+n)k^* \tag{18.18}$$

and

$$e^* = [(\gamma\tau^* - \beta)f(k^*) - \gamma\tau^* k^* f'(k^*)]/(n-\alpha) \tag{18.19}$$

respectively. Under Assumption (b) the timeless version of (18.13) simplifies to

$$\begin{aligned} u'[(1-\tau^*)w^* - s^*]e^* &= \gamma b(1+n)^{b-1} u[h(s^*)]/(1+\rho) \\ u'[(1-\tau^*)w^* - s^*] &= (1+n)^b h'(s^*) u'[h(s^*)]/(1+\rho), \end{aligned} \tag{18.20}$$

where $u(x) \equiv U(x,1)$.

In (18.18), (18.19) and (18.20) we have a system of four nonlinear equations in four unknowns (τ^*, s^*, k^*, e^*). To solve for the steady state equilibrium we express τ^*, s^* and e^* in terms of k^* and then determine the value of k^*. Combining the equations in (18.20) and keeping (18.18) in mind, the timeless version of (18.14) becomes

$$e^* = \gamma b v(s^*)/[(1+n)v'(s^*)] = e(k^*), \tag{18.21}$$

where $v(s) = u[h(s)]$ and $e'(k) > 0$. Substituting (18.21) into (18.19) it is possible to express τ^* in terms of k^* alone as

$$\tau^* = [(n-\alpha)e(k^*) + \beta f(k^*)]/\{\gamma[f(k^*) - k^* f'(k^*)]\} = \tau(k^*). \quad (18.22)$$

The value k^* is then determined by the equation relating to the steady state consumption of a representative young person (detailed derivations are provided in the Appendix), given by

$$\begin{aligned}(1-\beta/\gamma)f(k) - kf'(k) - (1+n)k - (n-\alpha)e(k)/\gamma \\ = \varphi\{(1+n)^b v'[(1+n)k]/(1+\rho)\}\end{aligned} \quad (18.23)$$

where $\varphi \equiv (u')^{-1}$.

Since φ and v' are both strictly decreasing functions of *k* (recalling that $h' > 0$) and $\lim_{k\to 0} v' = \infty$, the graph of the right-hand side of (18.23) is a rising curve which is tangent to the *k*-axis as *k* approaches 0. Now, it can be shown that, as long as the sustainability condition (18.17) is satisfied for all *k*, the graph of the left-hand side of (18.23) must initially rise (with vertical slope at the origin) then fall and eventually intersect the *k*-axis at some positive value of *k*, say k_M. It is clear these two curves intersect once and only once. Thus we may state the following proposition.

Proposition 4: *If the sustainability condition* (18.17) *holds for all k, the economy possesses a unique steady state.*

It is worthwhile to reiterate the role of Assumption (b). Without it, the necessary conditions for the steady state depend on the (growing) size of the labour force and will not have a solution. It seems sensible that a steady state can only exist if the sustainability condition is satisfied. If the sustainability condition does not hold, then the graph of the right-hand side of (18.23) lies below the *k* axis for all *k* and thus no steady state can be found.

5.3 Some comparative statics

Suppose that a unique steady state exists and is stable. In principle, the comparative statics of the steady state can be studied by implicit differentiation of (18.23). It can be shown that $\partial k^*/\partial\alpha > 0$, $\partial k^*/\partial\beta < 0$, $\partial k^*/\partial\gamma > 0$, $\partial k^*/\partial\rho < 0$, $\partial k^*/\partial\delta > 0$ and the sign of $\partial k^*/\partial n$ is ambiguous (see the Appendix). To summarise, we may state the following proposition.

Proposition 5:

(i) The greater the autonomous growth of the environment (higher α), the higher is the steady state capital-labour ratio.

(ii) The greater the rate of environmental degradation by productive activities (higher β), the lower is the steady state capital-labour ratio.

(iii) The more effective the environmental maintenance technology (higher γ), the higher is the steady state capital-labour ratio.

(iv) The more severely economic agents discount their future utilities (higher ρ), the lower is the steady state capital-labour ratio.

(v) The greater the rate of capital depreciation (higher δ), the higher is the steady state capital-labour ratio.

The above results appear to be sensible. For example, a higher rate of autonomous growth of the environment (α) means that the environment is more capable of correcting itself from human productive activities. In this case, the young generation can afford to save more, which will in turn increase the level of capital per worker. Similarly, an economy with better environmental maintenance technology (higher γ) has higher capital-labour ratio. In contrast, an economy in which production causes greater environmental degradation (higher β) experiences lower capital per worker. Not surprisingly, when the young people are impatient and discount future utility more heavily, the economy will end up with less capital per worker. With respect to capital depreciation, young people will need to save more to compensate for a higher depreciation rate.

Keeping (18.18) and (18.21) in mind, the above conclusions also apply to s^* and e^* and similar interpretations can be made. The direction of the relationship between k^* and τ^* is ambiguous in general. However, in the specific case of a Cobb-Douglas production function and utility function, k^* and τ^* vary in the same direction so that Proposition 5 also applies to τ^* in this specialised case.

6. CONCLUSION

This chapter has presented an investigation of the equilibrium behaviour of an overlapping generations economy in which a stream of one-period perfectly democratic governments make decisions on environmental maintenance programs and capital accumulation to maximise the lifetime welfare of a representative member of its constituents. Further work is required to study the stability of the steady state of the model. In addition, the model can be extended in several different directions.

First, it is assumed here that parents leave no bequests to their children. It would be interesting to develop a model in which parents' welfare depends on the well-being of their children. Alternatively, it may also be worthwhile to investigate the behaviour of the economy in the presence of an infinitely long-lived government that seeks to maximise a discounted sum of utilities defined on per capita consumption and the environmental stock.

Second, the present chapter focuses on production externalities while John et al. (1995) only consider consumption externalities. The patterns of pollution and economic growth observed in the empirical data suggest that both production and consumption externalities should be incorporated into the model. However, this extension should not alter the results obtained here in a fundamental way.

Third, the assumption that the rates at which human activities degrade or improve the environment are exogenously constant is somewhat too restrictive. It is perhaps more useful to treat β (or γ) as being dependent on the environmental stock and the level of output (or taxation). More generally, we may allow for technical progress in the pollution abatement technology through either learning by doing or deliberate investment in this activity.

Fourth and finally, the model assumes the aggregate output is independent of the environmental stock. It is rather artificial, as the final output is likely to be positively related to the natural capital stock as suggested at the beginning of the chapter (e.g., clear water helps to increase output). A more comprehensive approach would be to treat the environmental stock as a factor of production.

ACKNOWLEDGEMENTS

We are grateful to Professors Murray Kemp, Ngo Van Long, Koji Shimomura, Alan Woodland and an anonymous referee for their helpful comments. All remaining errors are our sole responsibility.

REFERENCES

Bovenberg, A.A. and B.J. Heijdra (1998), 'Environmental tax policy and intergenerational distribution', *Journal of Public Economics*, **67** (1), 1-24.

Coase, R. (1960), 'The problem of social cost', *Journal of Law and Economics*, **3**, 1-44.

Cropper, M.L. and W. Oates (1992), 'Environmental economics: a survey', *Journal of Economic Literature*, **30** (2), 675-740.

Dasgupta, P. (1996), 'The economics of the environment', *Environment and Development Economics*, **1** (4), 387-428.

Hartwick, John M. and Nancy D. Olewiler (1986), *The Economics of Natural Resource Use*, New York: Harper & Row.

Hotelling, H. (1931), 'The economics and exhaustible resources', *Journal of Political Economy*, **39** (2), 137-75.
John, A. and R. Pecchenino (1994), 'An overlapping generations model of growth and the environment', *Economic Journal*, **104** (427), 1393-410.
John, A. Pecchenino, R., Schimmelpfennig, D. and S. Schreft (1995), 'Short-lived agents and the long-lived environment', *Journal of Public Economics*, **58** (1), 127-41.
Kemp, M.C. and N.V. Long (1979), 'The under-exploitation of natural resources: a model with overlapping generations', *Economic Record*, **56** (154), 214-21.
Kemp, Murray C. and Ngo Van Long (1980), *Exhaustible Resources, Optimality and Trade*, Amsterdam: North Holland.
Kemp, M.C. and K. Shimomura (1995), 'The apparently innocuous representative agent', *Japanese Economic Review*, **46** (3), 247-56.
Meadows, Donella H., Meadows, Dennis L. Randers, Jørgen and W.W. Behrens (1972), *The Limits to Growth: A Report for the Club of Rome's Project on the Predicament of Mankind*, London: Potomac Associates.
Pearce, David W. and R. Kerry Turner (1990), *Economics of Natural Resources and the Environment*, Hemel Hempstead: Harvester Wheatsheaf.
Perrings, Charles (ed.) (1995), *Biodiversity Loss: Economic and Ecological Issues*, Cambridge, New York: Cambridge University Press.
Solow, R.M. (1986), 'On the intergenerational allocation of natural resources', *Scandinavian Journal of Economics*, **88** (1), 141-49.

19. Why Trade Matters to Development: A Learning Model

Henry Wan Jr

1. INTRODUCTION

By conventional wisdom, trade is conducive to development. For example, according to Lucas (1988, p. 41), 'The dramatic...success stories... have all been associated with increase in exports ... [of]... goods not formerly produced in these countries'. For more formal statistical corroboration, see Lau and Wan (1994). Bhagwati (1999) summarises the main arguments for such a conclusion.

The importance of the role of trade may be seen in a highly aggregative analysis of Clark (1993), in which both the downfall of the centrally planned economies and the success of the East Asian economies are traced to the failure and success in harnessing trade for technical progress, in the face of Western advances in research and development (R&D).

But although circumstantial evidence suggest that trade benefits development, the analytic findings of Young (1991, 1993) showed that the theory of learning-by-doing may actually imply the exact opposite. The conclusion is seconded by Stokey (1991, p. 79): 'Suppose that human capital is acquired through learning-by-doing and so is stimulated by the production of high quality goods, then, free trade will speed up human capital accumulation in the North and slows it down in the South'. The elegance of such logic appears persuasive among most theorists, judging from the treatment in Aghion and Howitt (1998). Thus the plot thickens.

In principle, trade may benefit development through channels other than learning (see Van and Wan 1997), such as:

1. The pro-competitive effect. Trade brings competitive pressure against oligopolists and monopolists and hence improves allocative efficiency.
2. The scale effect. Trade may allow a fuller exploitation of scale economies; the opposite can also happen under the Graham Paradox (Helpman and Krugman 1985).
3. The accumulative effect. Trade enhances the marginal product of capital and stimulates investment, which increases output.

4. The technological spill-over effect. Trade facilitates the information flow and allows developing economies to emulate the best practice in production and management.

Young and Stokey have never denied that trade may benefit development through non-learning channels. Chuang (1998) – a student of Stokey – showed the spill-over benefit may dominate the negative influence of trade through learning. Young himself also showed that with three or more countries, trade might benefit one developing country through learning, at the expense of an even less developed economy. We believe that the topic deserves further analysis, because, while Young's three-country case is analytically valid, it is not what drives the episodes of the East Asian economies cited by Lucas. Their trade expansion reflects *trade creation* with the developed economies, not *trade diversion* from other developing areas, like South Asia or Africa. To leave matters as they are will lead readers to believe that, for developing countries, trade tends to be beneficial for non-learning reasons, but harmful through learning. That ambivalent general impression is not warranted.

It will be shown that the conclusions of Young and Stokey come from two crucial assumptions, namely, (a) all economies – rich and poor – share consumption patterns that are sufficiently similar for the present purpose, and (b) their production requires no imported or domestic input. In significant aspects, both (a) and (b) differ from the facts of life. In East Asia, a developing economy may thrive by supplying outputs its home market cannot absorb, using inputs it cannot yet efficiently produce. Experience may be gained in supplying services for one export today, which helps to export others later. Once (a) and (b) are relaxed, the same reasoning in the contributions of Young and Stokey can be extended to reach the policy assessment of Lucas and Bhagwati, that is, trade may benefit developing economies through learning, even in the (two-country) North-South context.

In the next section, we present a simple model, to be followed by three examples. The first example captures the essence of the special assumptions of Stokey and Young. Unsurprisingly, one reaches their conclusion that trade harms development. Once those special assumptions are relaxed, the next two examples show the opposite result that trade benefits development. Final comments are offered in the Conclusion.

2. A SIMPLE MODEL

Learning-by-doing is intrinsically a dynamic effect, and the international division of labour is inherently an issue of general equilibrium. In comparing different trade regimes under the impact of learning, it is understandable that Stokey and Young have adopted their simplifying assumptions. On the other hand, development policy is concerned with the welfare of the world's least fortunate. On such issues, one must hope that tractability of the analysis can be balanced against the veracity of the policy assessment. We cut the analytic Gordian knot by considering a very simple model of our own. Insight and not generality is our present goal.

Consider the choice of policy regimes of a small, developing economy, taking as given certain initial conditions at the time of choice. For simplicity, we adopt the following simplifying assumptions.

2.1 Assumptions

(1) *Policy regimes:* There are two policy choices $C=A$ for autarky and $C=T$ for free trade.
(2) *Primary input:* There is a single primary input labour, x_0, supplied in the fixed amount of unity.
(3) *Technology:* There are $N>1$ goods, each producible in the economy with a no-joint-output technology, and representable as a fixed coefficient (Leontief) production function given by

$$x_i = \min\{x_{ji}/a_{ji}\}, \quad 1 \le i \le N, \quad 0 \le j \le N,$$

where x_i stands for output *i*, x_{ji} stands for input *j* used to produce output *i* ($j=0$ stands for labour) and a_{ji} stands for input *j* required to produce 1 unit of output *i*.
(4) *Learning:* The input-output coefficient $a_{ji} = f_{ji}(X_1,...,X_N)$ is a non-increasing function for all $1 \le i \le N$, $0 \le j \le N$, where X_k is the cumulated amount of output *k*, $1 \le k \le N$.
(5) *Bounded learning:*

$$\partial f_{ji}/\partial X_k = 0 \quad if \quad either \quad X_k \ge X_k^* \quad or \quad X_i \ge X_i^*,$$

where X_k^* and X_i^* are respectively the 'learning ceilings' for industries *k* and *i*, in that once the cumulative output reaches the ceiling, the technology of this industry is called 'mature'. Further output accumulation in this industry provides no useful experience, and experience from any other industry can no longer reduce input requirements for this industry.
(6) *The non-triviality of learning:* If $X_i < X_i^*$ then $\partial f_{0i}/\partial X_i < 0$, in that for any industry not using mature technology, output accumulation at least reduces labour requirement.
(7) *Preferences:* All agents in this economy share both the input endowment and Geary-Stone preferences representable by the utility index

$$u=\sum_{i=1}^{N} b_i \log(c_i+\delta_i), \quad b_i \geq 0, \quad \sum_{i=1}^{N} b_i = 1 > b_1 \ ; \quad \delta_i \geq 0,$$

where c_i stands for the consumption of good i. If good i is not for consumption, $b_i = 0$.

Remark: An intuitive interpretation of (7) is that the representative agent consumes not commodity c_i, but 'characteristic' $(c_i+\delta_i)$, in the sense of Lancaster (1971), with δ_i being the latent endowment of the characteristic. Let the i-th characteristic denote 'mobility' then any person who walks is endowed with a quantity δ_i of that characteristic. This may be augmented by renting a bicycle, a car, or purchasing an air ticket, provided the price is right.

(8) *Given world prices:* The country being *small*, one can always normalise by selecting the units for goods and set the unit world prices of all goods to unity.

(9) *Balance of trade:* Each period, the aggregate consumption must equal the aggregate value-added

$$\sum_{i>0} c_i = \sum_{i>0}\left(x_i - \sum_{j>0} x_{ji}\right).$$

2.2 Definitions

I now introduce some definitions.

Definition 1: *The set of industries with mature technology is*

$$M = \{i \in \{1, N\} : \ X_i \geq X_i^*\}.$$

Definition 2: *Policy $C(=A \ \ or \ \ T)$ causes the economy to be shut-out (or stagnation) if:*

$$\forall i, \ x_i^C > 0 \ \ then \ \ i \in M,$$

where x_i^C is the value for output i under policy C.

Remarks:

1. In this model, a *shut-out* means no progress in technology for the present.
2. Further, a *shut-out* under autarky is permanent.
3. Since *no shut-out* dominates *shut-out*, one can rank policies in a situation if one policy causes a *shut-out* but the other does not.

For our purpose, we find the concept *shut-out* very useful (Wan and Weisman 1999). In each situation, our attention can now be focused upon the pair of policy-dependent current output vectors given by

$$x^A = (x_i^A)_{\forall i} \quad and \quad x^T = (x_i^T)_{\forall i}.$$

By short-circuiting the need for a fully dynamic analysis, we can retain tractability, even after relaxing the special assumptions of Stokey and Young.

We now have all the building blocks for our three examples, with the result of a double *shut-out*. For Example 1, *shut-out* is the outcome under free trade but not under autarky; for Examples 2 and 3, *shut-out* is the outcome under autarky but not under free trade. Further, Example 1 has the special assumptions similar to Stokey and Young. These are relaxed in Examples 2 and 3.

3. EXAMPLE 1 (INTERNATIONAL SUBSTITUTABILITY)

We now adopt four more assumptions, in the spirit of Stokey and Young. The first two establish why their conclusions rest in a very special case, and the second two lie at the heart of their reasoning.

(3') *Ricardian technology:* There is no intermediate input, traded or produced:

$$a_{ji} = 0, \ \ \forall j > 0, \ \ \forall i.$$

(7') *Mill-Graham preferences:* There is no Engel effect:

$$\delta_i = 0, \ \ \forall i.$$

Remark: One implication of (7') is that no matter how rich or poor, everyone consumes every good in positive amounts and must produce every good under autarky.

It is now clear that Assumptions (3) and (7) of the Leontief technology (a generalisation of the Ricardian) and the Geary-Stone preference (a generalisation of the Mill-Graham) not only provide computational convenience but also highlight the special nature of Assumptions (3') and (7'), which underlie the conclusions of Stokey and Young.

Next we adopt the simplest specifications sufficient to portray the reasoning of Stokey and Young.

(10) *Comparative advantage:* $a_{01} = 1 < a_{0i}, \ \forall i > 1.$

(11) *Maturity of technology:* (a) $1 \in M$, (b) $N \notin M$.

Assumptions (10) and (11a) together capture the reservation of Stokey and Young against free trade: the force of comparative advantage drives the developing economy to a production pattern that provides no useful experience. In contrast, (7), (7') and (11b) jointly imply that, under autarky, the developing economy – however poor it is – will consume every good, including some that will yield valuable learning.

This establishes the following proposition.

Proposition 1: *For Example 1, the economy is* ***shut-out*** *under free trade, but not under autarky.*

Proof. For free trade, $\forall i \notin M$, $i > 1$. Thus, for such a good, the value of marginal product of labour $= 1/a_{0i} < 1/a_{0i} = 1 =$ the value of marginal product of labour in good 1 and hence, $x_{0i}^{T} = 0$. For autarky, $x_N^A = c_N = (b_N)(1)/a_N > 0$ (by routine computation) where, by (11b), $N \notin M$.

4. EXAMPLE 2 (INTERNATIONAL COMPLEMENTARITY)

In this section and the next we show that the mere relaxation of the special assumptions (3') and (7') may yield results diametrically opposite to Example 1. Briefly, this is accomplished by constructing special examples with chosen numerical values. Two examples are given, each representing a case important in real life.

We first consider the effect of internationally traded inputs. There are two consumption goods, the traditional good 1 (abacus or sandals), which is produced directly and the modern good 2 (calculator or plastic shoes) which is costlessly fabricated from good 3 (simple parts) and good 4 (sophisticated material such as silicon chips or petrochemical powder) each requiring half a unit for each unit of output. Both intermediate inputs are produced by labour alone. The processes yielding both final goods 1 and 2 use *mature technology*; the processes producing the intermediate inputs, goods 3 and 4, do not.

The economy has a comparative advantage in good 3, but not in good 4, nor in good 2, which may be viewed as a mixture of goods 3 and 4. In fact, under Engel's effect, good 2 will be neither consumed nor produced in autarky. More specifically, we adopt the following assumptions.

(3") *Production functions:*

$$x_1 = x_{01} / a_{01}, x_2 = 2\min\{x_{32}, x_{42}\}, x_3 = x_{03} / a_{03}, x_4 = x_{04} / a_{04}.$$

(7") *Utility index:*

$$u = (1/2)[\log c_1 + \log(c_2 + 1)] \quad (b_1 = 1/2 = b_2;\ \delta_1 = 0,\ \delta_2 = 1).$$

(10") *Comparative advantage:* Input coefficients satisfy the inequalities $a_{03} < a_{01} = 1 < a_{02} < a_{04}$, where $a_{02} = (1/2)(a_{03} + a_{04})$ is the domestic unit labour required for good 2.
(11") *Mature technology:* $M = \{1,\ 2\}$.

We can now establish the following proposition.

Proposition 2: *For Example 2, the economy is* ***shut-out*** *under autarky, but not under free trade.*

Proof. For free trade,

$$1/a_{03} = \max\ \{1/a_{0i} : \forall i\}, \quad \text{[Assumption (10")]}$$

so that to attain the highest value of the marginal product of labour, all labour will be allocated to produce good 3, using a technology which is not mature. Thus the economy is not shut-out. For autarky all we need to verify is that $x^A = (1,\ 0,\ 0,\ 0)$ or, equivalently, that $(c_1,\ c_2) = (1,\ 0)$ is a *corner solution* for the consumer's equilibrium under the constraint that $(c_1,\ c_2)$ must be non-negative. Now, at (1,0), the marginal utilities per unit value of labour are

$$(1/2)(1)/(a_{01}) = 1/2 \quad \text{for good } 1,$$
$$(1/2)(1)/(a_{02}) < 1/2 \quad \text{for good } 2,$$

proving what we desired. Thus $x_i^A > 0$, only for $i = 1 \in M$, so the economy is *shut-out* under autarky.

In the world of globalised production of today, those developing economies with sustained rapid growth either export parts under subcontract or import sophisticated components from the advanced economies (see Hobday 1995). In such context, the logic of Stokey and Young implies that trade plays the indispensable role for the developing economies to gain useful experience in production. Due to Engel's effect, an autarkic economy can scarcely afford those sophisticated goods, which alone provide their producers with valuable experience.

Remarks:

1. Nothing is changed if one assumes that the process producing good 2 uses some labour.

2. By the above analysis, customs unions among the developing economies may not bestow much benefit in providing valuable production experience. At best, one may replicate the domestic markets of an India or a China, which in themselves have never provided much benefit: most of what is sold there is produced with *mature technology* and generates no valuable experience.
3. It is also clear why the insistence on requirements of a 'high local content' (like Brazil used to demand for computer-related products) does not always benefit development.

5. A GRAPHIC ILLUSTRATION OF EXAMPLES 1 AND 2

Consider a small developing economy in a world with two final goods: good 1 for an abacus and good 2 for a calculator, with $c = (c_1, c_2)$ denoting the consumption bundle for the representative agent who has a fixed supply of one unit of labour. By normalisation, each unit of every good, whether or not it is for final consumption, is worth the same value on the world market. Both goods are produced with labour under constant returns: abacus is produced with mature technology; calculator consists of mechanical and electronic components, the technology of producing neither is mature. Presently, the unit labour requirements of these are as specified in Table 19.1.

In Table 19.1, each calculator uses half a unit of mechanical component as well as half a unit of electronic component, where each unit of the former requires half a unit of labour and each unit of the latter requires seven half units of labour. Thus, within each unit of calculator, the labour requirement is one-quarter unit for the mechanical part and seven quarters for the electronic part. So the total is 2 units of labour for each calculator.

Table 19.1 Unit Labour Requirements

(1)	(2) Component /Unit	(3) Labour/ Component	(4)=(2)×(3) Product	(5) Labour /Unit
Abacus				1
Calculator				
Mechanical	½	½	¼	
Electronic	½	3 ½	1 ¾	
Sum				2

Now consider the following two examples specified in Table 19.2. Intermediate inputs are traded in Example 2, but not traded in Example 1. Thus, under free trade, the developing country specialises to produce the good in which it enjoys a comparative advantage. This is abacus in Example 1, yielding a per capita income of 1/1 = 1 and mechanical components in Example 2, yielding per capital income of 1/(1/2) = 2. Thus the free-trade budget line in the consumption space will always have a negative 45 degrees slope, with intercepts 1 and 1, or 2 and 2 under Example 1 and Example 2, respectively.

Table 19.2 Comparison of Examples

	Example 1	Example 2
Production	Integrated	Fragmented
Utility	$\log c_1 + \log c_2$	$\log c_1 + \log (1 + c_2)$

As shown in Figures 19.1 and 19.2, the production possibility frontier under autarky is always linear, with intercepts $c_1 = (1,\ 0)$ and $c_2 = (0,\ 1/2)$.

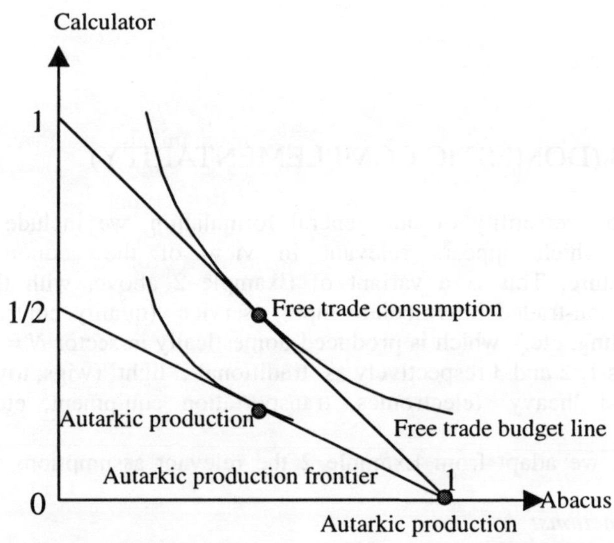

Figure 19.1 Example 1

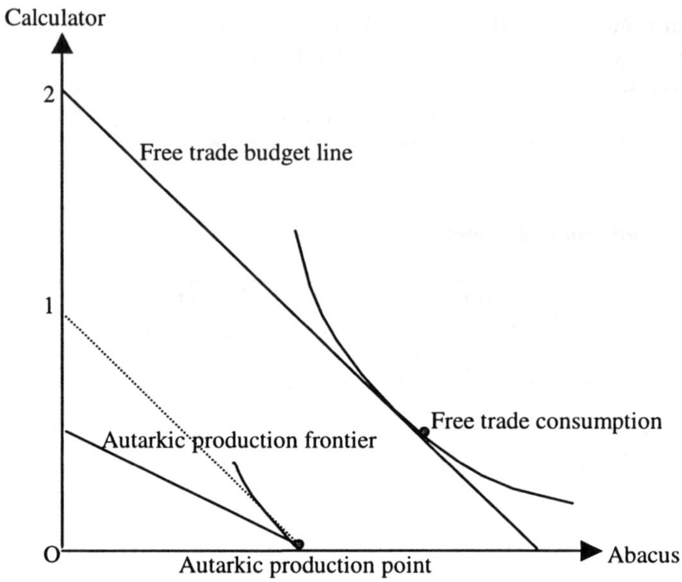

Figure 19.2 Example 2

6. EXAMPLE 3 (DOMESTIC COMPLEMENTARITY)

To demonstrate the versatility of our general formulation, we include a further example, which appears relevant in view of the economic development literature. This is a variant of Example 2 above, with the introduction of a non-traded intermediate input, 'service' (quality control, production scheduling, etc.), which is produced domestically in sector $N = 4$. We identify sectors 1, 2 and 3 respectively as 'traditional', 'light' (wigs, toys, parasols, etc.) and 'heavy' (electronics, transportation equipment, etc.) industry sectors.

For illustration, we adapt from Example 2 the relevant assumptions as follows:

(3''') *Production functions:*

$$x_1 = x_{01},\ x_2 = (3/a_{02})\min\{x_{02}, 2x_{42}\},$$
$$x_3 = (3/a_{03})\min\{2x_{03}, x_{43}\},\ x_4 = x_{04}/a_{04}.$$

Remark: One may reinterpret x_0 and x_4 as direct and indirect labour respectively.

(7''') *Utility index:*

$$u = (1/2)[\log c_1 + \log(c_3 + 1)], \quad (b_1 = 1/2 = b_3; \;\; \delta_1 = 0, \;\; \delta_3 = 1).$$

Remark: Noticeably, at the early phase, the light industry exports of developing economies are not much demanded in their home markets.
(8''') *Given world prices:* The unit price of all *traded* goods 1, 2 and 3 are normalised to 1.
(9''') *Balance of trade:* Each period, the following must hold:

$$\sum_{i=1}^{N} c_i = \sum_{i<N} \left(x_i - \sum_{0<j<N} x_{ji} \right).$$

(10''') *Comparative advantage:*

$$a_{01} = 1 = a_{04}, \; a_{02} < 1 < a_{03},$$

but,

$$(1/3)a_{03} < (2/3)a_{02} < 1.$$

To complete our example, we retain the following assumption.
(11'') *Mature technology:* $M = \{1, \;\; 2\}$.
Thus, under free trade, current learning takes place in sector *N*.

By routine computation, similar to that employed for Example 2, we can establish that

$$x^A = (1,0,0,0,0) \;\; \text{and} \;\; x^T = (0,1/a_{02},0,1/3).$$

In view of Assumption (11''), we have proved the following proposition.

Proposition 3: *For Example 3, the economy is* ***shut-out*** *under autarky, but not under free trade.*

Corollary: *The comparative advantage of the economy will shift to good 3 (the product of 'heavy industry') when a_{04} has been reduced sufficiently.*

Observation: By Assumption (11''), a_{01} remains at unity, but a_{04} declines with learning. The comparative advantage of the economy lies with good 2 (the 'light industry' product) only if

$$[(2/3)a_{01}+(1/3)a_{04}]a_{02}<1<[(1/3)a_{01}+(2/3)a_{04}]a_{03}.$$

Remarks:

1. In the modern world, there are two types of jobs: the skilled and the unskilled. Only for the former type does experience improve productivity and reduce manpower requirement.
2. In modern industries, there are two types of products. For one type, relatively more skilled work is required; the accumulation of output makes the production more efficient; the operations are yet not standardised, making it difficult for less developed economies to compete; the output satisfies the sophisticated needs of the people. These are often classified as 'heavy industries' as distinct from the others, which are referred to as 'light'.
3. In developing economies, there are two types of trade regimes. For one type, the heavy industries are promoted by trade restrictions so that their output may be absorbed by the domestic market and not the world market. This is the import substitution regime, with autarky as its idealisation. The other is called outward-oriented, with free trade as its ideal form.
4. In centrally planned economies, the trade regime is consciously designed to serve the long-term goal of an economy. Understandably, import substitution policy is usually pursued to promote the heavy industries.
5. Historically, many East Asian economies started their development program under severe balance of trade pressure. They exported whatever they could: toys for Hong Kong, wigs for Korea and parasols, etc. for Taiwan.
6. Four decades after World War II, central planning is abandoned by most economies as a dead end, in New Delhi no less than in Beijing, in Moscow no less than Brasilia. Foreign technology and foreign investment are universally welcome with tax holidays, etc. At the same time, East Asian economies have become competitive over time in automobiles, computers and consumer electronics.
7. Part of the explanation may lie in the need for imported key parts and components (engines for cars, central processing chips for computers) when developing economies embark on industrialisation. That is where Example 2 comes in. But the other part is the gradual building up of human capital (for management and marketing) in 'light industries' to lay the foundation of heavy industrialisation. In business literature, the availability of satellitic industries for industrial suppliers are repeatedly cited nowadays as an advantage of East Asia as industrial sites. Example 3 is an attempt to explain such a mechanism in analytic terms. For related trade literature, see Jones and Kierzkowski (1990).

7. CONCLUSION

On policy issues that affect the world's least developed countries, this chapter has studied how trade influences learning with three examples and has come up with conflicting conclusions. As researchers in trade theory, when perplexed, we seek guidance from the life work of Murray Kemp, the trade theorist *par excellence* of our day, and ask how he might have handled it when conflicting theoretical possibilities coexist on issues of significant welfare consequence.

Two points soon become clear.

1. Economics is an empirical field. Economists discipline arguments with theory, yet policy assessment must still be anchored on evidence, a task no different from what faces the trial lawyer or the historian. Kemp (1964) ended the first edition of his trade theory with an unwritten chapter, reserved especially for econometric evidence. It is his methodological statement for all ages.
2. Econometrics is not merely applied statistics. Structures are drawn from economic analysis to form specifications and help the processing and assessment of evidence. For example in his joint study (Hadley and Kemp 1966) on transportation cost and trade, Kemp arrived at the most comprehensive and realistic formulation of the topic, even to this day.

In short, thoughtful empirical work should be made on the trade-learning nexus, in proportion to its policy relevance.

We now turn to two lines of empirical research on learning. First, Backus, Kehoe and Kehoe (1992) found significant learning effects only with disaggregated, manufacturing data. Also a high index of intra-industry trade (a situation closer to free trade) is seen to benefit growth performance. This is to be expected. By our Examples 2 and 3, any productive activity using mature technology (like making sandals) yields output value but not valuable experience. Thus, significant learning effects can hardly be found from aggregate data.

Second, Krugman (1994) cited econometric studies that attributed East Asian high growth to investment, and not to trade or productivity gain. Now such results involve both the East Asian economies where, by Lucas, launching new export industries is a signal characteristic, and the aggregate production function, about which one should quote Solow (1966, pp. 1259-60) in full:

> I have never thought of the macroeconomic production function as a rigorously justifiable concept... It is either an illustrating parable, or else a mere device to handle data, to be used so long as it gives good empirical results, and to be abandoned as soon as it doesn't, or as soon as something better comes along.

Thus, by his criterion, we can conclude that the aggregate production function no longer 'gives good results' in identifying the cause for growth, if in launching new industries, the importance of learning and trade can be independently established by other means.

An informative example is well documented in Stern et al. (1995): the 1986 entry of Hyundai Motors into the American car market. Believing that the expected learning from its US sales would be crucial to its viability, Hyundai both (a) invested heavily to meet the US emission standard, and (b) prepared for an initial loss of US $1000 per car. The gambit paid off after efforts over the period 1974-1986, when its first sales happened to incur no loss. Since the project may benefit any firm in the industry beyond the one making the first sales, this justifies the generous loans from Korean government banks, by the Kemp (1960) criterion.

Here, the expected productivity gain, investment, export sales and realised gain are indispensable links which form a virtuous circle. Exports must be an integral part of the investment plan, or else spending would never be targeted on a specific foreign emission standard. There must be expected benefit from learning, but not from scale economies or else there would never be the need nor the rationale to prepare for losses on initial sales. History proved that the expectations were rational. The gambit paid off. To analyse the cause for growth, the aggregate production function approach claims that investment is all-important, which we accept, but dismisses as unimportant the causes of investment in the first place, namely, learning and trade. That is certainly not giving good results.

In real life, each investment project involves a flow input and flow output model, with the anticipated productivity gain built into the output stream. The closest approximation in the growth literature is the putty-clay model, like that of Kemp and Thanh (1966).

We present below some further observations, which are both tentative and second-hand.

First, exporting to the most 'demanding' markets is essential to learning. According to Morawetz (1981), style is crucial for garments sold in America, but not inside the Andean Group. Catering to American fashion, East Asian suppliers have acquired the capability for punctual delivery, which their Columbian counterparts cannot match. Thus, autarky would be ineffective for learning.

Second, the import of key components is essential to the sales of up-scale goods. According to Chu (1997), when Taiwan's exports of bicycles expanded, its local content percentage fell. Thus, internationally traded inputs help learning.

Third, the skill developed in exporting certain products appears to be transferable to other, more valuable, products. According to Kim and Leipziger (1993), Handok, a Korean firm, moved from exporting wigs to computer parts in just a few short years. Thus, domestically supplied (export) services help learning, irrespective of what is initially exported.

As such, these are certainly inconclusive in themselves, but they may offer a basis in the future to organise a search for systematic evidence.

It is apropos to note that the focus of the present study is on the policy implications of the learning mechanism and trade regimes, as a response to the work of Young and Stokey. Time and space do not allow a full exploration here into the analytic relationship between the models used here and the gains from trade literature covered in Kemp (1995).

ACKNOWLEDGEMENTS

I would like to acknowledge the helpful comments of Simone Clemhout, the useful advice of an anonymous referee and the stimulation gained from reading the forthcoming paper 'Learning-by-doing, trade in capital goods and growth' by Goh Ai-ting and Jacques Olivier. I am thankful for Mrs Paulette Calisle's patient assistance in preparing this paper. All remaining errors are my responsibility.

REFERENCES

Aghion, Philippe and Peter Howitt (1998), *Endogenous Growth Theory*, Cambridge MA: MIT Press.

Backus, David K., Kehoe, Patrick J. and Timothy J. Kehoe (1992), 'In search of scale effects in trade and growth', *Journal of Economic Theory*, **58**, 377-409.

Bhagwati, Jagdish (1999), 'The miracle that did happen: understanding East Asia in comparative perspective', in Erik Thorbecke and Henry Wan, Jr (eds), *Taiwan's Development Experience: Lessons on Roles of Government and Market*, Norwell, MA: Kluwer Academic Publishers.

Chu, Wan-wen (1997), 'Causes of growth: a study of Taiwan's bicycle industry', *Cambridge Journal of Economics*, **21**, 55-72.

Chuang, Yih-Chiy (1998), 'Learning-by-doing, the technology gap and growth', *International Economic Review*, **39**, 697-721.

Clark, Carol (1993), 'Relative backwardness in Eastern Europe: an application of the technological gap hypothesis', *Economic Systems*, **17**, 167-93.

Goh, Ai-ting and Jacques Olivier (2002), 'Learning-by-doing, trade in capital goods and growth', *Journal of International Economics*, **56**, 411-44.

Hadley, George and Murray C. Kemp (1966), 'Equilibrium and efficiency in international trade', *Metroeconomica*, **18**, 125-41.

Helpman, Elhanan and Paul Krugman (1985), *Market Structure and Foreign Trade: Increasing Returns, Monopolistic Competition and the International Economy*, Cambridge MA: MIT Press.

Hobday, Michael (1995), *Innovation in Asia: A Challenge to Japan*, Aldershot: Edward Elgar.

Jones, Ronald W. and Henryk Kierzkowski (1990), 'The role of services in production and international trade: a theoretical framework', in R.W. Jones and A.O. Krueger (eds), *The Political Economy of International Trade: Essays in Honor of Robert E. Baldwin*, Oxford: Blackwell.

Kemp, Murray C. (1960), 'The Mill-Bastable dogma', *Journal of Political Economy*,

68, 65-67.
Kemp, Murray C. (1964), *The Pure Theory of International Trade*, Englewood Cliffs, NJ: Prentice-Hall.
Kemp, Murray C. (1995), *The Gains from Trade and the Gains from Aid*, London: Routlege.
Kemp, Murray C. and Pham Chih Thanh (1966), 'On a class of growth models', *Econometrica*, **34**, 257-82.
Kim, Kihwan and Danny Leipziger (1993), *Korea: A Case of Government-led Development*, Washington, DC: World Bank.
Krugman, Paul (1994), 'The myth of Asia's miracle', *Foreign Affairs*, **73**, 62-78.
Lancaster, Kelvin (1971), *Consumer Demand: A New Approach*, New York: Columbia University Press.
Lau, Man-lui and Henry Wan, Jr (1994), 'On the mechanism of catching-up', *European Economic Review*, **38**, 952-63.
Lucas, Robert E. Jr (1976), 'Econometric policy evaluation: a critique', *Journal of Monetary Economics* (supplement series), **1** (2), 19-46.
Lucas, Robert E. Jr (1988), 'On the mechanics of economic development', *Journal of Monetary Economics*, **22**, 3-42.
Morawetz, David (1981), *Why the Emperor's New Clothes are Not Made in Columbia: a Case Study of Latin American and East Asian Manufactured Exports*, New York, NY: Oxford University Press.
Solow, Robert M. (1966), 'Review of Capital and Growth', *American Economic Review*, **56**, 1257-60.
Stern, Joseph J., Kim, Ji-hong, Perkins, Dwight H. and Jung-ho Yoo (1995), *Industrialization and the State: The Korean Heavy and Chemical Industry Drive*, Cambridge, MA: Harvard University Press.
Stokey, Nancy L. (1991), 'Human capital, product quality and growth', *Quarterly Journal of Economics*, **106**, 587-616.
Van, Hoang Pham and Henry Y. Wan, Jr (1997), 'Interpreting East Asian growth', in Bjarne S. Jensen and Kar-yiu Wong (eds), *Dynamics, Economic Growth and International Trade*, Ann Arbor MI: Michigan University Press.
Wan, Henry Y., Jr and Jason Weisman (1999) 'Hong Kong: the fragile economy of middlemen', *Review of International Economics*, **7**, 410-30.
Young, Alwyn (1991), 'Learning-by-doing and the dynamic effects of international trade', *Quarterly Journal of Economics*, **106**, 369-405.
Young, Alwyn (1993), 'Invention and bounded learning-by-doing', *Journal of Political Economy*, **101**, 443-72.

20. The Effects of Growth of its Trading Partners on Malaysia

Siang Ng

1. INTRODUCTION

In the current world of globalisation, the importance of international trade is undeniable. The benefits of free trade have been much emphasised and demonstrated by the fast economic growth of many trading economies, especially in Asian economies such as Japan, Singapore, Taiwan, Korea and Hong Kong as reported by the World Bank study (1991). This is an area where Professor Murray Kemp and other trade theorists have made significant contributions. In this chapter, the following question is asked: does the growth of one country/region benefit another? More specifically, the effects on Malaysia of the enrichment of its trading partners will be examined empirically.

It is possible that a 'growing' country itself may also be harmed (though then other countries as a group will be better off), as revealed in the well known 'immiserising growth' literature. In his book, Kemp (1964) analyses the likely effects of economic expansion. As a result of growth, the increase in the ability of a country/region to produce more of some goods may benefit or harm another, depending on the specific cases. If one of our trading partners develops a new technology allowing her to produce at a lower cost a good, which she bought from us previously, we may lose our export opportunity. On the other hand, if the new technology reduces its costs of supplying a good it sold to us, we may gain from the lower price charged. Thus, it is not possible to show that growth always makes others better off. However, using the traditional analysis, Ng (1996) shows that a proportionate enrichment (an increase in the ability to produce all goods proportionately) of a country or region benefits the rest of the world as a whole in its general thrust, both for the case of perfect competition and that with monopolistic power. The analysis is quite general. No assumptions are made regarding the returns to scale, substitutability of products, single versus multiple outputs from an industry and the like. The main condition needed to relax the qualification 'in its general thrust' in the description of the main result above is that of 'strong non-inferiority'. This condition is more demanding than non-inferiority but less demanding than homotheticity of preferences or the requirement that the income consumption path be a ray from the origin. For the abstract case, the bias from homotheticity may be in any direction. Hence, the qualification of 'in its general thrust' really justifies the assumption of homotheticity. Thus, the assumption of 'strong non-inferiority' is really very reasonable in the context. The condition is needed to ensure that, as a country enriches itself proportionately and hence is able to consume more of all goods, it wants to consume more of all goods (at unchanged relative prices) to a sufficient extent that it wants to export more of its original exports to, and to import more of its original imports from, the rest of the world. This makes the terms of trade move in favour of the rest of the world and hence makes it better off.

Ng and Ng (2000) extend the above analysis and show that whether a proportionate enrichment of a country or region benefits/harms another particular country depends on whether the latter exports and imports different/similar sets of goods as the former. If this particular country exports and imports similar sets of goods in comparison to the enriching country, it loses from the proportionate enrichment as the enriching country increases the quantities of exports/imports and hence reduces/increases the international equilibrium prices of the exported/imported goods. On the contrary, if the two export a different set of goods, it will gain. In the next section, we apply this result to examine whether the enrichment of a specific country (selected from a number of Malaysia's trading partners) will benefit or harm Malaysia economically. In the concluding section, further research on the topic is discussed.

2. THE EMPIRICAL RESULTS

Applying the theory of enrichment effect, we now examine the case of Malaysia and a group of selected economies by looking at the actual empirical data.

The export/import commodity categories of Malaysia and the economies under study are grouped according to the SITC (Standard International Trade Classification) classification at three-digit level. For example, telecommunications and sound equipment are classified under Division 76 which is divided into 761 television receivers, 762 radio broadcast receivers, 763 sound recorders and 764 telecommunication equipment. The detailed list of export/import commodity groups included in this study is available in the *International Trade Statistical Yearbook* published by the United Nations. We then examine the differences between the export/import categories of different economies with Malaysia for the period 1994 to 1998. These economies are Argentina, Australia, Bangladesh, Belgium, Bermuda, Brazil, Brunei, Canada, Chile, China, Costa Rico, Egypt, Fiji, France, Germany,

Guatemala, Hong Kong, India, Indonesia, Italy, Jamaica, Japan, Jordan, South Korea, Kuwait, Mexico, Morocco, Netherlands, New Zealand, Nicaragua, Pakistan, Panama, Philippines, Poland, Portugal, Qatar, Russia, South Africa, Saudi Arabia, Singapore, Sri Lanka, Taiwan, Thailand, Turkey, United Kingdom, Uruguay, United States and Zimbabwe. Having calculated the percentages of total exports/imports for each export/import commodity group for each economy, the differences in export/import shares in each category for each economy with Malaysia is computed. The absolute differences over all commodity groups are then summed to derive the coefficient of differences. (Since the figure for each group is already in the form of percentages of all imports or exports, no weighting is needed.) The formula for the coefficient of differences between any two countries *a* and *b* may be written as

$$c \equiv \sum_i \left| s_i^a - s_i^b \right|,$$

where s_i^a is the share of group *i* in the total exports or imports (as the case may be) of country *a*. The coefficient takes the value of 0 (no difference in the pair's export/import shares) to 1 (complete difference in the pair's export/import shares). The value of 0.5 may be taken as the dividing line of more differences than similarities. The larger the coefficient of difference, the more the growth of one will be beneficial to the other. That the coefficient of differences can be calculated in the way used has been shown to follow from a set of reasonable axioms in Sun and Ng (2000). Previously, some studies (e.g. Finger and Kreinen 1979, Xu and Song 2000) have used the coefficient of similarity (which equals one minus the coefficient of difference) in international comparisons. However, as far as I know, no conceptual justification of the formula used has been made before Sun and Ng.

The coefficients of differences of different economies with Malaysia can then be compared to show that the economic growth in which countries will tend to benefit Malaysia most. The changes in these coefficients over time can also be used to give a dynamic perspective. The results are summarised in Tables 20.1 and 20.2.

Table 20.1 Coefficient of Differences (with Malaysia) in Exports

Country	1994	1995	1996	1997	1998
Argentina	0.7872	0.7951	0.8020	0.7962	0.8064
Australia	0.7715	0.7588	0.7566	0.7603	N/A
Bangladesh	0.9392	0.9161	0.9294	N/A	N/A
Belgium-Lux.	0.7273	0.7103	0.7037	0.6938	0.6928
Bermuda	0.9934	0.9875	N/A	N/A	N/A
Brazil	0.7602	0.7607	0.7561	0.7595	0.7566
Brunei	0.9187	N/A	N/A	N/A	N/A
Canada	0.6504	0.6364	0.6207	0.6219	0.6362
Chile	0.8479	0.8601	0.8547	0.8543	0.8572
China	0.6358	0.6252	0.6042	0.6026	0.5915
Costa Rica	0.8256	0.8297	0.8380	0.7827	N/A
Egypt	0.8430	0.8487	0.8455	0.8500	N/A
Fiji	0.9124	N/A	N/A	N/A	N/A
France	0.6520	N/A	0.6386	0.6287	0.6190
Germany	0.6642	0.6532	0.6509	0.6502	0.6518
Guatemala	0.8269	0.8372	0.8186	0.8125	0.8254
Hong Kong	0.6231	0.6147	0.6310	0.6340	0.6544
India	0.7898	0.7860	0.7773	0.7836	N/A
Indonesia	0.6174	0.6242	0.5926	0.5996	0.6473
Italy	0.6776	0.6796	0.6802	0.6878	0.6821
Jamaica	0.9305	0.9357	0.9397	0.9430	N/A
Japan	0.5824	0.5576	0.5546	0.5601	0.5625
Jordan	0.8866	0.8928	N/A	N/A	N/A
Korea (South)	0.5357	0.5169	0.5302	0.5227	0.5625
Kuwait	0.9176	0.9361	0.9322	0.9180	N/A
Mexico	0.5815	0.5860	0.5760	0.5737	0.5568
Morocco	0.8661	0.8789	0.8796	0.8939	N/A
Netherlands	0.6516	0.6277	0.5944	0.5569	0.5628
New Zealand	0.7556	0.7651	0.7674	0.7654	0.7267
Nicaragua	0.9286	0.8793	0.8571	0.8774	0.9376
Pakistan	0.9028	0.9082	0.9096	0.9096	0.9136
Panama	N/A	0.9241	0.9226	0.9286	0.9325
Philippines	0.6392	0.6227	0.4308	0.5795	N/A
Poland	0.7353	0.7371	0.7262	0.7125	N/A
Portugal	0.7236	0.7121	0.7127	0.7103	0.7135
Qatar	0.9271	N/A	N/A	N/A	N/A
Russia	N/A	N/A	0.7829	0.7889	N/A
S. Afr. Cus. Un.	0.8516	0.8077	0.7873	0.7841	N/A
Saudi Arabia	0.9115	0.9061	0.9071	N/A	N/A
Singapore	0.4178	0.3853	0.3787	0.3561	0.3524
Sri Lanka	0.8401	N/A	N/A	N/A	N/A
Thailand	0.5442	0.5249	0.4762	0.4747	N/A
Turkey	0.7837	0.7757	0.7534	0.7513	0.7421
UK	0.5672	0.5621	0.5437	0.5517	0.5864
Uruguay	0.8609	0.8381	0.8393	0.8333	0.8427
USA	0.6056	0.5859	0.5782	0.5771	0.5800
Zimbabwe	0.8527	0.8394	0.8363	0.8416	N/A

Source: United Nations, International Trade Statistics Yearbook.

Table 20.2 Coefficient of Differences (with Malaysia) in Imports

Country	1994	1995	1996	1997	1998
Argentina	0.4598	0.4735	0.4679	0.4662	0.5304
Australia	0.4624	0.4463	0.4531	0.4612	N/A
Bangladesh	N/A	0.6637	0.6360	N/A	N/A
Belgium-Lux.	0.5255	0.5157	0.5069	0.5091	0.5557
Bermuda	N/A	0.7143	N/A	0.7048	N/A
Brazil	0.4993	0.4791	0.4454	0.4202	0.4553
Brunei	0.5759	N/A	N/A	N/A	N/A
Canada	0.4680	0.4577	0.4492	0.4452	0.4915
Chile	0.4729	0.4833	0.4673	0.4749	0.5257
China	0.3724	0.3848	0.4037	0.3817	0.3976
Costa Rica	0.5175	0.5239	0.5147	0.4980	N/A
Egypt	0.5460	0.5618	0.5522	0.5254	N/A
Fiji	0.5767	N/A	N/A	N/A	N/A
France	0.4696	0.4708	0.4661	0.4616	0.5004
Germany	0.4656	0.4649	0.4616	0.4650	0.5036
Guatemala	0.5650	0.5627	0.5440	0.5285	0.5811
Hong Kong	0.4635	0.4571	0.4672	0.4614	0.4885
India	0.5810	0.5656	0.5879	0.5756	N/A
Indonesia	0.4716	0.4822	0.4654	0.4639	0.5495
Italy	0.4542	0.4351	0.4349	0.4496	0.4994
Jamaica	0.5667	0.5636	0.5326	0.5575	N/A
Japan	0.5784	0.5636	0.5456	0.5378	0.5397
Jordan	0.5373	0.5550	N/A	N/A	N/A
Korea (South)	0.3938	0.3927	0.3824	0.3901	0.4168
Kuwait	0.5687	0.5988	0.5852	0.5876	N/A
Mexico	0.4059	0.4145	0.3955	0.3811	0.3953
Morocco	0.5079	0.5411	0.5415	0.5498	N/A
Netherlands	0.4961	0.4956	0.4911	0.4737	0.5186
New Zealand	0.4748	0.4741	0.4741	0.4771	0.5231
Nicaragua	0.5980	0.6237	0.5823	0.5875	0.6521
Pakistan	0.5799	0.5797	0.5622	0.5993	0.6261
Panama	N/A	0.5665	0.5586	0.5479	0.5887
Philippines	0.4571	0.4361	0.3520	0.3887	N/A
Portugal	0.5008	0.4906	0.4971	0.4885	0.5327
Qatar	0.6280	N/A	N/A	N/A	N/A
Russia	N/A	N/A	0.6169	0.6002	N/A
S. Afr. Cus. Un.	0.4825	0.4815	N/A	0.5453	N/A
Saudi Arabia	0.4822	0.4825	0.4845	N/A	N/A
Singapore	0.2862	0.2797	0.2909	0.2790	0.2784
Sri Lanka	0.5846	N/A	N/A	N/A	N/A
Thailand	0.3169	0.3142	0.3051	0.2832	N/A
Turkey	0.4673	0.4930	0.4607	0.4407	0.4828
UK	0.4541	0.4536	0.4429	0.4481	0.4810
Uruguay	0.5490	0.5653	0.5464	0.5343	0.5879
USA	0.4854	0.4650	0.4596	0.4710	0.5152
Zimbabwe	0.4929	0.4672	0.4805	0.4918	N/A

Source: United Nations, International Trade Statistics Yearbook.

It may first be noted that, as Singapore is to a significant extent serving Malaysia as an entrepot, the simple comparison of total exports and imports of these two countries does not give a true picture of the net (of entrepot trade) exports and imports. The gross figures exaggerate the similarity. Except for this special case of Malaysia and Singapore where the coefficients of export differences lie between 0.4178 (1994) and 0.3524 (1998), from Table 20.1, it can be seen that during the period of study, the structure of commodity exports of Malaysia and that of the other economies studied are highly different, in particular, with the following countries: Bangladesh, Bermuda, Chile, Costa Rico, Egypt, Guatemala, Jamaica, Jordan, Kuwait, Morocco, Nicaragua, Pakistan, South Africa, Saudi Arabia, Uruguay and Zimbabwe. In 1994, the values of the coefficients of differences between Malaysia and this group ranged from 0.9934 (with Bermuda) to 0.8256 (with Costa Rico). The data for the next group (Argentina, Australia, Belgium, Brazil, Canada, China, France, Germany, Hong Kong, India, Indonesia, Italy, Japan, Korea, Mexico, Netherlands, New Zealand, Philippines, Poland, Portugal, Thailand and Turkey) also show significant differences in their exports with Malaysia: the 1994 values of the coefficients of differences lie between 0.7898 (Malaysia and India) and 0.5357 (Malaysia and Korea). In 1995, the values of the coefficients range from 0.5249 (Malaysia and Thailand) to 0.9875 (Malaysia and Bermuda). Though the coefficient of differences in exports between Malaysia and Thailand, and Malaysia and Philippines, are slightly lower, the empirical results for the next three years (1996-1998) continue to show high differences in exports between Malaysia and the rest of economies under study. In 1996 and 1997, the lowest coefficients are the case between Malaysia and South Korea with the values of 0.5302 (1996) and 0.5227 (1997), while the highest coefficients are the case of Malaysia and Jamaica showing the values of 0.9397 (1996) and 0.9430 (1997). The case for 1998 is very much similar with the previous years with the highest difference between the exports of Malaysia and Nicaragua (0.9376) and the lowest difference between the exports of Malaysia and Korea (0.5269). Due to incomplete data, it is not possible to compare the export differences between Malaysia and Bermuda, and the case of Malaysia and Jamaica.

Malaysia's exports and that of its major export markets (USA, Japan, Hong Kong, United Kingdom, China and other European economies) are significantly different. The former five economies, Netherlands, India, Belgium and Australia are the trading partners with which Malaysia also registered the highest surpluses in late 1999. For the period under study, the values of the coefficients for Malaysia and the United States range from 0.5771 to 0.6056; Malaysia and Japan: 0.5546 to 0.5824; Malaysia and United Kingdom: 0.5437 to 0.5864; Malaysia and China: 0.5915 to 0.6358; Malaysia and Netherlands: 0.5569 to 0.6516; Malaysia and Belgium: 0.6928 to 0.7273. The exports of Australia and Malaysia are also significantly different as shown by the statistical data. In the case of Malaysia and Hong

Kong, it was 0.6231 in 1994, 0.6147 in 1995, 0.6310 in 1996, 0.6340 in 1997 and 0.6544 in 1998. For Malaysia and India, the coefficients range from 0.7898 (1994) to 0.7836 (1997). The study also shows that there are big differences in the exports of Malaysia and other Asia-Pacific economies. These include ASEAN countries, such as Indonesia (0.6174 in 1994, 0.6242 in 1995, 0.5926 in 1996, 0.5996 in 1997 and 0.6473 in1998), Philippines and Canada. The exports of New Zealand and Pakistan are also highly different from that of Malaysia as shown in Table 20.1. With the expansion of world trade, the importance of the economies in Africa, Latin and South America have increased. As can be seen from the table, the exports of Malaysia and this group of economies are very different, especially for Argentina, Brazil, Chile, Costa Rico, Egypt, Guatemala, Nicaragua, Panama, South Africa, Uruguay and Zimbabwe.

Although the coefficients of differences in imports shown in Table 20.2 are not as large as that of Table 20.1, there are significant differences in imports of Malaysia and most of the economies selected, in particular, with Belgium, Egypt, Guatemala, India, Jamaica, India, Kuwait, Morocco, Netherlands, Nicaragua, Pakistan, Panama and Uruguay.

The statistical analysis clearly shows that economic growth in Malaysia or the other economies under study will benefit each other. Malaysia and its trading partners export and import different sets of commodity groups. This is further supported by the five-year average figures presented in Table 20.3. Examining the average of the averages of the export and import coefficients, only less than 10% of Malaysia's trading partners (excluding Singapore) have a coefficient below 0.5: they are Thailand (0.4049, the lowest), South Korea (0.4608), Philippines (0.4853) and Mexico (0.4866). However, it is important to point out that the statistical differences in the coefficients presented above do not reflect the complete differences in exports and imports, as there are differences in quality even in the same commodity category. Furthermore, the current analysis focused on the benefit from trade only and has not taken into account of benefits from direct investments, as the enriched economy also tends to benefit others through investment and the transfer of knowledge. The mutual benefits from the enrichment effect will be greater if the benefits derived from direct investments and technological transfer are included.

Table 20.3 Average of the Coefficient of Differences (with Malaysia) in Exports and Imports, 1994-1998 *(see next page for explanatory notes)*

Country	Coefficient for Exports[a]	Coefficient for Imports[a]	Average of Coefficients[a, b]	Trade with Malaysia (%, 1999)[c]
Argentina	0.7974	0.4796	0.6385	0.1831
Australia	0.7618	0.4557	0.6088	2.2565
Bangladesh	0.9282	0.6498	0.7890	0.9382
Belgium-Lux.	0.7058	0.5226	0.6146	0.8187
Bermuda	0.9990	0.7095	0.8500	-
Brazil	0.7586	0.4599	0.6092	2.5035
Canada	0.6330	0.4623	0.5477	0.6730
Chile	0.8548	0.4848	0.6698	0.1204
China	0.6118	0.3880	0.4999	2.9705
Costa Rica	0.8190	0.5135	0.6663	0.0183
Egypt	0.8468	0.5463	0.6966	0.2155
France	0.6346	0.4737	0.5541	1.2959
Germany	0.6540	0.4722	0.5631	2.7008
Guatemala	0.8241	0.5562	0.6902	0.0075
Hong Kong	0.6294	0.4675	0.5485	3.6126
India	0.7842	0.5775	0.6808	1.7120
Indonesia	0.6162	0.4865	0.5514	2.1816
Italy	0.6815	0.4546	0.5681	0.7000
Jamaica	0.9372	0.5551	0.7462	-
Japan	0.5635	0.5530	0.5583	15.6292
Jordan	0.8897	0.5462	0.7180	0.0695
Korea (South)	0.5265	0.3952	0.4608	3.9422
Kuwait	0.9926	0.5851	0.7555	0.0473
Mexico	0.5742	0.3984	0.4866	0.2352
Morocco	0.8796	0.5351	0.7073	-
Netherlands	0.6598	0.4949	0.5468	3.1462
New Zealand	0.7632	0.4847	0.6240	0.3507
Nicaragua	0.9896	0.6087	0.7524	0.0005
Pakistan	0.9088	0.5894	0.7491	0.3800
Panama	0.9629	0.5654	0.7462	0.0818
Philippines	0.5681	0.4025	0.4853	2.1786
Portugal	0.7145	0.5019	0.6082	0.0450
Russia	0.7859	0.6085	0.6972	0.2391
S. Afr. Cus. Un.	0.8077	0.4692	0.6385	0.2763
Saudi Arabia	0.9083	0.4831	0.6957	0.3920
Singapore	0.3781	0.2829	0.3305	15.8805
Sri Lanka	0.8401	0.5846	0.7123	0.1227
Thailand	0.5050	0.3049	0.4049	3.4322
Turkey	0.7612	0.4689	0.6151	0.2219
UK	0.5547	0.4559	0.5053	3.1011
Uruguay	0.8429	0.5566	0.6997	0.0158
USA	0.6585	0.4792	0.5323	19.9476
Zimbabwe	0.8425	0.4832	0.6628	0.0060

Notes to Table 20.3:

a. The data are 5-year averages except the following: for Australia, Costa Rica, Egypt, India, Jamaica, Morocco, Panama, Philippines, S. Africa, Thailand, and Zimbabwe, 4-years average; Saudi Arabia, 3-year average; Bangladesh, Bermuda, and Russia, 2-year average.

b. The figure in this column is the simple average of the average coefficients for exports and imports presented in the two previous columns.

c. The % refers to the economy's total trade with Malaysia (exports to Malaysia + imports from Malaysia) out of Malaysia's total trade (exports + imports), calculated from the trade data of Ministry of International Trade and Industry, Department of Statistics, Malaysia. Figures for Indonesia, Philippines, Singapore and Thailand are for April 2000; and 1998 figures for Australia, Fiji and New Zealand.

Source: United Nations, International Trade Statistics Yearbook

3. CONCLUDING REMARKS

The evidence of this chapter shows that there are large differences in the sets of goods exported and imported by Malaysia and most of its important trading partners, suggesting that a proportionate enrichment of most of these countries will tend to benefit Malaysia. While the growth of any country is unlikely to be proportionate, in most cases we do not have the knowledge on the direction of bias of the future growth of a country. In the absence of such knowledge, we may take a proportionate enrichment as the expected benchmark case. Where knowledge regarding the specific growth pattern is available, it could be incorporated to increase the accuracy of the prediction of the effects of growth. Moreover, our analysis understates the benefits in the following respects. First, there are differences in variety, quality, etc. of goods classified under the same category that are ignored in our analysis. Secondly, a country may benefit from the enrichment of another other than through the terms-of-trade effect. On the other hand, our analysis ignores the existence of some competition effects between goods of different categories. The analysis of different degrees of substitutability between different categories of goods is beyond the scope of this paper.

Our analysis also ignores the possibility of entrepot trade, that is, the analysis here does not take into account the situation where one economy's significant proportion of exports and imports are done through another as entrepot. Hence, pairs of economies may export/import very similar sets of goods as appear in the statistical data. Due to this special trade relationship, the actual mutual benefits will not show. In terms of our conceptual framework, it means that, in the presence of significant entrepot trade like Singapore, what Singapore exports are mainly its services of entrepot business, not the whole set of goods re-exported from Malaysia. Thus, an obvious refinement of our method is to examine exports in terms of value added. However, for the cases of Malaysia and other trading partners, the problem created by entrepot trade should be small.

The analyses of Ng (1996) and Ng and Ng (2000) that forms the conceptual basis of this chapter are based on the traditional analysis of trade gain from exogenous comparative advantage. Yang and Ng (1993), Ng (1998) and Ng and Ng (1999) have analysed trade gains based on the endogenous advantage of division of labour due to the economies of specialisation. The principal results of the last paper are that, if the enrichment consists of a higher ability to produce goods, this tends to benefit others; if the enrichment consists of an improvement in the transaction efficiency, the result is ambiguous.

ACKNOWLEDGEMENTS

Thanks to Professor Alan Woodland and an anonymous referee for their useful comments on the paper.

REFERENCES

Finger, J.M. and M.E. Kreinin (1979), ‘A measure of “export similarity” and its possible uses’, *Economic Journal*, **89,** 905-12.

Kemp, Murray C. (1964), *The Pure Theory of International Trade*, Englewood Cliffs, NJ: Prentice Hall.

Ng, Siang (1998), ‘Economies of specialisation and trade', in K.J. Arrow, Yew-Kwang Ng and Xiaokai Yang, (eds), *Increasing Returns and Economic Analysis*, London: Macmillan, pp. 127-44.

Ng, Siang and Yew-Kwang Ng (1999), ‘The enrichment of a sector benefits others: the case of trade for specialisation', *International Journal of Development Planning Literature*, **14** (3), 403-10.

Ng, Siang and Yew-Kwang Ng (2000), ‘The enrichment of a sector (individual/region/country) benefits others: a generalisation', *Pacific Economic Review*, **5**, 299-302.

Ng, Yew-Kwang (1996), ‘The enrichment of a sector (individual, region or country) benefits others: the third welfare theorem?’, *Pacific Economic Review*, **1,** 93-115.

Sun, Guang-Zhen and Yew-Kwang Ng (2000), ‘The measurement of structural differences between economies: An axiomatic characterisation’, *Economic Theory*, **16** (2), 313-22.

World Bank (1991), *World Development Report*, Washington, DC.

Xu, Xinpeng and Ligand Song (2000), ‘Export similarity and the pattern of East Asian development’, in Peter Lloyd and Xiao-guang Zhang (eds), *China in the Global Economy,* Cheltenham, UK and Northampton, MA, USA: Edward Elgar.

Yang, Xiaokai and Yew-Kwang Ng (1993), *Specialization and Economic Organization: A New Classical Microeconomic Framework*, Amsterdam: North Holland, pp. 117-46.

Index